247

GROWING UP
IN THE BLACK BELT

GROWING UP
IN THE BLACK BELT

Negro Youth in the Rural South

CHARLES S. JOHNSON

WITH AN INTRODUCTION BY ST. CLAIR DRAKE

Prepared for The American Youth Commission
AMERICAN COUNCIL ON EDUCATION

SCHOCKEN BOOKS • NEW YORK

All the names of persons used in the interviews and case histories in this book are pseudonyms. In no instance does a name refer to any person now existing, or having existed in the past.

AUTHOR'S ACKNOWLEDGMENTS

THIS study is in a significant sense a collaboration shared by colleagues and assistants, from the patient and intimate interviewing of rural youth in the field to the construction of the special tests and the analysis of the considerable volume of statistical detail. Prompt and appreciative recognition is given to the tests developed by Eli S. Marks, psychologist and statistician of the department of social sciences, with the assistance of Lily E. Brunschwig of the department of education of Fisk University. These provided a valuable and essential structure for the study.

A full list of the field and staff workers of this study appears at the end of the volume. All of them rendered excellent service. Particular reference, however, might appropriately be made to the contributions in this connection of Estella H. Scott, Anne DeBerry Johnson, and Edmonia White Grant.

This volume memorializes with deep felt gratitude the services of Lincoln Sawyer who was drowned in a treacherous quarry lake in Coahoma County while swimming with the boys whose water games are described in Chapter VI.

In each county the work with the youth began in the rural schools and this was possible only through the cooperation and assistance of the school principals and superintendents. In acknowledging their valuable aid it is especially fitting to give particular mention to principals J. B. Wright, Coahoma County Training School, Clarksdale, Mississippi; John A. Galloway, Pearl High School, Nashville, Tennessee; W. R. Collins, Johnston County Training School, Smithfield, North Carolina; and to C. F. Baber of Greensboro, Georgia.

Dr. Harry Stack Sullivan was throughout this study an invaluable counselor, and Hortense Powdermaker made sound and vital contributions from the field and on the method of the

47921

study. From the beginning of the study Robert L. Sutherland has been unsparing of his time and energy and patience in the constructive discussion of both method and materials. Perhaps the greatest debt of gratitude is to Robert E. Park whose maturity of wisdom, wealth of suggestions, and helpful criticisms have been as vital to this and other work as they have been constant.

Valuable assistance in the early organization of the details of the investigation was given by Melissa Elliott Forrester. Hattie McDaniel Perry, Martha Harris, and Annie C. Owen typed this and other versions of the manuscript. The drawings were made by Vincent Saunders, Jr., and Sidney J. Apfelbaum.

It would be difficult to overestimate the persistent and painstaking assistance of Bonita H. Valien to the entire study. She has kept the myriad threads of the full study in efficient orderliness, followed each detail of the statistical analysis and testing, read the proof, made the index, and otherwise guarded the text from certain errors difficult of detection. For all of these services the nominal author of this volume offers grateful acknowledgment.

CHARLES S. JOHNSON

CONTENTS

Introduction to the 1967 Edition

BY ST. CLAIR DRAKE

"**H**OW CURIOUS a land is this—how full of untold story, of tragedy and laughter, and the rich legacy of human life; shadowed with a tragic past and big with future promise! This is the Black Belt of Georgia." Dr. W. E. B. DuBois wrote these words in 1903—over sixty years ago. They appear in a well-known collection of his essays, *The Souls of Black Folk*, in one of two absorbing chapters on Negro life and race relations in rural Georgia ("Of the Black Belt" and "Of the Quest of The Golden Fleece"). Although he was trained as a historian, DuBois had acquired broad social science interests and, after publishing *The Philadelphia Negro* (1899), became the first Negro American to organize a series of sociological studies. Despite inadequate facilities and finances he managed to produce sixteen high-level papers and monographs around the turn of the century—the Atlanta University Studies of the Negro. But DuBois was at his best in his essays, and in those dealing with life in the Georgia Black Belt he transmuted sociological data into lyrical prose and turned controlled observations and more casual impressions (what he called "car-window sociology") into convincing generalizations and perceptive predictions. There is a prophetic note as well as a highly relevant query in one of his comments: "A change is coming and slowly but surely, even here, the agricultural laborers are drifting to town and leaving the broad acres behind. Why is this . . . ?" DuBois posed the basic problems for significant future research on both the Southern Black Belt and the Northern Ghetto.

Over a quarter of a century after the Atlanta University Studies appeared, the first professionally trained Negro sociologist with access to funds and adequate facilities for large-scale social research, Dr. Charles S. Johnson of Fisk University, was able to widen the scope of inquiry on the American Negro to include the entire Southern Black Belt, not just a few Georgia counties. Out of his interest in the change which DuBois had seen coming, and a concern for the "Why?" he produced two important books, *Shadow of the Plantation* and *Growing Up in the Black Belt.* (Incidentally, in *The Souls of Black Folk,* DuBois had written of "the shadow of an old plantation . . . forlorn and dark.")

In temperament and life-styles these two men were at opposite ends of the spectrum. The older man—DuBois—militant, passionate, and impatient, left the Black Belt for New York after the Atlanta race riots in 1906, became one of the founders of the National Association for the Advancement of Colored People (NAACP), and, as editor of *Crisis* (a magazine sponsored by the organization), thundered away at exploiters and lynchers below the Mason-Dixon Line. The younger man—Johnson—highly restrained and incredibly patient, was a graduate student at the University of Chicago when race riots erupted in the Midwestern metropolis in 1919. He conducted research for *The Negro in Chicago,* a study of the causes of the riot with recommendations for the future. But, within a few years, he too was in New York, editing a magazine, *Opportunity,* the official organ of the Urban League, a social work agency devoted to the adjustment of Negro rural migrants to life in the city. Neither of these organizations, nor their editors, conceived of each other as rivals, but rather as agencies and men having different but complementary functions in the process of social change and Negro advancement. Both DuBois and Johnson used their strategic positions to encourage young Negro writers and artists, to stress the value of education, and to publicize the achievements of successful Negroes. Neither of them, however, could find complete intellectual satisfaction as a journalist, and both of them eventually returned to the South.

DuBois made "the return" during the early Depression years, going back to Atlanta at the age of sixty-four to lecture and to edit *Phylon,* "a journal of race and culture." While there, he finished his scholarly but controversial Marxist reappraisal of the post-Civil War period, *Black Reconstruction* (1935). In his old age he left to others the type of study he had envisioned when he wrote "Of the Quest of The Golden Fleece":

> We seldom study the condition of the Negro to-day honestly and carefully. It is so much easier to assume that we know it all. . . . And yet how little we really know of these millions—of their daily lives and longings, of their homely joys and sorrows, of their real shortcomings and the meaning of their crimes! All this we can only learn by intimate contact with the masses, and not by wholesale arguments covering millions separate in time and space, and differing widely in training and culture . . .

Johnson, in the meantime, had accepted a post at Fisk University in Nashville, Tennessee, on the edge of the Black Belt, and he was able to do what DuBois says so bitterly in *Dusk of Dawn* he had never been given the opportunity to do. With generous foundation funding, IBM machines to handle mass data, and the encouragement of the New Deal political milieu, the young scholar, in the 1930's, could accomplish what the pioneer could only dream of. He developed a center at Fisk that won an international reputation for research on varied aspects of Negro life and race relations, and that produced not only studies of the Black Belt, but also publications such as: *The Economic Status of Negroes* (1933); *The Negro College Graduate* (1938); *Patterns of Negro Segregation* (1943); *To Stem This Tide: A Survey of Racial Tension Areas in the United States* (1943); *Into the Mainstream: A Survey of Best Practices in Race Relations in the South* (1947).

Charles S. Johnson visualized the role of social science as one providing both data for the planners and human interest documents to evoke popular understanding and to help create a favorable climate of opinion for change induced by legislation and executive order. A constant stream of articles and a number of significant books were produced by the Fisk social science center between the two World Wars. One of the most important and influential of these was *The Collapse of Cotton Tenancy* (credit for which Dr. Johnson shared with Edwin F. Embree of the Julius Rosenwald Fund and Will Alexander of the Agri-

cultural Adjustment Administration as a bit of practical wisdom
in winning a hearing in government circles). The leg work and
much of the preliminary drafting of manuscript for these studies
were done by graduate students and junior colleagues who, with
the cruel humor of apprentices and subordinates, sometimes
referred to the Fisk social science department as "The Plantation" and to Dr. Johnson as "Massa Charlie." But they worked
together as a highly competent team, with a sense of being a part
of history-in-the-making. The end product was always Charles
S. Johnson's, not a ghost writer's job. From the mass of data at
his disposal he wrote not only books, some of which (like
this one) have become social science classics, but also numerous
articles for academic journals and occasional ones for a wide
variety of magazines, discussing problems of current interest,
such as, "Should we Expect More From the Negro in the Solution of His Own Problems?" or "Negro Youth's Dilemma."

Growing Up in the Black Belt is a historic document. It is one
of several studies sponsored by the American Council on Education between 1935 and 1940. Hundreds of thousands of American youth were unemployed, and the number of Negroes among
them was greatly out of the expected proportion. The New Deal
had established a National Youth Administration (NYA) and a
Civilian Conservation Corps (CCC) to provide emergency employment, but both educators and government officials were concerned over the long-term welfare of the nation's young people.
(About 200,000 Negro youth served in the CCC between 1933
and 1939.) The American Council on Education organized an
American Youth Commission to conduct research and to recom-
mend action. It was recognized that Negro youth had special
difficulties and that the psychological component was extremely
important, involving as it does the problem of motivations to
achieve. The key question selected for study was, "What are
the effects upon the personality development of Negro youth of
their membership in a minority racial group?" Several prominent
social scientists were invited to participate. W. Lloyd Warner
and his collaborators, Buford H. Junker and Walter A. Adams,
contributed a volume, *Color and Human Nature,* based upon

interviews with Negroes in Chicago. E. Franklin Frazier concentrated upon the Upper South in *Negro Youth at the Crossways.* Allison Davis and John Dollard, in *Children of Bondage,* focused upon social class differentials as they affected personality development in urban areas of the Deep South. Dr. Johnson chose to study the problems of youth in the rural Black Belt, especially those living on plantations producing cotton. His title emphasizes the point that an understanding of the process by which lives are shaped and molded is as significant for Georgia as for New Guinea, and that the way in which people come of age in North Carolina is as important as the socialization and maturation processes in Samoa.

The neatness of the research design and the coherent style of presentation of results make *Growing Up in the Black Belt* a model worth studying by readers with an interest in understanding how some sociologists go about their work. Fisk had the precise data at hand needed for scientific sampling within the Black Belt, something no other institution except the University of North Carolina had. Eight counties in five Southern states were selected for intensive study, six of them being "cotton counties" and two others having patterns of diversified farming. Two of the "cotton counties" were chosen to exemplify traditional plantation systems (Bolivar and Coahoma in Mississippi); two were typical of plantation systems in decline (Macon in Alabama and Greene in Georgia); one was near a major Southern city, Memphis; and, in another, Negro tenants were competing against white owners in a nonplantation setting. Six questionnaires were administered to over 2,000 young people distributed throughout these counties and representing various types of households and social status levels. These were designed to lay bare racial attitudes and personal attitudes and values, as well as reactions to skin color differences among Negroes, and to determine the I.Q. for each individual. Every respondent was given an opportunity to talk freely to an interviewer, as were parents in 916 families. The data was analyzed in such a way as to relate attitudes and I.Q. to each other, and both to geographical and social class variables. A unique feature of presentation was the inclusion of the questionnaires in an appendix, thus making it possible for readers (especially school teachers) to administer them in other social contexts if they wished to do so.

Detailed statistical tables were provided for those who cared to examine them in detail, but clear interpretation of the data made their study unnecessary for the general reader. One of the most attractive features of the book is the extensive and vivid documentation provided by interview material that is given almost verbatim. These comments, scattered throughout the book, may be read either as individual examples of fascinating self-revelation by young people, or as part of the narrative into which they have been skillfully woven. Many of the comments are spontaneous, frank, and refreshingly naïve. For instance, Amanda was thirteen years old when the interviewer visited her. She hadn't been to school for five years, having dropped out when her mother died so she could help her sharecropper father take care of the seven younger children. She revealed her fantasy life freely: "The only thing I think about, and I think about it a lot, especially at night when everybody is asleep, if I just save some money and leave from here. I just hate this place and I get so tired of working in the field and doing that heavy washing outdoors over the fire. I want to go North. . . . Sometimes I get real mad and curse everybody, including my father. . . . If it wasn't for papa, I could go . . . [but] when I get mad and say I'm going he always tries to show me how much he needs me. . . . I want to be a teacher . . . like Miss Benton. She is so kind and good . . . I just want to 'mount to something some day." George was fifteen years old. His father was a farmer, and the house was "very run down," but it was *theirs*; they owned it, unlike their sharecropper neighbors. George was a dreamer, too, confiding to the interviewer, "I want to be a doctor so I can help people get well"; and, revealing an unusual fantasy life: "I would also like to be like God. He can do powerful things. I would make poor people be better off than they are. I would fix it also so colored people would not have to work for white people."

Not all the youngsters interviewed showed the extreme reactions of Amanda and George or revealed the streak of idealism mingled with self-interest they displayed, but there are dominant themes: a desire for money, for husbands with good jobs, and for love and affection often denied. And there is a universal protest against the boredom and isolation of rural life. Cries of anguish frequently burst out from these pages as well as caustic criticisms by the youth of a world they never made, and bitterness over the legacy of the past bequeathed to them by a hostile white society and by impotent Negro institutions: disorganized families that could not help them to get ahead (a third of the homes were broken and had female heads) and churches that tried to fix their eyes upon heaven and were dominated by preachers whom the youngsters often say they could not respect. But fun and laughter and pride in work are present too, as a chapter on "Youth at Play" makes clear.

The book begins with ten "personality profiles" of young people living in varied geographical and social settings. The cases highlight the variations around a basic theme—that "escape is the primary goal of individual activity and is sought in sex and shouting religion by some; in physical flight from the country to the city and from South to North by many (only one person in four stated a desire to continue living in the South); and by accumulation of money and education where possible. Both youngsters and parents reveal a persistent and almost pathetic faith in education as the magic key to attainment of "a better life" and the professional and semi-professional occupational status that more than half of these farmers' children yearned for. Fragments of conversation quoted throughout the book reinforce the impact of the profiles. They reveal the thoughts of young people groping for a feeling of dignity within a social system that makes them ambivalent toward themselves and other Negroes. But persistently they search for their identity, full of irrepressible vitality and animated by a drive to escape either by upward social mobility, physical flight, or both. Readers will find other examples to add to the few quoted here:

> "Some day I'm gonna get away from this place and go where they have some real libraries."

"I'd like to have a house that don't leak. . . . I'd like to have some clothes like other girls, too."

"I calls anybody 'Sir' if they be a man. I got just as much right to call a colored man 'Sir' as I is a white man."

"Most dark people are dumb and don't know nothing and I'd rather not be fooling with them." (Comment by a mulatto boy.)

"I'd rather be black than anything. All Negroes belong to the African race . . ." (Comment by a very dark girl.)

"I hope to do some traveling before I marry."

"I want to marry a doctor then we can work together in a hospital."

"I'm willing to co-operate and go to vote but the white people don't want that."

"What I'd really like to do is to go to an engineering school. . . . If I had the money I'd go up North. They don't care up North if you're colored."

Amanda and George, and the other young people growing up in the Black Belt twenty-five years ago, lived under the shadow of what the author called "the all-pervading psychological and social implications of the traditions of race and class." They were all affected, too, by "the deep margins of poverty and the prestige and glamor of those who have escaped it." There was visible evidence of the possibility of escape in the few well-to-do Negro farmers; and in school and church they were made aware of Negroes elsewhere who had "got ahead." And everyone knew of people—often relatives—who had gone to the city. Amanda is thirty-eight years old now, and George is forty—if they have survived. We shall never know their fate or the fate of the more than 2,000 other young people who were studied. But coming to know them as they were twenty-five years ago provides a base-line from which to measure change; and it gives an insight that aids in understanding the contemporary world. Amanda may never have escaped from the Black Belt to the North, but over a million Negroes did leave the South between 1940 and 1950, and another million during the next ten years (half of Mississippi's young adults left between 1940 and 1950, and not all of them went into the armed forces, either). The Black Ghettos of the

North are full of Amandas and their children. This book helps us to understand why they preferred the Black Ghetto to the Black Belt, and why some of the features of urban Negro life are what they are today. George probably abandoned his unrealistic wish "to be like God" (and it is most likely that he never had the chance or the academic preparation to become a doctor). But thousands of Southern Negroes eventually did find a way to "fix things" in the Black Belt—marching behind a new type of preacher and singing "We Shall Overcome"; or going to jail alongside young people from the North. If George never joined "the movement," it is entirely possible that his children did. Some of them may even be in the Black Panther Party in Alabama or members of SNCC or CORE, or have become Watts-type rioters in some Northern or Western ghetto. Reading *Growing Up in the Black Belt* deepens our understanding of black marchers trudging the road from Selma to Montgomery, or registering to vote under the glare of hostile white officials in some Black Belt county.

Dr. Johnson concludes the book with characteristic caution and understatement, suggesting that: "In general the Negro continues to occupy a subordinate position, but the fact that he is struggling against this status rather than accepting it, and that the white group is constantly redefining its own status in relation to the Negro, indicates that in the future, if one cannot safely predict progress in race relations, he can at least predict change." This was, in part, a polemical shaft hurled at those scholars who used the term "caste" to describe the status of the Negro in the South, for Dr. Johnson was impressed by the fact of change—however slow it seemed to be—rather than by the rigidity of the system. It was his conviction that fundamental economic changes were undermining traditional patterns of race relations in the South, and that the attitudes of the youth were accelerating those changes.

At the time, neither he nor DuBois had any way of knowing the extent to which those changes would be sped up by another World War and its aftermath, or that an emerging national concensus would be in the direction of progress in race relations.

DuBois eventually became convinced that only a socialist revolution could free the Negro from his disabilities, but Charles Johnson worked closely with a small group of Southern white men and women who were dedicated to the "separate but equal" doctrine. He, himself, believed that such an ideology was bankrupt (and he paid the price for his patience and restraint at innumerable "conferences on interracial cooperation" in the form of migraine headaches), but he had faith that his own scholarly work and that of others would help to prepare the way for more dramatic changes inevitable in the future, when the forces of political interest and economic necessity, coupled with Negro protest and white idealism, had reached full fruition. And his work—and that of other scholars—was extremely influential during the gestation period before the great break-through of the 1950's and 1960's.

That *Growing Up in the Black Belt* has the power still to speak with meaning across the years was driven home to me when I was preparing to write this introduction. My research assistant (Miss Odessa D. Thompson, a recent college graduate and a social work intern) was reading the book for the first time in order to prepare abstracts. She, herself, had been born in the Black Belt, but her family left for Chicago when she was eleven. She began to reflect upon what it would have meant for her if she had not left, and upon the conditions of those who stayed. The book "rang a bell"—evoking not only memories of her childhood but also of other reading she had done. It was she who suggested that to fully appreciate what Johnson had to say one ought to re-read *The Souls of Black Folk*. She remembered that it was DuBois' book that first stirred her reflections upon the milieu in which she was born, although he wrote forty years before her birth. And so it was that while I was completing this introduction, my assistant who had spent part of her childhood in the Black Belt and "escaped" came to a decision to "return" to join the march from Memphis to Jackson after the attempted murder of James Meredith. She wrote in her diary that the reading of *Growing Up in the Black Belt* had set off thoughts and impulses which demanded an act of commitment, and thus became a catalytic agent in her decision-making process. She returned to Chicago with a feeling of depression over the fact that so much of the South looks so very much the same, but also of optimism because of the action people were taking to change the conditions of their existence. Most of the readers of this re-issue of Johnson's book will have no opportunity for such a unique personal experience, but many, no doubt, will feel impelled to contribute to the process of change in their own way.

The Black Belt is being transformed by technological changes as well as by the civil rights movement. In 1950, 99 per cent of the cotton was picked by hand. Twelve years later, over half of it was being picked by machine. Urbanization and industrialization are proceeding rapidly. The exodus from the South continues, but may be slowing down as prospects for a decent life in the Black Belt are improved. All too often hope is betrayed, however, both for those who stay and those who leave. To look again at that hope through reading this book may strengthen the resolve that these betrayals end—and end quickly.

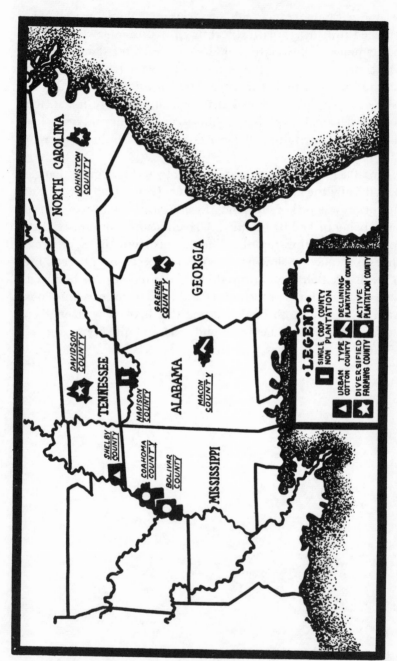

Location of eight selected counties by type of agricultural area.

INTRODUCTION

THE FRAMEWORK within which we have studied the problem of personality development of southern rural Negro youth is that of the relation of personality to culture. Personality is conceived as the organization of the individual's habits and behavior patterns in adjustment to his environment and in his effort not merely to survive but to achieve a career. Since the emphasis of our study is upon the minority racial status of Negro youth, we are interested in defining the social environment in its racial implications. The indices considered most important in characterizing this environment are those indicating adjustment or lack of adjustment to the community in which the individual finds himself. It is assumed that in the process of personality development the individual strives to maintain a certain integrity of personality and a comfortable functioning relationship with the social group in which his life interests are set. Where there is adjustment there is no emotional conflict; where there is lack of adjustment there is some incompatibility between the individual's behavior and the social sanctions of the group in which he seeks some form of recognition and status.

In our approaches to Negro youth we are seeking indice. to conflict situations, indications of concern for status, for prestige, for security in their society; we are interested in their fears and wishes, their personal attitudes in relation to specific social values and the behavior prompted by these, whether successful or unsuccessful in accomplishing adjustment. In the social environment we are attempting to define the social sanctions of the intimate social group as well as the conditions under which identification with the dominant cultural group is achieved. In the dominant white group we seek to define the taboos, compulsions, attitudes, and behavior which, in turn, define the racial status of Negroes generally and Negro youth in particular.

The racial position of Negroes in the South is a part of the institutional organization of the South and reflects a long history of racial conflicts and accommodations. The attitudes and the behavior prompted by them may be said, in turn, to be a reflection of general economic and cultural factors. The situation is aggravated by the generally low economic condition of the area and the resulting inadequacy of provisions for education, housing, health, and similar social measures which operate to maintain these social disparities. The response of Negro youth to this situation is the objective of this study.

The census indicates that in 1930 there were in the United States 2,803,756 Negro families, and that 2,193,357, or 78.2 per cent, lived in the South. The number of rural Negro families in other sections of the country was negligible. In the North and West there were only 67,418 rural Negro families, including both farm and nonfarm. In the rural South there were 962,401 Negro farm families, and 80 per cent of these were tenants, living for the most part in the plantation areas. In addition to these were 445,767 Negro families classified as rural nonfarm families. This group included those not engaged in agricultural pursuits and living in small towns which are for the most part outside the one-crop commercial agricultural areas. It is significant that of these rural families not engaged in farming, 32.2 per cent were home owners as compared with 19 per cent of the farm families. The cities, South and North, have drawn large numbers of Negro families. In the urban areas of the South were 785,189 and in those of the North, 514,187 Negro families. Sixty years ago 80 per cent of the Negro families were not only southern but rural. Today only 50.2 per cent of the Negro families are in rural southern areas.

Omitting those usually classified as border states, there are eleven states in the "Solid South."[1] These eleven states had 2,817,137 Negro youth between 10 and 25 years of age in 1930. In fact, more than half (57.1 per cent) of the Negro population in this area was under 25 years of age. There are, however,

[1] Virginia, North Carolina, South Carolina, Georgia, Florida, Alabama, Mississippi, Tennessee, Louisiana, Arkansas, and Texas.

interesting differences between urban and rural areas. In the cities, 48.2 per cent of the population was under 25 years of age as compared with 62.8 per cent in rural farm and 54.5 per cent in rural nonfarm areas. The youth are definitely dominant in the villages and on the plantations. In the urban areas only 18.8 per cent of the population was between 10 and 20 years of age as compared with 26.7 per cent in the rural farm and 20.6 per cent in the rural nonfarm areas. In 1930 there were in all 1,497,950 rural Negro youth in the South between the ages of 10 and 20 years.

Eight southern counties were selected for the intensive study of Negro youth in their cultural setting. The selection was designed to include the major types of southern agricultural life of which they, with their families, are a part. Since our emphasis is on the rural South, special attention has been given the single-crop cotton, or plantation cotton counties, which, although they constitute only one-third of the total number of counties in the South, contain one-half of the rural Negro population of the South. Six cotton counties were selected for study: Bolivar and Coahoma in Mississippi, Macon and Madison in Alabama, Greene in Georgia, and Shelby in Tennessee. This area, however, is by no means homogeneous. The principal variations within the area are the presence of towns, usually commercial centers for the surrounding rural districts, and the stage of development or disintegration of the plantation society. As a result of declining soil fertility and the general economic disorganization in the cotton areas, a partial breakup of the traditional system of cotton tenancy has occurred. Macon County, Alabama, and Greene County, Georgia, were selected because they represent areas in which the plantation system has been in the process of disintegration. In these areas the collapse of tenancy has produced a shift to smaller ownership units, increased use of wage laborers on farms, and increased insecurity for owner and tenant alike. The breakdown of the plantation system is most advanced in Greene County, Georgia. Bolivar and Coahoma counties in the Mississippi Delta are active and comparatively flourishing plantation areas not yet seriously affected by the forces which have brought about disorganization in the other areas. Despite falling cotton prices and general unrest, the exceptional adaptation of the delta to the plantation system has preserved the traditional order with only slight modifications.

Shelby County in Tennessee represents an urban type of cotton county. It includes the city of Memphis, which is the major trade center for the rich cotton areas of the delta and of Arkansas. This county, therefore, presents an interesting combination of the dominant cotton culture and the influence of urbanization. Madison County, Alabama, is a single-crop cotton county outside the direct influence of the plantation. It represents an area of white operators and tenants working small farms with poor soil in competition with Negro tenants. In this area the Negroes are both less dependent and more insecure than in the other areas; they have, nevertheless, higher ownership rates.

Counties with diversified farming contain about one-third of the rural Negro population of the South. These counties are less homogeneous as a group than the plantation counties. In so far as they can be typified, Johnston County in North Carolina and Davidson County in Tennessee represent this group. The dominant crop of Johnston was cotton in 1929 and corn in 1934. In both years tobacco was an important crop. In 1934 Johnston County produced the second largest tobacco crop of any county in North Carolina, the state which leads the United States in tobacco production. Davidson County lies outside the cotton belt and its principal crops are grain and forage, with considerable crop diversification. The rural population is, however, largely nonfarm. Only one-fourth of the rural Negro population of Davidson County is farm population.

Southern counties with urban centers (cities of 25,000 population or over) have special significance for this study. These counties have only about one-tenth of the rural Negro population of the South but they have one-fourth of the total Negro population. They are centers from which cultural changes are introduced into the other sections of the South. Davidson and Shelby counties in Tennessee represent this group. Both contain large urban centers (Nashville and Memphis respectively). They differ in that, as mentioned above, Shelby County is an urban type of cotton county while the agricultural economy of Davidson County is noncotton and highly diversified.

These eight counties, when related to the groups of counties identified as having similar characteristics,[2] may be said to represent approximately 80 per cent of the rural Negro population of the South. The selection of "typical" counties in this manner for intensive study serves two important purposes: it makes possible a more intimate description of the social setting of the Negro youth who are included in this study, and it provides a statistical frame of reference within which accurate sampling of the total Negro population can be obtained. The youth sample is based upon the total youth population in the county, male and female, in and out of school. The sampling procedure was followed rigidly to insure a balanced and accurate representation from the different social classes of the Negro population. This study is based upon the experiences of over 2,000 southern rural Negro youth, who were given six tests,[3] five of which were specially devised for this study. The tests were followed up with intensive interviews of about 20 per cent of these youth and, in addition, 916 of the families of these youth were interviewed.

The scheme of this volume is to present by way of introduction to the study of the personality development of southern rural Negro youth, brief though fairly complete pictures of ten youth in their intimate setting. This is followed by a description of the rural South in which the lives of these youth are set,

[2] Charles S. Johnson and others, *Statistical Atlas of Southern Counties* (Chapel Hill, N. C.: University of North Carolina Press, 1941).

[3] A description of the tests and testing procedure appears in Appendix B. Most of the youth tested took all six tests. However, only 1,834 of the rural youth took the intelligence test and a few failed to take one or more of the other tests. Most of the tables shown are based on the 2,250 youth who took the Personal Values Test. Most of these 2,250 youth also took the Personal Attitudes Test and the Race Attitudes Test. The Personal Attitudes Test was only scored for the 2,156 youth who took both it and the Personal Values Test. The Race Attitudes Test was only scored for the 2,096 youth who took both this test and the Personal Values Test. However, tabulations of responses to individual items on all tests were made for *all* youth taking the given test. For this reason the total number of cases shown in tables giving responses to individual items is slightly larger than the number shown in tables giving test scores.

with its characteristic economic institutions and patterns of life, shaping inevitably the patterns of family life into which the youth are born and from which they get their first directions for living. Since the experiences of these youth find more exact and realistic interpretation in the significant framework of the interacting social groups within the population, this social definition is presented and followed by more detailed analyses of these experiences in the familiar institutions of community life. The final section deals with the vital patterns of race contact and relations which both inspire and define much of the behavior which characterizes the minority status of the group of which these youth are a part.

CHAPTER I

PERSONALITY PROFILES

Descriptions of ten Negro youth are given in this first chapter by way of introduction to the study of the personality development of southern rural Negro youth. The common everyday experiences of these young people on the plantations and in the other rural areas of the South are described in these profiles, frequently in the words of the young people themselves. These particular young people were not selected because they are striking or unique but because they are typical and have problems common to the section. The profiles include boys and girls from all types of areas and from all classes of the Negro population in approximately their true proportions in the area. The remaining chapters of the book deal more specifically with those social and economic factors affecting southern rural Negro youth in general and with the responses of these youth to the stimulation and restraints of their environment.

HESEKIE PARKER: PLANTATION YOUTH

Coahoma County in Mississippi has a teeming Negro population, vast plantations, and a complete and traditional devotion to the cultivation of the commercial crop of cotton. Three-fourths of the rural population of the county are Negroes and practically all of them are tenants and sharecroppers. Hesekie Parker is a youth of 18 who lives with his grandparents in the Yazoo-Mississippi delta section of Coahoma County, which has rich and well-nigh inexhaustibly fertile soil.

He is well built physically and is still boyish and lively. He talks with a thick accent and a careless drawl, and his complexion is so dark his associates have affectionately labeled him "Crow." He does not object to this label. Hesekie grew up in a little community of sharecroppers called New Africa. By the time he was 6 years old his mother had taught him how to milk a cow. At 10 his father had started him chopping cotton.

> First, I wanted it, but after a week I was ready to quit. I had to go to the fields though, 'cause they made me. The same year I commenced a-pickin'. Mama was fixin' sacks and she just made me one. I was glad to get it then. I reckon I was pickin' 'bout fifty when I started.

When he was 12 he began plowing.

> I used to watch 'em and figured I could do it. When I asked Dad to let me have it he was breaking with four mules, but I knew I could handle them. He gave it over and I been plowing since. Every evening when I come home from school I'd plow till dark. I still like to do it better than anything else around the place.

Family Trouble and Separation

When Hesekie was 13 years old his mother and father separated. He does not know why. They never told him and he did not inquire. One day his mother just went off and did not come back. His father found her in a nearby town, but she refused to return. Later his father left for Illinois. His mother went back to him once, but she did not stay because by that time he had two children by another woman. Now both have remarried and Hesekie is living with his grandparents who, as tenants go in this section, are fairly well off.

Routine of Work on the Farm

Hesekie's working schedule is typical. In the spring and summer he rises at four o'clock and feeds the chickens, hogs, mules, and cows. Then he milks the cows, eats his breakfast of molasses and bread and milk, and goes to the fields. In the spring he starts "breaking." When chopping time comes it is his job to plow up the center of the rows and "dirt" behind the choppers. ("Dirting" is done with a double-shovel or a Gary plow. The chopping hands loosen and pull the dirt away from the cotton and "dirting" is simply throwing it back again.) At twelve o'clock he stops for dinner, the heaviest meal of the day—greens, beans, corn bread, middle-pork, molasses—and returns to the field at one o'clock, to remain until sundown. This is his schedule until cotton picking begins.

In the middle of August picking begins. In the early morning and late evening working conditions in the cotton fields are tolerable, but in the late morning and early afternoon the sun beats down mercilessly, and there are few hands, young or old, who can be indifferent to it. They stop work and rest under the shade of a convenient tree, or trudge back to the cabin for a nap and dinner. Where several children are picking cotton they can sometimes make a contest of picking—a nickel or a dime for the winner. This is their pay and they are lucky if they can get that.

During the "laying-by" season, when work is slack, Hesekie has a lighter schedule and he may go to the nearest town to visit friends or just for a lark.

Acquiring New Skills

At 18 Hesekie is tired of farming, but just keeps on. "I reckon that's because I been doing it all my days," he says. He likes carpentry and has been "trying a hand to it for seven or eight years." He began by making log play wagons at home. Now he can shingle a house, build a chicken coop or hog pen, and do various kinds of ordinary "fixing." He learned to shoe a mule, but does not like it. His grandfather taught him to drive a well. He says the rope and rigging and pulleys "wore him down."

Once he and his brother Bennie tried to escape from the farm by selling fish. They would go along the Mississippi and buy the fish caught by men who liked to fish for fun. It was a good idea but the capital of larger traders put them out of business.

With his cousin he worked a cane mill for a while. His job was feeding the cane to the mill. The improvised mill which they operated consisted of a couple of spools with a long pole attached which was turned by a mule. He can cut and strip cane.

At home with his grandparents he is comfortable but not happy. His total personal possessions consist of one suit, two extra pairs of trousers, two pairs of shoes, four shirts, and an old twelve-gauge shotgun left by his father.

> My grandpa don't have much to say 'bout things, 'ceptin' his own business. He runs that and nobody tells him nothing. He could do better, but I dassen't tell him. That's one reason I don't want to stay on the farm with him. Long as he's boss I can't make nothing, and he ain't doing much. He's nice enough to all of us, but he can't give us much and we sure have plenty of work to do.

Hesekie's teachers call him ambitious and energetic, and say that he does a pretty fair job of anything he tries.

Religion and Play

When Hesekie was 11 years old he followed the pattern of the community and "got religion" and joined the church.

> I just went to the mourners' bench because my brother was there. 'Course I got 'ligion. I don't know how it happened or what it was, but I just felt somepin in me and I wanted to jine. Grandma was glad and kinda cried when I got 'ligion.

In the fall of the year he and his gang pick hickory nuts and pecans for fun. They sit on the river bank and eat them and then go swimming. They also hunt rabbits, birds, coons, and possums, and steal cane from the fields and carry it into the woods to eat.

Thoughts of Escape

He thinks he would rather be up North "where you don't have to say 'Yes, suh' and 'No, suh' to every white man." "If you don't do it here," he says, "they are going to try to see what's ailin' you." These observations, thoughtfully made if crudely expressed, suggest the influence of his racial past upon his present behavior and outlook.

> Now, the white folks that lived in front of us was good. There was fifteen of them in the family and we never had any trouble. Lots of white boys around would pick fights with colored boys because they wouldn't do too much fighting back. I fought plenty of white boys and whipped 'em too. Some mean, poor white folks around would ketch niggers' cows and sell 'em, or do other mean things.

Niggers and white folks often get into it and kill each other. Well, one day a white man came to see a colored woman and a nigger was there; so he got mad and went home for his gun. Time he got back the nigger was out in the field working. The white man shot the nigger, then another old nigger got on the white man's side and said that the white man was going to hunt ducks and the nigger told him he couldn't hunt around his place. He said the nigger drawed for his gun and the white man had to kill him to save his life. That wasn't so 'cause that colored man never even had a gun. A little later the white man's own son killed him for beating his mother.

Some white men fool around with Negro women and nigger men are too scared to do anything. 'Course once in a while niggers kill 'em up. Then they got to take to the bushes and go ahead. If they ketch him, they just hang him to a bridge. Lynchings often happen. They are different to what they used to be, though. They used to be big mobs hunting for a nigger, but now you just hear about some nigger found hanging off a bridge.

They came right through by home one evening. I reckon there was 'tween thirty and forty men riding on horses, with guns and pistols. They was men from 'round that go for bad. They didn't make any fuss, just rode quiet like. I didn't do nothin'— just set on the porch and looked. Them mobs don't hardly bother nobody 'ceptin' the one they're after, 'lessen they figger you know somethin' 'bout who they want. Now if you happen to run up on 'em at night they are more than apt to kill you, 'cause when they holler for you to stop, you gets scared of the mob and cuts out runnin'. Then they shoot you down. If you do stop some bad white man is likely to kill you for sport.

Sometimes the agents ride at the head of a mob, but round here there is a bad scoundrel called Dan Ashby who usually gets mobs together. They only get them after niggers—I never seen or heard tell of one after any white man.

Some white folks are just natcherly low-down and no good. A white man next to our place did something that wasn't right to his own daughter and his son killed him for it. There was a little white girl 4 years old down in Duncan what asked a little nigger boy about 3 to pull her bloomers up for her. They was just little kids playing along together. Some old white man saw it and grabbed up the little boy and castrated him. Then he took the boy and threw him in the lake. Nobody ever did anything about that.

I never had much to do or say with white people, and I don't either like or dislike them. I ain't scared of them, though, like some niggers. I fight white boys quick as they meddle with me.

Thousands of youth are "dammed up" on the farms of the South. They are unable to make a satisfactory living there and are unwanted in the cities and industrial centers. Hesekie represents a class of rural Negro youth in the plantation area capable of growth and confident in his rural skills but bound in by a complex of barriers, small in their separate details but fairly paralyzing in their totality. He is, however, a part of the raw material from which the cities recruit their surplus populations and which the rural South all too casually loses to the city.

SADIE RANDOLPH: GIRL IN A SHARE-CROPPER FAMILY

Sadie Randolph's family is one of the thousands of Negro sharecropper families living along the Yazoo in Bolivar County, Mississippi. She is a placid girl of 18. Her complexion is dark-brown and she has short, straightened hair. In her new gingham dress, which she herself made, she is neat and clean.

The house in which she lives is a four-room frame dwelling in fairly good condition, although about twenty-five years old. Its chief defects are a leaky roof and a broken back door. Beside the house is a small well-kept vegetable and flower garden. In the back yard is a motor truck, worth about $300. There are many chickens, nine hogs, and two cows—a conspicuous affluence by the standards of the Negro community. The family cleared $160 from the cotton crop last year.

Sadie Randolph is interesting because she belongs to one of the numerous sharecropper families that find it necessary to compromise with the conventions in order to achieve a practical economic unit for sharecropping. The fact of irregular family organization is often noted statistically. The effects of such organization on the personality of youth is not so often indicated.

The head of the house is David Freeman, who, although not married to Sadie's mother, is accepted as Sadie's stepfather. He is a pleasant-looking, medium-brown man of about 30 years of age, with short, crisp hair, and an honest, independent, good-humored air. His education ended at about the third grade. Sadie's mother is darker, with unkempt hair, a hard face, and a surly manner. There is also a 10-year-old boy in the household, David Freeman's son by another woman at the time he was living with his first wife. The boy's mother gave the baby to David's first wife because the wife had no children and the mother had too many. An uncle and aunt of Sadie's also live in the home. The uncle is Sadie's father's brother, and the aunt is Sadie's mother's sister. The uncle assists on the farm and is an essential part of the economic unit of the household. The aunt, often ill and the victim of "spells," works when she can.

Sadie's lineage is complicated, but her mother explains it tonelessly and apparently without emotion. When the girl's grandmother married Randolph, her second husband, she already had a grown daughter by her first marriage and Randolph similarly had a grown son. These two became Sadie's parents although they never married because Sadie's mother did not like the man.

Working for a Negro Farmer

The stepfather is sharecropping with a Negro farmer who rents his land from a white man. He says:

> I'd rather work with my own color. They talk to you like you was a man. The white man talks to you like you was a boy. The colored boss don't cuss you out, neither. I make a better showing here than where I was before and get more out of my crop 'cause I'm working for a colored man.

Before he came to the present place he worked on a white man's plantation. It was, he said, "a one-man town, all owned by one white man, and too tough" for him.

Whatever Sadie decides to do as a career, the stepfather does not want his own son to follow him in farming, because "he would not get enough out of it." He would rather have him be

a "carpenter or something mechanical." What is needed on a cotton farm is a large family, but his wife is emphatic about a small family. She says bluntly, "I don't like children much."

Daily Routine of a Girl on the Farm

Sadie's daily duties get her up at 4:30 in the morning. Her mother prepares breakfast—usually fried okra, salt pork, tomato gravy, and bread. The ailing aunt washes the dishes. By five o'clock they are all in the field. The blistering heat sends them in about eleven, and dinner is cooked—turnip greens, cornbread, salt pork, and sometimes pie. They lie around and rest until about 1:30, then return to the field until sundown. Supper consists of the left-overs from dinner.

Sadie walks to the local school, located four miles from her home, to attend the five-month school term. The school is an old, two-room, frame structure, with two teachers—the principal and his wife. The principal is also a house painter in his spare time. Sadie is in the eighth grade and likes her school work, such as it is, when she can attend. Her favorite subjects are arithmetic and spelling. English and arithmetic, she thinks, will be most important to her after school because " you always have to talk and to count."

Worries about Being "Saved"

She "got religion" when she was 8 years old but saw no "visions" or anything of the sort. "They don't have visions in the Church of Christ," she said. Her main worry is whether she will be "saved." She is afraid of the devil and fire and brimstone, and she wants to go to heaven which, she says with conviction, is filled with milk and honey. The only complete books she has read are church books. She does not dance nor go to the movies because her church forbids it. Her recreation is playing such simple games as "buzz seven," "minister's cat," and "eleven hands," at home or at church parties. However, there are times when she wishes she had never been born, for then she would not have to worry about school or being saved. The worst sin, she thinks, is having a baby before marriage. Then "I'd miss heaven

and go to hell, and I'm working to go to heaven." The next worst
sins in the order named are drinking, killing, and stealing.

Resentment toward Stepfather

The last time she saw her real father was in 1926, when she
was 6 years old. She wants very much to see him again and says
that she loves him more than her stepfather, although the latter
does more for her than her real father. But she would not like to
live with her real father because "he drinks so much and stays
drunk." She does not know his present "wife," but she knows
that this woman takes care of him when he is drunk.

With a vagrant and consciously irrational vehemence she asserts, "I love my father 'cause if it hadn't been for him I wouldn't
of been here," and adds, "I'd rather mamma to be married to
him, and then I could have stayed with my father." When she
visited her real father in 1926 he wanted to come back home
with her, but her mother would not permit it. The resentment
in Sadie's tone shows rather obvious jealousy toward her stepfather. She refers to her own father as "Daddy," sometimes
"Father," and to her stepfather pointedly as her mother's husband, or her stepfather.

Attitude toward Self

She is sensitive about color and prefers a light-brown complexion, but adds, "I like my color [dark-brown] but would like
to have long hair." Her own hair is short. However, she thinks
color is more important than hair, "because you can fix hair
and make it look pretty, but you can't change color." She does
not like white because "it wrinkles quick." Although she likes
her own color, she recognizes that whites have more opportunities and that is the only reason she might like to be white. If
she were white she would like to be a bookkeeper. Being what
she is, she thinks she will probably sew and cook, or get married
and not have to worry about a job.

Attitude toward Whites

Sadie says "the poor white men are after the colored women
on the streets. They ought to be after their own color if they're

after anybody." She recalls walking down the street with a friend in Clarksdale on one occasion when two white men in a car stopped them and asked if they wanted to make a dollar. The girls did not reply. When the other girl's mother, who was walking behind, came up to them the men drove off. Sadie says:

> Whites are all right in their place and ought not to bother colored folks. I am scared of whites when they don't stay in their place. They like the colored women.

She says some whites are good and mentioned particularly a man whose office her mother cleaned. "He wasn't stingy, and he paid good," she said.

The mother says that she did not let Sadie play with white children after she was 8 or 9 years old. Before that age she thinks the white children do not know about color, but after that their parents teach them. Then they run to their parents with tales and there is danger of a fight in which the Negroes will inevitably suffer. They have as neighbors an Italian family. This farmer is a renter and lives across the road from Sadie's home. The stepfather says he is "good friends" with this family and often goes to their house and they come to his. He says that he eats with them "right in their own house." He likes them and "gets along fine" and the two little boys "play fine." But he will not allow his boy to go over to the Italian neighbor's house. It is all right for the Italian boy to come to his house, but not for his boy to go there.

> They treat us good so far, but we don't know what is to come. If the boy goes over to the Italian's house and something happens . . . maybe the Italian man might say something he didn't like. I'd know what to do . . . I'd come home, but the boy, he wouldn't know what to do.

Ambitions and Outlook

Sadie's chief ambition is to go to the Saints Industrial School near Lexington. This school is run by the Church of God in Christ and imposes a very rigid discipline on behavior. That is why she wants to go there and also why her mother prefers it; they have not been able, however, to save enough to cover the expenses of $4 a month. If her mother and stepfather cannot send her to the Industrial School, she hopes they will let her work her way through. This is her driving ambition at present and it overshadows every other interest. She does not plan to get married until late, but when she does she says she would prefer a husband a bit lighter than she is and would like to marry a doctor; she says, "Before I marry a farmer I wouldn't marry at all." After marriage she says she would like to have just one child because "then I could dress her like I want to."

The large number of families in which there are stepparents gives importance to Sadie's experience; her response to this fairly typical cultural situation is a neurotic one. From all present indications she will not be able to realize her ambition to get out of the farming class. This she has recognized to some extent and has taken refuge in religion.

ESSIE MAE JONES: SISTER IN A TENANT FAMILY

Large families are necessary in the cotton economy, but this often means two or three incompatible sets of children in the household. The home of Essie Mae Jones is located about three miles from the little community of New Rising Star, in Macon County, Alabama. The one-story frame dwelling occupied by the family shows obvious signs of age and deterioration, but in spite of this its cleanliness and a fresh coat of whitewash make it appear attractive. Inside there is very little furniture. The two front rooms contain only beds, but these are neatly covered with white sheets. A large pallet is stretched across the floor. The crude furnishings are accentuated by the neatness. The floors have recently been scoured with a disinfectant, giving the place a sanitary, clean odor. There are no chairs in the house, but several small home-made benches are lined up on the porch. The yard and garden, like the house, have been made attractive. Flowers are growing and serve to relieve the gaunt and bare house. Despite the apparent poverty, it is obvious that the family takes pride in its home.

Essie Mae is 17 years old, tall and black. She wears a plaid dress patterned in intense shades of red, yellow, green, and pink.

Her short, crinkly hair has been untwisted and combed free so that she appears to have a fringe around her head.

Her own mother died when she was 8 years old and her father has remarried, so with the new additions there are two sets of children in the houshold. Mrs. Lake Erie Jones, the wife, is a slender woman of dark-brown complexion who, possibly from work or lack of care and the rapid succession of child-births, or all of these, appears much older than her 28 years. She smiles frequently revealing teeth that are large and tobacco stained. The father is a small man of brown complexion, very pleasant and sincere. He is considerably older than his wife. Their interest in their children and their ambitions for them are manifest. The wife attempted to name the children in the household. She made two attempts to do so and finally gave up:

> Lord, we got so many of 'em here, seems like I can't keep 'em straight. Now I ain't the mother of these older children. Essie Mae, James, Lessie Belle, Liza Belle, and Thelma belong to Mr. Jones' first wife. She's dead. She died 'bout six or seven years ago. She was going to have another baby and taken fits the night the baby was born. Well, she and the baby both died 'fore we could get the doctor. I know, I was right here. See, she and me was first cousins so I was all the time right here with her. Then, Mr. Jones, he needed some woman to help him with all them little children, so he and me got married.

There are three sons of the husband who are almost as old as the wife, but they do not live at home. They are Essie Mae's full brothers. One of the boys is in Detroit and works in a barber shop. Will, Jr., is married and lives in Heflin, Alabama. Both of these boys write home and occasionally visit, but Tom, a third son who went to Atlanta several years ago, is completely out of touch with the family.

Stepmother Trouble

When the boys are on visits to the family they accept the wife and obey her mild orders. But Essie Mae is different, the step-mother says:

> Seems like since she's getting older she don't want to do what

I tell her. Sometimes I don't understand that girl. As long as her father be 'round she do well. He makes 'em all mind me— his own and ourn; but Essie Mae kinda mean like. Reckon she don't mean no harm, but she's lazy. She won't do no work less I keep right behind her, and then she gets mad and declares I ain't her mother. Well, a stepmother's got as much say as a mother when a girl ain't got no mother. I never show no differ- ence to her or my own, but seems like she kinda feels I love mine best and tries to be hard on me. Mine is just little and naturally we pets 'em. Essie Mae is a envious kind of girl. She be right proud of her father. Well, she gets "railed" [angry] when Will puts my children first. She don't like that at all. Lessie Belle, Thelma—ain't none of the rest like that. I think Will always let Essie Mae have her own way, and now she just showing herself. I never has no trouble with her and the boys— nothing like that. She's just envious and jealous like, and I tell her that's dangerous. Folks get to killing and get in trouble when they get all worked up like that. I likes her fine myself. I tries to be just like a mother to her, but she ain't 'preciative. She be right good to these children. She plumb in love with this baby boy, Roosevelt. This is my knee baby. Ludie, my lap baby be sleeping.

Alma, the 5-year-old child, came out on the porch carrying Ludie, the baby. The wife exclaimed:

Lord a'mighty—the cat's got the kitty [she hurries to rescue the baby]. Alma's just crazy 'bout this baby. I have to watch her or she's carry him everywheres. You know she'll drop that baby and make him lose his good sense.

Conflict among the Children

Essie Mae and Lessie Belle sleep together in one room. Mr. and Mrs. Jones, Clarence, Roosevelt, and Ludie sleep in another room which has two double beds in it. James, the older son, has a cot in the third bedroom, and the double bed is occupied by Thelma, Liza Belle, and Alma. The family always sits down at the table together for meals.

It is obvious that Essie Mae is acutely aware of the brother and sister relationships in the home and emphasizes a prefer- ence for her own sisters and brothers. She says decisively:

I like papa best of all. He does what I tell him to do, and he don't make me do nothing I don't want to do. If I want anything all I got to do is ask papa and he will give it to me. Next I like my mother best. I don't mean that one out there. She ain't my real mother. She's only my stepmother. She's nice, I guess, but I don't like her like I do mama. She was kind and liked us all the same. My stepmother likes the little children better than she loves us because them is her children. Papa loves us best. Sometimes my stepmother tries to make it hard on us. She tells papa we don't behave and tries to make him punish us, but he don't. When she scolds Liza Belle I get mad and try to fight her. Liza Belle is the baby and I have to see to her.

She does not recognize the youngest child in the family as the baby.

That's my stepmother's baby, but it ain't my mother's baby. I'm talking 'bout my own mother. Liza Belle is my own mother's baby and my real sister. I tell Thelma and Lessie Belle and Liza Belle that ain't our real mother and just to talk to papa 'bout things we want. James is my real brother but he stays away most the time. This mother is kind to me, but I just can't like her like I did mama.

Liza Belle is Essie Mae's favorite sister, because she is "the baby" and James is her favorite brother "because he is my only real brother." Essie Mae is, nevertheless, very fond of her step-sisters and stepbrothers, and although she places them after her "real" ones in her affection, she fails to show the same resentment toward them that she shows toward her stepmother. This resentment grows stronger as Essie Mae grows older, and there is real jealousy for her father's affection. A neighbor said:

I been knowing Essie Mae for a long time. That child won't leave her papa. I declare she is just crazy about her papa. Mr. Jones is a fine man, too. I ain't seen many men as kind and good to his children as that man. He just loves every one of them. 'Cose, I think Essie Mae is his favorite. When the mama died Essie Mae comforted him so much and, little as she was, she'd cook and do 'round for him. You can't get her far away from him. Now, Lake Erie Jones she be fine to all them children. Don't make no difference at all between them. Essie Mae's a little headstrong and wants things her way. I reckon her papa's made her selfish. He gives her nice clothes and spending money for school, but Lake Erie Jones do just what a mother would for them.

Tensions based upon jealousies sometimes arise where there are different sets of children in the family. The majority of rural Negro households are in some degree mixed. Thus, in the youth's earliest and most intimate group the sense of emotional security is qualified by problems of family organization.

Color as a Social Problem

Essie Mae has rationalized her color. She says:

Black is the best color. I'd rather be black than anything. All Negroes belong to the African race and if you are black you look more like an African, and people can tell you got pure blood. I'm glad I'm dark-skinned. I think colored people what look white is the worst. It shows they are mixed and been with white men. They call them people bad names. I don't like to say it but the children says white colored people is all bastards, and I believe it because if you belong to the black race you should be black. I like some light-skinned people, but it just don't look good to me.

Her best friends are of very dark complexion. She says she prefers going with dark-skinned girls because "when they get mad at you they don't call you 'black'." Tangerine Smith, a close girl friend, is dark. They play together and like to go to church and Sunday school "and don't fight."

Family Income and Educational Opportunity

The father went as far as the fourth grade in school, and his wife as far as the sixth grade. They both had to leave school early to help on the farm and never went back. They want their children to get all the education they can, at least to go through high school. Essie Mae wants to go to Selma University. The father wants her to go, but times continue to be hard. He said:

Farming ain't like it once was. Things is pretty tight now. There was a time when a man made a right smart living on crops, but now we work just as hard and long and don't have much to show for it. I rent this place and pay $80 a year for that and the house. 'Cose, I ain't got more than 30 acres under cultivation. Last year I raised eight bales of cotton. We got two prices on that. My best cotton brought 'bout 12 cents a pound. Reckon I raised just about four bales of that. Then

I got 'bout 8 cents for the rest. I take mine and get the best price I could, so I don't get nothing more. I used 'round about two and a half tons of fertilizer. That cost me $70. That was just for cotton. I paid $15 for fertilizer for corn.

He has no idea as to the amount of money he cleared last year. According to his figures it would have been about $330 for cotton. The corn is used for the stock and for food at home; he also has a fine garden. His wife cans vegetables and fruits, which reduces the food bill. The family raises its own meat.

Well, you see [explained the father] we trades up our food bill at the store. Then at the end of the season I pay it out in cotton. That takes plenty, and we got to pay $80 for our rent. That don't leave much. The rest we usually spend for clothes, and getting the children in school. Right now we spends just about $9 a week for food. All our meat is out, and we won't kill the hogs till late fall.

The Negro Community

The community in which Essie Mae lives provides few recreational facilities. All social gatherings are held at the church. Essie Mae likes to dance but knows it is frowned upon by the community.

Folks here say if you dance, you dance to the devil. The most I do for fun is go to town sometimes, fish, and, when I'm in school, play volleyball.

She reads the *Country Home* magazine sometimes, and the newspaper every day, but she has gone to the movies only once in her life, and she did not like it.

I don't like to sit still and look at fighting and things like they have in the movies, so I wouldn't go even if we had one out here.

She has never traveled. Once she visited Montgomery for a few hours, but she can remember nothing about the visit except that she went to a woman's house, ate dinner, and kept wishing she was back home. She insists she never wants to go away from home unless it is to go to Selma to school.

Relations with Whites

The pattern of the white community is accepted by the father, but not by Essie Mae. The father says:

> White folks are all right long as a man stays in his place. Down here in the South a Negro ain't much better off than he was in slavery times. We work all the time but don't get nothing for it 'cept a place to live and a plenty to eat. Some can't get that. Now you asked me 'bout voting. I'm willing to co-operate and go to vote, but white folks don't want that. They don't think much of Negroes voting. I ain't got nothin' 'gainst white people, but they won't give Negroes a chance. We all equal and ought to have a equal chance, but we can't get it here. In this settlement there ain't no white folks. You won't find a white family between here and Red Gap—that's up the road six or seven miles—so we don't have no trouble. Folks live peaceably here and tend to their own business so I consider it a good place to be. I don't know any place else I'd rather be. This suits me fine. I was born in Montgomery County but was raised here in Macon County. Reckon I was 'bout 5 years old when I come into this county, and I've stayed right here.

Essie Mae avoids all contact with white people. She says:

> I don't like them. I don't know why. There ain't no reason except they think they are better than colored and try to keep colored people down. Maybe all white people ain't alike, but I don't like none of them.

WILLIE BRAYBOY: CHILD OF A FARM HAND

Farm hands are the lowest class of agricultural workers, and escape, even through education, is difficult for the children. Willie Brayboy is the type of youth who can be seen any day ambling aimlessly along the highways that wind through the great cotton estates. He is 15 years old, is in the third grade, and is one of a family of seven children. They are farm hands and they live in Bolivar County, Mississippi. William is about 5 feet tall and weighs about 125 pounds. His hair is harsh and set in tight spirals and is, apparently, never combed. His complexion is dark and rusty from want of bathing. His bare feet are caked with dirt and tough as leather. But he has sparkling, mischievous eyes and a wide playful grin which discloses decaying yellow teeth and coral-pink gums. He is dressed in a soiled and ragged polo shirt and blue denim overalls.

Willie is a dreamer, and his conversation is filled with fantastic accounts of travel, of people, and of escape.

> Yestiddy I went to New York. . . . Yes, sir, I went to New York in an automobile. No, it war'nt; it was a airplane I went to New York in. I saw the President, but he didn't see me. Yes, sir, he knows me. . . . I been to his house. . . . I didn't shake hands with him 'cause he was busy. I saw lotta other people, but they didn't see me. . . . I just walked around, and saw things and come back last night. . . . I come back 'bout two o'clock and took my airplane home. I don't know whether or no I'm going again.

Social Insecurity at School

Willie avoids school whenever he can. The children do not play with him. He knows them all, but has not been to their homes. He plays only with his brothers. "I don't hardly know none of the girls," he says. He adds, "I know some of them, though; but I ain't never kissed nair one of them." He feels the snubs of the boys directed at his very lowly social status, and finds some escape from the humiliation in fantasy and daydreams.

> None of these ole boys'll fight with me, 'cause they know I can beat 'em. I don't like none of 'em, and most of 'em don't like me.

The reason why he does not want to go to school is made very clear in a sudden burst of enraged self-pity.

> Everybody round here pokes fun at me. Everybody says why don't I comb my hair, 'n why don't I wash up. My mother don't got no comb for me to be usin'.

He wants to be an electrician some day, and likes to tinker with wires. He actually repaired a lamp for Mrs. Miller, one of the few kindly women who do not "make him feel bad."

> Yes, suh, if I could go to school and learn how to be a 'lectrician, I'd go every day.

The Dreary Refuge That Is Home

Willie's home is a two-room dilapidated cabin. It leans perilously to one side and seems about to collapse at any moment.

There are two cots, one bed, and two chairs in the house. The boys sleep on the floor in the kitchen. A pile of freshly picked cotton is in a corner of one room. The walls are bare, and the sunlight streaks in like yellow blades from great cracks in the roof and sides.

The mother is a well-built and muscular woman. Her hair sticks out from a handerchief tied around her head. Her teeth are snuff stained. She wears a soiled and worn white dress, and shoes with so much of the tops cut off that almost her entire foot is exposed. On her legs are large pellagra scabs the size of a half dollar. She talks earnestly and sadly about her children, for their poverty is complicated by the father's vices of desperation.

> I want them children to get education and behave theyselves, I honest do. But it's just like this—they father take up all the money he make and gamble it away and drink it up. When I send them to school they learn or they won't go at all. Last year I just didn't have money to send 'em at all. You know yourself if you ain't got no shoes to wear and can't dress like the other children, and all the other children making fun of you, you wouldn't go neither.

Without comfort, security, or prospect of a better future, the ambitions of the youth of this level are diverted to empty dreams of escape.

STANLEY BYRD: MULATTO YOUTH

There are relatively few mulatto youth on the plantations, and they are proud of their color. Stanley Byrd is a Coahoma County youth of 19, tall, muscular, and well-built. His complexion and hair are a light terra-cotta brown which Negroes sometimes call "meriny." He is lively and prankish, and frequently gets into trivial arguments but rarely fights. He walks with a slow shuffling gait that gives one the impression that he is always tired, and his habit of keeping his head lowered heightens this effect. He is, on the contrary, quite active and energetic when he is engaged in some sport. His heavy brows, full lips, and pug nose highlight his yellowish complexion.

Long arms hang heavy and low from his shoulders, and his hands and joints are large and thick. His feet are of exceptional size. He wears misshapen, cut away old shoes that exaggerate the size of his enormous flat feet. Stanley's usual dress consists of a much worn and faded green flowered shirt, blue denim overalls with shoulder straps, and a sweat-stained and discolored collegiate felt hat that originally was white. When Stanley is dressed up he wears a white shirt, open at the collar and with the sleeves rolled up, white washable slacks, and white shoes. He always wears the discolored felt hat. He wears socks only when he is "dressed up," and they are usually white.

He began farming—slopping hogs—at the age of 7. Then he learned to cut wood for the stove, and later to milk the cows and feed the mules. At 12 his father and older brother taught him how to plow, but he was 15 before he had full responsibility as a plow hand. The family lived at first on a farm "in the hills," and at 6 he started to school in that community.

He stopped school when he was in the seventh grade. His oldest brother was sickly and could do very little work around the farm. Another brother was headstrong and unreliable, and usually went his own way. Stanley, the most dependable one, finally quit school after being interrupted so often in his schooling that he became discouraged. He has been out three years and talks vaguely of going back at some time, but actually never expects to return.

His mother is a deeply religious woman who reads the Bible regularly to the children, prays constantly, and sincerely laments the fact that the father, a normally genial parent while he lived, was a sinner. She is the moral strength of the household. She would say, "Turn favors if people do something for you, and don't run over folks or take advantage of them." She has taught them that lying and stealing are sins. Stanley says, "Mamma said God hates a liar and you has less chance to get into heaven if you is a liar."

Behavior Problems

There is an interesting ambivalence in Stanley's attitudes on sex relations. He would not marry a girl "if she had something to do with other fellows." However, at 19 he has a son 4 years old. He says:

> I see him often, and his mother too, but I don't have nothing to do with her no more. She just told me about it, but didn't try to make me marry her. I didn't want to marry her because she was too dark. I wasn't thinking about marrying, and would of tried to get out of it if she had wanted me. Lots of people know it's my kid. Her oldest sister often gets after me about it, but doesn't do nothing. People 'round don't make no difference, though some don't have too much to do with the girl. They never act like they think I ought to marry her though.

The attitude of the community toward certain types of behavior is not well defined. There is a general feeling of objection to drinking and gambling, but unless the offenders run afoul of the law and are put in jail not much control is exercised because both are rather common. Stanley says:

> There even was a little old preacher around that wasn't doing much at preaching, and he took to rolling dice. He said he could make more money gambling than he could preaching. Nobody did anything about it either. They didn't run him off or nothing. Some of the people won't have no more to do with him, but lots of 'em do.

Absence of Guides to Behavior

According to Stanley, there are no leaders among the young people in his community.

> Young folks don't travel much together, and each one does about as he wants to. There ain't no clubs and such things for anyone to head up. The only place they get together is at the church, and the old folks practically run that.

> There ain't much amusement either 'ceptin' dances or ball games. There is a little ball team that plays some. Fact, there ain't much to do. See, we live about half way between Lyons and Jonestown, and neither one is much. We even have to come into Clarksville to go to the show.

The only place that he has ever gone is Memphis, Tennessee.

> I went up there one time to see my aunt when she was sick. I like it pretty good. I didn't get to go around much 'cause I

didn't stay very long, but what I saw was all right. I'd like to go and see some more places, like New York.

All the Boys Quit School

Stanley's father died five years ago of heart trouble. Since his father's death his mother has been running the farm, and is afraid to marry again because a stepfather might not be kind to the children. She had ambitions to have all the children go to college; but one quit because he did not like rural schools, another because he was not interested in anything, and Stanley quit because he had to work.

Color Troubles

He is conscious of his color difference from most of the boys of his acquaintance, and has adopted a pronounced attitude on the matter. "Dark people," he says, "are hard to get along with." He goes with a dark girl, but does not take her out publicly. He says, "Most dark people are dumb and don't know nothing, and I'd rather not be fooling with them." Once while he was tossing fruit from an orchard to some of his companions, a peach struck the hen house and broke and a part of it struck a dark boy. Stanley apologized and forgot it promptly. A little later while they were standing near each other, the boy picked up a croquet mallet and asked him challengingly why Stanley had hit him. Thinking that the boy was playing, he laughed it off and apologized again. The dark boy struck Stanley on the temple, knocked out a tooth, and fractured his jawbone. He was rendered unconscious and "laid up" for several days.

> He had no cause to hit me and I wasn't expecting it, but black niggers are just mean that way. I ain't never goin' to fool with one no more. People used to tell me black was evil, but I didn't pay it no mind. I sure believe it now. Some black niggers are just naturally mean—like that boy that hit me.

Empty Future

Stanley has no plans for the future; he has never thought of being anything except, perhaps, a house painter. He recognizes that education probably plays an important part in getting a good job, but he says:

Color makes a lot of difference too. You notice that they put all white on the good jobs and give niggers no 'count jobs like working on the highway or doing hard and dirty work that white folks ain't particular about doing.

His general lack of foresight also applies to his child. He says:

I ain't never give it a thought. Her mamma and her people will take care of him. I might help it some day, but I hadn't never thought about it.

JUANITA AND CLINT: MARRIED

Early marriages are frequently unfortunate, socially and economically. Juanita Sawyer is 17 and her husband of three months is 19; they have a baby one week old. Young couples have a difficult time because there are not enough hands available for work in the fields to support them as sharecroppers. The worn-out land is too poor to offer a living unless there are many members to work the crop. For this reason young people usually remain with one or the other of their parents, or defer marriage until they can fit more comfortably into an economic unit. Young girls frequently marry men very much older than themselves, and are most fortunate when they can get a widower with children.

Juanita is a large girl of dark-brown complexion, with a broad face and a wide mouth. Her white and even teeth are small for her face. She looks weary and spent. The two-room cabin in which she lives with her husband and child, in an isolated section of Macon County, Alabama, is dilapidated and musty with age and long use. The roof over the bedroom hangs low and has some holes in it. She sits by the window helplessly indifferent to the decay around her. She and her husband have begun to try to get a foothold as a cropper family.

Her husband, Clint Sawyer, is of slight build, youthful and sophisticated in a rural sense, and a bit shifty. He was introduced to Juanita while she was in school by a girl friend at whose home he had lived. He had been a beau of this girl friend but she preferred not to get married.

Juanita's Family Background

Juanita's parents have been separated for five years, and the father has remarried and lives in Detroit. There is a little brother, born to her mother two years after her husband left. Juanita does not know the father of her youngest brother.

The school which she attended is sixteen miles from her parents' home, and she was sent to board in the home of a friend of the family nearer the school. Here she met her husband, and their marriage was as accidental as their meeting. When the principal of the school discovered that Juanita was pregnant, he let her complete her grade and take her examination; he insisted, however, that she should get married, and Clint agreed. She said, "I spec he didn't mind or he wouldn't of married me."

At home with her mother she had been unhappy. Her mother was a quarrelsome woman. Juanita said, "I think if my mother wasn't always quarreling and fussing my father would of stayed at home; but she treated him so bad he just left." She had wanted to run away but had no place to go. Now she is married. Marriage meant escape of a sort, but it also brought new responsibilities and a new definition of her economic role. She said:

> When you marry you suppose to live where your husband live, and he found this home. Some of his folks give him a bed and table and the white man he work for give him a stove. Mamma give me the chairs. I reckon we'll get along all right.

Founding a Cropper Family

There is a well-worn iron bed on one side of the room which is covered with a clean quilt. There is a slight hump in the center of the bed. Juanita rises slowly, as if in a daze, goes to the bed, pulls back the quilt and sheet, and reveals a tiny five-pound baby, who has been completely covered in spite of the humid heat. The baby's color is an unnatural red. She picks it up gently and gazes at it and sighs, "It's so little." The baby's eyes are filled with a thick yellow secretion. Juanita says casually, "Seem like something the matter with her eyes, I have to keep wiping out pus." She takes a corner of her dress and mops out the child's eyes. It cries feebly. Juanita looks puzzled, replaces the child on the bed, and draws the covers again.

> I just have to keep her covered up, these flies so bad they jest worry her so she can't sleep.

Clint has had trouble getting a good contract because he does not have enough hands to work the cotton. When he married he found a side job helping a white man who runs a café on the highway; he gets $2 a week and such food as he can occasionally "get away with." The baby is a burden. The young mother complained:

> Once I liked babies. I likes other folks' children, but seem like I just can't like this baby. I been trying, but I just don't love it. I don't think it's cute. She is ugly—I be very kind to her but it just look like I can't love her like I do other people's children. I don't never want no more.

Juanita's life pattern is set in terms of the dominant Negro community. She joined the Mt. Canaan Baptist Church after an operation for appendicitis when she was frightened at the thought of dying before her "soul had been saved." She does not want her husband to work for Negroes "cause they are all poor just like us, and after he works they may not pay him." She prefers white people. "They be fine. They give us a living." The wife of her husband's employer gave the baby all the clothes it has, a box of baby powder, and some oil.

In school Juanita was about like the average simple plantation girl—heavy, placid, and uninspired in school work, but well enough behaved to be permitted to complete her work even after her condition was so noticeable that it was the object of good-natured joking by her classmates. The principal said with bored resignation, "I've seen it happen too much. She'll have a baby every year and struggle along somehow."

DAVID HILMAN: MIGRATORY YOUTH

David Hilman was born just across the creek from his present home in Greene County, Georgia. His family has been highly mobile; during his 17 years he has covered by truck, with his parents and their essential stock and household property, most of the hopeful spots of three southern states. Now he is back home again.

When he was about 3 years old the family migrated to Birmingham, Alabama. David does not know how his father ever heard about "out there." The boll weevil had struck in Greene County and left black havoc.

> Colored people couldn't furnish themselves and white people wouldn't let them have any money 'cause they didn't believe they could make good crops.

In the delta area larger capital might have taken a chance, but not in the impoverished old South where white owners were also poor. After three years in Birmingham they returned, partly because his mother was ill and partly because his father had a temperament less adjustable to the power plants in which he was working than to the soil. The stay was long enough to permit the oldest son to break away from the family and seek a career. He found a job in a barber shop in North Carolina and got married.

Trek to North Carolina

David's family remained on the farm six years, and when hard times struck again they packed their belongings and left for North Carolina.

> The crops we were making weren't much and the landlord couldn't help us. And then the house was in a awful condition. My brother was living in North Carolina. I don't know how he got up there. He said they were making good crops there and he wrote my father about it.

There were eleven members in the family party that set out for North Carolina. A sister's husband and a brother's wife were members of the economic household. They left in two trucks—one carrying the family, the other a mule, a cow, and some furniture. David was ill on the trip, and the party stopped in Hartford, Georgia. It was cold. The women folks went to look up a first cousin who was a preacher, but he was in the throes of a revival and could not see them. David stayed in the truck and in the early morning a policeman investigating the strange truck heard his groans and carried him to the jail to warm him up. The next morning they set out again and got as far as Greenville, South Carolina. The sickening fumes from the old truck nauseated the whole party, but it was David again who became really ill. Then the motor stopped running. They flagged a passing car and were dismayed to find it driven by a white woman. To their surprise she offered to take one of the brothers to the nearest town for help.

A New Home and New People

On the long North Carolina trip David got a deep fright. His father, who was an ardent reader of the Negro papers, had read aloud to the party the story of a white woman who had gotten a Negro to strike a white relative of hers over the head and kill him for his insurance. Listening to his father's vehement discussion of this case, David received his first dramatic introduction to the white world. His father had been angered because a mob wanted to kill the Negro, completely ignoring the white woman's responsibility. David developed a morbid fear of white people and fancied thereafter that he saw the white woman dogging him through the fields to bait him for a mob.

When they finally reached North Carolina the whole party of eleven moved into a two-room house. Nine of them slept in the two beds and two on the floor. David's father began sharecropping on halves. The location of their home was especially fascinating to David. Trucks came out from town regularly to dump garbage and trash. The boys from all around came to watch the trucks unload. They were mostly white boys, and one of their games was throwing bottles at the colored children to see them run.

> One time one of my little brothers lost his shoes, he was running so fast. His shoes were old and cut out, and they just come off while he was running.

When they got home on this occasion an older brother got his gun and went back to find the white boys but they had gone.

> My brother-in-law told my brother he shouldn't have carried a gun over there 'cause he might of got in some trouble. We were afraid to go over there after that, and we just stayed around the house, or went to the field.

Once a white boy who was a neighbor met him in the field and walked home with him. In the back yard they stumbled upon a leather strap, and David picked it up. The white boy said, "Give me that strap!" and tried to take it; he said his grandmother had been promising him a strap for his school books and he needed it. David said, "No," and ran with the strap. For days he hid, in a sweat of fear, expecting the white boy's grandmother to have him punished, perhaps killed. When nothing happened his fears abated and he regained confidence in himself.

School Problems

The children did not attend school in North Carolina because they did not have presentable clothes. They were already retarded because their father had withdrawn them for a year from the Georgia school when the principal had wanted them to "act monkey" for the white superintendent at a "concert."

Trouble with Whites

Their biggest problem in North Carolina was trouble with lower-class white people. Impoverished white neighbors removed the tires from their trucks and sold them, and stole their hunting dogs, but nothing could be done about it. In North Carolina the father was free to sell his cotton anywhere—a respite from plantation discipline, but all mills were alike. Always the white man would figure himself into a large share in the cotton. David recounted one incident:

> The white man figured how much my father owed him for ginning. He cross figured and all like that, and got my father all mixed up. He beat my father out of $100 or more. The white man's father-in-law come out and started raring around too. He said they'd never had a nigger come up there to a white man's house to settle up, 'cause they always stayed on the place and took what he give them. My father stayed down there and tried to get a settlement, and every time the white man come down there he would figure it up real fast and say he was in a hurry and had to go, so my father got tired of that and went over to his house for settlement.

The landlord thought David's father was a blustering novice and counted him out for the next year. When the crops came in good order, he saw his mistake and tried to get him to stay.

But being defrauded of $100 and getting the worst mules and the last use of the wagons, discouraged him. His father said "he wouldn't stay if he gave him the whole plantation."

Trek Back to Georgia

So they went back to Georgia. On the return trip the mule and the cow were in the truck with the family and the furniture, because they could afford only one truck on this trip. They found their old place neglected and surrounded by weeds. The new owner lived in New York and came down only once a year. When the credit merchants refused an advance to the family, they managed to borrow money from a bank.

David welcomed the return home. In North Carolina they could not go to school, could not hunt without a license, and could not make cotton baskets from anything except dead trees.

David is now a full grown farm hand, getting up at four o'clock to feed the stock and, since his mother fell through the floor and injured herself, he helps with preparation of breakfast. He walks three miles to the highway to catch the school bus every time it runs. When the families cannot pay the driver's charge of $1.00 a month for each child, the driver cannot buy gas to run it. After school David helps his father in the field, and in winter cuts wood enough to keep fires going all day and night.

Family Links

David's family is linked with interesting characters and events in the history of the county. His mother's father was white.

> I used to hear my sisters say "I got some white blood in me," but I didn't know it was true until I went up and got my grandmother the other week. On the way back she told me how her father was white too.

He has a cousin who killed a man and escaped to Alabama. Another "cut up" a man and escaped. Two female cousins had children before they married. The sister who went farthest in school is now a stenographer in Detroit. "I guess we most proud of her," he said. The local preacher is an uncle who owns large parcels of land which he bought up as people fled before the boll weevil. This preacher was illiterate until a few years ago. It was an unsuccessful romance that goaded him into literacy. He wanted to marry one of the local girls who had graduated from school, and since he could not write he asked David's sister to write the proposal. The sister disliked the girl and wrote an insulting letter instead of a proposal of marriage, and shattered Uncle Wilbur's romance beyond possibility of repair. He decided to learn to do his own writing.

Conflict with the Community

The family is in a constant struggle with both the Negro and white communities. The Negroes dislike the father because he is a renter and the whites because he asserts himself when he believes he is right. David said:

> Colored people don't like my father because he is a renter, and a lot of them is just hands. So they tell the white man a lot of things about my father. They said he would steal things. Some of them is my kin people, and some of them knew him all his life.

The neighbors could blame their smaller crops for the landlord on the depredations of the Hilman hogs. Once the hogs actually broke out of their pens during a rain storm and got into a white man's corn. The white man sent for David's father and angrily accused him of letting his hogs run wild all the year. When his father disputed him another white man shouted, "Nigger, you know you called a white man a liar!" A fight started and David's father neither apologized nor ran. He was a strong man and could handle them both so long as they were without their guns.

The family now behaves with great caution, knowing well that they are a marked group and that the next time any white man starts something he is going to take the precaution of supporting his status with his gun and his white neighbors.

MADGE HICKMAN: A SUCCESSFUL FARMER'S DAUGHTER

Diversified farming areas permit more independence, greater freedom of ownership, and securer subsistence, and these bring new responsibilities. Johnston County in North Carolina is outside the plantation area and its farmers do not depend wholly upon any one crop. They raise their own food and may even give some of their time to nonagricultural pursuits. Along with subsistence crops they raise some cotton and tobacco, which are essentially cash crops. Over 90 per cent of the Negroes of the county are rural and over 70 per cent of them live on farms. The Negro families in the county have a comparatively high tenancy rate, but this is not so likely to be a matter of fixed status as in the plantation counties, for it is more often possible to do other work along with farming.

Home Setting

Madge Hickman lives on her parents' 102 acre farm, about six miles out from a small town in Johnston County, in what is called the Good Samaritan section, because of the presence there of the Good Samaritan Baptist Church. Her grandmother owns an adjoining farm of 140 acres, and both produce cotton, tobacco, grain, and food stuffs.

The five-room house is well furnished. The living room is a mixture of old and new furnishings, reflecting at the same time respect for modern conveniences and a sentimental regard for the battered treasures from earlier days and generations. The basic furniture is an overstuffed suite consisting of a davenport and two chairs, upholstered in deep blue mohair, an end table, and a large console radio. Beside the radio is an old cane-bottomed armchair, painted blue to match the furniture. Across the room is a huge dresser, also old, and an elaborate hatrack. On the tiny center table is a very old kerosene lamp which supports a new and modern parchment shade. A pale green and yellow straw rug partially covers the floor. On the walls are pictures in aging hand-carved wooden frames or in tortoise shell frames which are cracked and curled with age; there is one large gilt frame holding a collection of recent pictures. The center art piece is a vivid, curiously fanciful tapestry representing George Washington apparently leaving a group of soldiers and riding toward the Statue of Liberty. On the mantel and table are a thick array of bric-a-brac, colored paper flowers, artificial oranges, animals blown from glass, and a collection of white elephants.

Madge's mother is a large, friendly, brown woman who is dressed neatly in a well-fitting blue and white cotton print dress. In her rapid, lisping speech are marks of schooling and some urban influence. The father, Mack Hickman, is a brown man with slightly wavy hair and a serious face. In the household also are a cousin, Pensy, who is 15 years old and named for her maternal grandmother, Pensacola, and the grandmother herself, a proud old woman of about 65. The pictures on the walls are an important link with the past. The hand-carved and tortoise shell picture frames belonged to Mack Hickman's mother, and her mother and grandmother had them before her.

In one frame is a picture of Mr. Hickman's mother, who has been dead about five years. She has the physical traits of an Indian. In another frame is a picture of Mr. Hickman, rigid and severe with his high collar and handle-bar mustache. There is another picture of two white men, dressed in military uniform and holding rifles. They are relatives of Mr. Hickman's, a generation removed. The cane-bottomed chair belonged to Mr. Hickman's great-grandmother.

Madge is 17 years old, tall and thin, with a nut-brown complexion, large brown eyes, and brownish hair that has been straightened and bobbed. Her manner is mild and childishly immature for her age. She has been humored from birth by her grandmothers and her father. She calls her parents by their first names and her grandmother "mamma."

Family Training

Madge describes some of the incidents of her childhood as follows:

> When I was about seven years old I went to a funeral. Lil [her mother] had just bought me a great big doll, she paid $8.50 for it; and it came in a big box. Well, we children decided to have a big funeral. Two of my cousins helped me. The boy was the preacher. The girl and I cried and cried and brought

piles of flowers. We had a big funeral and buried the doll. Lil kept asking me where the doll was, but I told her I didn't know. I thought the doll was dead and I didn't want to dig it up. Then one day Mack [her father] was plowing and plowed up this doll and brought it to the house. He said "Lil, here's that doll you paid $8.50 for." It was all streaked and cracked, almost eaten up. Lil wanted to whip me, but my grandma took me in her apron and run off with me.

I didn't start to school until I was 8 years old. Once the teacher whipped me because I didn't know my alphabet. She didn't have to whip me but once. I came home and I learned them. After that I always learned enough to get promoted. I stayed in the seventh grade two years, but that's the only grade I ever got left in. I couldn't pass the state examination for the seventh grade, so I had to take the seventh grade work over. The next time I was sick at examination time and one of the teachers gave me the examinations, and I passed.

When I was little, Mack built me a playhouse and I tried to get Lil to let me have the victrola out in my house, but she wouldn't. Then one day she went away and I took the victrola out in my house. It rained and the records got wet and the machine too. It got so wet the spring broke, and after that I had to put my finger in it to make it run. Lil certainly was mad when she saw it, but Mack wouldn't let her whip me. He happened to be there when she saw it.

Daily Routine

Madge describes her day as follows:

In the winter I get up about 6 or 6:30. I sleep in the room with my grandma and Pence. Grandma sleeps in her bed and Pence and me sleep together. Pence helps me to clean up the bedroom. Then we eat breakfast. We have bacon and eggs, cornflakes, and biscuits. Some mornings I cook breakfast, usually on Wednesday morning. I like to give Lil a rest from cooking sometimes, so I cook. Then I dress; I take a sponge bath every morning and a bath in the tub twice a week. I don't want to smell. After that I dress.

I leave here at 7:45 every morning and drive to school. I get there at 8:30. I stay in school from 8:30 until 12:30, when we have lunch. Every day I spend about 25 cents for lunch. I buy apples and drinks and cakes or peanuts—just trash. Sometimes

I buy so much I can't eat it all during lunch hour, and I eat in class afterwards. Once or twice the teacher has sent me out to finish eating. I hate that. But I like to eat in school; it tastes so much better.

We stay in school until 3. In the afternoon I play basketball. I play on the school team—forward. I play fairly well. In games last year I made 64 goals. In one game I made 15 out of 21 scores. I take typing too, some afternoons.

I like arithmetic best. I can understand that, but some of those other subjects, I just don't like—like history and English. I don't like either one.

Well, I leave school at 3. As soon as I get home I eat a boiled dinner—collards, home-made meat, bread, and something sweet. Then usually I have to go off somewhere for Mack. He just saves the things for me to do. Most of the time I'm back home by 6. Then I drink a pint of milk and study. Nobody helps me. I study each subject about 30 minutes, but I don't have any regular plan. I study awhile then walk around with Pence, and go back. I study sorter haphazard. I never study English unless we're going to have a test. I hate it. If we're going to have a test, I'll study it for 45 minutes. I go to bed at 9:30.

Flowers are my hobby. All those in the yard out there, I planted them. I just love flowers. I like to play all kinds of games—baseball, basketball, football, and soft ball. We play out here every Saturday. We have a girls' soft ball team out here, and some team plays every Saturday. Lots of people come and watch the game. Next Saturday we're going to Piney Grove to play the girls there. We do that just when school's out in the summer time. I like to swim and play cards too. I don't like to read. Sometimes I read western stories and *True Story*, but not often. Usually I read the newspapers.

I spend lots of time doing things for Mack [her father]. I get his money and pay his men. I keep up with the money for him. One time they sent him too little money and I counted it before I started paying the men. I told Mack and went back and asked for the rest. The man gave it to me, and said he was sorry he made a mistake. But I notice that when he makes mistakes it's always in his favor. I count it first every time. I take out about $5 or $10 a week for myself, and I've got $140 in the bank.

Ambitions and Personality

Madge's school principal says that she is very neat, is very spoiled as a result of family indulgence, and is never rude. "She never admits anything about herself, even things that are nice." She is ambitious and she says she wants to have a career, but this is not convincing. She seldom gets angry, and when a boy once said something very mean to her she just looked at him and laughed tolerantly. She is timid and quiet but likes a good time, and is the most popular girl in school.

SAM CALLOWAY: SMALL FARMER'S SON

Rural areas within the influence of large cities attract the city's vices along with its advantages. Davidson County, Tennessee, has more urban than rural dwellers, for the city of Nashville is located in it. The rural Negro population tends to concentrate on the periphery of the city and just outside the borders, and usually in settlements. A few of these settlements, however, are ten to fifteen miles from the city, far enough to continue as self-contained communities, but close enough to the city to be accessible to its influences.

Sam Calloway lives in one of these settlements with his mother, father, and a sister 12 years old. Their house is a one-and-a-half story structure of four rooms, very much in need of paint, wall paper, and general repairs. The family owns this house and another equally defective one nearby. Inside, the furniture has been shifted to escape the water which comes in through holes in the roof. Sam's father works in a lumber yard and leaves the farming to the family. The mother is large and genial; the father tall, awkward, and casual in his movements. There are two older sons who are now away from home; all the children were born where the family now lives.

Sam is 15 years old, but weighs 165 pounds and looks 17 or 18. He dresses in blue overalls, and walks with a heavy, slow tread which again belies his youth. His brown face is chiseled sharply and his eyes show dark rings. Farm labor has made him muscular. He works about as a laborer on farms, especially during harvesting time, doing anything the farmers will give him to do.

Now at 15 he is considering leaving school when he finishes the eighth grade. In the first place, he feels that he is too large to be sitting in class with students so much smaller. Then, the money he can earn means more to him than what he is getting from school.

> What I'd really like to do is to go to an engineering school. I sure wish there was one around here, then I'd want to go to school. If I had the money I'd go up North to one. They don't care up North if you're colored.

Recreation and Religion

What worries his mother just now are his coughing spells and his companions. When he was 12 years old the doctors said he had tuberculosis, but she thinks "it's all gone now." Nevertheless she says:

> I don't think it would be good for him to set in class all day, with that cough he have now. When he's out in the open air I feels a lot better about him.

The other problem involves the whole community. There are three "taverns" which accommodate the local people as well as the people out from the city for a lark. The nickel-in-the-slot phonographs play "hot numbers" and cheap bootleg whisky can be bought. Sam says:

> We go to the taverns and joints around here. We drink beer, smoke, and dance with the girls. I don't like beer much; I just drink because the other guys drink it. We dance with the girls and play around with them. Ain't nothing else to do but that. The folks out here don't say nothing about us fellows and gals going to the taverns. Most of them do the same thing under cover. You can get a gal there and proposition her if you want to.

Some of the girls are hardened tavern habitués. One of them has a reputation for having "cut up" three men at different times in her romantic career. The community does not provide organized recreation for its youth. During the school term the children play baseball and football, but these are very largely spectator sports.

Sam seldom goes to church, and when he does it is to meet his girl friend. "Old people make too much fuss over religion," he thinks. Moreover, he does not have very high regard for the ministry.

It ain't just the poeple in the church that don't do the way the preacher says they ought to do, but the preacher don't move quite right himself sometimes. If you look around long enough you'll see the preachers making plenty "creeps" [trysts]. I know one who makes them every week.

Attitude toward Whites

He is not uncomfortably aware of the white community.

White folks don't worry me. I just don't bother them and they never bothered me. The white folks live down the highway mostly.

Ambitions

Sam goes on dreaming of becoming an engineer, or perhaps the owner of a car factory, or even a car salesman, because "you know a lot about cars then and can drive all you want to." He does not want too much education.

I think too much schooling, like going to college, does a lot of people harm. You can make money doing what I want to do.

But he cannot get away to begin his engineering study, and so he thinks he will just give it up.

When I read in the mechanic books sometimes about the places where they train engineers, I feel kinda bad. If I was white I could go to Vanderbilt or some other place right here in the state.

CHAPTER II

THE SOCIAL WORLD OF YOUTH

THE SOUTH is distinguished from other regions of the United States by significant cultural, climatic, economic, and population differences; within the South itself there are great variations. One cannot comprehend the life experiences and the intimate adjustment difficulties of the rural Negro without an understanding of the physical and the social worlds in which he lives. A unique environment fashions, in ways both subtle and direct, his personality and his destiny.

In a broad sense, the personalities of Negro youth are shaped by interaction with the social institutions characteristic of the South. Their personalities are profoundly influenced in a more realistic way by their familiar round of work and play, by the character and composition of their immediate families and their cliques, and by the level of education, the skills, and the social habits of their parents and all others who influence them. The significant physical environment is not alone the houses in which they live, but the highways and winding footpaths that link these families with their neighbors, the relentless sun and the violent or lazy rivers. Their lives are linked obscurely but inescapably with the seasons and prices. Overshadowing the daily round of life is the heavy imminence of illness and violence and death. Inevitably their personalities and careers are influenced by the fears, hopes, and expectations bred by their status; by their isolation from the stimulating currents of a growing world; by the deep margins of poverty and the prestige and glamour of those who have escaped it; by the moral, aesthetic, and religious standards to which they are exposed; by the complex etiquette of race; and by the all pervading psychological and social implications of the traditions of race and class.

In this study we are dealing with diverse types of southern

rural areas. The patterns and style of life in these areas, as they take form, cannot become really intelligible until the personalities are viewed in their community and family setting. The purpose, therefore, of this chapter is to present some of the characteristics of the areas and to relate these to the organization and structure of the families of the youth who are intimately exposed to their influence.

THE SOIL AND THE PEOPLE

The eastern rim of the South, along the coast, is the gray and mottled sand of the flatwoods and the gray and sandy loam of the coastal plain, stretching from Virginia to Florida. Bordering it closely is the sweeping Piedmont crescent from north Georgia across North Carolina to Danville, Virginia. It is in this area that capital began to erect mills to utilize both the product of the nearby cotton area and the landless, propertyless whites of the mountainous and infertile countryside. This area grows and manufactures 85 per cent of the tobacco consumed in America, and has lured the textile industry from New England.

The great Piedmont plateau, red clay belt, rolls along across North Carolina, South Carolina, and Georgia. It is cotton and tobacco country, with good tobacco and only middling cotton crops; three-fourths of the farms are operated by tenants. Here was once the heart of a great empire of cotton, now gone westward leaving only the pleasant memory of the past, and worn-out land which requires almost as much fertilizer as it produces in crops. There is now the new South, with its cotton mills and progressive spirit; the long isolated rural population has been drawn into the mill towns. Great wealth is concentrated in the ownership of the mills. The real population of the area, however, is made up of the mill workers and the many Negro tenants who farm half of the cotton land; they are ruled by the new leaders who came to supplant the old aristocracy.

In the infertile stretches of the coastal plains, in pine barrens and sand hills, live many of the poor whites who were pushed back long ago from the richer plantation land. Schooled to an inadequate diet and to eking a scant living out of a poor soil, they live on "Tobacco Road," fighting hookworm, proud toward upper-class whites, and inhospitable to the Negro.

The old plantation cotton belt has been one of the richest in the region and is now one of the most seriously depleted areas in the entire nation. The soil is practically worthless, but the population remains and, ironically, continues to have a high birth rate. To use one example, in Georgia this area embraces some 35 counties between Athens and Atlanta in the north, and Augusta, Macon, and Columbus in the south. It was a prosperous plantation area in 1860, with more great estates and slaves than any similar area in the South. Putnam County was opened to white settlers in 1812 and by 1847 only 200 acres remained in virgin forest. Two-thirds of the upland had lost from three to eight inches of top-soil, or as much as had been laid down by virgin forest economy in a period of from 2000 to 8000 years. One-fourth of this plantation land has now fallen into the hands of creditors, the white and Negro tenants are impoverished, and the landlords debt ridden or land poor.[1]

The cotton kingdom represents virtually a culture of its own, which embraces the alluvial delta stretches of Mississippi and Arkansas, the new fertile areas of Texas and Oklahoma, and the worn-out areas of the Southeast. It is characterized by its type of agriculture, which is rigidly built around the single commercial crop of cotton; a vast Negro population inherited from the plantation economy of slavery, in some areas constituting as much as 90 per cent of the population; a large and mounting white tenant class; a population organization—a rigid cycle of life, a network of accessories in gins, compresses, warehouses; unbalanced food distribution; and a low level of living for half of the millions of producers of the crop. Vance[2] calls this a "cotton culture." The cotton kingdom stretches from the Carolinas to Texas and covers an area 1,600 miles wide and 300 miles deep.

[1] W. A. Hartman and H. H. Wooten, *Georgia Land Use Problems* (Georgia Experiment Station Bulletin, No. 191, May 1935), as discussed in Arthur Raper, "Gullies and What They Mean," *Social Forces*, XVI (December 1937), 203-4.

[2] Rupert B. Vance, *Human Factors in Cotton Culture* (Chapel Hill, N.C.: University of North Carolina Press, 1929).

Alabama is in this cotton country and was once the center of the political South. It has its plantation area, still peopled by Negroes and a waning planter class, and its poor cotton lands in the northern part of the state where no plantations could prosper, and which became a white section of small farms. Birmingham, however, is a new growth, an outpost of northern capital which recruited its industrial workers from the unprofitable areas of the cotton country and from the mountains of North Carolina and Tennessee. It has become the battleground of competing and speculating capital in mines, furnaces, and railroads as well as for the labor market.

Mississippi is the heart both of the great cotton system and the agricultural South. Here there is the best soil and climate for cotton, a land constantly enriched by the slow accretions from the alluvial deposits of a rich river system. Here is the delta, the richest cotton soil in the whole South and, as would be expected, here may be found the greatest plantation area and the greatest concentrations of Negro tenants in the South. The largest cotton plantation in the world (37,000 acres) is at Scott, Mississippi.

There are areas of the South remarkable for the absence of Negroes just as some are remarkable for their presence in large numbers. The southern highlanders live in the double pronged thrust of the great Appalachian chain. On the west these mountains extend from Kentucky down to Birmingham, Alabama, and on the eastern flank stretch from Maryland down to Spartanburg, South Carolina, embracing an area of 111,000 square miles. Here are southerners who have lived generation after generation near the margin of subsistence, with their log houses, their violent patterns of life, their feuds, their low literacy, their fundamentalism, their codes of family honor and distrust of law, and their rugged individualism. This society has tolerated comparatively few Negroes. In fact, many of the families sought the mountains to escape the slave system in which they could not participate profitably. It has the lowest proportions of Negroes in the entire South.

Texas, the western outpost of the cotton kingdom, has an

area larger than France or Germany, and is rich in cotton, oil, and cattle. A neighbor of Mexico, Texas shares her population. Thousands of Mexicans remain unassimilated in the area which was once theirs. The rich "black waxy" land of the state has drawn its population from the states of the Southeast. Vast open country has fostered a frontier spirit. Texas is one of the comparatively new areas of the South, and it took over the cotton culture without taking over the full plantation pattern of the old South. It got its population not so much from the planter class as from those independent small farmers who were seeking to escape from the domination of the plantation. While there are no plantations in the manner of the old South, there are astonishing concentrations of land. There are 215 holdings averaging 52,168 acres each. A group of 647 holdings accounts for an area equal in size to the whole state of South Carolina.[3]

THE ECONOMY AND THE PEOPLE

The general social institutions of the South rest upon the basic economic structure. There is, and has been over a number of years, a constant draining off of the population in the active ages (after the area has supported their nonproductive years as children) to more promising industrial regions. In the last decade the largest per cent of population increase has been in the upper age groups, suggesting an increasing burden of nonproductive persons. There are fewer industries in the South than in the North for the absorption of the population and for the creation of the necessary additional wealth. There is smaller buying, earning, and tax-paying power per capita in the South than in any other section of the country. The wealth of the area is the lowest in the country and the money income is from a third to a half less than the national average. This is the first index to the provisions for education, health, and general well-being possible for such an area. In 1929 the lowest incomes in America were registered in the southern states, with the Carolinas, Mississippi, Arkansas, Georgia, and Tennessee at the very bottom. Most important, the dependence upon the staple

[3] T. J. Cauley, "Agricultural Land Tenure in Texas," *Southwestern Political and Social Science Quarterly*, XL (September 1930), No. 2.

crops of the area not only keeps the rural population dependent upon uncertain fortunes, but it has also created in addition a high rate of tenancy which has become notorious for the evils associated with this status. In the South as a whole, 42.4 per cent of the farms, and in the cotton belt 60 per cent, are operated by tenants. Nearly half of these tenants are croppers. The rates of tenancy range from 28.1 per cent in Virginia to over 72.2 per cent in Mississippi.[4] In the profitable growing of cash crops a cheap labor supply is regarded as essential. In times of depression not even the availability of cheap labor helps and no expedient the federal government has yet devised has been able to improve very much the condition of the 60 per cent of all cotton farmers who are tenants, that is, beyond temporary relief for those who have failed.

Considered as a whole, the rural areas of the South have remained nearer the economic margin of subsistence than any other major section, and they have felt general changes more severely. The South Atlantic and East South Central states have 15 per cent of the land area and 21 per cent of the population, but only 11.7 per cent of the income. Ten southern states, for example, lead in the incidence of pellagra—well named "hidden hunger." Social institutions and particularly public facilities provided through taxation are necessarily inadequate. In the South will be found the most rapid increase in numbers of children in both the elementary schools and the high schools, the highest birth rates, and the largest families. More than half of the total rural farm population of the United States lives in the South and a fourth of all southern families are Negroes.

THE PLANTATION SYSTEM

The South, cotton, and the plantation are associated in popular conception. No single unbroken stretch of territory in the South may be designated "the plantation area." "Plantation" is a term employed to designate a system of exploitation of the natural resources of a territory in which land is owned in large units and organized for the mass production of raw materials.

[4] Figures used throughout this book are from United States Census material unless some other source is specified.

The location of areas of large scale ownership or undivided control is determined chiefly by the adaptability of such areas to large scale production. In the South, Virginia, Kentucky, and most of Tennessee, as well as the mountainous areas of North Carolina and Georgia, have no large scale tenant operations. The rolling upper Piedmont section has very few plantations. Few are to be found in the Muscle Shoals area, the Mississippi ridge, and the interior plain west of the Mississippi. The regions of heavy plantation concentration are: the level lands of eastern North Carolina; the lower Piedmont; the upper coastal plain of South Carolina, Georgia, and Alabama; the delta and loess bluff regions of the Mississippi and its tributaries in the states of Mississippi, Louisiana, and Arkansas.[5]

The largest contiguous plantation area in the South is in the flood plain of the Mississippi River. The delta, so-called, consists of a series of basins of rivers which flow into the Mississippi.[6] In Arkansas the delta area is determined by the basin of the St. Francis River, and the junction of the White and Arkansas rivers with the Mississippi. In Mississippi the Yazoo River marks off a delta area. In Louisiana the Ouachita, Red, and Atchafalaya basins belong to the delta. The alluvial lands of these streams, together with the flood plain of the great river to which they are tributary, constitute the Mississippi Delta. Here the plantation survives with smallest deviation from the traditional pattern. Soil conditions and historical influences have produced in other areas forms of exploitation in which many of the essential features of the plantation system appear, but nowhere else are the economic definitions and social institutions of this agricultural system so closely related.

The plantation is described as "a large landed estate located in an area of open resources, in which social relations between diverse racial or cultural groups are based upon authority, involving the subordination of resident laborers to a planter for the purpose of producing an agricultural staple which is sold in

[5] T. J. Woofter, Jr., *Landlord and Tenant on the Cotton Plantation* (Washington: WPA Division of Social Research, 1936), p. 1.

[6] Rupert B. Vance, *Human Geography of the South* (Chapel Hill, N.C.: University of North Carolina Press, 1935), p. 226.

a world market."[7] This definition embodies the salient characteristics. The plantation is distinguished from other forms of large scale exploitation in areas of open resources, mining, for example, by being primarily agricultural. Like mining, however, it is dependent upon the world markets and upon the importation if not the eventual regimentation of its labor supply.

It is difficult to secure complete statistical information on the extent of plantation development in the South. The general practice of the census in enumerating farm statistics on the basis of the operation unit rather than the ownership unit has not produced a clear picture of the situation. The Census of Agriculture for 1910 and the Woofter study[8] in 1935 give a partial enumeration of ownership units involving a selected group of counties. The 1910 census selected 325 counties in which 39,073 plantations were enumerated as fitting the following description:

> A tenant plantation is a continuous tract of land of considerable area under the general supervision or control of a single individual or firm, all or a part of such tract being divided into at least three smaller tracts, which are leased to tenants.[9]

The Woofter study analyzes a sample of 646 plantations which fit the same definition. They are located in 40 counties selected to represent the several plantation regions in the South. While the boundaries of these plantation regions have not been clearly drawn, their characteristics are well known and are seen reflected wherever cotton is grown.

In romance the great historic plantations of the South were famed for the culture and wealth of their owners, the luxury of their households, and the contentment of their slaves. In reality there were few estates that achieved such grandeur, and over recent years the pattern itself has been profoundly modified by economic and other circumstances. As the economic

---

[7] Edgar T. Thompson, *The Plantation*, Ph.D. Dissertation, University of Chicago, 1932.

[8] Woofter, *Landlord and Tenant on the Cotton Plantation*.

[9] *U. S. Census of Agriculture: 1910* (Washington: U. S. Bureau of the Census, 1911), Vol. V, p. 925.

structure has weakened, it has required increasing effort to maintain the original social organization. Many of the older plantations have passed successively through many hands; the planter class has been invaded by speculators from various social and occupational classes; the center of social life has shifted to the towns and cities. The plantations are today, for the most part, large scale commercial farming ventures. Life has changed materially for all groups except those who provide the labor. The tenants and sharecroppers who work the land have been held to the soil by habit and ignorance and poverty.

The plantation system as it exists today is organized, as it was originally, so as to control practically the entire life of the families living within it. Work is seasonal and, for tenant and landlord alike, dependent upon a variety of factors—flood, drought, pests, market prices. Essentially, the great bulk of workers must be tenants and, if the system is to continue with labor as the chief source of power and skill, they must remain tenants. Under the conditions which the system imposes, tenants live by credit advances; with costly credit advances and usually low returns for the labor invested, few of them end the year with enough of a cash surplus to begin the next year. In a bad year the landlord may lose money, but he is able, nevertheless, to maintain a decent standard of living, and he has credit for the next year. The tenant when he fails, loses all.

The plantation tenant families have no stake in the land and no voice in determining what or how much they shall plant, when or where the crop will be sold. Since they keep no books and have no interests beyond the daily routine, they have no strong incentives to self-improvement. Food crops are taboo on rich cotton land, gardens are meager, cows are scarce; this shows up in the chronic inadequacy of the diet of the families and in the prevalence of pellagra. Cotton farming is a commercial enterprise devoted to the production of a single commodity which must pay for all the other services its producers require. So, on his meager earnings on shares a cotton tenant must feed, clothe, and provide all necessities of life for a family. Actually, fewer make a net profit than "break even." As recent studies show, a third or more of the families usually go into debt.

The intimate social life of these families is linked to this low economic level. The status of dependency permits the landlord to determine, in large measure, for the tenant family its politics, the education of the children, and its habits. Dependency, from which the cotton tenant apparently cannot escape, has bred a state of chronic insecurity which makes being in debt a safeguard against complete separation from the soil, the sole source of income.

FAMILY PATTERN

Where there has been little education or contact with the active currents of life, where there has been little communication, the patterns of life—the social codes and experiences, the social attitudes and self-estimates—set in the economy of slavery, still control the life of the people. It is a lowly level, but still American. It is a lowly plane of the American culture.

A typical Negro tenant family in one of the older plantation counties is that of Dexter Washington. His home can be seen across the dusty tops of the growing cotton for a long distance. It is one of several gray and worn cabins that dot the wide expanses of the cotton fields. Dexter Washington lives in a three-room cabin with his wife and six children. The room to the left, off the "dog run," is the center of the home. There is a large brass bed in one corner, covered with a patchwork quilt. Opposite is a large fireplace with one dusty log resting in it, waiting for the cold winter months. A broken dresser is piled high with paper and a jumble of clothing. Stretching across the fireplace is a broad shelf, covered with an ancient strip of velvet and holding a profusion of pictures, cheap bric-a-brac, old cigar boxes, fragments of cups and saucers, and some one's Sunday hat. There is an extension or lean-to in the back that accommodates two of the older children. The whole family, with the exception of the two youngest children, have been in the field all day. After a supper of crisp fat hog meat, molasses, and corn bread, they are in a mood to talk about themselves. The mother is uncertain about her age, although she appears to be about 45. She comments vaguely on the problem of keeping ages in order when children are growing and changing ages every year.

> I don't know how old I is; I'm a po' guesser. Bennie's 'bout 17; I don't know how old Oscar is. There's one dead between Bennie and Oscar; I guess Oscar's 'bout 19.

Bennie comes into the room and observes, indifferently, that he is 15, but all are somewhat confused about the ages of the other children.

Dexter Washington is a deep, dull-brown colored man of medium height and weight, but staunchly built, with deep wrinkle grooves in his face, and thinning hair. His hands are large and hard and scarred. He wears blue overalls that have been washed and patched so often they retain but little of the color beneath the fresh dust of the day's work. He speaks of his working terms and earnings with diffidence:

> We made 'leven bales of cotton last year, but we turned it to the man. I had a patch and I made about $20; that's all we had left. You know, I believe we didn't owe him all that. He jest kept it. . . . The house is all right, but I want it full of furniture inside.

His wife supplements the account of the family working arrangement. She said:

> We works from Christmas to Christmas. Dexter, he been working from Monday morning to Saturday night. See, they works you tight like they did back in slavery time. The only difference they ain't got a whip over you, whipping you like they done then. This house and patch was give to him free of charge to work out by the day. We just buys groceries out of that. Sometimes he gits money and sometimes he don't. We didn't have no money a-tall last year. I ain't never keep no 'counts a-tall. We worked on Captain Nichols' place years. We jest decided to come over here, 'cause we thought we could do better.

Looking around with a very critical eye, Mrs. Washington points to the room across the "dog run."

> That room there needs a chimney in it. It don't rain in here unless a big rain comes blowing in. All the children is healthy

but that oldest boy; he complains of headaches and a misery in his breast.

I ain't been plowing much myself this year, 'cause I wasn't able. The white folks took my cow away from me two years ago. I feel like the best friend I has is gone. I owed a little mortgage, it was only $7.00, and my husband had done paid about $4.00 of that; but they took my cow for that. 'Course I knowed 'twas wrong, but I didn't want to cause no row. Heap of wrong these people do. We ain't got time to hurt nobody and we don't want nobody to hurt us.

The plantation has molded a family pattern, and it has developed characteristic Negro types. There are, of course, the listless, illiterate, hard-working, and apathetic ones. They go on from year to year, frequently without acute consciousness of race, perplexed by their poverty if it becomes acute, content to go on, taking such satisfactions as they may from the social life of their group as long as they can maintain animal security. There are those who manage to rise out of the status of tenants into ownership of their farms. Their children have more incentive for education and fit less easily into the pattern of the plantation. If they cannot make adjustment they move to the towns and cities, or even to the North. There was a loss of 380,595 Negroes from the farms of the South between 1920 and 1930.

OUTSIDE THE PLANTATION AREA

There are at least 400,000 Negro families in the South engaged in farming outside the plantation area. Some of them are in cotton areas where small independent farmers predominate. These farms are usually on the poorer or exhausted land, where the plantation no longer functions. Some are in mixed farming areas where crops other than cotton or tobacco are grown. The Negro families in the nonplantation areas, in spite of the fact that they live on poorer land, show greater diversity in types, have higher farm ownership rates, a somewhat higher standard of living, a higher educational level, and a larger measure of family organization in terms of the dominant culture patterns. It is characteristic of the areas of mixed agriculture that there is wider occupational differentiation, increased currency and trade, more subsistence farming, and greater mobility.

A statistical study of the characteristics of counties of the South has made it possible to group these counties by crop specialization.[10] There are 357 counties in which cotton is the only crop cultivated. They might be assumed, in the absence of exact census figures, to represent the plantation counties, since in the very nature of the plantation no other major rivals are permitted.

Comparing the counties of the South which have two or more crops with the single-crop counties, generally regarded as the plantation counties, we find in the former somewhat lower population density, a decreasing total population, and a general absence of urban population. These facts are related to the type of changes going on in the areas of diversified farming. Some of the counties in these areas are former plantation counties. As the soil has lost fertility the plantation system has given way to a system of smaller ownership units, frequently with the owner also the operator of the farm and, possibly, with one or two helpers. The large tenant population has moved either to the cities or to other areas where the plantation still flourishes. Although ownership units have decreased in size, operation units have become larger and, consequently, population density is lower.

FAMILY ORGANIZATION AND STATUS

The rural areas outside the plantation system reflect significant internal differences in Negro family organization. Negro farm ownership is conditioned by traditional race relations and the fact that fertile plantation land is not for sale. One result of this is that where Negroes are able to buy land it is likely to be less desirable, even though they pay more for it than other buyers. Thus, the percentage of Negro farmers who own the land they till ranges from 61.6 in Virginia, a nonplantation state, to 12.4 in Mississippi, a plantation state. The two well-defined Negro ownership areas, according to Vance,[11] are the

[10] Charles S. Johnson and others, *Statistical Atlas of Southern Counties* (Chapel Hill, N. C.: University of North Carolina Press, 1941).

[11] Rupert B. Vance, *The Negro Agricultural Worker Under the Federal Re-*

Atlantic coastal plain and the interior coastal plain. The first of these is the decadent plantation area, and the second, for the most part, cheap undeveloped land.

The results of a number of studies of areas of mixed farming are available which point to pronounced social and cultural differences in the Negro population in these nonplantation areas.[12] We may select Williamson County in Tennessee as an example; 23.1 per cent of the population was Negro in 1930, and 50 per cent of the farmers were owners. Ownership tends to be concentrated in communities within the county with high proportions of Negro population. It is a mixed farming area and the chief crops are cereals and, more recently, tobacco. The food supply is ample though there is little money. Families raise hogs, and corn to fatten them. Chickens are raised for eggs and food, and many of the families can foods for the winter. Study of the Negro population of the area showed, in contrast to the plantation areas, a wider range in the size of dwellings, larger proportions of the families with such facilities as sanitary pits, kerosene lights, and stoves instead of open fireplaces. Five per cent of the landowners had farms of 100 or more acres. Of the families studied, about 88 per cent of the owners had lived in their homes over five years, and 40 per cent had lived in their homes more than twenty years—pointing to greater stability. The owner-families possessed the rudiments of a family tradition. They were more responsive to community organizations and took pride in membership.

In North Carolina there are 71 counties in which there is no crop specialization in agriculture. Of 33,633 Negro farm operators, 12,578 or 37.4 per cent are owners. In Georgia the 56 counties of nonspecialization have 9,559 Negro operators, of whom 3,527 are owners. In 10 southern states[13] there are 584 counties in which there is no dominant crop specialization, and

---

habilitation, prepared for the Committee on Negroes and Economic Reconstruction, 1934. (Mimeographed)

[12] Unpublished studies of the Negro population in the Tennessee Valley Area, Department of Social Science, Fisk University, 1934.

[13] North Carolina, South Carolina, Georgia, Alabama, Mississippi, Tennessee, Arkansas, Louisiana, Oklahoma, Texas.

in these counties are 266,636 Negro operators, of whom 77,712 or 29.1 per cent are owners. In the Southeast 48.7 per cent of the farmers in the cotton counties are Negroes, but only 11.2 per cent own their farms. In the noncotton areas 32.4 per cent are Negroes, but 22.6 per cent own their farms.

SMALL TOWN FAMILIES

Negro families in the small towns begin to show definitely the transition from rural to city ways—from homogeneous racial grouping to class divisions shared in sentiment and interest by other groups, from low money economy to wage labor and direct trade, from control of behavior by habit and custom to control by the impersonal regulation of laws and ordinances and codes of industrial practice. From a variety of possible patterns, we select as examples a group of small market and industrial towns which have received large Negro population accretions from rural areas. Selecting the occupational field in which there is the largest group of Negro workers, we find the composite picture of the families of this group is as follows: the median Negro industrial worker's family has 3.1 members and lives in a three-room house, for which it pays $9.75 a month rent. The total weekly family earnings are $11.93. The average family is behind in rent, and those in arrears owe for an average of 13.2 weeks. Three-fourths of the dwellings need repairs. One in every 4 families has an inside toilet, one in 4 has a radio, one in 9 has a bath, one in 31 has a telephone, one in 17 has an automobile, and one in 16 owns its home. One in 3.5 families has had a birth within the preceding five years, one in 3 has had a serious illness over the past year, and one in 4 has had a death during the preceding five years.

The movement from plantation to open rural settlement, then to town, and finally to city is marked by a variety of crises. It is, however, culturally a progressive development in spite of the new problems created and the difficulties of readjustment encountered. Each step brings a broadening of the range of attention and interest and responsibility. Development is possible, however, within the rural areas. It is possible to the extent that education, communication, ownership, family stability, and an increasing identification of group and personal interest with the area itself permit such development.

HOME ENVIRONMENT

The description of the homes of southern rural Negro youth which follows is based upon a study of 916 rural Negro families in eight counties of the South. These counties were selected, as noted earlier, on the basis of economic, cultural, and population characteristics which made them significant for a general study of rural Negro youth. The families were selected by a process of sampling which permitted, so far as possible, an equal distribution of all classes of the Negro population.

ECONOMIC LEVEL

The most distinguishing feature of the rural Negro family is poverty. Other elements of the American population are poor, but the poverty of the southern rural Negro is undoubtedly more extreme and involves a larger proportion than is true of any other group. This poverty appears not merely in figures on income. It is underlined by all indices of living conditions. In education, recreation, housing, religion, and other forms of institutional life, the influence of low economic status is evident.

The low economic status of rural Negroes is complicated by the biracial system. Although some rural Negroes have relatively comfortable incomes, these incomes do not permit them to escape the restrictions of Negro life. In education, in cultural life, and in religious life, the facilities available are determined by the economic level of the mass of the population, and the inadequacies of these facilities rest alike upon the lower, middle, and upper class. Individual achievement provides an escape from group poverty on the material side, but complete escape is not possible within the rural South, and migration to other areas brings only a partial solution.

The houses in which the great majority of Negroes live in the rural South are notoriously wretched. The reason for this condition is, of course, that the rural Negro family is impoverished.

Every index of living conditions emphasizes this poverty. The median annual income of 681 rural Negro families covered by this study was, for example, only $452. Even this low figure is an overestimation, since 235 families could not provide reliable data on their income.

Variations in income exist among the counties studied. The very lowest incomes appear in the two decadent plantation counties: Greene County, Georgia, with a median income of $329, and Macon County, Alabama, with a median income of $352. Shelby County, Tennessee, also shows a low median income ($386). In this county the cotton economy is in decline, although the nearness of a large city (Memphis) provides an influence tending to delay general economic collapse. The two counties where the plantation system still flourishes (Bolivar County and Coahoma County in Mississippi) have relatively high median family incomes ($554 and $604). The income level in Johnston County, North Carolina, and Madison County, Alabama, is about the same as that in Bolivar County while the highest median income is $667 in Davidson County, Tennessee. In these three counties the plantation system has been partly replaced by more diversified agriculture carried on by independent farm owners and by hired farm labor.

Low as the family income is, it is maintained only by combining the earnings of several wage earners. In 398 families (43.5 per cent) there were two or more gainfully employed adult members. This figure does not include the unpaid family workers in farm families, where only very young children are exempt from labor in the fields.

The family's marginal economic position is a primary influence on the development of the personality of Negro youth. This position implies, first, that youth must begin to act as supplementary wage earners at an early age, and second, that the opportunities for education and economic advancement are sharply curtailed. Educational and economic opportunities are also limited by the fact of being a Negro. The combination of racial discrimination and economic hardships is only rarely surmounted.

SHELTER AND THE CONVENIENCES OF LIVING

The climate permits primitive structures to serve as shelter. A few of the pioneer log structures remain inhabited on the plantations. The predominant type of house, however, is the "box house," which is constructed of rough lumber, frequently providing through structural defects ventilation which cannot be controlled. A large number of rural homes are not equipped with glass windows, but have crude wooden shutters which serve as coverings for window openings. Unpainted and weathered a drab gray, these three- and four-room structures offer but little more than shelter. In these homes the open well, the kerosene lamp, the fireplace, and the privy are standard equipment. For the most part homes of this description are inhabited by tenants. A few small owners live in houses of this type, but as a rule owners improve their houses more than do tenants, and there is a sense of permanence with owners. Their improved housing is indicative of stability and better organized family life. Many owners, however, have incomes which are so small that they are prevented from establishing homes that meet good standards.

There can be but little beauty in the lives of people who live under such conditions. The drudgery of farm work which requires the labor of the children leaves little leisure for the enjoyment of the advantages rural life offers. The family circle may soon be broken by the children, who early seek more satisfactory living conditions in the urban areas. It is only in the prosperous areas that conditions are developed to provide satisfying experiences in the development of family life among the rural dwellers.

Low economic status is more apparent in living conditions than in income figures. Of the 916 families studied, only 69 or 7.5 per cent lived in houses with no major physical defect; 509 families (55.6 per cent) lived in houses over twenty-five years old; 407 (44.4 per cent) lived in houses which had never been painted, and in an additional 135 instances the house had not been painted for over twenty years. In over half of the houses the roof leaked; in nearly half of the houses there were broken porches or steps and defective floors. Only 5 houses, however, lacked floors completely. Screening was absent or inadequate in over half of the houses.

Only 53 families (5.7 per cent) had running water inside the house. Only 9 of these were farm families, and 5 of the 9 were farm owners. Most of the other families had wells, although 51 families used springs and 174 (18.9 per cent) had no water supply on the place. Sanitary provisions are primitive. Nearly two-thirds of the families had an open privy only, and 93 families (10.2 per cent) had no toilet on the premises. Only 43 families (4.7 per cent) had inside toilets and 191 (20.8 per cent) had a septic tank or sanitary pit outside.

Only 17 families (1.9 per cent) had a telephone; 14 (1.5 per cent) had electric refrigeration; 10 (1.1 per cent) had a washing machine. Electricity was used in 120 houses (13.1 per cent). More families (199 or 21.7 per cent) had an automobile than any of the above conveniences; 4 families had automobiles valued at over $1,000; 2 of these 4 were farm owners and the other 2 were among the small number of white-collar workers.

Half of the families had no musical instruments at all. For the remainder, the most common musical instruments were the victrola (in 27.6 per cent of the homes) and the radio (in 17.4 per cent of the homes). Less than 15 per cent of the families owned instruments requiring musical skill for their operation. About 30 per cent of the homes had no books of any kind. One-fourth of the families subscribed to a daily newspaper and another fourth subscribed to weekly papers, farm journals, or general magazines.

THE TYPICAL CABIN AND FAMILY GROUP

Of the families studied 12 lived in one room and 7 of these had four or more members. There were 382 families with only two or three rooms in their home, and 195, or more than half of these, had six or more members in the family. Of 283 families with eight or more members, 191 (two-thirds) lived in four rooms or less. There were 30 families with ten or more members living in two- and three-room houses. Although the median size of family was 6.03 persons, the median number of rooms was only 3.72.

Some of the discomforts of rural Negro life are taken for granted, but others are resented. With one or two exceptions, the families living in badly overcrowded houses mentioned the need for more room. The exceptions were families at the very bottom of the social scale who had settled into apathetic acceptance of almost subhuman conditions.

Typical of the worst homes in the group studied was that of the Roberts family in Shelby County, Tennessee. Saul Roberts, his wife, and their seven children lived in a two-room board house. The house was in an extremely dilapidated and decaying condition. A dresser, with a newspaper covering the top, an old leather couch, and a rickety iron bed were the only pieces of furniture in the room used for living purposes. There were two chairs in the house. The wife said:

> We all sleeps in the one room. The kitchen ain't large enough to sleep in so we makes pallets on the floor at night. All of us piles in the one room. I hope some day to get a better place to live, with more room and furniture.

The family was at times bitterly conscious of poor living conditions. Such attitudes of hopeless resentment in the parents were transmitted in many families to the children.

The Connells, a family of seven of Bolivar County, Mississippi, lived in a two-room cabin. There was one large bed in the front room and a small bunk in the kitchen. The place was infested with vermin which defied all their moneyless efforts to eradicate them. Long boards hung from the ceiling. The walls were papered with newspaper. The wife said:

> The whole house need to be torn down. Hit ain't fit to live in. This house used to be a cook's house on the white folks' lot, and we moved it over here. You know five children [the youngest was 8 years old], a mother and a father is too many to be livin' in this two-room shack.

The husband added:

> Folks must wonder how we lives in such a place. I jest can't do no better. I be's sick most all the time. I ain't had a regular

job in six years. My trade is carpentry but hit's very seldom that I gits that kinda work. I been trying to get a WPA job, but these peckerwoods jest won't give me a chance.

The two families described above are very near the bottom of the social scale. However, about half the rural Negro families in the South live under conditions only slightly superior to these.

In contrast to these families, though considerably less numerous, is the type represented by the Moody family, in Johnston County, North Carolina. Their home was below that of the upper-class Negro, whose standard of living is similar to that of whites in the professional class, but it was superior to the average sharecropper's or domestic servant's home. The exterior of the Moody house was neat and clean and not unlike that of their white neighbors. Inside, although it was crudely furnished, the house was also neat and clean. Mrs. Moody was very proud of the place, and explained that a serious fire burned their home about three years ago and the owner, an unusually considerate farmer, built this new house on the old site for the family.

FAMILY CONSTELLATION

In the lower socio-economic groups the family is more often dominated by the woman than by the man. To be sure, upper- and middle-class families usually follow what might be called a patriarchal setup like that of white families of corresponding social status, but the matriarchal organization (in the popular sense) is more traditional among Negroes generally. Under the slave system, the Negro woman frequently enjoyed a status superior to that of the man. Formal marriages were not customary and illegitimacy carried no social stigma. Children (whether by white or Negro fathers) took the social status of their mothers and were reared by them. In many cases the children did not know who their fathers were; when the father did live with the family he usually possessed little authority.

In the lower-class families today a pattern similar to that of the slavery period persists. This is not simply a carry-over of traditional mores, although historical factors play a part. The real key to the organization of the Negro family today is found in the relative economic positions of men and women. Particularly in towns and villages, Negro women are better able to secure work than are Negro men. The bulk of Negro workers are in domestic service and in unskilled labor. While jobs for men are increasingly closed to Negroes, the Negro woman still maintains a monopoly of domestic service positions in the South. These jobs are very poorly paid but they bring in more money than the odd jobs upon which the man must frequently depend.

Even where the woman is not employed, it is conceded that she is capable of economic independence. This is true also of farm families (except farm owners). The woman is an economic asset on the farm. She works in the field and contributes a "man's share." She and her husband are well aware that, if she is deserted or dissatisfied, she can easily find another husband glad to get a "good wife." Children are no barrier to remarrriage since husbands readily accept children of their wives by a former marriage or even illegitimate children. Particularly on the farm, children are also an economic asset. As early as 5 or 6 years of age they can be used as field hands at seeding or picking cotton.

The "independence" of Negro women is complemented by "irresponsibility" in the men. The man knows his family will get along without him. When deserted, the woman makes no attempt to force the man to support her or his children. Legal recourse is expensive and violates community mores; the social stigma upon the man who neglects his family is not pronounced.

BROKEN FAMILIES

Of the 916 rural Negro families included in this study, 18.3 per cent had female heads. In Greene County, Georgia, the per cent of female family heads was 32.3 per cent. The proportions were also high (over 20 per cent) in Macon County, Alabama, and in Bolivar and Coahoma counties in Mississippi. These are the counties which preserve to the greatest degree the traditions of the plantation system. Although in Greene and Macon counties the system has collapsed, nothing has appeared to replace it. In Greene County the economic disorganization is highest and this seems to be accompanied by a high degree of family disorganization. In this county it is not unusual for the men to migrate in search of better economic opportunities, leaving the women to support the families.

Except in upper- and middle-class families, desertion is common. At least a third of the families were "broken" families. Desertion is in many instances an extremely casual process:

> I don't know what happened to my husband. He just went off. One day he come in and said he was going to town. We ain't heard a word from him since. I kept looking and looking for him but that was going on over a year ago and he ain't turned up. I don't think nothing happened to kill him or somebody would of let us know. I think he planned leaving all the time because he just sold his cotton and had done right well. . . . I know he'll come back some day. He wasn't satisfied and kept wanting a job what paid some money without all this work. I figure he's off looking for a job, and when he gets one he'll send for us. I ain't got no hard feelin' for him because I think he's trying hard to get hold to a good living.

Mrs. Daniels, the mother in another family, commented:

> I only get $6 a week, and that ain't much with a family and her [the daughter who was interviewed] in school. Her father don't do a thing for 'em. I have to buy everything they got. Bennie's childlike. Mr. Daniels [the husband] gi'e 'em some candy or some little something what don't amount to nothing, and they think he's keeping 'em. Ain't neither of the children seen him in a time now, and I ain't seen him in a long time either. I hear he lit out of Memphis. I don't try to get him to help none. He never was no-account; just won't work, so I let him go.

The children's attitude toward separation of parents is often unemotional. A few youths (2.9 per cent of the boys and 3.7 per cent of the girls) said that they hated their fathers. In most cases, however, criticism of the father was unemotional. The youth may say his (or her) father drinks or is "no-account," but there is no expression of antagonism. Edith, Mrs. Daniels' 15-year-old daughter, said:

> I see my father in Memphis sometimes but he never did help us none. He likes my little brother and gets him clothes sometimes, but he won't do nothing for my mother or me. I like him because he is my father, but I don't like him like I do my mother or brother.

A 13-year-old boy in Coahoma County mentioned the fact that his mother hated his father, but the boy seemed quite undisturbed by the situation:

> My mama and papa separated a long time ago, when I was 4 years old. Papa is still up dere farmin', but mama live down here on Blank Street. I believes they hate each other. I lives with mama 'cause I'd hate to have to stay up dere on the farm.

Frequently, when families are broken the child is turned over to some relative other than the parents. When the father deserts the family, the mother must find employment since very few families have any incomes aside from weekly wages, and cash reserves are practically unknown. In many cases the relative who assumes responsibility for the child is a grandmother or an aunt. When the mother dies, a similar solution of the problem is often adopted. One 14-year-old boy said:

> I have got more whippings from my grandmother. I have been with her ever since I was 2 years old. I be mischievous and get whippings. I like my grandmother best. I haven't been with my mother much. Mother said the other Sunday that it looked like me and my brother both cared more for my grandmother than we did for her. My mother said she started to get me something but she knew my grandmother had something better.

Another youth explained:

> My mother been dead a long time. I don't know why she died. She got sick and stayed sick a long time. I was real small but I remember. She was good to me and I cried. I don't know where my father is. I ain't seen him in a long time. I 'spect he be in town [she didn't know what town]. I reckon I love my grandmother best. She helps me grow. She is the one what looks after me.

In the case of remarriage of a parent, the children often appear to get along quite well with the stepfather or stepmother. Resentment of a mother or father's new mate, if present, may not be expressed. This is largely due to the fact that second marriages are customary and acceptable among rural Negroes. Children are familiar with the idea of stepparents and regard remarriage as normal and proper. Furthermore, stepchildren are not necessarily regarded as a burden, and a woman or man is usually quite willing to care for children of the mate. Lillie Sanders, a 14-year-old girl in Davidson County, Tennessee, expressed considerable affection for her stepmother.

> She is the one I like best. I take her all my problems. I don't go to my father for very much because he's not home much.

This stepmother is very fond of the children, particularly of Lillie's younger sister. Mrs. Sanders makes a pet of the younger sister, who is, consequently, rather spoiled.

Children may sometimes build up strong attachments to stepfathers. Annie Ewing, a 13-year-old Johnston County, North Carolina, girl, was more attached to her stepfather than she was to her real father. Although she had not seen her own father since she was a little girl, Annie remembered him quite well. She called him "papa" and her stepfather "daddy." On each birthday and holiday her real father sent her boxes of clothing. Annie said that "daddy" was "real nice," and since she had been "around" him most of her life she felt closer to him and liked him better than she did her own father.

When friction with stepparents occurs, it is based on personal dislike. Antagonism toward stepparents is based on much the same causes as parent-child frictions, and there is little hatred of a stepparent as a person displacing the child's own parent. When George Wade was 18 he quarreled with his stepfather and ran away:

> I just couldn't get along with him. He made me do a lot of work and I couldn't get my hands on any money and I needed clothes. He was mean, too. He'd fuss at me, whip me, and make me do a heap of work. One day he started to whip me, and I

left. Mama didn't want me to leave, but she couldn't stop me then.

In a few cases, separation of the parents leaves the child without supervision. This usually occurs when the mother must work out and no other relative is available to assume responsibility for the child.

There ain't nobody for me to mind since my poppa and mama been away from each other. I sleep back there in the kitchen, and my mama sleep up here. In the winter time we sleep together because it is so cold.

FAMILY ORGANIZATION AT HIGHER ECONOMIC LEVELS

The man is usually the head of the household in upper-class families. In these families responsibility for family support rests upon the father. The mother may work out, but the man is recognized as the primary wage earner and ultimate family authority. The Wilson family is typical. Mr. Wilson is an unusually well-educated farmer in Madison County, Alabama. He completed graded school and went to an agricultural and technical college in the state for a year. Mrs. Wilson accepts her husband's decisions without question. She says little and plays the role of housekeeper and bearer of children, having had ten in fourteen years. Her major interest is the children.

In the Andrews family the husband has a good job as foreman in a bottling plant. The mother does not have to work out:

No, I don't work out. I could get something, but my husband won't hear of it. You really don't make anything much, and he wants me to stay at home with the children and keep a clean, attractive home.

This family belongs to the middle class and is typical of this class. They have only two children and intend to give them all the education possible. One boy is in college, and the 16-year-old girl who was interviewed, is to enter in the fall. The father is proud of his children, and ambitious for them. He says:

They're good kids, both of them, and I mean to give them the best even if it is kind of expensive. After they finish college,

I expect them to support themselves, but if they don't get jobs, I'll continue to look out for them.

The parents have traveled extensively, and have taken the children with them. They usually go away on a trip each summer. The home is modern and well furnished. Money is ample for all wants, and the children are given a weekly allowance. They have enough clothes, and are always well dressed. The daughter said:

Papa is the boss. He makes all the money and has the most to say about things. He decides if we are going to school and all big things; but mama decides the little things. She plans the spending of the money, but daddy pays all the taxes and tends to all the business. I haven't had a whipping since I was so small. I get punished now by having to stay at home. My mother is my favorite. I take up all my problems with her. I think it is easier for a girl to talk things over with her mother. Of course papa comes next.

This family and other middle-class Negro families have living conditions and a family setup similar to white families at the same level. In general, however, the upper-class Negro families live more harmoniously together than white families on the same level. The youth of such families realize the superiority they enjoy over lower-class Negro youth. Parental achievement is not taken as a matter of course as it is in white families. The white upper- and middle-class youth does not often come in contact with youth from other levels. He compares his family with other families on the same economic level. Family restrictions are therefore not related to superior advantages in the white youth's thinking. The upper-class Negro youth is thrown into contact, through the schools and in almost all social groups, with youth from all levels. Although the youth may rebel against family restrictions, the rebellion is mild since it is accompanied by a realization of the tangible benefits which membership in the family affords.

RESPONSE TO HOME ENVIRONMENT

Home adjustment problems of rural Negro youth fall into two groups: problems common to all American adolescents, and problems distinctive of rural Negro youth. The latter will be considered in detail in Chapter III so that attention will be confined at this point to the former classification. Family problems of adolescents in general revolve around the establishing of status as an independent adult. During this period parents shrink in the eyes of youth from omnipotent, perfect beings to ordinary stature as human beings with customary human faults. Frequently, the shock of this transition leads to the exaggeration of parental defects in the youth's thinking. During adolescence the youth becomes critical of his (or her) family and also becomes more conscious of outside criticism. Although the youth is himself more critical of the family, outside criticism is resented. The adolescent is still closely identified with the family and feels compelled to defend it against criticism. In part, this compulsion may be satisfied by projecting one's own criticism on the community. If the criticism is attributed to the community, it can be properly resented. On the scale of home maladjustment the most commonly endorsed complaint was that people said untrue things about the youth's family. Of 1,388 girls, 70.4 per cent checked this as true, and of 853 boys, 64.3 per cent checked the statement as true.

Victorian regulation is the exception rather than the rule in rural Negro families. Except in upper-class families or in very religious households, comparatively few restrictions are placed on the conduct of the adolescent. In one family the mother forbade her children to dance or play cards. The children would go out and play cards clandestinely, but when the mother found cards among their belongings she would burn them. The 16-year-old girl interviewed in this family found home life unpleasant and often thought of marrying as an escape.

Most of the youth interviewed enjoyed considerable freedom, although parents attempt to keep the children, especially the girls, from getting in trouble. In lower-class families the adolescent is relatively unsupervised. Despite this freedom, the youth studied share with other adolescents the feeling that parents restrict their movements and social life. The usual adolescent feeling that "My folks won't let me do the things other girls (or boys) do" was shared by 70.7 per cent of the girls and 63.8 per cent of the boys. The slightly higher percentage of girls is probably due to the stricter supervision imposed upon them. Forty-one per cent of the girls and 40.6 per cent of the boys agreed that their families are always making the youth do things that they "don't want to do." Where home restrictions are particularly severe, the complaint is voiced that "My folks treat me like a baby." About a fifth of the boys, or 21.6 per cent, and 37.5 per cent of the girls felt that this was true. Irene Jackson is typical of this adolescent reaction:

> My mother doesn't understand the things, nothing I want to do. She still thinks I'm a little bit of a baby. You see, most of my friends live in town when I was at school, and I would want to spend week ends with them, and she wouldn't let me. After all, I'm old enough to know what I want to do. When I'm home and there's no place to go and nothing to do, she's all right, but as soon as I get away from her she's so particular about what I should do and what I shouldn't do. I'm going to get away from here as soon as I can.

About one-third of both boys and girls felt that "My mother can't ever understand the things I want to do." As in other groups, boys are given more freedom than girls. Except in the most disorganized families, attempts are made to keep the girls "out of trouble." While 27.4 per cent of the boys said "I never stay around home unless they make me do so," only 17.9 per cent of the girls stated that this was true.

Although both boys and girls resent outside criticism of their families, a number of youth endorsed as true the statement that "Most other boys (or girls) have better homes than I have." This was endorsed over twice as frequently by girls as by boys, the proportions being 31.6 per cent for girls and 12.3 per cent for boys. The statement, "Most of my friends get more from their folks than I do," was endorsed by 26.6 per cent of the boys and 20.2 per cent of the girls.

DISSATISFACTION WITH HOME

The group endorsing statements implying dissatisfaction with home constitutes between one-eighth and one-fourth of the youth tested. Nearly one-fourth of both the boys and girls felt that "My mother could do more for me if she wanted to"; 13.7 per cent of the boys and 9.7 per cent of the girls said their brothers and sisters "think they are a lot better than I am"; 19.8 per cent of the boys and 20.0 per cent of the girls said that sometimes they loved their "folks" and other times they hated them; 14.7 per cent of the boys and 11.7 per cent of the girls said that "People are always praising my brothers and sisters and not me."

The reactions thus far discussed are probably common to adolescents in all sectors of American society, but among Negro youth the criticism of family seems unusually severe. In response to three rather extreme statements concerning the father, surprisingly high numbers replied "true"; the statements and figures are given below:

	Percentage Responding "True"	
Statements	*Boys*	*Girls*
My father spends too much money for liquor.	15.2	14.1
My father doesn't amount to much.	13.7	11.0
I am scared of my father.	12.7	13.0

References to the father's drinking are not uncommon in the interviews:

> The old man is all right. He just don't know what he's talking about half the time. He lays around drunk most every night. He can't tell me nothin' about no school.

> Daddy didn't never stay home. He had two things he loved to do, drink whisky and chase after women. When he did come home it was always a row. I guess that's why I don't like whisky. . . . He got in jail once for hauling whisky. He swears it was another man's and that's the only thing he ever told me that I didn't believe was the truth. I told him he was lying, and he knocked me down. I still believe it was his whisky. He didn't never help take care of us much. So we just decided to help mama get her divorce from him.

The effects of bad home situations appear in the reactions of the youth included in this study. The wishes of these youth, as recorded in one of the tests employed in the study[14] centered around items directly concerned with escape from their present situation. Only 26.1 per cent of the girls and 23.3 per cent of the boys wanted to live in the South, and about half of them wished to live in a southern city. Specific northern cities were mentioned as preferred residences by more than one-third of the group. Other responses were more vague, specifying "the North" or "Pennsylvania," without mention of a particular city. The North remains for most rural Negro youth the Promised Land, where the restrictions and discomforts of life in the rural South may be left behind.

One of the most extreme cases of revolt against home conditions was that of Selma Hale in Greene County, Georgia, whose home was on the very lowest level. On the Personal Values Test[15] Selma wished for "a happy life, home, and to be well cared for." Asked, in a later interview, what she implied in her wishes, Selma replied:

> I'd like to have a house that don't leak, a house with no leaks in it anywhere. I wants a comfortable house, a house you won't freeze in in winter. I'd like to have nice things in the house, nice furniture so you could be comfortable. I'd like for it to have smooth floors, not big loose planks.

> By being well cared for, I meant to have enough to eat. To have something to eat every day. Lots of days we don't have nothing to eat. It must be nice to have enough to eat every day. . . . I'd like to have some clothes, too, like other girls.

It should not be supposed that this picture of an extremely impoverished home life is typical of all rural Negro youth. Such conditions are, however, not uncommon. In families with a more secure economic position, a fuller and more satisfactory home life appears. This comment from a girl in one of the better homes illustrates the contrast.

> At home we have fun with our daddy. The biggest time we had was on Father's Day. We gave him a surprise party, and he was so pleased. . . . We gave him lots of gifts. We always

[14] See Appendix B for the testing procedure which preceded the interviews.
[15] See Appendix B for the testing procedure which preceded the interviews.

have lots of fun telling jokes at the table. When he's out we play games with the little children and try to teach them how to play cards and tell jokes and things. My sister and I play whist. . . . My oldest sister and I sleep in a room alone, but we have the same bed. My daddy sleeps by himself, but my two little brothers have a bed in the room where the lady who stays with us sleeps; and one of my little sisters stays with my grandmother.

HOME MALADJUSTMENT AND SOCIO-ECONOMIC LEVELS

The relationship between maladjustment scores and socio-economic levels is by no means perfect. This is due partly to the fact that the home score is a composite and therefore is only a rough measure of home maladjustment, and partly to the inadequacy of the indices used to show socio-economic level. It is, nevertheless, significant that youth whose fathers are in professional occupations show the lowest average home maladjustment score. The highest average maladjustment is that of youth with fathers in clerical occupations. This average, however, is based on only 26 cases. In addition, it must be borne in mind that the occupational grouping does not always give a true picture of the status of a family within the Negro group. The next highest maladjustment average is that of youth who gave no occupation for their fathers. The bulk of this group is composed of children of broken families (where the father is dead or has left the family) and youth whose fathers are employed on odd jobs so no definite occupation can be reported. A high average home maladjustment score is also shown by youth who reported their fathers as unemployed.

Youth with fathers in the "servant" group show a low home maladjustment score. Contrary to opinions ordinarily held, Negro men who are servants enjoy a preferred social status. Negro women in domestic service are usually cooks or maids, earn very low incomes, and have little security. However, Negro men in domestic or personal service are chauffeurs, butlers, pullman porters (porters in stores are classified as unskilled laborers), and waiters. These are preferred occupations, paying wages above those of unskilled labor and offering some amount of job tenure.

A relationship of the home maladjustment score to parental education is also evident. Youth whose mothers had completed less than three grades in school show a home maladjustment score of 6.50. (The highest possible maladjustment score is 16 and the lowest 0.) As the mother's education increases the home maladjustment score decreases. Youth whose mothers completed the tenth or higher grades show an average score of 3.90. A similar relationship appears between the home maladjustment score and the father's education, although the differences are less marked, and the trend is less regular.

The type of problem encountered by Negro youth of different social classes differs considerably. In the lower classes the problems are those of poverty, economic deprivation, poor living conditions, and a very unstable family organization. In the upper classes these are not the common problems. As other sections of this study indicate, upper-class youth, freed of the family and economic difficulties encountered by youth at lower social levels, are more acutely conscious of difficulties in the spheres of race relations, education, sex and marriage, and social relations within the Negro group.

CHAPTER III

STATUS AND SECURITY

A CENTRAL problem of the adolescent Negro is that of status. In our dynamic American society many emotional tensions are associated with social rank and position. No group in America, however, is experiencing a more rapid or profound internal change in its social composition than the Negro group. Over a comparatively brief period the cultural level of this population group has been considerably advanced. Illiteracy and mortality rates have declined markedly, the standard of living has been raised to some extent, there has been a pronounced advance in the organization of family life, and there have been other equally significant changes. The external evidences of improvement have been accompanied by a less conspicuous but nevertheless intense struggle of the members of the group for position and recognition within the group. Negro youth are a part of this bitter struggle, and the period of adolescence is one in which the tensions engendered by feelings of personal inadequacy and social insecurity register their most violent shocks.

The gradual change in the cultural basis of Negro life, and the variety and uncertainty of the institutional aspects of Negro-white relations, act together to give unique character to the problems of adolescence of Negro youth. All youth are expected to be sensitive to situations involving conflict of the normal impulses to recognition and status with varieties of external circumstances. The youth may make successful adjustment, or seek to escape from the conflict by various devices. They may succeed in devising ways of protecting themselves from the more serious emotional shocks or, in their desire to escape, they may simply retreat helplessly into the shadowy security of a make-believe world. These adjustment devices have important implications for the shaping of personality, and for that wholesome integration of personality and the social world which gives one a sense of adequacy and gives life meaning and satisfaction.

The focus of the intra-group struggle for status is around social class lines, and is supported by the complex processes by which social differentiation within the Negro population at present is developing. Under normal circumstances class mobility produces certain tensions and prompts compensations of various sorts. In the case of Negroes class mobility is complicated by a variety of patterns and intensities of race relations, and by the fact that, for this group, social class mobility upward is not only a symbol of cultural change, but of escape from a traditional racial status. The impact of this conflict upon youth is at times devastating.

Few individuals escape some variety of social or personal insecurity. Negro youth are exposed not only as individuals but also as a group to acute conflict situations heightened by the chronically low economic level of a very large proportion of the race. They respond in various ways to the persistent tendency of the white world to regard them as a single homogeneous type in spite of a wide range of cultural levels and group orientations. They are affected by the cleavages within the Negro group and between classes of the Negro and white groups as new relationships are defined. In order to understand the basis of these tensions it seems necessary to discuss the process of social differentiation occurring within the rural Negro population.

SOCIAL DIVISIONS OF THE POPULATION

To a superficial observer the Negro population in rural areas might appear to be homogeneous. Agriculture offers a limited range for specialization, and particularly so in cotton growing. The most obvious line of cleavage is that between farm owners and tenants. Most Negroes, of course, are tenants. Keener scrutiny of the rural Negro, however, dispels the notion that they are all alike. Outside the areas where life is regimented by the traditional plantation system the differences among the Negroes become more apparent.

In all the areas included in this study there were found a few

Negro property owners, some of whom had large holdings and secure financial connections to differentiate them sharply from the mass. Moreover, such class differences within Negro society are based apparently on more than a simple occupational classification. One of the earliest historical distinctions was between house servants and field hands. This was reinforced both biologically and culturally as a result of closer contact, intimacy, and identification of the household servants with elements of the white population having unquestioned prestige. The association involved at times not only blood connections of these Negroes with white families of high social prestige, but in many cases a favored position for the Negro with respect to (*a*) ownership of property, (*b*) education, (*c*) color, and (*d*) an earlier free status. All of these factors still play some part in defining the group of highest status and prestige within the Negro society.

UPPER CLASS

The upper class of the Negro population is that group possessing in general a family social heritage known and respected by the community, a substantial amount of education, an occupational level which is achieved by special formal preparation, a comfortable income, ownership of property, stability of residence, superior cultural standards, a measure of personal security through influential connections, or the ability to exert economic or other pressure in the maintenance of this security, or *any combination of most of these characteristics*. Further, this group is conceived by itself as a class and is so recognized by others; it is recognized by similar groups in other areas; and is regarded, whether with approval or disapproval, by other classes as a different and an exclusive society. In this classification are usually the Negro doctors' families, some teachers and school principals, successful landowners, and even families without large possessions but with superior education and a significant family history. The distinction may be clarified by the observation that the typical rural preacher, although a "professional," does not normally belong in this class. The physician almost always does. Most of the preachers, especially in the southern rural areas, are about as unlettered as their congregations. Further, the economic and social limitations of their calling restrict their entree to this class.

MIDDLE CLASS

This is a small but growing group. Its members have some of the characteristics of the upper class and are often the church and community leaders. They have a high regard for education as a means of achieving fuller cultural emancipation and escape from racial status. Their children avoid contact with whites and seek economic independence in professional careers. In this group may be found small owners and proprietors, some successful farm owners or renters, teachers, skilled artisans, insurance salesmen, white-collar workers, managing artisans, and some preachers who earn a comfortable living.

LOWER CLASSES

Upper-Lower Class

The upper-lower class, comprises the great bulk of the rural Negro population. They are the tenants and renters, unskilled and semiskilled workers, personal and domestic workers earning barely enough to live and not enough to live comfortably. They have little education, but have urgent ambitions for their children, who are in both voluntary and enforced association with the more successful Negroes of the upper classes and with the unsuccessful lowest classes. They are constantly aware of the struggle to keep up with the upper classes in material and cultural advantages, and avoid the conspicuous symbols of lower-class status. They are ambitious to own their own homes, although they are seldom able to do so. They understand the advantages of living on a self-respecting level, but their poverty and cultural isolation give them only a confused understanding of what that level is. They belong to a church and regard this as a symbol of respectability. Major concerns are "staying out of trouble," getting some education for their children, and advancing into the next highest classification. They are conscious of their group status and respond to it, sometimes by emulating and sometimes by ridiculing what they regard as the pretenses of the upper classes. They are the rank and file of the rural Negro population.

Lower-Lower Class

The lower-lower class is made up of individuals who lack most of the major characteristics noted above, and who recognize the other classes as different and having more advantages. They have little or no education and skill, although they may be hard working. Their standard of living is very low and their resources are meager. They are the tenants, sharecroppers, and laborers on the farms, and the unskilled laborers and domestic servants in the towns. They add to the low economic level a thorough cultural poverty with confused values. Frequently they are condemned to permanent economic incompetence because of their family structure. In this class are also the chronic relief cases.

The "Folk Negro"

Within the lower classes a distinction should be made between the "folk Negro" and the rest of the population. This distinction is important and more cultural than economic; it refers to the family habits and values evolved by the Negro culture under the institution of slavery. Many of the naïve traits and customs of the "folk Negro" are out of line with the practices of the larger society, but were at times in the past essential to group survival in cultural isolation. Stripped of their basic African culture by the exigencies of life in America, they evolved a social life and a culture of their own which was adequate for survival in their peculiar status in America. The customs, beliefs, and values developed have been a response to their limited roles within the American social order, even when many of the traits of the group have been borrowed from early American settlers and crude pioneers in the cotton country. In a sense, they have been repositories of certain folkways now outgrown by those groups which were more rapidly absorbed into the larger currents of American life. The patterns of life, social codes and social attitudes, set in an early period, have because of the cultural as well as geographical isolation continued to be effective social controls. In the social consciousness of the group and in its social life, there has been a considerable degree of organization and internal cohesion.

The "folk Negro" organization of life and of values has been essential to survival and to the most satisfying functioning of the members of the group in their setting. Many things for which the larger dominant society has one set of values, meanings, and acceptable behavior patterns—marriage, divorce, extra-marital relations, illegitimacy, religion, love, death, and so forth—may in this group have quite another set. This helps to explain types of personalities developed under the peculiar circumstances of life of the "folk Negro" and makes their behavior more intelligible. The increase of means of communication and the introduction of some education is breaking down the cultural isolation of this group.

THE UNDERWORLD

The "underworld" is a group which does not, perhaps, constitute a class, but which, nevertheless, is a social category. It is composed of individuals who fall outside the recognized and socially sanctioned class categories, that is, those persons who are free from the demands of society—the "wide" people, the vagabonds, the "worthless" and "undeserving poor" who are satisfied with their status, the "outcasts," the "bad niggers," prostitutes, gamblers, outlaws, renegades, and "free" people. Life in this underworld is hard, but its irresponsible freedom seems to compensate for its disadvantages. These are the people who create the "blues" and secular songs of the demimonde. They are the ones who have in greatest measure a sense of irresponsibility. Persons in this category may be criminal or merely loose. Some of them are even protected and used by white persons for their own ends, and as compensation are licensed to be "hellions" in the Negro community. This category also cuts across classes.

CLASS MOBILITY

There is a fairly easy mobility between the social classes proper, but perhaps the most significant changes to be observed are those from the naïve "folk Negro" group to a formal middle-class status, and from the middle to the upper class. In the present situation of the Negro in the South, the two values within control of an individual which can do most to facilitate class mobility are wealth and education. Ancestry and color, which are sometimes associated with social status, are factors beyond the control of living individuals struggling for status. Wealth is theoretically possible of control, but actually a remote possibility. Education is within reach and, consequently, it is invested with almost magical properties by both the ambitious parents and the youth. It is an escape not only from social position within the group, but from an unfavorable racial status.

STATISTICAL INDEX TO SOCIAL DIVISIONS

On the basis of occupation, income, education, family organization, relationship to property, and general community recognition of standing, the estimated percentages of Negroes belonging to the different recognizable social divisions of the southern rural population are as follows:

Upper Class	6 per cent
Middle Class	12 per cent
Lower Class	82 per cent

In our sample, selected in a manner designed to secure a cross section of the rural Negro population of the areas studied, the physical indices correspond roughly with the division given above. There were 102 families in the 916 studied, or 14.8 per cent, with annual family earnings of $1,000 or more; 18.2 per cent who were voters; 12.4 per cent who owned real estate other than their homes; 20.7 per cent who were in the occupational range of professionals, skilled workers, foremen, businessmen, or farm owners (not all farm owners, however, are in the upper social or economic classes); 4.4 per cent had some member of the family with more than high school education; 17.4 per cent had radios; 13.1 per cent had electricity in their homes; 21.7 per cent had automobiles; 8.7 per cent had libraries of more than 50 volumes; 8.4 per cent had pianos; 12.4 per cent subscribed to general magazines. These are indices to the upper and middle classes.

On the other hand, 83 per cent of the heads of families had less than seven years of schooling, and 44.3 per cent had less than four years; 55.3 per cent read no papers or magazines; 89.5 per cent had no bank accounts.

CHARACTER OF TENSIONS AFFECTING YOUTH

The child gets his first emotional security in the family. Here are formed the first affectional ties and here he secures what James S. Plant so aptly describes as the sense of "belongingness." This "security" is something intangible and irrational, and is emotionally linked with individual and group status. There is an immediate problem for Negro youth in the disproportionately large number of irregularly organized or broken families. One of the greatest threats to emotional security in the family setting, in the sense described, is the one-parent family, whether this irregularity is due to death, desertion, divorce, or failure of the mother to marry. Frequent moving is another threat to security, and one of the characteristics of Negro farm families, especially tenants, is their high mobility.

There is abundant evidence of the irregular family organization in which these youthful personalities get their first fashioning. A large proportion are reared by grandparents and stepparents. In the group of families included in this study, 50 per cent were "natural families," made up of two parents and their children. The other 50 per cent of the families were of various types: mother or father with children, grandparents and children, three or more generations in a household, the natural family with other related and nonrelated persons in the household. The effects of these irregular structures upon youth at the very beginning of socialization are inescapable. They appear in the chronic friction and unrest within the family, the frustrations, timidity, overcompensations, and various antisocial activities, as well as in what Gertrude Stein once referred to as "nothingness."

For example, in the home of Sarah Cole, a 15-year-old Madison

County, Alabama, girl, live her father, stepmother, stepsister, great-aunt, and a lodger. In a discussion of her relationships with other members of the family Sarah said:

> I got a half-sister, too. My mother was her mother, but my father was not her father. . . . No'm, she wasn't married before she married my daddy, but she already had my sister. She never stayed with us. My mama gave her to a lady when she was a baby. She just told me I had another sister and my daddy carried me there once and told me that was her. She's married now. That's my half-sister, but this is my stepsister here. . . . Yessum, I get along all right with my stepsister. Sometimes I let her boss and sometimes I tell her mother on her when she won't do what I tell her. She has more clothes and things than I do. I feel bad about that, but I never said nothing about it. . . . No'm, I never talked to my daddy about it. I have about five dresses to wear to school, but she got a lot of 'em. I got four Sunday dresses, but she's got more of them, too. She's got lots more toys, and she gets more things Christmas than I do. I guess she's been staying here with us about two years. Sometimes her mother brings her candy and somethin' t'eat and don't bring me none. Sometimes she brings me some, but most of the time she just bring it to her. I guess it's 'cause she likes her best. My father treats us about the same. Sometimes when she won't do right I wish she wasn't here, but she's all right most of the time. Sometimes she helps me wash dishes and sometimes she won't. If she say she's not gonna help, my stepmother don't say nothing. My daddy never says nothing to her either when she won't help me, so I just go head and do it myself. Sometimes she just gets mad and says she ain't gonna dry the dishes for me. Sometime she's nice to me and let me play with her little doll dishes. I don't have none. She'll be 8 years old this month.

The school principal's statement about Samuella Hill, of Macon County, Alabama, points to another type of undesirable influence upon the child of the kind of family environment created by sex irregularity on the part of the parents, and particularly on the part of the mother. The school imposes a different standard for sexual behavior, and conflicts in the youth result.

> I'd say she was easy to lose control too. Well, now, I don't like to talk about this but she's a problem. She constantly has sex relations with the boys and I've even caught her doing so on the school grounds. Well, she is a good student so I send her home

for a few days and she comes back and starts over again. Seems like she's a real sex problem. She started long ago and just got a bad name from being with boys. Her mother is a bad example. She's just loose morally. I can't tell you whose children these little ones are. I doubt if Mrs. Hill knows herself. When she wants a man she goes out and gets one and the children know that. I imagine Samuella doesn't even think it's wrong to have relations with boys but she should as much as I've talked to her about it. Our greatest sex problem is with the children 12 to 16.

In the south the proportion of Negro women heads of families is very high when compared with other elements of the population and with other localities. Southern rural nonfarm Negro families with female heads constitute from 20 to 30 per cent of Negro families. Similarly, the illegitimacy and separation rates are high. The importance of these social factors, when taken in conjunction with the normal problems of minority group status, comes out most clearly in the context of the social divisions within the Negro group. For it is to be noted that one of the most pronounced features of the stratification of Negro society is the different evaluation put on certain items of behavior.

UPPER-CLASS YOUTH

The higher the social classification and the more intelligent the person, the more acute his adjustment problems. It is not possible for youth in families of this group to utilize the simple escapes which are possible in families of whom less is expected. Moreover, the social difference between this class and others operates to exaggerate the advantages of the upper class. Since to deny these fictitious values would disturb the class distance, they are not discussed, and the families remain exposed to the criticism of other groups based upon their estimates of the advantages enjoyed.

Limited Associations

Joyce Barnes is the only girl finishing her high school who will go to college immediately. She is of brown complexion, with straightened and bobbed hair. Her father is a successful business-man. At school she has her small clique. She says:

> There are three of us. I guess we dress better than any of the other children. We all have nice clothes and extra spending money. . . . Most of the other children's parents let them run the streets, but none of us can. . . . We three were all reared together, and I like their personalities.

There are not enough eligibles in the area. The result is when they give parties it is necessary to invite friends of similar status from other areas. If they attend a public function at the high school, the three girls and their carefully selected escorts dance together. "But," Joyce explains, "we're nice to the others; we just don't associate with them." One of the neighbors of the Barnes family said:

> I know that Barnes gal—been knowing her since she was born. She's a sweet thing but spoilt. Always had everything she wanted. Her pa's got a lot of money. She ain't selfish, but they make her feel like she's better than the others. Tain't good for things to come too easy for a gal.

There is nothing for Joyce to do in her home county when she gets her education but teach, and this is not attractive to her. Her mother explained:

> The principal here is sort of backward, you know. Won't let new ideas come in. Just afraid he'll lose some of his standing with the whites if he gets too free handed.

This outlook has dulled some of Joyce's ambitions in school, but she remains a fairly good student. Her only recourse is to go away as her brothers have done, or stay and get married. Since the more ambitious of the boys of her group go away, eligible husbands are scarce, and she does not view with much satisfaction the prospect of settling down with what is in sight. Regarding a possible career Joyce said:

> I really would like to be a social worker. I'd like to go around and help the poor and things like that, but here there isn't much chance of a colored girl getting that kind of job—only whites.

Once she thought vaguely of becoming a missionary to China, but this notion soon flitted away. She has no plans now but to go on to college, because it is the expected thing for one of her status to do.

The pressure of the larger group from below, however, brings its problems. The Barnes family is accused of "trying to act like white people" and often is exposed to white antipathy and humiliation as a result of stories told to whites by vindictive Negroes. Humiliation of upper-class Negro children by whites helps to reduce the social distance within the Negro group. Since upper-class Negro fathers are usually businessmen and professionals, and depend upon other Negroes for their livelihood, the children must avoid giving offense to other Negroes. Failure to associate with others on their own level can constitute offense.

> The folks say that I'm uppity since I don't associate with the children, but I just don't like to visit and be bothered with them. There are no school functions, and there's nowhere to go out here. You can't do anything that everybody doesn't know and talk about. Some of my friends from town come out on Sundays, and I may go riding with them. The folks here think it is a sin and terrible for a girl to go riding on Sunday, especially when I ought to be in church. I'm not happy here.

The strong influence of the rural church is felt by families of this class very largely because the church remains a symbol of respectability. However, this class does not take the church seriously though it does not escape the effective censure it imposes. The available churches are usually unattractive to this group because of the uneducated ministry and the primitive character of the services. Nevertheless the local church may condemn this indifference with some effect.

Avoidance of Whites and Other Negroes

The simplest method of getting along is by limiting association with whites and other Negroes. Since common occupations are limited for upper-class youth, they stay in their homes or seek the greater vocational freedom of cities or northern areas. Their families are subjected to severe criticism from other Negroes and from whites, and they have little opportunity for retaliation. Not uncommonly the situation creates definite neurotic conditions as in the case of Myrtle Suggs, whose parents are well-to-do farmers living in attractive surroundings. She is 14 and is devoted to her parents, but has developed a marked fear of getting out of their sight. They have to force her to school, to make friends outside, and even to leave the house. Although large for her age she refuses to abandon many infantile habits, and has as her one dominating passion a desire "to remain the same age forever." Arguments of her parents that she should prepare for independent living are of no avail. She refuses to relinquish the parental protection in each detail of living.

The avoidance of other Negroes serves a further purpose of escaping identification with lower cultural levels. This is at times rationalized by criticism of the social behavior of other classes, and at times frankly explained as necessary to the preservation of exclusive status. In turn, upper-class youth are criticized for being unsympathetic to their own color and for being more heartless exploiters of labor than white employers. As one father said of a well-known Negro attorney, without much apparent justification:

> He's a crook and ain't fitten to lead nobody. He'll kill you. I don't mean kill you really. But killing you by not helping you and all like that. That's worse than killing you.

The children of these upper-class families further respond to this criticism by observing that other Negroes "will not cooperate."

Class Control over Future Vocation

In a study of 5,512 Negro college graduates in 1938,[1] it was found that although the professionals in the Negro population were only 2 per cent of the Negroes gainfully employed, 27 per cent of the employed fathers of college and professional graduates are professional men. The present study shows that 81.3 per cent of the children of professionals and successful businessmen who form the upper class planned to enter the professions

[1] Charles S. Johnson, *The Negro College Graduate* (Chapel Hill: University of North Carolina Press, 1938), pp. 75-76.

as careers. The selection of vocational careers for rural Negro youth is often a serious problem. One mother said:

> I tell Victoria she should take home economics in college, and then she can teach anywhere in the state, if she wants to work. Of course they ought to have men teach in these schools because it's really too hard on a woman. I hate to see them have to do it. It makes them unfit for marriage.

> My boy I should like to see get a Ph.D. It would not be comfortable for him to have to work under some of these people here even while he is getting prepared, and if he gets his Ph.D. he will have an undeniable advantage.

Absence of Social Incentive in Education

There can always be striving on the part of the Negro mass for the exclusive status and apparent immunities of the Negro upper class, but for the children of these upper-class families the limits tolerated for one of the Negro race have been reached, and new occupational advances involve new racial conflicts. Further advance would be tantamount to moving the frontiers of the whole race problem. Only the most sturdy of the youth can face this prospect with much hope of success. Lacking the incentive to higher status, and faced with the frequent poverty of school facilities and curricula, they take school less seriously. Carver Bowman's father is troubled because his son now has every material advantage but carelessly fritters away his time and refuses to take school seriously. His father's concern is expressed in the following comment:

> I can't keep him on his books. We were actually afraid that he would not make his grades. He just likes to play all the time.

His father wants to send him to college, but the boy does not cooperate. He plays defiantly throughout the school hours and says the only thing he likes about school is the recess period. The youth seems to feel that "there isn't much use of working hard in school. What's it going to mean to you down here?"

Carver has no enthusiasm for his upper-class role in the South. He has traveled and can make comparisons.

> Here it is not like it is up North where you just say "yes" and

"no." You talk to white people up there just like you do to colored. Down in Macon, Georgia, it's still worse. If you don't just play ignorant and humble to white people they want to string you up for the buzzards. I would like to beat up some white people and get away with it.

The father said:

The Negroes around here do not act very friendly toward us because we own a bit of land and have an income that is beyond their reach to interfere with. Some of them have even asked me how much income I have. They want the information for the white people, who are just as curious but have no way of asking. If they could stop it they would. That's another reason why I do not discuss my affairs with them any more than necessary for the thing at hand.

MIDDLE-CLASS YOUTH

There are comparatively few Negro families who might be described as "upper class" in the rural areas because these areas are not at the present time capable of supporting professions. A slightly more numerous class is that described roughly as "middle." Some of the indications of recognition of this class appear in various comments by these youth. In one of the areas the president of the Negro school is classified as upper class in a sense implying both social distance and benevolent interest in the group as a whole. Next in importance as a type is Mr. Cosby, "He draws money from the government." A 17-year-old boy giving his estimate of the most important Negroes in the county pointed to another local figure:

He has most money for a colored man. . . . I don't know what kind of work he does, but he just has plenty of money. He made it when he was young—that's what the folks say. He is kind and will turn people favors.

In another county the most highly respected class is made up of individuals with money, occupational distinction, and some position in the church.

Mr. Miller is the biggest Negro around here. I don't know what he did but he's got lots around him. Lots of money and he's deacon in the church.

The most effective test of status is, however, something quite vague and unmeasurable. The description of a family of high position is given briefly by one youth of 16.

> I guess the biggest man here is Mr. Simons. He *stands* for something. Lots of the people around here don't stand for nothing and don't try to make their children do anything, but he does.

In one of the plantation counties the three families most frequently mentioned as having highest status were a farmer ("Mr. Rolf makes pretty good around here"), a doctor ("Dr. Simpkins does pretty good too, he get $3.00 every time he looks at somebody"), and an undertaker ("He makes a lotta money too").

An interesting example of recognition of Negro middle-class status by both Negroes and whites appears in the comment of one youth's father, who regards himself as belonging in the social middle class. He said:

> We don't call each other "niggers" ourselves. Sometimes the real low-class whites call us "nigger" and use other slang terms. If an old man or a person born around the Civil War period should call us "nigger," "Sambo," or anything like that, you wouldn't get mad and mind it, because it is one of his old habits and he doesn't mean any slang or meanness in it.

> The good white people will sooner help a laboring Negro than a laboring white man. A middle-class white man is going to help another middle-class white man before he helps anybody. I could go out here right now and borrow $10 or $100 before any laboring white man could. A laboring white man would have to have his boss sign a note or speak for him before he got anything. I wouldn't have to trouble my boss at all to borrow anything.

Conflict Situations

Middle-class families have achieved their position by hard work and foresight, and resent the envy and borrowing habits of the carelessly improvident. If the social distance were greater and had a longer history, some of the problems would probably prove less acute. A daughter in one of the middle-class families rationalized her position as follows:

These folks around here don't visit us because they say we try to be white folks. Just because we can hire them to pick peas. Now if you worked hard and bought a kodak would you want to lend it to somebody after you had sacrificed to get it? We sacrifice for the things we get. If they would try to save instead of baking ten or twelve cakes and chickens they would have money too. Our folks make me so sick! As soon as they get a penny they run to these stores around here and get a box of crackers and a hunk of old bologna, and they are satisfied.

And when they get a little at settling time all they think about is baking cakes and inviting everybody in to have a feast. People around here think you ought to let them borrow your tools, and if they break them they can't fix them. . . . When I wouldn't lend Martha Cole a nickel she said to me, "If you all didn't act like white folks and have us picking peas I could be in school, but I got to stay home and mind the baby just on account of you all."

Some of the more vocal of the lower economic groups take no pains to hide their resentment of the "pretenses" of this class. One mother whose daughter was not faring so well in school referred to the principal as "that old, bald, black devil of a principal nigger." Canaan Hawks' father explained why he had to be so careful in his dealings with other Negroes:

About here I must be very watchful. Some of these colored folks are pretty treacherous. They run and tell the white folks everything. There was a time I'd sit and talk to my own folks, and before the day was over the white folks would know every word I said. They'd come up here and caution me. . . . White people help each other and keep the Negroes where they want them. Negroes don't do that. They run to help the white man keep the Negro down.

Struggle to Maintain "Respectability"

Mildred Reed says there are definite things a girl of her position cannot do and keep her respectability.

It's bad for a girl to smoke or drink. Boys can do it sometimes if they do not carry it too far. People do not think much about girls who hang around street corners and go to the cafés. It's all right to be around boys and go with them if they have nice people and they do not take a girl to rough places, but there aren't many nice boys now. Most of them do not respect girls.

Mrs. Angie Minton Simon says she has had to bring up her girls "to be intelligent like white people, so they would behave anywhere no matter where it is." She does not permit them to sit on their beds or "stand over the table when they are eating."

Struggle to Attain the Symbols of Higher Status

Julia Minton's father died and left his family a comfortable amount of government insurance. Under good medical care he lived for several years before succumbing to tuberculosis. Julia was 14 when the family inherited this legacy. Before the father's death he had said to his wife:

> Rhoda, we got to get our kids through college so they will be somebody. Some goes to college and thinks they be better than anybody else, and go 'round with their heads up ignoring the less fortunate. Well, I don't want my children like that. I just want them to learn enough to make a good living and carry on what we give 'em.

Julia's mother was an efficient, if only moderately literate farmer's wife, but she was ambitious in a social way. The legacy provided the first real opportunity to project herself and her family into a set which she had admired and worshiped from a respectful distance all her married life and had tried vainly to attract with noisy flattery. She invested her funds immediately in the physical symbols of the status to which she had so desperately aspired. She bought 40 acres of land and built a large house on it. She said:

> There wasn't a nigger out here then. We was the first to build in this section. Well, it wasn't no time 'fore all the muck-a-mucks—I don't mean the white folks—I'm talking about the niggers—come driving by to see what was going on. Them big shots all try to stop and talk then. Long as we didn't have nothing they didn't bother.

Her central room was finished in stucco. A large baby grand piano in the middle of the room nearly filled it. The furniture was teakwood, with elaborate decorative carvings.

> It's all antique and costs lots of money. Lots of them big niggers up at the school use to pass on by me 'cause I ain't got all them

figures and letters of education, but they soon stop and want to see my house.

On the sleeping porch was an immense gilded sofa and a large armchair with a massive gold frame.

> Now that cost me $500. It's a bargain. It's suppose to be worth thousands. It came out of a Jewish synagogue. The gold on it look kind of dull, but I'm going to have new gold put on it. What I want to do is use the best taste in furnishing my home.

> Now that imported rug, the Chinese wove it all by hand. I got a white man what really knows to pick it out, and you can be sure it's real, 'cause it's got "Oriental" stamped right on the back.

She pays her hired man $25 a year and board. The children have to help her work the farm. They scrimp on clothes and education to keep up the taxes and repairs. The mother is happy and the children bored and indifferent. She goes on:

> I figure where we might as well get a good place for the children so they would have a home to be proud of. I'm going to send them to college. Catherine going to take nurse training. She naturally will be bringing her friends home, and I want them all to have a home they won't be ashamed to bring in high class folks.

The total outlay for the place was approximately $15,000. The girls want to drop out of school, and they do not want to stay at home. Julia confides this story of her attempt to escape:

> Last year I wasn't doing nothing so I got a job in town, looking after some white children. The lady what I was working for was real mean. I had to wash all the clothes and cook and everything. She was supposed to pay me $2.00 a week. The first week she give me my money. Then on Friday of the next week she come running into the yard, screaming I stole her ring, and if I didn't give her the ring she would put me in jail. I didn't have no ring. I ain't even seen no ring in her house, so I couldn't give it to her.

> She called the police and they put me in jail. I stayed there all night, and I cried all night. They kept telling me if I didn't give them the ring they would burn me, and I didn't have no ring. The next day the white woman came to the jail and said

she found the ring at home, and they let me out of jail. I asked her for my $2.00 and she cussed me.

When I got home mama was mad but she didn't do nothing. She said white people is funny, and if we caused trouble they would burn up this house and all our furniture. That's exactly why I hate white folks. Mama would be fighting mad if I ever told this. She say it would disgrace us two ways.

This family story requires no further comment than perhaps that of two members of the class which she was trying to impress. One said:

She is a kind-hearted, ignorant woman who has made the error of trying to buy friends and a place for herself where she doesn't fit. Once she would give parties and invite people she had never seen. Many ignored her, but some would drive out just to see what she was going to do.

Another said:

Farmers around here regard her as rich, but she is a "striver," outwitting her own purpose by trying to impose herself on people who do not want her but "use" her. This has made the children sad and broken targets of ridicule.

Education as a Symbol of Improved Status

All classes strive to escape their status through education. For many education becomes a fetish for which they are willing to make any sacrifices. The content of education is less important than the symbolic value of "making the grades," or getting a certificate, or a degree. This formalism encourages the rote learning process which many teachers find a convenient device. School failure under these circumstances can take on an intense social as well as academic importance. Parents urge the children relentlessly to become educated, remind them constantly of the economic loss to the struggling farm unit while they are getting this vital education. The children, however, not infrequently see no relation between the instruction and the acclaimed objectives of education. In the poorer schools the relationship is even farther removed. In some instances, the children have absorbed the faith of their parents. Mark Strothers, the 15-year-old son of a Shelby County, Tennessee, farmer says:

If you have an education it will make you have a lot of things.
... I wouldn't want to be a cook or chauffeur because anybody
with no education could do that. Them's about the onliest jobs
you can get.

From the point of view of the parents, education is an escape
and its devices and formulas are seldom questioned by them.
Willie Sanders, a Macon County, Alabama, youth, says, "It looks
like you can't do nothing today or get a good job without an
education." Rosamond Jones, now in high school, thinks that
if he finishes college he can get more money, be a teacher,
and help at home. "I want to be somebody big," he says, "so
people will know me everywhere."

Harvey Goodson is a hard handed, hard working small owner
living in Greene County, Georgia, with his five children. He
has saved a little money, and he says that his success is due to the
simple philosophy back of his hard work. The philosophy is
this: "Go on getting what you can slow and be quiet about it."
He has pride in his ancestry and family. His father was a slave
but had "powerfully good stock, strong as a mule and he lived
to be a hundred." He looks with mingled respect and contempt
upon upper-class Negroes.

I could have lived a high nigger life and built me a house with
electricity, but I wants to have something for my children.

He has learned to avoid trouble with whites and Negroes alike
by "keeping my mouth shut." His one driving ambition is to
have his children get "book learning." He says "I wants them
to school they way through life." All but the youngest of his
children, however, have quit school, and he is a disappointed
man.

An ambitious mother expressed a similar concern for
lifting the family's level through the children's education. She
said:

We be doing all we are able to keep these children in school. It's
important to have an education nowadays. Robert [the hus-
band] didn't never go to school and I only went to the fifth, so
we want the children to do better'n that. All of 'em do right
well in school. That's why we trying to hold to a little money.

We got a little in the bank, 'tain't much but it's a start. I got it all planned out. Emma keep on saying she wants to be a trained nurse. 'Cos, I don't think much of that kind of work for girls— calls for too much heavy lifting, and it's hard, but if that's what she likes we going to help her get it. I want James to be a dentist, and Albert to be one of those eye doctors, but he keeps talking about he want to be a carpenter. I want to send all my children away to school, and there ain't no reason of going to school if you ain't going to do nothing but cut lots.

Grandmother Dudley says:

I don't care what the children want to be so long as they get an education. Nowadays you can't get nowhere less you edu- cated. I tell the children they should go to school as long as they is able.

Rufus Redding's children have gone out in the world, and with his approval. He does not require them to work on the farm with him because it interferes with their education. He said:

I support two children here and another daughter in Chicago, and will go on doing it as long as she is trying to make some- thing of herself. I would wear overalls till they was quilted just to see my children educated and bein' somebody. You see, I really knows the value of education. You can't do nothing to- day without it, and I am doing all I can for my children.

Social Maladjustment in School

Amanda Alford is a 15-year-old girl and belongs to a hard working family in Madison County, Alabama, that has just recently attained the new, if costly, status of home owner. In this distinction they acquire a conspicuous symbol of improved social status. There are seven children in the family, most of them now old enough to work. The shortening of the years of schooling of the older children was one of the prices paid by the family for the symbolic security of a house of their own. Amanda, who is one of the younger girls, is the family gesture to the educational symbol of upper-class status. She is a shy and sensitive girl, of brown complexion, with short, crinkly hair. The large family is crowded in a four-room house. She has a serious disadvantage at school in her inadequate clothes, which contrast noticeably with those of other children. She said, "When

I go to school I don't have as nice clothes as the rest of the children, and some of them make fun of me."

In the effort to relieve her embarrassment, one of her teachers gave her some of her own daughter's discarded dresses, which the other children immediately recognized. They made remarks about Amanda's clothes which humiliated her. Even in recounting her school experiences she whimpered and finally broke into sobs:

> I felt bad because all the rest of the children would be laughing at me, and I'd cry and go on off by myself. They picking at me about it every two or three days all through the year.

Her mother and sisters tried to console her, saying that she should "pay them no mind" and that when her schoolmates discovered that she ignored them they would forget to laugh at her. But the children did not forget. When she was compelled by lack of any other clothes to wear the dresses recognized by the students, they would resume their teasing. Amanda could not stop school and thus disappoint her parents and defeat her own ambition, largely compensatory, to achieve scholastic superiority; and yet she could not be happy at school. She retired into herself, shrinking from all the children and living constantly on the brink of tears.

The children who troubled her most at the beginning have now tired of overt ridicule, and one or two of them have explained to her that they were just having some fun. Amanda cannot forgive them. She observes that although she plays with the children occasionally in school games, the children have never yet accorded her acceptable recognition.

> In hygiene class we have to look up games and learn how to play by the next class time. One of them I looked up was called the King's Court. They choose a king and queen and the king and queen choose two listeners, and the listeners put their ears to the floor and the other players have to come in one by one and try to make it to the King's seat. He is not supposed to make a noise, and if he does—like a floor squeaking or anything—he has to turn round and go back. The listeners and the others will tell if they have made any noise. I've never been a queen. I was a listener, once.

Amanda has a girl friend who is not a member of the set that "runs the school" either. One of Amanda's greatest fears is getting into a fight. She says, "They try to start a fight with me sometimes, and I just go on off. They say I'm a coward, but I don't care, I just go on off to myself."

She has become decidedly unpopular with the children; in spite of the careful defenses against injury which she has developed, every contact with the children becomes a fresh reminder of her earlier experiences. She wants to go on as far in school as she can. "I want to get a Ph.D. I just want to get one and I don't want to marry."

The greatest number of children in the school population are drawn from the largest economic class in the community—the struggling families of low economic status. They respond variously to their economic and emotional insecurity in school. One of their emotional outlets is that of badgering the few children of better circumstances. Rachel Thompson's parents own their small home and send her to school well dressed. In school Rachel displays a surly manner and is referred to as "a girl nobody likes." She finally quit school, and this was the reason.

> I hate all them children up there. I couldn't get along with them. We was always fighting. You don't know how evil they is. There's Sadie Moore. She got a baby now, and I'm glad of it. She's married, but I ain't saying when she married. We had a fight in school and she tore all my clothes off me and scratched my face. She is bigger than me. The teacher came out after the fight and I told her I wasn't never coming back to the old school, and I didn't. I hated them, and I do yet.

Sadie's mother had her own explanation of this school difficulty:

> The trouble is Sadie looks a little better than most these children and we own our place and they're just jealous of her. You know a jealous nigger is a dangerous thing.

Conflict with Community Folkways

George Lester is a struggling farmer in Madison County, Alabama. He has brought up a family of girls in a community in which the social standards are lax, and he has invested hard earned money in their education. He says:

> The reason I work hard is so my children can have something. I want them to get all the education they can, and I'll keep them in school till they finish up high school, if I live. I'd send 'em on to college, but I got to be doing lots better than I'm doing now to manage that. But that's what they need, plenty of college education. I didn't have it but I watch them papers as close as if I did. The only thing is that now days these girls get boys in the head, and you can't do a thing. Well, I got out my shotgun and told 'em the first no-account nigger I find here I'd shoot him, and I mean it. These boys now days don't mean a girl no good. All they think of is getting full of whisky and fightin' and killin'. . . . I ain't had no trouble with Metro. She don't seem to care 'bout 'em yet. . . . She and all the others know I'd kill any boy I find messin' with 'em. . . . Libby Lee is slick, but I ain't caught up with her yet. I think she gets to meet 'em. She's at the age now when she can get ruined. . . . If any man ruins my girls I'll kill him. My children can live with me when they grow up, but if they marry they got to live and look after themselves. . . . I want them to marry, but none of these scoundrels around. They just give the girl babies and won't work and feed the kids.

Impatient Social Drive of Parents

Under the impatient urging of the parents, some of the youth, instead of progressing in school, become hoplessly distressed, shy, and sulky; in the end they tragically defeat the family purpose and their own chances of effectual escape through the medium of education. One such girl is Mattie Coleman, who is 15 and in the fourth grade. The family now considers her a hopeless problem, and are loud and persistent in their expressions of disappointment and apology. The mother said:

> Mattie is not as bright as some of the other children. She feels it too and she's always complaining of her head "every month."

The father, equally embarrassed by Mattie's backwardness said, impatiently:

> All the children are bashful and slow to talk up and say what they got to say, but Mattie is the worst of them all. I'm always after them about it 'cause I can talk to anybody.

Mattie's head and spirit alike are bowed most of the time. She had "been left" twice in one grade.

> My teacher said I didn't read good enough, but look like she was picking on me 'cause I was doing the best I could. I didn't say anything 'cause if I'm going to stay in school I have to just take it.

> Mother said look like I ought to pass on to another grade but she didn't go to see the teacher or do anything about it. I just never talk about it now. I know there wasn't no need of raising up a bug after she didn't pass me.

Strong minded, excessively articulate parents have effectually cowed her at home. In school she is nervous, hesitant, easily flustered, and goes blank with fright when a question is asked. She has concluded that they are all right in their judgment of her. She tells herself that she cannot learn and discovers that the simplest things escape her understanding.

Carrie May Hawkins has two younger sisters. Her parents have to struggle to keep them all in school. Carrie's life is one long, fretful worry, and for this reason:

> Ma and my father are going to send me to college, but then they say I'll have to come out and work and send my other sisters through. That worries and scares me, because I wonder what will happen if I get through college and then don't get a job, and can't send the other girls through.

Her worry, which seems deep rooted and persistent, is that her failure will disrupt the family plans to educate all the children.

Color and Economic Status

The Rhodes family in Shelby County, Tennessee, has members with light and dark complexions, and four of the six children are boys. They are cotton farmers with a very low income and the parents seem more or less resigned to their prosaic roles in the economy of the country. Two of the older Rhodes boys stopped school "because they wasn't getting nowheres here" and drifted away to Chicago. The father, however, says, proudly,

> My boy in Chicago, he don't do nothing, just dresses up in fine clothes and be a sport. He the one what done well. Don't have

to hit a lick, and got all the shoes he can wear 'til he's dead. I don't know what he do for money, but I know he ain't got to work.

Pride in the escape of the oldest son from the South and from work was in no apparent sense qualified by the fact that neither this son nor any of the others shared their good fortune to lighten the hopeless economic situation of the rest of the family. The father has mild contempt for the son in Detroit who "had to work hard and then didn't have nothing." The youngest son has attained the most conspicuous recognition—in a negative direction, however. The father says, "My youngest boy—that's the bad one. He got three men to his credit. I mean he done kill three." This boy like the others decided early that staying in school was futile. He did not like farming and he saw that even if he finished school there would be nothing but farming for him to do. He did not go away to the city, but has "gone bad" in the country.

He just totes a gun for the sport of it. The first man he killed in defense of himself. Seems like he got caught with this man's woman, and the man pulled a gun, but my boy got to his'n first and just pumped him full of lead. They let him go 'cause the other man pulled the gun first.

Pauline Rhodes is 17, and stopped school the middle of last year when she was in the seventh grade.

I just got tired of school. I wanted to be a beauty culture, and I wasn't learning that in school. I ain't never going back.

She is of light-brown complexion, with heavy features, and a pimply face. Her family has the double handicap of low social and economic status; this has restricted her outlook for the future. The family has also received unfavorable distinction because of the boy who stayed at home and "went bad." Her social resentments, however, are bitterly transformed by Pauline into defense against the antimulatto sentiments of her school associates, most of whom are of dark complexion. She says, "Black is ugly. Black girls can't make up and use powder and lipstick, and I don't think it looks good."

One of her first cousins is a very fair mulatto, and another is light-brown. The former can "pass for white."

> Ain't no way in the world to tell she ain't white, less you just know her. She's got light hair and real white skin, and the same green eyes I got.

A visitor from the North told this cousin that she was pretty, that there "warn't no sense in staying here being a nigger," and that she should "go to New York and pass for a white woman, and she could get anything she wanted." The cousin went to New York and eventually got a job "selling in white folks' stores, and had plenty of folks working under her." The light-brown cousin wrote her, complaining of the difficulty of life in the country; soon afterwards she received train fare from her fair cousin to join her in New York. The tragic sequel is told in Pauline's own words:

> When Emma got there she couldn't get no job selling, but Pinkie got her on as a maid. It made her so mad that she didn't have as good a job as Pinkie she went to the boss and told it all —told him Pinkie wasn't nothing but a nigger like herself. 'Course that wasn't right after Pinkie had helped her. They put Pinkie out the store and she come back home and lost her mind worrying over it. Right now she in the state place for the insane.

LOWER-CLASS YOUTH

Poverty and ignorance imprison the lowest economic classes in a low cultural and social world. In the lower economic group of the rural Negro population, the families are not only poor but on the whole disorganized socially. It is important to keep in mind in reference to this class the "folk Negro" types who represent a low degree of assimilation to American standards, but who nevertheless retain some measure of family organization and internal group cohesion in the framework of the "folk Negro culture." Although the lower class is the most numerous class in the rural Negro population, more attention is given in this chapter to other social classes because among them the problems of status, as such, appear to be more acute.

Irresponsibility

The youth from lower-class families have greater difficulty than the youth of other classes in moving into the next higher group. The hopelessness of their status contributes to a type of free living that acknowledges little responsibility to accepted standards. Education is used by the lower classes less as a means of escape than as a means of handling some urgent practical problems like counting and reading notices. With less opportunity for recognition through education, money, or status, the youth of these families may seek their self-assurance in free sexual activity, in a reputation for physical prowess or for being a bad man, and in other forms of antisocial behavior. The "bad men" who can cut and kill and get away with it, the ones without conscience concerning various types of sexual behavior, the hopeless ones seeking to escape their troubles and status through chronic drunkenness, are likely to be found more frequently in this category than in the others.

This does not mean, however, that all members of this group are morally disorganized. Many of the families are merely uneconomic units which are incapable of self-support, because the number of young children, old persons, or other nonearning members is too great for the earning capacity of the breadwinners. They may be sensitive to community values but forced to live only as conditions permit, whether their social behavior is sanctioned or not.

One father in this group, with eight children, said with a shrewd sense of realism, "We can't feed all these children, but having children is the only freedom we got." Marriage is not always convenient or desirable in this group. The mother of one 14-year-old girl said, rather philosophically:

> I got a man frien' and he do all right. If'n anything come up between us, I kin get another one. I don't think I wants nary nother husband. See, I don't have to be bother 'cept when I want to be, like it is now, but wid a cold old husband you always gotta be thinking what he does and what he thinking about you. Dey all right, but jes' like everything else, dey soon gits in the way.

Family Conflicts Based on Poverty

Laura Gresham's father once had a small piece of property, but his brother took it over for an old debt. The family lives miserably, and Laura hates her father as well as her home.

> Just looks like to me like I oughta be getting a little more out of life than I do. . . . These clothes, they're all rags. I don't ask for any good clothes. Since my mother can't give them to me, what's the use asking her. It worries her too.

Simple poverty is a major feature in the difficulty. But beyond this are the inevitable emotional tensions inherent in the process of socialization within the narrow limits of the Negro youth's world.

The circumstances under which the youth in this class live are given briefly by Hester Lee, in describing her own family. There are in the family a father, a mother, an unmarried sister and her two children, and two other sisters. Hester says of her sister, "Jane ain't married but the kids' papa supports them. She just didn't want to get married." Of her father she said, "He drinks a lot and when he's drunk he and mama get into fusses and I have to tell them to shut up. They listen to me." She is dissatisfied with some of the things her family does, but she thinks her father is doing "the very best he can—he gives us a place to stay and something to eat." She had to stop school to go to work when her father got into trouble and was put in jail. They finally got him out, but they had to hire a lawyer to do it.

The comment of Susie Boyd's grandmother about Susie's father is an eloquent definition of his status and character. It suggests the difficulty of ever getting out of this lowly status. She said:

> He's a low-down nigger. He's lower than any animal you see. He ain't never done nothing for Susie, not even bought her a pocket hancher. Susie look just like him, like as if he spit her out'n his mouth. She even stan like him, and I git after her for that.

Susie has a good mind and "keeps her nose stuck in a book," but she cannot go to high school, nor can she sustain her ambitions against the constant demands of reckless relatives who run afoul of the law. Susie had one bright spot in her memory, and it was short-lived:

> My grandmama and grandpapa saved me some money once but Uncle Hunk got in trouble and they needed the money to get him out. He's always getting into trouble. This time he stole something from the drugstore, and they sent him to the pen.

The boys in these families drop out of school early because they are more in need of money and less hopeful about the values to be received. The girls, while they remain somewhat longer, are similarly disillusioned and place their hope of escape or adjustment in marriage and children to help with the work. Thus the cycle goes on.

SUMMARY

Beyond the problems of racial status, a large proportion of Negro youth face economic insecurity; as individuals they face intense status struggles within the Negro group, involving economic, personal, and social insecurity. All these special problems make a wholesome integration of personality and the social world difficult. The external behavior of Negro youth at all social levels bears unmistakable relationship to the internal fears, worries, anxieties, and feelings of inadequacy and frustration which reveal themselves in the individual cases cited in this chapter. It is not unlikely that these obscure emotional snarls, whether petty and persistent or violent and transitory, are at least in part the source of those characteristics which distinguish the Negro most sharply as a unique cultural phenomenon in American life.

CHAPTER IV

YOUTH AND THE SCHOOL

NEXT TO the family, the school is the social institution that most strongly influences youth. Modern education has broadened its aim to include, not only the imparting of subject matter, but also the development of wholesome, well-rounded personalities. In what is called "the traditional school" the aim is principally to teach the curriculum and to enforce the conformity of each pupil. Relatively few concessions or adjustments are made to the interests and capacities of a particular individual in the class. Modern schools, on the contrary, emphasize attention to the individual differences among pupils and seek to develop worthy interests, aptitudes, incentives, and appreciations.

THE SCHOOLS

What about the schools for southern rural Negro youth? How far does the public school compensate for the disadvantages of poor homes and neighborhoods, economic distress, and lack of opportunity for personality development? As we shall see, the public schools open to southern rural Negroes can contribute very little to the elevation of these youth.

FINANCING

Although the rate of taxation is relatively high in the southern states, there is not enough tax revenue to maintain governmental services comparable to those in other states. Nowhere is this inadequacy more evident than in the funds appropriated for rural Negro schools. To be sure, a school which carries out a progressive program of education is costly, and one should not expect to find excellent school systems in impoverished states. The point here, however, is that in the South the school funds, which are usually insufficient to support one good school system, are unequally divided. Only a small amount of the available tax revenue is expended on Negro education.

It is, of course, regrettable that, whereas the average annual expenditure for schooling (current expense, interest, and capital outlay) per pupil in average daily attendance in 1937-38 was $99.70 in the United States as a whole, in the South where separate schools for Negroes and whites are maintained it was $60.61 in the 17 states and the District of Columbia. It is more unfortunate that the per capita expenditure for Negro youth in average daily attendance is only $23.00 in the 12 southern states where information is available.

The situation in Alabama is a good illustration of this inequality of support. In 1937-38, $37.81 was spent for current expense, interest, and capital outlay for each pupil in average daily attendance. The amount spent on each white pupil was $49.37 and on each Negro pupil $14.75. When expenditures for new grounds, buildings, and equipment are compared, the inequality is more striking. For each white pupil in average daily attendance the capital outlay was $2.85; for each Negro pupil it was 58 cents.

Under present methods of taxation the southern states cannot afford to maintain school systems comparable to the best in the United States. Yet, the available funds in the South support the white schools much more liberally than the Negro schools. White teachers in Alabama, for example, receive the low average salary of $827; but Negro teachers receive an average salary of $393. This is one more illustration of inadequate support for the schools that serve rural Negro youth.[1]

Throughout the South the county superintendents usually find that tax revenues are too meager to support even a single efficient school system. Legal requirements and tradition have complicated this problem by the biracial educational system. Inevitably the outcome is that Negro schools are allotted only a small share of funds which, even on an equal division, would hardly suffice. It is frequently explained, by way of justification,

---

[1] Data on school expenditures from unpublished material in the United States Office of Education.

that this inequality is necessary because the Negro is too impoverished to pay school taxes. The fact remains, however, that the burden of indirect taxation falls as heavily upon the Negro as upon anyone else.

QUALITY OF INSTRUCTION

The homes of rural Negro youth are, with few exceptions, dismally inadequate. Their schools, which have the support of the state, are scarcely better. Unattractive schools and a lack of supplies for class work do little to inspire pupils with aesthetic feelings or to induce teachers to put forth their best efforts. Teachers on a bare subsistence income, and often with a minimum of preparation, are hardly qualified to foster the development of wholesome, well-adjusted personalities in their pupils.

A typical rural Negro school is at Dine Hollow. It is in a dilapidated building, once whitewashed, standing in a rocky field unfit for cultivation. Dust-covered weeds spread a carpet all around, except for an uneven, bare area on one side which looks like a ball field. Behind the school is a small building with a broken, sagging door. As we approach, a nervous, middle-aged woman comes to the door of the school. She greets us in a discouraged voice marred by a speech impediment. Escorted inside, we observe that the broken benches are crowded to three times their normal capacity. Only a few battered books are in sight, and we look in vain for maps or charts. We learn that four grades are assembled here. The weary teacher agrees to permit us to remain while she proceeds with the instruction. She goes to the blackboard and writes an assignment for the first two grades to do while she conducts spelling and word drills for the third and the fourth grades. This is the assignment:

> Write your name ten times.
> Draw an dog, an cat, an rat, an boot.
> Draw an tree, an house, an cow, an goat.
> Draw an book, an apple, an tomatoe.

While the children are complying with these instructions, the older ones are reciting:

Teacher: What is a contraction?
Pupil: A word with a letter left out.

Teacher: What word would rhyme with "hung"?
Pupil: Rung.

Teacher: Give me a little word that we make longer by adding "ing."
Pupil: Read.

Teacher: How would you write "G-o-d"?
Pupil: Capital "G."

Teacher: How can you pluralize the word "jelly"?
Pupil: Change "y" to "i."

Teacher: You add "er" to what word to make it longer?
Pupil: Old.

Teacher: Now we have the word "win." To add "ing" what do you do?
Pupil: Double the last letter in the word.

Next, the arithmetic class is called up for recitation. These fourth-graders have to multiply and to check their products. One boy demonstrates the method of checking. He multiplies 32 by 4 and obtains 128; he then writes 32 down four times and adds to check the answer. To be doubly sure of their answers the children all count on their fingers in addition. We inspect a child's paper and read as follows:

a.
$$\begin{array}{r} 158 \\ 4 \\ \hline 632 \end{array} \qquad \begin{array}{r} 158 \\ 158 \\ 158 \\ 158 \\ \hline 632 \end{array}$$

b.
$$\begin{array}{r} 204 \\ 6 \\ \hline 1{,}224 \end{array} \qquad \begin{array}{r} 204 \\ 204 \\ 204 \\ 204 \\ 204 \\ 204 \\ \hline 1{,}224 \end{array}$$

Another class comes forward to recite on the day's reading lesson. Haltingly a boy retells the story which the group had been assigned to read:

Fred was a little boy. He went to the city to work for a man. The man told him if he worked he would pay him. Fred worked

three years. The man paid him only three pennies. Fred said . . .
Fred said . . . The man paid him only three pennies. Fred
said. . . .

The poor boy could get no further; he simply could not recall
what Fred had said. Obviously the story had been studied in
rote fashion, as no amount of questioning by the teacher served
to refresh this pupil's memory.

In the English class there is a "review" on the kinds of verbs.
"How many kinds of verbs are there?" the teacher inquires. A
volunteer opens the lessons by replying, "Abverbs . . . " but is
interrupted by the teacher. "There are two kinds of verbs,
aren't there?" she says. "Yes," the class agrees. "They are transi-
tive and intransitive, aren't they?" And again the class agrees
with her. So the lesson proceeds with the teacher answering
as well as asking the questions and the class voicing their agreement.

At another school in the county the teacher came forward
with her face wrapped up in a white cloth. "I am suffering from
neuralgia," she explains. "We have no substitute teachers here,
and when one of us gets sick we just have to keep right on. I'll
just keep the children busy today. I don't feel like teaching."
So she requests the fourth-graders to write all they know about
fish—where they live, how they are caught, and how they are
canned. Second-graders have two assignments: first, they must
draw three boots, two eyes, and a stone; then they are to use
one, two, three, girl, boy, baby in sentences. At the board the
teacher draws in crude fashion these objects which the first-
grade children are to identify: an apple, a pear, an eye, an ear,
a spider's web, and an ice cream cone.

No doubt, the very low salaries paid to Negro teachers in the
rural districts are one cause for instruction such as is illustrated
by these typical examples. Few well-trained persons would be
attracted to teaching for the amounts paid, and few teachers
could spare money to pay for necessary in-service training. Another reason for such low quality instruction is that appointments are often made on the basis of political influence and personal manipulation. Often county superintendents are not parti-

cularly interested in the Negro schools within their jurisdiction, and they make appointments in a most casual manner. Personal acquaintance with the superintendent, a reputation for efficiency in domestic or personal service, and recommendations from influential white citizens often carry more weight than training and experience.

The results of such a lack of concern for the professional qualifications of applicants for teaching positions in rural Negro schools are plainly evident. In 1931 Horace Mann Bond gave the Stanford Achievement Test to 306 Negro teachers enrolled in summer school who had been teaching during 1930-31 in the public schools of six Alabama counties. He reported that these teachers made an average score below the national norm set for ninth-grade school children. Elizabeth Moore depicted the situation in more dramatic language when we interviewed her:

> The teachers in Boyle [Mississippi] were worse than they are in Alabama. You won't believe this, but it is the honest-to-God's truth. We had one teacher who didn't know her multiplication tables. She didn't mind telling us that she didn't know. She'd say to us, when we'd ask her what a certain number multiplied by a certain number was, "Oh, go away, child, I am tired and can't be bothered with you. If I tried to remember all that study and stuff I'd go crazy." We soon found that she didn't know a lot of things so we always thought of hard things to ask her so she would be embarrassed 'cause she didn't know them. I told mamma about this when I got home and she decided to move to Bolivar. Here the schools are better, the terms longer, and the teachers are better. We have the best school in the county. If I hadn't been thrown back in those other schools I would have finished before I was 18.

As Elizabeth has said, the school term in many rural districts is very short. Four Alabama counties had an average term of less than five months, and the average term in Negro schools throughout the state was about seven months in 1936-37. The teachers are, themselves, the products of an inadequate system, and merely help to perpetuate its unfortunate results.

AREA DIFFERENCES WITHIN THE SOUTH

The South is no more a homogeneous unit socially than it is geographically. There are wide differences in wealth, economic activity, and culture. Naturally, therefore, there are considerable differences in educational opportunities for Negro youth. The schools reflect the cultural setting of several divergent situations.

First, there are the plantation areas represented by Bolivar County and Coahoma County in Mississippi where tradition is strongest. Here there is little demand for change, and the rural elementary school remains on a low level. In a few centers there are fairly good consolidated schools. The high schools, poor as many of them are, nevertheless do come into conflict with the old plantation system. The most telling evidence of this fact is that few high school graduates are interested in going back to work as tenant farmers on the plantations.

Madison County, Alabama, which is very poor in agricultural products, is an unusual area. Here the Negroes have developed their own life. They have purchased more farms than would be possible in the delta area, and several Negroes own very large tracts of land. They operate their farms with little outside control and are less dependent upon supervision over their affairs. They have learned how to raise a small part of their food, along with the commercial crop. Though their schools are poor, particularly on the elementary level, they seem to feel a need for more education in order to work out their own agricultural problems.

In Johnston County, North Carolina, and Davidson County, Tennessee, where there is mixed farming, the Negroes have an even greater degree of independence and a greater diversity of habits. In these two counties, as in Madison County, there is much unemployment and economic insecurity. As the Negroes in these areas begin to compete with similarly placed economic groups of white people, they see the need for improvements in their schools

RURAL EDUCATIONAL PROBLEMS

The southern rural Negro school faces special practical problems in addition to inadequate funds and unqualified teachers.

The general poverty of the population, the demands of the farming system, the poor health of many of the children, and the long distances between homes and the school all contribute to the difficulties of rural education.

SCHOOL AND THE FARMING SYSTEM

Schooling for Negro youth is controlled by the exigencies of cotton. Throughout the cotton belt a late cotton picking season may empty the schools. In the northern cotton belt, for example, in Shelby County, Tennessee, the divided session plan provides from two to three months of schooling for children in the summer off-season between hoeing and picking, in addition to the winter term of less than five months. In spite of this adjustment, whenever work must be done on the farm, parents feel they have the right to keep the child out of school. The county truant officer is unable to cope with the problem of poor attendance. Both the parents and the plantation owners protest if he attempts to carry out his duties as indicated in the law and school regulations. A white truant officer in Shelby County said:

> It just isn't safe for me to go on a plantation to bring students to school. The landowners show absolutely no concern and they tell me to let the "niggers" work.

A tenant parent explained:

> The children need all the education they can get, but we need them to help on the farm. If you don't make your crop the white man will put somebody else here to do the work. The children go to school when there ain't no work for them in the fields, but when there is work, they has to stay home and do it.

The functional relationship in Shelby County between the Negro school and the farming system appears in small details of administration. The time for the closing of the school, for example, is not a predetermined date as in the case of white schools, but depends upon the condition of the crop. Neither the pupils nor the teachers know when the school will close or open very much in advance of the signal given by the landlords as they watch the maturing crops. In the spring and fall the internal school program is changed to accommodate the system.

Chapel exercises, lunch hours, and recreational periods are either shortened or eliminated entirely in order that school may close at an earlier hour to let the children get away to the farms. The average length of the school year for Negro children, including these adjusted days, is 161 days. For white children there is a nine-month session of 180 days, and the schools are closed during the three months of the summer heat.

Many of the families expressed their belief in the benefits of education, although they felt their children were forced by economic necessity to attend school irregularly before completing the elementary or high school grades. The following comment of the mother of a nonfarming, home-owning family of Shelby County, where the husband holds a responsible job, is typical; her family includes an 18-year-old daughter attending business college, a younger girl in high school, and a son, the oldest child, who has stopped school and is now employed as an errand boy.

> Of course, our boy didn't get a college training, but my husband and I are both anxious to give our children the best. If we couldn't get it, still we want them to have it. That's why I work too. I don't make but a little, but that helps with the clothes, and I like to send them out looking nice and not feeling slighted.

In other counties as well, rural parents have to keep their children out of school in order to have their help on the farm, though these parents may deplore the economic necessity which interferes with opportunity for education. The wife of a Coahoma County, Mississippi, farmer expressed it this way:

> I believe children ought to get all the education they kin. I'd like to see 'em all finish the twelfth grade at least. My daughter is the only one that goes now. The rest have to chop and pick right now, but they be going 'long soon.

Another Coahoma County mother said:

> I believe in education. I really do. That is one thing that hurts me. My boys is got to forsake their schoolin' to help out they daddy.

A farmer in Johnston County, North Carolina, said:

Last year, I kept my boy out three weeks. I hope he won't have to miss so much this year. Staying out makes him miss so much he ought to have. Farming people don't have much time to spend in books.

Another Johnston county farmer with six children describes the conflict between future educational needs and immediate economic demands, and sets forth the manner in which he is attempting to resolve it:

I keep all of them out of school in the fall to work in the field. None of them go to school before the first of November. I don't allow the younger ones to go until they are all ready. The other children on the bus would treat them terrible and I wouldn't give them a chance to get at my children like they do some of the other little children. The children enter school always late, but they attend regularly until school closes in May, except when I keep them out a day or so to work or set out tobacco in the spring. They need all the education they can get until they finish up high school, at least. They should go on through college, if possible. My children are going to school as long as we can just half support them. I mean to let them stay in school, and all of them that wants a chance to go will get that chance.

Excessive retardation in the rural schools is the inevitable result of the demands of the economic system. Regardless of how strong the desire to attend school may be, it is secondary to the demands of the system. Every member of the family who is old enough must work until the crop is in. Edith Moss, who is 17 years old, is still in the fifth grade although she should be much higher. Each year she loses from four to six weeks out of school because she has to complete her work on the farm first. Edith's ambition is to become a teacher, but her present status is anything but encouraging to her. She has become pessimistic.

I just don't think I'll ever be what I want to be. I really want more than anything else to be a teacher, but to be a good teacher you really ought to go to college. Having to stay out of school and farm makes me so far behind in my school work I don't see any need of keeping on trying to plug away like this and getting no place. I'm old enough either to be in college or have a man's size job. Since I just know I'll never get to college I feel like just dumping the whole thing and getting a job some place. My folks don't have any money to be keeping me in school anyway.

REGULARITY OF ATTENDANCE

The important causes of irregular attendance are economic in origin. Prominent among them, after the apparently inexorable demands of the farm situation, are the health conditions of the rural South. Horace Mann Bond found in his Alabama studies that sickness played an important part in curtailing the regular attendance of Negro school children. In one county located in the Alabama River valley, he observed that the schools were practically deserted for several weeks. The usual explanation given by teachers and those children who did come to school was that the children "had the chills and fevers." Malaria was expected in this community every fall as a normal part of the life cycle. The sickness and morbidity rates were even higher for Negro children than for adults, although both were excessive when compared with rates for whites.

The influence of ill health is clearly revealed in the following cases. A Coahoma County, Mississippi, boy said:

> I been out of school for three years. I quit in the fifth grade because I was sick. I took sick and stayed sick a good while, for about a year. I had terrible pains in my stomach. When I got up I just wasn't interested in going back to school. I ought to and needs to. I like school, but I just don't know if I'll get back.

A 15-year-old second-grade farm boy in Greene County, Georgia, said:

> I used to go to school right smart when I got through picking cotton. It would be done started, but it wouldn't be going on long before I'd start. My daddy would keep me and my oldest sister out to pick cotton, but he'd send the other children all the time. School starts in November and it would be open just a week or maybe two before I'd get started. We have to stop out in the spring to help plow and chop, but he would let the little ones stay in until it closed. I don't know whether it closes early or late, and I don't know when it closed. Last year I didn't go hardly at all 'cause I had a rising in my head.

TRANSPORTATION

Lack of school transportation is another major factor. The remark of 14-year-old Bessie Young is typical, "I didn't start to school until I was 9. I wasn't living close by a bus line so I couldn't go to school." Only in those areas where progressive and fair-minded county superintendents have extended the consolidation movement to Negro schools are transportation facilities available to Negro children. For the most part, rural Negro youth still must either walk from five to ten miles daily or not go to school at all. Even when the child is willing to walk the distance, bad weather and bad roads often make regular attendance impossible. Fifteen-year-old Maggie Red "just loves to go to school" and walks a distance of twelve miles daily, but, she complains:

> Sometimes it rains so hard I just can't go. It's mighty hard walking so far when it's cold, too, but that ain't nearly as bad as when it's raining. If I just had some way of getting to school when it rains I'd be so much further along in school than I am now.

Negro youth in counties which provide no transportation facilities for them are aware of the racial implications of such a situation. Beulah King, 14-year-old sixth-grade pupil, says she, "just gets so mad" every time she sees the white children riding to school in a bus when she has to walk. The thing Beulah cannot understand is this:

> Now if they ain't got money enough to buy a bus for both white and colored children to ride in I don't see why they couldn't let some of the colored children have some of the seats in there [the white bus], and ride. It just don't seem fair to me for them to let the white children ride and make us walk. 'Cose it ain't so bad when the weather is good, but I just get so mad I want to cry when it's rainy and cold. The little ones at home can't go at all when the weather is bad.

Seventeen-year-old Charles Webster, who "ain't gonna be bothered with no schooling," presents the problem faced by a large proportion of rural Negro youth when he says:

I'm just getting tired of trying to go to school. When it's warm enough to walk, you got to stay out and work on the farm, and when all the farm work is done, it starts being cold and rainy. I just don't see no need of making yo'self sick trying to go to school in all the bad weather. I'm gitting so I ain't gonna be bothered with no schooling. At the rate I'm going I'll be 40 before I'm done with the grades.

Johnnie Mae, a sixth-grade pupil, reveals an important reason why Negro education in her community often stops at the seventh grade.

The seventh grade is as far as they go in our school here. Most of the boys and girls around here just stop altogether when they finish up here because we don't have any way to go to the high school. I'm going to try to go on when I finish up here, but if they don't have a high school put up here by then I'll have to walk all the way to Greensboro to attend school. That's about nine and a half miles.

In rare instances the family, often by making tremendous sacrifices, is able to board the child at a place near the school or could pay for private transportation. Mary Lynn's family was able to board her at Mrs. Dunn's house near the school for $1.50 a month. But Mary Lynn's family is not the typical rural Negro family. For the most part, the average rural Negro youth is doing well when he can attend school "after the crop is in" and the "weather isn't too bad" for him to walk his five to fifteen miles daily. His going to school is, in the first place, a tremendous sacrifice, and if, in addition, money must be expended, further schooling becomes "out of the question."

Even in a section that provides conveyances, the child is often kept back because the location of the home is such that access to the school bus is difficult. In such areas, the handicap works its greatest hardship on smaller children who cannot walk unaccompanied the long distances to the highway where the bus stops.

ATTITUDES TOWARD EDUCATION

The results of our study indicate that the presumed practical values of education have become a motivating force for both parents and children to a remarkable degree, even in the plantation area. Their reasons were varied. Some wanted an education so they could "live in town," some "to make a living." One boy said, "Everybody needs to know how to read and count." The increased possibility of securing desirable work was perhaps most common. A 12-year-old seventh-grade Johnston County, North Carolina, girl, whose family is economically well-off according to community standards, thought, "Everybody ought to go to school and get educated. If you get a heap of schooling you get plenty of jobs when you finish." A 17-year-old tenth-grade Shelby County, Tennessee, boy said:

> I like school just fine because it tells you how to do the right thing at the right time. An education will tell you whether to farm this year or to do something else.

From this same area another youth expressed the view that:

> An education is good to have. You might get a job in Clayton and you will have to know how to count and you can make better change.

Although many reasons for their interest in "schooling" were given, in general, education appears to have two vital meanings for most of these youth and their parents. First, education makes people literate. These people believe that their poverty is largely attributable to their inability to read and write. Hence, for them education meets an immediate, practical need. It protects them against frauds often practiced upon ignorant people who are tenant farmers.

A Johnston County, North Carolina, farmer of high standing in the community explained the attitude of parents who themselves had not had extensive education:

> I didn't get far, but I am anxious for my children to remain in school until they finish high school at least. I would like for them to attend college. I intend to send them, too, if my health keeps up. Children need plenty of education these days so they can go into business without folks cheating them.

A Bolivar County, Mississippi, tenant farmer said:

> Children need all the education they can get and ought to get

enough to keep people from cheating them. They should go through high school, and farther if they can. Especially the boys; they is the ones that need the education, 'cause they has to make a living.

Secondly, education is regarded as a means of escape from the prospect of an unpleasant occupation which is frequently associated in the minds of Negroes with a low racial status. The hope that education may offer a way of escape is expressed by a deserted, sharecropper mother of six children:

> I plan to let the children keep on in school as long as they want, until they want to leave. It sure is hard, but I'm willin' to struggle along to help them all I can. If a child ain't got a good education now days it be mighty hard on them. If I'd a had more of it I wouldn't be so hard put now. I went to the sixth and had to come out to work. I don't know nothin' but farmin' and it's hard makin' a livin' on the farm. My girl is the oldest and I'm goin' to help her stay in school. She's smart, too.

A 16-year-old eighth-grade plantation girl of Macon County, Alabama, commented:

> I'd rather go to school than farm. I really like school. My folks are going to try and send me to Tuskegee and I want to go, too. It costs a lot of money and I can't say I'll get to go, but I sure do want to go, for I'd rather do anything than farm, and if I go to school I can do something else.

Another youth said, "Everybody ought to have an education. If you don't have an education, you'll have to work on a farm all the time." A 12-year-old fifth-grader remarked:

> If it weren't for schools Negroes would be in a terrible shape. If there weren't any schools, Negroes wouldn't know anything and would have to always work on the farm.

A mother in a Madison County, Alabama, tenant family, living nine miles from the nearest school, further illustrates the escape aspect of education when, speaking of her daughter, she says:

> 'Cose there ain't much for a girl this far in the country, but we get on pretty good. We been so anxious for her to get her schooling we just pay a man $2.50 a month. He picks her up and a few others on the highway ever' morning. I wants to see her keep getting educated. I didn't go no higher than the fifth grade

or I'd not be here on a farm today. I sho' don't intend for her to have to work on no farm.

A Macon County, Alabama, mother, viewing education as the chief avenue of occupational escape, said:

I didn't get very high in school, went to 'bout the sixth grade. My husband, he only went as far as the fourth. I had to come out and help my folks farm and just didn't get back. I wants all these children to get all the education they can. They ought to finish high school and that's what we be planning on—sending them to high school and college, too, if they hold out and stay in school. Trouble is, today most young folks don't want no schooling. All they want is a good time. I say you got to have education now to get a job what will pay any money.

Apparently no sacrifices were too great for the majority of the parents to make in order to secure for their children the advantages of an education. A widowed domestic day worker in Davidson County, Tennessee, said:

I want Bennie to stay in school just as long as I am able to send her. That's why I sent her out there to the boarding school. Like it be with me working out, girls can get into so much trouble and I felt that out there she would be watched over and be learning all at once. It takes all I can make, for ain't nobody to keep the children but me, but I want Bennie to get learning.

In this same vein, another widow from Macon County said:

I want my girls to finish high school. I'll send them as long as I can, but I can't tell how long I'll be able to keep them. It's right high [expensive] sending children to school and boarding them out, but I want them to get some learning.

Some parents are so solicitous of their children's welfare that they personally supervise their educational progress. One Shelby County, Tennessee, farmer said:

Every year when school opens I goes down to the school and see his new teacher. I tell her what I want my son to learn and how I want him to act. My boy is a good student; he gets his lesson fine. If something goes wrong at school I goes down and see what the trouble is.

Other parents make no attempt to hide their disgust or sorrow when their children lack interest in school. A Bolivar County,

Mississippi, resident spoke strongly of his son's lack of interest in school.

> I don't know what is the matter with that blockhead. Me and his mother done everything for him, but he just won't do no good. He ain't been near no school for three years and he's 17 now. I just wish I had the opportunity he had when I was coming along. The world expects more of him than it does of people like me. I'm going down and he's coming up, but he won't go to school.

The wife of a Macon County, Alabama, farmer of moderate circumstances said proudly:

> Our daughter wants to try and go to Selma University, down here at Selma, and her father will sure try to send her, too. If he half-way got the money and she really want to go, he'll sure send her.

In some cases, even after the child had married, the parents still wished to have the process of formal education continued. One sharecropping widow in Coahoma County, Mississippi, who had four daughters said:

> I wanted Baby to finish her schooling. I wanted her to go all the way. I went to Tuskegee in 1925 on a visit. I wanted Baby to go to school there. It don't make no difference about her being married. I want her to go there if she don't do nothing but learn a trade and then she will be able to take care of herself. Lots of people go to school after they are married. Sometimes they do better because their mind is settled.

Although the hostile, indifferent "folk" attitudes toward education are rapidly giving way in the face of new conditions, need for the children's labor not infrequently is rationalized in terms of a lack of need for education. This attitude appeared most frequently in areas within the shadow of the plantation. An interesting example of this attitude appears in the comment of a struggling, illiterate sharecropper in Bolivar County who has seven children, all but one of whom are illiterate.

> I ain't so worried 'bout my children getting all this schooling. They ain't going to do nothing nohow but work on the farm. I'll send them upon consideration up to the sixth grade, then they got to come out and help me. I went as high as the seventh,

but it didn't do me no good. Unless you can go on to college, schooling ain't no 'count. My children just as well be home as chasing over there to that school house wastin' time and money.

The child's reaction to this attitude was both wistful and pathetic:

I like school. I always want to stay in school, but I reckon after this year I can't. Maw thinks I am big enough to stay home and work, and schooling costs so much. Sometimes I dream that when I am bigger I am going off and finish school, sometimes it seems like I am away at school.

A rationalization for her failure to attend school, presented by an 18-year-old Coahoma County girl who had been married for three years, combines a disrespect for the value of education in plantation life and for the school facilities that are available to Negroes:

Education is all right for those who wants it for somethin' they want to do. If you gonna farm all your life, though, you jus' wastin' your time goin' to school. And that's what most of 'em gonna do. Dey gonna stay right here on some of these planta-tions all their life anyhow. Colored school ain't near 'bout doin' much good nohow. They open way late after the white school done opened and dey close up 'fore the white schools shut down. Now how's school gonna do any good if you can't stay there as long as you oughta?

Further disapproval of modern education is voiced by a Boli-var County parent who said:

I believe education is like this: If it prepares you to do some-thing, then it's all right. Now, I believe a person ought to go as far as the eighth grade. After that he ought to take a trade—bricklayin' or plasterin' or something he can work at with his hands. All those people you see 'round Clarksdale and in the city what done finished up, walkin' 'round holdin' their hands, with nothing to do. What's the use of learnin' how to be a book-keeper if you ain't gonna never have no books to keep? That ain't for no niggers.

EMOTIONAL PROBLEMS

The economic and social insecurity of southern Negroes is reflected in the attitudes of school children. They seem to be timid and fearful, even in a situation where they ought to feel happy and secure. A 16-year-old girl who was in the third grade of a Madison County school told the interviewer:

> I remember the first day I started to school when I was 13. We played lots of games. I always feel scared when I go to school the first day. I think I'm going to get a whipping if I be late. I never did get a whipping on the first day.

A more graphic picture was given by another girl of the same age who was in the eighth grade:

> I first didn't like science and I failed it the first semester. I get nervous in school when it comes time to take a test. I must get scared. I don't know what makes me scared. The children used to talk about that school so much before I went there it just got me scared. I still get the jitters when exams time come.

That the school definitely constitutes a crisis situation for a large proportion of these youth is shown by the high percentage who list either "School work" or "Getting an education" as the first of their three greatest worries and the equal prominence with which "Success in school work" or "College or advanced education" figures in the first of their three greatest wishes. In Coahoma County, Mississippi, for example, 48 per cent of the boys and 53.3 per cent of the girls listed "Getting an education" and "School work" as the first of their three greatest worries. The smallest proportions listing these worries were 28.2 per cent of the boys and 35.2 per cent of the girls in Greene County, Georgia. In every county except Greene, one of these two worries—"Getting an education" or "School work"—was among the first three mentioned. Even in Greene County the first position was shared and not yielded: 17.9 per cent of the boys ranking "Family affairs" first and an equal proportion ranking "School work" first; 23.1 per cent of the girls ranking "Family affairs" as their first worry and an equal proportion of the latter ranking "Getting an education" first. In Shelby County, Tennessee, 13.7 per cent of the boys listed "Getting an education" as their first worry and an equal proportion listed "Money or material goods" as their first worry.

In Bolivar County, Mississippi, "Success in school work" or "College or advanced education" was the first wish of 35.1 per cent of the boys and 38.8 per cent of the girls. In Coahoma County, Mississippi, 36.5 per cent of the boys and 40.9 per cent of the girls listed one of these as their first wish. "Success in school work" or "College or advanced education" was the first wish of boys in Coahoma and Bolivar counties and Macon County, Alabama, and of girls in Coahoma, Bolivar, and Macon counties, Shelby County, Tennessee, Greene County, Georgia, and Johnston County, North Carolina. Only Madison County, Alabama, and Davidson County, Tennessee, girls failed to place one of these two—"Success in school work" or "College or advanced education"—first; these girls chose first "Personal professional success," which bears a close relationship to education. "Personal professional success" shared first place with "Money or material goods over $25" as their first wish in several instances.

Evidence of tensions revolving around economic insecurity lies in the fact that 17.9 per cent of the boys and 23.1 per cent of the girls in Greene County, Georgia, list "Family affairs" as their greatest worry. This is to be expected when we consider that only one out of every ten Negro farmers in this county owns any land; that their holdings are, as a rule, too small for subsistence; and that of the nine-tenths who own no land, about half are sharecroppers, owning no work animals or farm equipment. Nearly a fourth are farm hands, and only the remaining fourth are renters who own some work animals and farm equipment. The direct implications, therefore, between economic insecurity and "Getting an education" can be readily understood. This problem is given more detailed attention in Chapter II of this volume.

It is interesting to note that Davidson County, Tennessee, both urban and rural, and Johnston County, North Carolina (which ranked first and third respectively in average I.Q.'s), had the highest percentages of boys and girls who ranked "School work" as their greatest worry. Perhaps worry in this instance denoted deep concern rather than a sense of personal inadequacy.

The fact that a relatively low proportion of both sexes in all counties ranked "My future" as their first great worry, in contrast to the consistently high percentage which designated "Getting an education" as their first worry probably indicates that these rural youth are keenly aware of education as the most immediate and effective instrument for escaping the vicissitudes of their present economic plight, and for assuring them of future security.

TEACHER-PUPIL CONFLICTS

Retardation and withdrawal from school were often explained by the demands of the economic system, but other comments were offered as, for example, by the child who complained, "Our teacher was mean!" Unqualified teachers have frequently relied upon fear as the means of enforcing discipline, and the Negro teachers in the rural South are no exception. Poorly trained teachers often try to conceal their ignorance and to terrify their pupils. Maggie Cole, a 13-year-old girl who has been retarded in school, gives a typical comment:

> I would be further along in school than I am now, but when I was small I stayed in the Primer three years. I was just scared of my teacher. She used to call on me and I'd know my lesson, but she was so mean that when she'd call on me I'd get scared and couldn't say nothing. Then she'd whip me.

There is little wonder that 14-year-old Charles King (along with many of his classmates) had failed in the fifth grade. The purposeless discipline meted out by the teacher has made Charles dislike school to the extent that he looks with dread upon the time for the opening of school. He said:

> I've failed in the fifth grade twice. I reckon it was because the teacher was so very mean. She used to maul boy's heads with a big old ring she had on her finger. She used to say, "I ain't going to whip you hard, niggers, but I'll maul your heads with this ring I got on my finger." All the kids was afraid of her. It seems like every time she'd call on me my head would just go blank, I'd be so scared. I'm getting so I just hate to go to school.

Large classes prevent the teachers from giving attention to

the needs of individual pupils. In the rural Negro schools, when all children are present, the harassed teacher may have sixty or more pupils distributed over seven grades. Frank Miller, who could not master arithmetic, felt the need of some special help. He said:

> I might could do better if Miss James woulda showed me how to work those fractions, but she would just pass me on by and let them that understood it work the problems all the time. She'd say she didn't have time to be bothered with trying to help all of us dumb ones who just didn't understand. She said we just oughta study more, but I know I studied all I could.

Many of the youth expressed a desire for a closer relationship between the school and their future work. They expressed dissatisfaction with the present curricular offerings which seem to have no bearing upon the needs of later life. The comments from youth in all areas reflect this dissatisfaction, occasionally becoming forthright and specific as in the case of the boy who complained:

> Looks like they ought to teach us something we can use later on like carpentry or something like that. The little we get up there at school ain't helping us none and we have to end up farming right on.

The obvious physical inadequacies, which are serious enough in themselves, tend to obscure these internal and personal problems of learning throughout the system. These problems, nevertheless, are frequently the source of the frustration and confusion that send these youth from the school back to the fields or to the streets before they have acquired the simple rudiments of an education. The seriousness of this maladjustment led to attempts to measure more carefully the extent and character of these problems, and to note, if possible, their relationship to other observed factors concerning the survival and internal status of these youth.

TESTING PROGRAM AND THE SCHOOL

A group of tests was given to rural youth by way of supplementing the interviews and providing a more exact index to the quantitative significance of the results. One of the tests used was the Kuhlmann-Anderson Intelligence Test. The I.Q. in this study was used merely as an indication of the effects of cultural and educational differences. The test of personal attitudes was especially designed for this study by E. S. Marks and Lily Brunschwig, both of whom are psychologists. In this test the youth were presented with 125 statements to be marked true or false. These statements were drawn from the common experiences of rural youth noted in interviews as being associated with maladjustment. Thus, to mark as "true" statement number 39, "I'd like to beat up my teacher," may be considered symptomatic of maladjustment in school. For convenience of comparison between groups, the numerical values were computed in terms of a score.

INTELLIGENCE AND ENVIRONMENT

The results of the use of the intelligence tests are shown in Table 1. In this table are shown the average I.Q. together with

TABLE 1

AVERAGE AGE, GRADE, AND INTELLIGENCE QUOTIENT
OF RURAL NEGRO YOUTH, BY COUNTY AND SEX

County	Average Age		Average Grade		Average I.Q.	
	Boys	Girls	Boys	Girls	Boys	Girls
All counties	15.14	15.08	7.32	7.63	77.47	79.60
Johnston, N.C.	14.57	14.78	6.61	6.96	79.15	80.65
Davidson, Tenn.	14.15	14.19	6.84	7.45	78.54	86.30
Shelby, Tenn.	16.02	15.59	9.06	9.10	80.20	80.43
Coahoma, Miss.	16.42	15.92	8.31	8.55	77.62	81.24
Bolivar, Miss.	14.93	14.92	7.16	7.54	75.23	77.38
Madison, Ala.	16.20	15.15	7.78	6.96	77.18	77.09
Macon, Ala.	14.43	14.89	6.37	6.62	75.00	75.24
Greene, Ga.	14.46	15.01	5.54	6.99	70.65	77.73
Number of cases	851	1,399	850	1,398	665	1,169

the average age, sex, and school grade for each of the counties. This table indicates that girls in Davidson County, Tennessee, had the highest average I.Q. Boys had the highest average in Shelby County, Tennessee, where there is an appreciable tendency to move from the country to the city. It is apparent that the relative excellence of the consolidated schools in North Carolina is of great benefit to rural Negro youth; Johnston County is one of the best examples. On the other hand, in Macon County, Alabama, and Greene County, Georgia, where the old plantation system is making a last stand, the relative level of achievement on intelligence tests is lowest.

It appears also that the brightest, or most alert youth, as measured by the intelligence tests, were frequently, though not necessarily, those from the professional or the white-collar classes. There seemed to be no indication that good socio-economic status invariably predicted better standing on intelligence tests. For example, in Coahoma County, Mississippi, the range of all scores was from 51 to 107, but youth from professional and white-collar groups were in the range from 70 to 93. Both the lowest and highest scores were made by children of farmers. In Bolivar County, Mississippi, the lowest and the highest scores were also made by farm children. One possible suggestion from this finding, confirmed in other observations, is that the type of area determines very largely the character of the school and the outlook of youth, and that this factor is more important than the socio-economic classification of the family alone in determining the children's learning interest and their alertness.

CHARACTER OF TENSIONS

The testing program revealed significant emotional tensions and feelings of personal inadequacy in the classroom situation (see Tables 2 and 3). The greatest emotional tensions, found in varying degrees in all counties and in both sexes, centered around problems arising from confusion, personal inadequacy, maladjustment to teachers and to other pupils, lack of interest in school, and general dissatisfaction with the curriculum as it is related to vocational aims.

The classroom experience has left its mark on these youth. Personal inadequacy is registered in the responses on the test which indicate inability to adjust to classroom work, or to understand it at all, and inability to make progress despite individual effort. There is registered also for some an acute consciousness of

TABLE 2

EXTENT OF MALADJUSTMENT OF RURAL NEGRO BOYS TO SCHOOL ENVIRONMENT

As Indicated by Proportions Responding "True" to Statements on Personal Attitudes Scale

Statement	Percentage Responding "True"								
	All Counties	Johnston, N.C.	Davidson, Tenn.	Shelby, Tenn.	Coahoma, Miss.	Bolivar, Miss.	Madison, Ala.	Macon, Ala.	Greene, Ga.
I find it hard to get along with other people in school.	25.4	30.2	14.4	20.2	19.4	34.4	19.4	31.6	31.4
I get all mixed up when the teacher calls on me in school.	25.0	26.6	35.9	13.2	24.3	32.8	19.4	18.9	31.4
It seems as if I can never answer my teachers' questions right.	22.4	27.1	16.3	13.2	32.0	26.2	14.0	20.0	28.6
My teachers make me do too much work.	21.3	36.7	16.3	6.1	25.2	27.9	3.2	15.8	25.7
I feel bad because I am bigger than the other boys in my class.	19.9	23.1	20.7	15.8	15.5	23.8	16.1	20.0	22.9
I always get blamed for everything that goes wrong in class.	19.2	24.6	9.8	14.9	17.5	20.5	18.3	20.0	28.6
My teacher is down on me.	15.8	32.2	10.9	7.0	8.7	9.8	14.0	13.7	17.1
I'd like to beat up my teacher.	14.4	17.6	16.3	11.4	17.5	19.7	4.3	10.5	11.4
The other boys in my class are smarter than I am.	14.0	21.1	7.6	12.3	13.6	13.1	14.0	11.6	8.6
I can't make good marks in school no matter how I try.	14.0	19.6	7.6	14.9	12.6	13.1	15.1	10.5	8.6
My teacher isn't fair to me.	11.6	17.1	10.9	6.1	6.8	10.7	12.9	11.6	14.3
The boys in my class make fun of me.	11.6	12.6	10.9	9.6	7.8	17.2	8.6	10.5	17.1
There is no use going to school since it won't help me any later.	11.4	13.1	9.8	12.3	7.8	11.5	9.7	11.6	17.1
They never teach us anything useful in school.	10.0	14.6	6.5	11.4	7.8	6.6	9.7	7.4	14.3
I wish I didn't have to go to school.	7.6	9.0	9.8	9.6	4.9	4.9	5.4	8.4	8.6
I'm not much interested in school work.	7.0	10.1	4.3	10.5	4.9	2.5	7.5	6.3	8.6
Number of cases	853	199	92	114	103	122	93	95	35

TABLE 3

EXTENT OF MALADJUSTMENT OF RURAL NEGRO GIRLS TO SCHOOL ENVIRONMENT

As Indicated by Proportions Responding "True" to Statements on Personal Attitudes Scale

Statement[a]	Percentage Responding "True"								
	All Counties	Johnston, N.C.	Davidson, Tenn.	Shelby, Tenn.	Coahoma, Miss.	Bolivar, Miss.	Madison, Ala.	Macon, Ala.	Greene, Ga.
I find it hard to get along with other people in school.	28.3	25.1	19.8	24.2	29.0	36.8	24.2	34.0	40.0
I get all mixed up when the teacher calls on me in school.	32.9	34.4	22.5	29.4	32.3	37.4	33.7	36.7	34.4
It seems as if I can never answer my teachers' questions right.	20.9	21.5	18.9	19.3	14.8	23.7	29.5	22.4	18.9
My teachers make me do too much work.	16.7	27.5	7.2	6.7	18.1	17.9	11.6	16.3	20.0
I feel bad because I am bigger than the other girls in my class.	13.9	18.4	8.1	9.7	9.0	15.3	13.7	18.4	15.6
I always get blamed for everything that goes wrong in class.	11.9	13.0	6.3	8.9	9.0	14.2	12.6	16.3	15.6
My teacher is down on me.	11.0	13.6	6.3	7.1	5.8	16.3	7.4	13.6	16.7
I'd like to beat up my teacher.	6.8	8.5	4.5	3.0	12.3	7.9	6.3	8.2	1.1
The other girls in my class are smarter than I am.	10.9	12.1	13.5	10.0	9.0	11.1	7.4	12.2	10.0
I can't make good marks in school no matter how I try.	14.2	16.9	7.2	14.5	9.0	14.2	15.8	14.3	18.9
My teacher isn't fair to me.	11.2	13.3	8.1	6.3	11.6	12.6	9.5	13.6	15.6
The girls in my class make fun of me.	13.3	10.0	9.0	11.9	12.2	13.2	16.8	19.7	22.2
There is no use going to school since it won't help me any later.	9.9	13.0	5.4	11.5	9.0	6.3	10.5	11.6	5.6
They never teach us anything useful in school.	8.8	8.8	7.2	7.8	7.7	6.8	10.5	12.2	12.2
I wish I didn't have to go to school.	6.5	8.2	10.8	3.3	6.5	3.7	7.4	6.8	8.9
I'm not much interested in school work.	6.5	8.8	2.7	5.2	5.8	5.3	5.3	9.5	6.7
Number of cases	1,388	331	111	269	155	190	95	147	90

[a] The statements are arranged in the same order as in Table 2, irrespective of their place in a declining percentage scale, in order to facilitate comparison between the two

intellectual inferiority in comparison with certain others, and social inferiority when they feel themselves the object of derision in the classroom.

MENTAL CONFUSION

The school experience of youth from culturally backward homes can become a serious and disturbing emotional adventure. In the first place, many of them have little experience in academic procedures, and are doubly confused when confronted with abstractions by poorly prepared teachers who control their pupils more by physical fear than by the interest they can inspire. These children simply go blank, or give indiscriminate answers when called upon to recite in the traditional manner of the rural classroom.

Perhaps the most striking finding derived from a comparison of Tables 2 and 3 is the strong general agreement, both as between the sexes and among the several counties. The statements most heavily checked "true" by girls and boys alike in all of the counties, though varying slightly in order and emphasis, all indicate lack of poise before other people and more especially before the teacher: "I find it hard to get along with other people in school," "I get all mixed up when the teacher calls on me in school," "It seems as if I can never answer my teachers' questions right," and "My teachers make me do too much work." The proportion checking each of these statements varied around one-fourth and one-third of the total number; the highest degree of school maladjustment displayed by boys occurred in Johnston County with respect to being overworked by their teachers (36.7 per cent) while for girls the highest degree of maladjustment was in Greene County over inability to get along with other people (40 per cent).

The same tendency toward agreement may be noted at the other end of the adjustment scale where less than 10 per cent of each sex, and for the most part in each county, checked as true the statements: "I'm not much interested in school" and "I wish I didn't have to go to school." An interesting sex difference appears however at this point. While the girls were practically indifferent in the aggregate to the statement "I'd like to beat up my teacher," the boys showed a similar indifference only in Madison County, and usually responded more positively to this sentiment. Instead of being one of the less common indications of maladjustment, as in the case of the girls, the statement occupies a position midway between the most and least weighty evidence of maladjustment for the boys. It will be seen that the reaction given to the other statements presented to these boys and girls bears out the same major tendency; such personal difficulty as they experience in school is due to social awkwardness and shyness rather that to lack of interest or faith in the values of education. While the method of scoring does not bring out the number of different individuals represented in the proportions checking closely related sentiments, it is nevertheless clear that at least a good third of these youngsters are seriously handicapped in school by these considerations.

SEX DIFFERENCES IN MALADJUSTMENT

The relative adjustment and maladjustment of youth in regard to the school is presented more concisely in the tables which show the total school scores by counties. The measure of school maladjustment used in this study is based upon the number of pupil endorsements of statements regarding the school which indicate varying degrees of maladjustment. These tables show that the average number of statements (indices of maladjustment) marked "true" by all girls was 2.31, with 25.7 per cent of the girls not marking any as "true," and 3.9 per cent marking 8 or more as "true." The counties showing the greatest amount of maladjustment among the girls were Macon County, Alabama, and Greene County, Georgia, with respective averages of 2.85 and 2.67 statements marked "true." The counties showing the least maladjustment among the girls were Davidson and Shelby counties, Tennessee, with averages of 1.71 and 1.83 statements marked "true" respectively. The proportions of girls who marked no statements "true," thus showing little maladjustment in school, were 26.7 per cent in Macon, 23.1 per cent in Greene, 38.5 per cent in Davidson, and 31.7 per cent in Shelby. Eight and two-tenths per cent of the girls in Macon, 5.5 per cent in Greene, 3 per cent in Davidson, and 2.5 per cent in Shelby marked 8 or more statements "true."

The average number of statements marked "true" by all boys was slightly higher than that for the girls, the boys' average being 2.52 as compared with 2.31 for girls. This difference suggests a slightly higher school maladjustment for boys than for girls. Eight or more statements were marked "true" by 5.3 per cent of the boys as compared with 3.9 per cent of the girls. Maladjustment was greatest among boys of Johnston County, North Carolina, and Greene County, Georgia, where the respective averages were 3.24 and 2.89; it was smallest among boys of Madison County, Alabama, and Shelby County, Tennessee, where the respective averages were 1.78 and 1.95.

Table 4 gives the average number of statements marked "true" by boys and girls in each county.

TABLE 4

ADJUSTMENT OF RURAL NEGRO YOUTH TO SCHOOL
ENVIRONMENT, BY COUNTY AND SEX

As Indicated by Average School Attitude Scores

County	Boys		Girls	
	Number of cases	Average score	Number of cases	Average score
All counties	805	2.52	1,351	2.31
Johnston, N.C.	182	3.24	325	2.58
Davidson, Tenn.	88	2.40	108	1.71
Shelby, Tenn.	111	1.95	258	1.83
Coahoma, Miss.	100	2.28	150	2.00
Bolivar, Miss.	110	2.83	187	2.49
Madison, Ala.	86	1.78	95	2.32
Macon, Ala.	93	2.35	142	2.85
Greene, Ga.	35	2.89	86	2.67

OUT-OF-SCHOOL YOUTH

The discussion so far has dealt with youth who are attending school, even though some of them may have been very irregular in their attendance. A serious problem of rural education, however, has been the rate at which these youth, and particularly the boys, have dropped out of school, and the reasons prompting this abandonment of schooling. In every county in which the study was carried on a large proportion of the children of school age were permanently out of school. These proportions of out-of-school youth were highest, of course, for the older age groups, but all too frequently included younger children. The level of education of these youth is important because they are a very significant element of the rural youth population of the South.

The largest number of out-of-school youth reported that they had completed the fifth grade, but there was a large concentration on the second grade level. The reasons given for stopping school varied, but usually reflected the precarious economic condition of their families. The following comment of a 15-year-old Coahoma County, Mississippi, youth illustrates the complex and subtle nature of those factors which account for the number of out-of-school youth:

> The reason I don't go to school is that when I stopped I had to help take care of the folks. My father had lost his job for some reason and wasn't nobody working but my older brother. My father had always been a farmer up 'til about ten years ago. Then he just got tired of that. He said he couldn't ever get ahead and couldn't never make nothin', so he just quit it down right. He traveled around, went to Memphis for a while, then down to Birmingham, and finally got back here. He finally got a job with Swift and Company and saved enough money to buy our house. I dropped out of school when he took sick two years ago.

An 18-year-old Greene County, Georgia, boy gave evidence of the desire to escape from the system and his inability to secure parental leave from the farm duties, which he disliked, in order to secure the education which he felt would make escape possible.

> I finished the sixth. I was 16 then and I didn't want to stop, but I had to go to work. I still want to go back to school. My father wished he could let me go but I had to help on the farm. I told him to spare me part of the day, for it would be better than not going at all, but all he said was "No." I want to go away, though, and get me some more schooling so I can leave the farm and work in Augusta.

A 17-year-old out-of-school youth from Madison County, Alabama, explained his situation:

> I started to school when I was 8 or 9, but I didn't get to go much. I had to work most of the time. I just went about two years straight, but I didn't go every day then 'cause I had to stop sometimes and plow and cut wood. . . . No, I didn't want to stop. I liked school. I want to go back to school and learn some more before I get grown. I want to learn how to keep folks from beatin' you out of things you own. I'd like to go to school up to the twelfth grade anyhow. I don't know if I can. I'd have to go to some high school I reckon. I could go to Normal if I had some money. Right smart of the children go to Normal when they finish up here. My father wouldn't send me. I guess I won't get to go no farther than I have. I went to the fourth grade. I want to try to go back this fall after pickin' but don't guess I'll get to go ever any more.

And from a 16-year-old Bolivar County, Mississippi, lad who stopped in the second grade, there is this weary confession of defeat:

> I like to go to school but I got to be workin' all the time. Miss Webb said she'd take me in any time I want to come. I went over there to night school for a while but I was too tired after I came home from plowing all day to keep that up.

Family disorganization, with its complication of economic problems, was prominent among the reasons for dropping out of school. A 16-year-old Coahoma County boy who stopped in the fifth grade and is the oldest of six children said:

> I want to go back to school some day if I can. My mother and father separated and I just had to stop to help mama and the children. I was in the fifth grade when I stopped.

The older children are more often the ones who must leave school in order that the younger ones may continue. An 18-year-old Madison county girl is only one case in many of this kind:

> I used to go to school. I finished the fourth and fifth grades but I had to stop school at 13. You see, I am the oldest child of nine children and I had to stay home and take care of my mother when she took sick. She was sick a long while before she died.

I help the younger ones all I can for they have to stop and help in the field and they have to walk four miles to school each way which makes eight miles every day. Sometimes when I think that I couldn't go to school I get real blue.

A Macon County, Alabama, boy who had stopped in the fifth grade, said:

I stopped going to school in 1932 when I was 12 years old. That year my father died and I stopped so I could help my mother. All of my older brothers and sisters had left school. By me stopping from school my little sisters could continue on going to school. I like school very much and hope that I can go back sometime and finish up.

The desperate struggle for existence, which precludes any serious consideration of such luxurious and abstract matters as education, is graphically portrayed in the following account given by a 17-year-old Bolivar County, Mississippi, girl who had stopped in the ninth grade:

I am the oldest of four children. My father deserted us about two years ago and we don't know where he is. I came here when I was two years old and have been here ever since. I went to school until last year when I had to quit because my mother wasn't able to send me. Both of us have to work every day to make a living. We work hard, too, but don't get much money. The people here don't want to pay you nothing for your work, but they want to work you like a slave all day. If my mother and I make 70 cents a day we feel like we been goin' some. I hate it because I had to stop school for I really liked to go. I wanted to continue until I finished but my mother told me she couldn't afford to send me another year. We don't know where my father is. If my mother knew she would try to force him to help take care of the children. We would like to move away up North but seems like we won't be able to go for a long time 'cause we can't save much money to go. I makes all my clothes and my sisters' too. If I didn't I don't know what we'd do 'cause bought ready-made clothes is too high.

In some cases the youth were unable to adjust satisfactorily to the school situation and, as a result, dropped out. Again, the inability of the youth to see the practical value in later life of their school subjects was another factor which sometimes accounted for dropping out of school. When there was no parental compulsion to continue, they left and turned to other interests.

SUMMARY

Some of the significant differences existing in the economy, the educational facilities, and the attitudes of various regions have been pointed out. In none of the areas is the physical equipment or the cultural situation adequate for real education. Present conditions in and around the rural schools are far from conducive to the proper personality development of these youth. The economic inadequacy of all but a few of the rural families and the gross lack of adequate transportation facilities are major factors in limiting school attendance. Poorly prepared instructors, unfit and untrained to cope with rural children and their problems even under normal circumstances, cannot succeed under such conditions. These teachers are expected to give the child an appreciation for a cultural heritage about which they themselves are generally unaware. A traditional, lifeless curriculum; the harsh, unintelligent disciplinary punishment; and the emphasis upon rote learning must share the blame with poverty for excessive retardation, and for the unrest and dissatisfaction of Negro youth.

The most hopeful aspect of the present school situation is the interest which pupils and parents continue, on the whole, to maintain in education, and the faith which they have in the power of education to confer prestige and to facilitate racial and occupational escape. These factors have, undoubtedly, helped to overcome in some measure the excessive odds against Negro youth in the disproportionate allotment of available funds for white and Negro education in the South. However, the pressure of this complex struggle upon youth has not been without its tragic effects. It has developed in many instances misshapen personalities which, to the casual and busy school administrator, sometimes seem to be evidence alike of the danger and of the meaninglessness of education for Negro youth.

CHAPTER V

YOUTH AND THE CHURCH

THE CHURCH has been, and continues to be, the outstanding social institution in the Negro community. It has a far wider function than to bring spiritual inspiration to its communicants. Among rural Negroes the church is still the only institution which provides an effective organization of the group, an approved and tolerated place for social activities, a forum for expression on many issues, an outlet for emotional repressions, and a plan for social living. It is a complex institution meeting a wide variety of needs.

In order to understand the behavior of rural Negro youth in relation to the church one must appreciate the cultural aspect of their religion. In the case of the Negro living in the rural South the religious conceptions and interpretations of doctrine which he expresses have been conditioned by his level of culture. Religious attitudes, like other social attitudes, are a part of youth's cultural heritage, and bear the stamp and limitation of the carriers of the culture. The first patterns have come from the parents, and these have been reinforced or redefined by the more formal agencies of religious instruction, the most important of which is the church.

Historically, the formal respect accorded Christianity in America has modified at significant points the expected patterns of treatment for a subject people. Under the slave system, religious gatherings were the first forms of association permitted Negroes, religious teachers were the first leaders allowed to develop, and reading of the Bible was the only tolerated excuse for literacy.

The Negro church came to serve a vital role linked intimately with the status of the race. The doctrine of otherworldliness provided an essential escape from the tedium and tribulations, first of slavery and later of economic serfdom. Educational limitations and the cultural isolation fostered by the rural life of the Negro and by the system of separate social institutions retarded the development of the Negro and stamped him with characteristics associated with the essential patterns of Negro life. Many patterns of religious expression were based upon the practices of white groups not far removed in culture. Frequently, the religious doctrines appropriated were in conflict with pragmatic social values.

The Negro rural church was useful to the older generation of Negroes. The economic homogeneity of the group gave it considerable cohesion. The indifference of the Negro church to current social issues and its emphasis on the values of a future life lent indirect but vital support to the race patterns of the early post-slavery period. The formal ban of the church upon dancing, card playing, and baseball did not seriously trouble the older members because these were not normal expressions of their impulses to recreation and diversion. Other codes of behavior, when in conflict with the folkways of the people, were less conspicuously enforced. The sex mores with which the rural Negro emerged from slavery were a direct result of a situation which prevented an organized family life and the development of personal habits in terms of the standards approved by white society. Through the early period of Negro family organization and the emergence of new values, inconsistencies have appeared between formal codes regarding "illegitimacy," marriage, divorce, and separation, on the one hand, and the requirements for the survival of an "economic family" reinforced by the strength of uncritical custom, on the other. The rural church has been more tolerant of sex mores which violated its codes of conduct than it has of certain forms of recreation such as dancing and card playing.

The introduction by the school of new values stressing literacy, economic improvement, and urbanization has brought significant changes in the role of the rural Negro church in the community. The institution itself has changed but little, but in its function it has a different impact upon new generations of Negroes. In the setting and atmosphere of a typical church and from observation of the character and content of the regular religious instruction, it should be possible to understand more adequately the nature of this impact and the basis for the religious attitudes of rural Negro youth.

A REGULAR CHURCH SERVICE

Mount Pizgah Church in Johnston County, North Carolina, is a large, gray, single auditorium structure, with high ceiling and long horizontal iron bars overhead to brace the walls. The altar rests at the rear of a small, semicircular platform. There are four chairs directly in front of the platform which are usually occupied by the members of the deacon's board. Back of the altar is a large, frayed, and soiled red plush chair with a high back, in which the minister sits.

The church is filled with perspiring worshippers, both young and old, who are cooling themselves with fans provided by the undertaker. The women are dressed in organdy and voile, and the men in wash pants and shirts. A few wear coats.

After the opening hymn, the congregation is seated; a hard-faced, wiry, dark man remains standing. He is Deacon Eppse, and he prays thus:

> Blessed Jesus, we thank you for life, the greatest blessing in the world, life. We thank you for the blood that circulates through our bodies. We thank you for the blood and the air so we can stand on our feet. We thank you for the loving hand of mercy bestowed upon us; that Thou are in our midst. Prepare us for our souls' journey through this unfriendly world, and when our life on this earth is ended receive us into Thy home which art in heaven.

The congregation sings, "We'll Understand It Better By and By." An elderly brown man of about 65 reads the scripture. There are groans and solemn exclamations from the four men in front of the altar, "Lord have mercy," "Amen." The reader interpolates:

> We have to slip and straighten up the wick in the candle and lamp. We have to straighten up a car. Just like we have to straighten up a wick so the light will burn, and the car so it

will run, we have to straighten up our lives so we can go the way
our Lord wants us to go.

They sing:

> Almighty God, Almighty God,
> Hold me in the hollow of your hand,
> I'll be your child, I'll be your child,
> Hold me in the hollow of your hand.

The minister comes solemnly forward to the altar. He is a
stout and pompous man who continuously rubs a large gold
watch chain extended across a prominent waistline.

It's a privilege of mine and a blessing to be here, my friends.
Since thirty days ago when we last met many things have been
done. Some have gone to their judgment since that time. Gone
to meet their Maker and stand in judgment before that stern
judge. I'm glad God has spared me to be here. There're some
who are sick today who desire this privilege we are enjoying.
[Amens] Since we met last, death has reigned right here in our
neighborhood. As sure as you see a man living, you see a man
who is going to die. You look around you and look at some men
and they look like the picture of health. The next thing you
know they're dead. That makes us know we got to get on our
traveling shoes so we can march right up to our heavenly glory.

You know, I'm a lot old times. I'm one of them that don't go
in for new fangled things. And one thing, I got that old time
religion, that old time religion that works by faith, that purifies
your heart. I ain't got no new religion, and I don't want no new
religion. Why, don't you know, with this new religion you can't
tell how you got it, and you can't tell where you got it? How
you going to tell you got religion at all? I got that same old
religion, I can go back to where I got it and tell you all about
it. I can tell you how I got it and where I got it any time you
ask me. And I can go back to that same old spark and refresh
myself and come out stronger in my old time religion. That's
what I do all the time—go back to that same old spark. It lighted
the way for my father and my mother, and it can light the way
for me. [Shouts]

He turns attention to his double text: "If a man die shall he
live again," and "I am the resurrection and the life," and dis-
courses at length on the life and trials of Job. The sermon then
gets down to everyday experience.

Now I've seen men in critical conditions, sometimes their finger-nails decay and come off and disease is destroying their bodies. Sometimes we say sin causes disease. But it's not always so. Sin in the hearts of men causes disease too. I'll make an example. Job was wrapped in sackcloth and ashes a'praying to God, and his wife said, "Look at old Job. He's no good to himself and nobody else. I'm tired of him being sick, and my children's all forsaken me." But Job heard her, and to Almighty God he said, "Lord, though you slay me yet shall I trust you." Job looked at his wife and his wife said, "Curse God and die!" But Job said to her, "Foolish woman, foolish woman. I brought nothing into the world with me and I'll take nothing out. All the time of my worriation has to be lived out somewhere. [The minister wipes his dripping face, and groans and gasps; the congregation groans and shouts.]

Job took his question to Daniel, and Daniel said, "I saw Him as a stone, hewn out of the mountain." But when Job asked him, "If a man die shall he live again?" Daniel said, "I don't know." Job kept on a'going till he come to Ezekiel, and Ezekiel said, "I saw Him as a wheel within a wheel. I saw Him in the haunts of women." But when Job asked him if a man die shall he rise again, Ezekiel said, "I don't know."

But here comes a man from a new country, a man called Jesus Christ. A man that said, "I am the Son of God, the friend of salvation. I am the lowly fisherman from Galilee. I've seen the face of God. I feed the leprosy cast out by yourself. I can cure the incurable disease. I can perform miracles such as the world has never known." And they brought out the leper, the man dying with that terrible disease, the man everybody shunned and let alone to die. And the Nazarene cured him. [Shouts] Blessed be His name! [Shouts and shrieks]

The congregation is now fully stirred, and its fervent chorus of assent punctuates dramatically the minister's spaced phrases. He refers to the loved ones who have departed, and stresses the certainty of death for everyone.

It don't matter how much you know or how high you climb, you got to die. Mr. Roosevelt, the president of this country's got to die, just like you and I. He can run all these things and do all them big things that everybody talks about, but he's got to lay down and die just the same.

The audience becomes sobered, the preacher lowers his voice:

If we fail to live the life in this world, it'll be too late when we come to cross the River of Jordan. It'll be too late then to get ready. Just like you start dressing at home in your room. You got to get dressed at home before you come out in the street, 'cause if you don't when you get out in the street without no clothes, they'll arrest you and take you to jail. It's too late to get dressed up then. Children, let's dress up and get ready for heaven and glory now. Now's the time to get dressed. Don't wait 'til it's too late. Let's be like Paul was when he said, "I've fought a good fight, I've kept the faith, and now I'm ready for glory."

Another deacon prays. The congregation sings a song about "True Religion" that has many verses, one of which runs:

> Where you going, Elias?
> Where you going, I say?
> Going to the River of Jordan?
> You can't cross there.

They sing of backsliders and cowards. The minister rises in excitement at the close and shouts, "That song is as true as my hand. It's true, true, true. There's not enough words to say it." He then extends an invitation to join the church; no one responds on this occasion. A deacon takes his place behind the collection table.

Whilst everybody is happy and enjoying this service, we come to you. We know you must have that true religion. But today we want $5.00. We want to get it right at once, quick. Now let everybody push hard while we sing. Let everybody give all he can to the service of the Lord.

The congregation sings a song with verses that could be extended indefinitely:

> It's the walk that you take
> That takes you home.
>
> It's the prayer that you pray
> That takes you home.

They raise $4.06. After three hours of this worship they go home.

Although the above case study of a Negro church in action during a regular Sunday morning service provides a background for understanding the religious culture in which Negro youth are reared, a still closer view of their relation to the church and of the conflict between the interests of the older and the younger generations in the conduct of the religious services can be had if one visits a special Children's Day program in which the participation of youth is the dominant feature.

A SPECIAL CHURCH SERVICE

It is the second Sunday in June and, by tradition, Children's Day at the Piney Grove Baptist Church in Johnston County, North Carolina. This introduces an exciting variation from the routine Sunday services. The whole day can be spent at church. The ten o'clock Sunday school session begins the day, and the regular church service follows around eleven. There will be a heavy basket dinner after the morning service and before the children's program at two o'clock. The young people appear to assume that they have a special privilege of expression on this day, both with respect to the program and the basket dinner. At regular meetings when baskets are brought, the elders have the first round of food at the tables; today there is a protest from the children who want priority rights to the food themselves. As a compromise for Children's Day, special tables are set up so that the young people may eat at the same time as the adults. A few of the liberal adults laugh good humoredly at "the spunk of the youngsters," but the majority of the adults make the concession grudgingly, fearing that one concession may lead to other demands. In many of the churches in the county the Children's Day privilege of eating at the same time as the elders has been flatly refused. The heavy handed domination of the church by the older people and their impatience with the claims of youth for participation are unquestionably responsible for some of the lack of interest on the part of youth in the church.

Children's Day offers a rare opportunity for the youth to parade their talents, in recitations, solos, and management, but there is a fundamental conflict with the deacon's board on the practical value of the occasion. The church needs money and, with all the expenditures for food, there will be little for the church collection. One deacon said, "If they'd put the amount in church they spend for baskets, the church would make some money." They cannot make the children see this, and the conflict increases and may find expression in the church service itself.

Children have come by various methods of conveyance from many sections of the county. They are eager, busy, and excited. The children's program is opened by an awkward youth of 18. He asks, in a shy monotone, if the congregation will sing a selection. Then, one after another, he calls on various youth to appear. They rush to the platform and recite, often in rapid monotone, a poem or a short essay memorized from the *Baptist Guide* (prepared for such occasions) or from various other books of poems. But, shrewdly, the deacons have their way. Between recitations there are competitions among young groups of choristers. As each group sings, a collection is taken, and the audience is urged by the deacons to register their appreciation in the amount of money contributed after each selection. The collection is recorded and contributed to the church in the name of the church or other organizations which the singers represent. After three hours of this program they go home.

Children's Day exercises are held at different churches in the county throughout the month of June. The young people may be observed following the exercises from church to church. Children's Day is their closest approach to self-expression in the church.

Thus far in this chapter we have gained a general understanding of the religious culture surrounding the development of rural Negro youth by observing the church in action both during regular services and during a special service on Children's Day. It would be a mistake, however, to suppose that all Negro religion in the rural South can be described by any one set of patterns. There are many differences in religious practice in the different localities. One of the major differences is between the churches in the plantation areas and those located in the nonplantation areas nearer the towns. The outstanding distinctions appear in the description of the plantation church.

THE PLANTATION CHURCH

The church at Riverton, Mississippi, stands bare and alone at the far end of Squirrel Hollow. It is small and neglected, with hard wooden benches and a rickety platform. The congregation is made up of hard working sharecroppers and a few struggling owners and their children. They arrive in wagons, old Fords, and by foot. Many of the members stand around outside the door of the church until the deacons and a few of the determined women members begin the meeting with singing. Most of the people are wearing their Sunday clothes. As they enter the building the minister talks familiarly with the members, but preserves a social distance by a set of mannerisms which appear to be a stereotyped pattern common to all rural preachers in this section.

The minister is Preacher Charlie Singleton—a tall, gangling man, about 45 years old, whose ministerial clothes fit loosely and are worn and greasy. In spite of his lowly appearance he knows how to handle his people, and can, on occasion, be frankly objective about his methods. He is untroubled by his illiteracy.

Various methods are used to impress the congregations in these localities, and the average minister is master of many histrionic devices. A favorite procedure is to intersperse the remarks with ceaseless gyrations which hold the attention of the tired congregation wearied by a week of toil in the field. One of the most striking of these dramatizations is the "acting out" of the journey to heaven in the "Heaven Bound" sermons. The minister's arms and feet go from slow to fast movements while the voice represents the sounds of a train. Other favorite devices are excited runs back and forth across the platform, quick jumps straight into the air, loud and prolonged shouts which often subside into a low unintelligible mumble, raised arms and dramatic gaze fixed upon the hypnotized audience.

The sermons of the average rural minister are long and repetitious. Phrases are emphasized by gestures and vehement expression. The congregation responds constantly with shouts of approval and conviction. It is expected that several persons, mostly women, will "get happy" and give expression to long hysterical seizures in the course of which they testify to their salvation, release some pent-up sorrow over deceased relatives, or bemoan a hard and hopeless life or the unjustified slander of their character in the community. The most emotional parts of the sermons are those which make reference to troubles and offer homely solace or inspired promise of reward or punishment by God, as the situation warrants.

A typical sermon is one made by Preacher Singleton:

I preaches the Lord's message as it is give to me. When I gits up here I don't know what I is goin' to say, but I jest has faith the Lord is a'goin' to put a message in my mouth to tell to you. I ain't like most preachers 'cause I jest cain't say anything jest to be sayin' somethin'. I has to wait for the Lord to send down his message to me.

I has to cry evertime I prays because I thinks of all the evil I has done an' then I walk alone with my arms a'folded an' sings this song, "Sometimes My Eyes Git Full of Tears an' Then I Has to Cry."

My text is: "Ask Him, He is of age." Has you all heard of that verse in the Bible where they was a'askin' the Jews if Jesus was their son an' they was scared to answer, so they jest said "Ask Him, He is of age." Ask yo' own self. That's just what hit means, 'cause you is of age an' you knows jest what is right an' what is wrong. Ef you don't you is plumb sorry an' better find out a way 'fore hit's too late.

The Lord told Solomon to go down to his gardens an' see how the pum'granites and the peaches was a'flourishin', and Solomon obeyed. Does you all know who Solomon was? He was the son of David an' the Lord done picked him out to build him a house. An' Solomon done it too, don't you fool you'self. Yas suh, the Lord told him to git on down in the gardens an' see how the pum'granites was a'gittin' along, an' see how the pears was a'gittin' along, an' er-r-r, see how the—apples was a'gittin' along, an' he done sent him down in the gardens to see how the peaches was a'gittin' along on the trees, an' see how the soil was a'gittin' on. You all know how soil is. Hit jest don't do right sometimes an' you has to git down and fertilize it an' make hit do what you wants hit to do. The worms gits in the peaches an' the apples, an' the pears, an' you has to git 'em out or pretty soon you ain't got no fruit. Go down, he say an' see how yo' pum'granites is a'gittin' on, an' see how all yo' other fruits is a'gittin' on, an' Solomon went on down an' seed how his gardens was an' fixed 'em up. He took all the worms outen his fruit an' fixed up his soil, and the garden growed right up.

The Lord meant fo' you all to go down in the garden of yo' hearts an' see how yo' soul is a'gittin' on. Go down, an' see how yo' pum-granites is a'gittin' on; go down, an' see how yo' apples an' yo' pears an' yo' peaches is a'gittin' on. Go down a'fore hit's too late an' git right with the Lord, an' see how the garden of yo' soul is a'flourishin'.

The taking of the collection in the rural churches is a protracted and, at times, irritating experience, lasting on some occasions as long as two hours. The people are poor and the preacher needy, unless he can combine farming with his ministry. Since farming would conflict with his role as leader, he usually prefers to cover a circuit of churches and get the maximum out of each group. The average congregation of 75 or 100 will yield about $3.00, except around settlement time when there is more money in circulation. The general impression this practice left upon youth was unfavorable, and it has led many to the drastic conclusion that the chief concern of the preachers is money.

THE CHURCH OUTSIDE THE PLANTATION AREA

Only a rough distinction may be drawn between the plantation and the nonplantation areas. On the plantations the social life of the Negro has been historically regimented, and to a large extent some of the influences from that period still survive. In the nonplantation areas, where Negroes engage in mixed farming or tobacco growing, the influence of towns and cities has been stronger. Thus these Negroes are somewhat less affected by old traditions and habits. The distinction is important in the discussion of Negro youth and the church because of the significant test results which show that respect for the church and the ministry is lowest in the plantation areas and highest in the other areas, varying in direct proportion to proximity to the towns and cities. This conclusion runs counter to the assumption frequently held that the more rural the Negro youth the more attached he is to the church. The rural churches outside the plantation and nearer the cities have their youth problems, but in general they provide a more intelligent ministry and a more progressive Sunday school in the sense that it is more open to new influences and provides more opportunity for participation by youth themselves in the religious exercises. The sermon is still directed to the older people, the church is still dominated by the deacons and other elders, emphasis is still on "old time religion," and many forms of innocent recreation are still banned; occasionally, however, there is a disposition to provide within the church a substitute for worldly pleasures denied, and at the same time there is, as a result of an improved cultural level, a more serious emphasis upon a code of conduct consistent with the standards of the larger culture.

From the foregoing characterizations of the types of organized religion presented to Negro youth in the rural South we now turn to the reaction of youth themselves to this part of their cultural environment. Pointedly, we ask this question: What are the attitudes of Negro youth toward the rural church?

ATTITUDES TOWARD THE CHURCH

Several significant factors appear in the attitude of Negro youth toward the church. These observations are based upon a group of tests given to 2,241 Negro boys and girls in the eight counties covered in this study and also upon personal interview data obtained in all of the counties.

DISTRUST OF THE MINISTRY

One test applied to rural Negro youth on their attitude toward the minister was their reaction to the statement, "The preacher tells you to do a lot of things that he doesn't do himself." This was endorsed as true by proportions ranging from 50 per cent of the boys in Davidson County, Tennessee, to 93.5 per cent of the girls in Coahoma County, Mississippi. The consistency with which this general point of view is held is striking, even when approached from special angles. In a list of

14 statements regarding the church, those relating to the minister stand out as revealing the most pronounced attitude of hostility.

Individual interviews tend to support and further explain this attitude. One 20-year-old youth in Coahoma County suggests that many of the young people go to church as a matter of habit, and he insists that it is important to belong to the church. He knows many excellent Christians in his community, but he dislikes the hypocrisy both of the church people, who are only trying to impress young people with their piety, and of the preachers, who are exploiting a sacred profession. "A heap of preachers," he said, "is looking for a job that is easy, and decide to preach. When they don't make much money then they quit, or turn to something else."

A 14-year-old seventh-grade girl living in Madison County, Alabama, gave an opinion which she felt to be prevalent among her own age group. She said she went to church regularly but did not belong; she deferred joining out of lack of proper respect for the preachers. She said:

> I guess some of them are good, but most of them do a whole lot they're not supposed to do. Some churches you see the pastor gets drunk and go to church and preach. He'll get up there and preach a long time then. Sometimes they be having conference and they can't get some of the people to agree on what they're talking about. Mama wants me to join, but if they keep doing what they doing now I may stay out forever. I just never feel like joining.

This criticism is directed more at the illiterate and ignorant preachers of the isolated plantation areas than at those in communities nearer the influence of a large city. The difference, for example, between 50 per cent criticism of preachers in Davidson County, which is within the influence of Nashville, and 72 per cent in Johnston County, North Carolina, which is outside the plantation area, and 93.5 per cent in Coahoma County, which is a rural plantation area, suggests the corresponding difference in the character of preachers available. In the nonplantation areas these preachers are better educated, frequently live in the towns and cities, and generally maintain better standards of living and conduct.

Turning now from the general attitudes of youth toward the rural minister, let us examine their specific criticisms of his work.

Stereotyped Sermons

The type of sermon presented is criticized by some of the young people. They not only object to the stereotyped sermons, but to the emotional antics of the leaders. A 17-year-old Shelby County, Tennessee, girl, daughter of a sharecropper, expressed a preference for useful advice about everyday living. She said:

> I think a preacher out here ought to preach today about things of today. He ought to give the people advice and help them out of their troubles by talking about things that happen today. I don't think a preacher ought to try to preach you into heaven. They had a funeral up at the church the other day, and the preacher tried to preach the body into heaven.

Double Moral Code

The double moral code which belonged to an earlier period of the Negro family is challenged by all types of rural youth, whether seriously as an evil, or in justification of their own indulgences. It seems clear from the comments of these youth that in spite of the persistence of unregulated sex habits in society, the church can no longer give to them the sanction of tolerance. This appears in their expectations of higher moral standards in the ministry. A 14-year-old eighth-grade Bolivar County, Mississippi, girl said she "guessed her pastor was all right," but she did not think he was "any better Christian than anybody else." A 16-year-old Johnston County, North Carolina, girl said:

> I believe part of what the minister tells you. They tell you not to drink, cuss, and yet you see them doing the same things when you get out of church. You be younger than the preacher, and he thinks you ought not to do these things, but I don't like that; he ought to practice what he preach.

An 18-year-old Madison County, Alabama, boy in the eleventh grade reflects the changed attitude and the critical viewpoint held by many of the older youth when he says:

> I don't belong to church. I don't know why. I just never did
> think I had religion. I don't like the way the preachers do
> neither—some of them, but that wouldn't keep me from church
> if I thought I had religion. Some of the preachers get drunk
> and treat their wives dirty; they go out with other women. All
> they is after is money. No, it really doesn't affect me; I go to
> Sunday school generally; and miss a lot of the nothing in
> church.

There is no more serious disillusionment over leadership than
is expressed by the Coahoma County boy who said:

> On lots of things the people mind the preacher. If he say some-
> body is all right, maybe it's all right and maybe it ain't. Some-
> times the folks do something the preacher don't like, but he
> can't do nothing about it and it's all right, 'cause so many be
> doing it, and maybe he be doing it too.

This recognition of the distinction between actual codes of
conduct and the role of moral teacher is sufficiently widespread
to be given recognition in a traditional song which is used
satirically to ridicule the distrusted minister:

> I know I've got religion,
> I know I was called to teach,
> Pay no 'tention to what I do,
> Just practice what I preach.

The extraordinarily widespread criticism of the rural Negro
preacher, it appears, is not a general criticism of the Negro
church. In the quantitative data a careful distinction appears
between churches, such a distinction being based upon their
policies and programs. In every type of community a distinction
was made between the churches with Sunday schools designed
for the participation of youth and the churches without such
Sunday schools. The cultural significance of this distinction is
evident when it is recalled that in many of the rural churches
school teachers, whose educational standards are rising more
rapidly than the ministers, are frequently in charge. Although
often at odds with the preacher and with the older church members on religious matters, these school teachers and better edu-

cated laymen are more intimately in contact with youth and have their respect. A 16-year-old farm girl in Madison County, Alabama, in her comments about the church indicated that many of the youth are not insensitive to the lag between the church and the school.

> I joined church when I was 14. It was during a revival. My mother took us and told us different things about religion. The Sunday school teacher talked to us about joining the church. If it hadn't been for them I wouldn't have joined. When I go I get more out of Sunday school than I do out of church, because you have a chance to discuss things. But in the church you just sit there. It's all right, I suppose, but people will wait till they get to church to bring up arguments, and if one discuss something better than the other, he's got to bring up another argument. People be running in and out, and they don't know what the preacher said. Some of the preachers try to go with the young girls too, and most of them are always after money and not trying to help the people. When they get the money they are satisfied. They never bothered me, but the biggest portion of them are like that.

THE CHURCH AND SELF-EXPRESSION

Domination by the elders and by a preacher who appeals to the emotions and superstitions of adults prevents the expression of youth during the regular church service. The Sunday school, on the other hand, offers more opportunity for youth to participate and feel a sense of importance. This conflict is brought out by one boy of 19 who appeared generally concerned about the indifference of the church to the needs of youth.

> I used to be very active in the church. I sang in the choir and was secretary of the Sunday school, but for the last two years I just have not bothered. I attend Sunday school most every Sunday, but I don't bother much about church services. There don't seem to be enough life in the church to suit me. I joined of my own accord; I am drifting away on my own accord. I know I'm a Christian, but I'm just a little rusty. The pastors aren't any good generally. Most of us around here don't go to church now.

ACCEPTANCE OF THE CHURCH AS AN INSTITUTION

Only a negligible proportion of rural Negro youth are antagonistic to religion or opposed to the church either as a social or a religious institution. About 80 per cent of the total group were critical of the ministers; half of them registered a belief that the main interest of the ministers was to get all the money they can from the people; a third objected to what seemed to them to be a bickering emphasis on church politics and on inconsequential, sectarian disputes; and half of the number made a distinction between churches, some of which they classified as all right and others as "all bunk."

TABLE 5

EXTENT OF MALADJUSTMENT OF RURAL NEGRO YOUTH
TO THE CHURCH, BY SEX[a]

As Indicated by Proportions Responding "True" to Statements
on Personal Attitudes Scale

Statement	Percentage Responding "True"	
	Boys	Girls
The preacher tells you to do a lot of things that he doesn't do himself.	80.1	76.8
All ministers want to do is to get as much money out of people as they can.	51.9	54.4
Some churches are all right, but others are all bunk.	50.8	51.9
People always fight in church over a lot of things that don't make any difference.	33.8	34.7
Going to church doesn't make people any better.	26.8	35.6
Most of the things in the Bible aren't true.	12.1	8.9
I only go to church because my girl (or boy) friend goes.	10.6	5.0
If you have to go to church to be good, I'd rather be bad.	10.0	.9.3
Praying never did me any good.	7.9	6.6
What the preacher says in church scares me.	7.0	5.6
I never understand what they are talking about in church.	6.3	7.2
Religion is a lot of bunk.	5.5	5.9
I wouldn't go to church if my folks didn't make me.	4.8	3.6
I hate going to church.	3.8	3.5

[a] Based on responses of 853 boys and 1,388 girls.

Table 5 presents briefly the results of the use of selected statements relating to the church in connection with one of the general tests employed in the study. This table employs phrases borrowed from the comments of rural young people themselves; they were embodied in a part of the Personal Attitudes Test (see Appendix B) and checked by 2,241 boys and girls in order to suggest the extent to which they were held generally. From the statistical results it will be observed that the boys are slightly more skeptical of the preachers than the girls, but both sexes show a high degree of disillusionment. The proportions in each category are strikingly similar for boys and girls.

There is an interesting variation by type of county area on the statement, "Going to church does not make people any better." The proportions endorsing this statement are low in the non-plantation counties and high in the plantation areas. In Davidson County, Tennessee, a nonplantation county, 18.9 per cent of the boys and 28 per cent of the girls endorsed this statement, as compared with 35 per cent of the boys and 49.7 per cent of the girls in Coahoma County, Mississippi, which is in the plantation area. Moreover, in the responses to this statement there are greater differences between the sexes than for any other statement. This fact is also borne out by the extended comments which many of the youth made.

The table further suggests that only a small number are actually skeptical about the value of religion in their lives. Only 5.5 per cent of the boys and 5.9 per cent of the girls believe that religion is unimportant or that it is an unfounded superstition. Few of them asserted lack of belief in the value of prayer—7.9 per cent of the boys and 6.6 per cent of girls. In spite of their attitudes, more youth attend church than stay away, but many of them attend with "reservations."

CONFLICTS BASED ON OUTMODED BEHAVIOR CODES

Rural areas are notoriously lacking in recreational outlets for youth. At the same time, the rural church imposes a strict ban upon dancing, card playing, baseball, and, in many instances, motion pictures, along with its other moral restrictions. There is an assumed condemnation of lying, stealing, immorality, and drunkenness, but these latter are more often sins that can be indulged in privately without immediate detection, whereas dancing, card playing, and baseball are essentially public pastimes. A result of this misplaced emphasis is that the more serious "sins" may be committed with such frequency as to defy control, and the emphasis of suppression falls upon the less serious "sins" and occasionally upon wholesome forms of recreation. When youth suspect the church members and even the ministers themselves of engaging in censurable behavior, while these same adults deny them what they consider legitimate pleasures, then youth begin to challenge the integrity and honesty of the people who make the rules.

This has had several significant results. One effect is that undesirable types of substitute recreation have crept into the rural communities in the form of taverns, roadhouses and "honkeytonks," where cheap whisky is sold and "hot" music is made available for dancing by dropping a nickel in the slot. Since the private homes of most of these young people are too small for dancing even if there were no religious taboo against it, dancing is possible only in town, in the consolidated schools of newer design, or in some of the disreputable rural roadhouses. The crowd hanging about the door of a tavern on Sunday, especially in early evening, looks outwardly very much like one of the church crowds; these places are actually dangerous, however, and witness many knife fights and murders. Whatever their attitude toward the church, upper-class Negroes must not frequent taverns if they would maintain their social prestige. Thus it happens that in a negative way the church connection still continues as a mark of respectability and class.

No adequate substitute social activity has been developed by the rural church to compensate for the denial to youth of dancing, card playing, and baseball. The resultant conflict is a dual one. Young people are unwilling to give up pleasures which they regard as harmless, but at the same time they fear the loss of respectability which the ban of the church can still inflict with pronounced effect. This is the sentiment of a 14-year-old girl from a middle-class family of Madison County, Alabama:

> Most of the girls here belong to church. I don't belong yet. The thing about the church is that they don't hardly want you to do anything much, and if you do much they will turn you out. I am not sure that I could stop doing all the things they don't want you to do if you join church. I go to church regularly, and I sing with the Sunday school choir, but I haven't joined yet. I am not sure that I will. I like to dance and have fun. I am not ready to stop having fun yet. Mame Allen, they

put her out of church for dancing, and it was such a mess. She didn't seem to worry much about it when Anna asked her how she felt about being turned out of the church, for she said "To hell with these old liars, some of them do worse things themselves than dance." Of course I don't think Mame was right the way she acts about some things, but I sort of agree with her a little about the people and the church members. Some of them do worse things, far worse than dancing. Dancing is one thing colored folks can do better than white folks, so I think the church folks ought to feel that it is all right to dance, because I really think it is a gift. My mother is the only one of us that is a member of the church. My father says "Nothing doing." He and I attend the revivals sometimes, but we never sit on the mourners' bench.

The comment of this girl stresses the current distinction between "going to church" and "belonging to church." She conforms to the social pattern of the community by attending, because she belongs to a middle-class family whose respectability is still linked with church membership. In Sunday school she finds response to her desire for some form of recognition. The girl who was turned out of church for dancing unquestionably felt the sting of censure from the church even though she did not believe in its honesty. This girl attempts, in her rationalization, to add to the recreational value of social dancing the virtue of a racial art, although actually the dancing in question is by far more social and recreational than artistic.

CONTINUING IMPORTANCE OF THE CHURCH

The parents of these rural youth frequently enforce church attendance as much from motives of respectability as of salvation for the souls of their children. From the testimony of many of these youth it appears that they draw little religious value from the enforced attendance. One 13-year-old Bolivar County, Mississippi, girl said:

Sometimes I want to leave church and come home, 'cause looks like to me like the preacher don't be sayin' much. He do a lot of hollerin' and shoutin'. Maybe if I could understand what he was talking about I would like church better, but I can't see what he's tryin' to say.

One 17-year-old girl in the same county made the following comment:

> I like the singing but I don't care much about the preachin', 'cause I can't understand what the preacher's talking about half the time. Seems like to me he's just sayin' a lot of words that just don't make sense. The older folks might understand them, though, 'cause they just shouts and hollers all the time he's preachin', but sometimes I wonder if even they know what it's all about.

Parental compulsion and community sentiment, rather than genuine interest in religion, bring these children to church each Sunday. A 13-year-old fifth-grade girl in Bolivar County said:

> I have to go every Sunday because my father makes me, but I want to leave and come home, though, for the preacher don't be sayin' much, 'pears like to me.

Another 15-year-old girl from a well-to-do Negro family in Coahoma County, Mississippi, complained:

> Mama takes me to church with her every Sunday. Church is all right, but you have to stay there so long, and I don't believe lots of what the preacher said.

In the same vein the 16-year-old son of a Mound Bayou filling station operator said:

> Oh, Mom sees to it that I'm sitting up in church every Sunday. I don't mind going sometimes, but I don't feel like sitting up there all day every Sunday. Ain't nothing special be doing, and I just get tired of sitting in church.

Economic Aspects

In the areas where the Negroes are of approximately the same economic status there is little evidence of social tension within the church based upon competition for office and prestige although the more prosperous and important members enjoy some honor in becoming deacons and stewards or in holding other offices. Where communities, however, are more heterogeneous and able to support several churches there is a tendency for social distinctions to develop even between the churches. Thus membership may, in one way or another, become an index to social position in the community. Much of the rivalry between churches of the same or different denominations, and the uneconomical multiplication of churches and cults, traces back to this ferment of competition for social position and prestige within the Negro community.

Some of the rural youth stay away from church because they do not have adequate Sunday clothes; others, because they have to work on Sunday, a practice which on the farm indicates low status; and others, because they are sensitive about their position in the economic scale. A 14-year-old Bolivar County girl, the daughter of a field hand, and too poor to take part in the normal activities of the community, says, with great conviction:

> I like church. I like to listen sometimes to what the minister say. It helps me. I never joined the church yet, but I pray. I pray for a lot of money, so I can be rich and travel and buy me lots of clothes. I'd help other people so I wouldn't be selfish. I would go to church if I had some clothes, but you feel funny with broken shoes, and the children all make fun of you so much I just stay at home.

Social Aspects

The social role of the church is still dominant for rural Negro young people. Although they may not "get saved," or believe in the sermons, or take the pastor seriously, and although they frequently look down upon the shouting, the church still provides them with most of their social contacts and approved entertainment. It is still the pivot of social life for Negroes as a group and for youth in particular. Many responded to the question concerning why they go to church with such replies as, "I go 'cause my girl's there," or "Most of the fellows go over and hang around there on Sunday, and that's where I see 'em at most," or "We got lots of clubs there and have a good time." Others supplemented these statements by being more definite, as in the instance of the 16-year-old eighth-grade Johnston County, North Carolina, farm girl from a moderately well-off family, who said:

> I enjoy church and go nearly every Sunday. That's how I get to see all my friends, especially during the summer. After church we have a good time just walking the road together.

Most of the stuff they tell in church about ghosts and spirits, that's foolish, but we have such a good time after the sermon that we sit and listen, for we know we're going to be together and have fun after the preacher gets through his say.

There were a few communities in which lay church leaders (with and without the stimulation of the ministers) provided special activities for the young people. One of the churches with a program for youth is described by an 18-year-old girl from a fairly well-off family.

We go to church regularly every Sunday. The whole family belongs. We spend about $1.oo a month in club dues. Me and my sisters sing in the choir and we belong to the B.Y.P.U. and the Y.W.C.A. We have such a good time at church.

In the winter we have candy pulling, chicken throwings, and a lot of other different kinds of entertainment. In the summer we have picnics and fish fries. We don't never have dances like they do in town.

COMPLETE ACCEPTANCE OF THE TRADITIONAL CHURCH

Not all rural youth are skeptical of the church and ministers. Some have adopted fully the pattern of their elders in their concept of religion, their deep emotional response to the church, and their adherence to its rigid doctrines, at least in theory. They are firm believers in the church as it exists in the rural areas today, its doctrines, precepts, and premises, and attempt to carry out its prescribed codes of behavior. They regularly participate in the revivals and in other phases of the church program. A 15-year-old sixth-grade son of a Johnston County, North Carolina, cash tenant said:

I go to church every Sunday. I believe in religion. I read the Bible once every week. The church will put you out for cussin' an drinkin'. It's a good thing to put people out for doing those things. They won't do them again, then.

In Greene County a rural boy of the same age testified to his conversion:

I belong to church. I joined it when I was 12. I done changed a whole lots. I stopped playing ball on Sunday and shooting marbles on the Sabbath day. I done stopped throwing rocks so much.

Fully accepting the religious mores of the rural Negro community, a 15-year-old girl explained:

I like church and don't ever miss. We have a good preacher. He is doing everything to help the people. I do believe the things he says are true. He tells the people how to live right, and I think that is good. All my family go to church. Even the baby goes, and we are all Christians. I think everyone should be a Christian or they won't go to heaven when they die. Heaven is up in the sky, and all the people what don't live right and don't follow the good word won't go there. If you don't do things like killing, stealing, and fighting, you will go to heaven when you die. I want to go there, that's why I do what is right.

The 13-year-old daughter of a farm laborer in Macon County, Alabama, expressed strong religious convictions in her reply:

I don't dance. It's wrong to dance. The preacher says them that dance will go to hell. My mother says so too. It's true. I wouldn't dance no time. The preacher tells us lots of things that be good to hear. It's a sin to tell a lie, or anything that ain't true, or steal, or say mean things on people. If you do you get punished for it.

Religious Emotionalism and Adolescence

One of the most striking facts about those youth who showed closest approximation to the traditional pattern of the rural church was the consistency in their ages. Most of them were in the early adolescent years around 14 or 15 and, incidentally, it was at this age that the most serious emotional shocks were observed in race attitudes and color consciousness.

Some of the most dramatic religious conversions occurred around the ages of 12 and 14. These children were deeply stirred by fear of hell, and being "black-marked" by God, and their religious experiences of visions and dreams were similar to those professed by their elders. An eighth-grade Macon County girl, the daughter of an electrician whose community status is very high both economically and socially, provides an excellent example of the sincere, full belief of the converted adolescent who has started "on her way to God" along the traditional path:

> I am a Christian. That was the best thing that happened to me, because now I will go to heaven when I die. I go every second Sunday. The pastor is a good pastor, because he tries to help the sinful folks. I just feel better since I joined church. Feel like I can't sin again. I do better since I joined too. Sometimes I want to talk back to folks, and I think that it is a sin and God will black-mark me, and then I don't say nothing. By black-marking, I mean a record is kept by God, and he puts down a mark every time you do wrong. I ain't afraid to die, and I'm not afraid of dead folks. They can't do nothing to you. I don't care about dying, but I don't want mama to die.

Some of the older youth professed full belief in the church and its teachings but were less intense about it. Most often the sentiment was bound up with some other factor, but the religious concern was nevertheless dominant. A 17-year-old Bolivar County, Mississippi, youth in the twelfth grade, the son of a local social club proprietor, explained:

> I get dressed most every Sunday and go to church. I don't go 'cause my father makes me, I go 'cause I want to. I think everybody ought to go to church, 'cause that's the way it is in the Bible.

Another youth, in the same age group, an eleventh-grade Greene County, Georgia, girl, from a moderately well-to-do family, said that she attended church regularly, sang in the junior choir, and belonged to the missionary society. She took part in most of the social activities and attended Sunday school regularly.

There were others who felt themselves to be "naturally religious," like this 16-year-old Coahoma County, Mississippi, boy who said:

> I'm kind of a religious person, so one day I was in church and got a feeling I should take church and religion more seriously. I felt like I ought to become a Christian, so I joined church. It has made a difference, for where I used to go to church only when I had to, after I got converted I became active and I go to church regular and really enjoy it. I think I am living a little better now.

Revivals and Conversion Experiences

Rural Negro youth appear to find revivals an interesting event, and attend them from the mixed motivation of fear of not being saved and the desire for excitement and diversion. Although perhaps not so far reaching in its influence as formerly, the annual revival meeting is for some of the present generation a welcome break in the monotony of rural life. The revival affords an opportunity for unhampered expression when the most emotional souls are envied for their skill in shouting and gesticulating. The "mourners' bench," the "visitations of the spirits," and the "visions" are associated with conversions on these occasions. The young people frequently enter into the spirit of the revival, some with deep respect for it, others because they are simply caught in a strong current and cannot escape. Often the conversion experience is stereotyped, the same for young and old all over the area. One 13-year-old Bolivar County, Mississippi, girl said:

> I sat up there and something say, "Now come to me, come to me now," so I just got up and went on down to the preacher and testified. It didn't strike me bad like it do some folks, but I went anyhow.

A 17-year-old fourth-grade Madison County, Alabama, farm youth told how he had a vision:

> I seen or dreamed something. I thought I saw some dogs, some lean hounds, and I thought that meant that old Satan was running me. So I knew I'd better get religion, and I been a lot different since.

A 14-year-old fifth-grade Greene County, Georgia, girl said that she knew she had religion because she felt "glad all inside" and now she doesn't dance, and she goes to church and Sunday school all the time. Another eighth-grade girl of the same age from Bolivar County, recounted her experiences that had come through prayer.

> I was 12 when I was baptized. I believe I have religion. I used to pray to the Lord to rid my soul of sin, so one day something inside of me said, "Your soul is clean, you're free now. Your

soul is white as snow." I felt glad all over and told my mother about it. She sure was glad.

The following experience of a 15-year-old Coahoma County, Mississippi, boy has a touch of realism to it:

A gang of us decided to go down to the revival meeting that was going on at the church. So one night we just went. After the preacher got done preaching he began talking—I don't know what it was like, but I just felt good. Directly he asked the sinners to come up front and give him their hands. I did that and began to cry. I don't know why, but I just remember that I was crying. That's all there was to it.

Along with this sincerity there is evidence, however, that other youth accommodatingly fall into the spirit of the occasion without very deep religious conviction. The youth just quoted added that several others boys "got religion" at the same time, but he was certain that they were just pretending in order to escape the further censure of the preacher and to impress the crowd. He said, "They walked up just like they was going to the movies. I don't think that does them any good that way."

The social pressure for "conversion" is not without important implications for ministers and youth alike. The success of the ministers is measured by the number of conversions. At the same time, rejection by the youth of appeals to conversion can brand the more persistent rejectors with the stamp of the hardened sinner, a stamp which all respectable members of the group find it socially comfortable to avoid. An interesting example of the effect of this pressure for conformity is the youth interviewed who had recently been converted at one of the revivals. He explained the procedure:

They put all the sinners on the mourners' bench, and they sing over you and pray till you join. They sang and prayed over me, and I didn't know nothing until I was up shouting. I don't know how I felt, just felt nothing. But they all shook hands with me and put me on the other side of the room, and two weeks after that they baptized me. I ain't shouted since.

Mama didn't say anything about me joining. She never shouts anyhow. I go to church all right. The sermons are all right, but just like all the others around here. I don't see why some of these preachers have to groan and hold their breath so long. I believe they do that just to excite the people.

HOW RELIGIOUS ARE RURAL NEGRO YOUTH?

The problem of reducing these varied types of experiences to their quantitative significance led to the development of a

TABLE 6

ADJUSTMENT OF RURAL NEGRO YOUTH TO THE CHURCH, BY SEX
As Indicated by Distribution of Church Attitude Scores

Church Score	Boys		Girls	
	Number	Per cent	Number	Per cent
All scores	851	100.0	1,399	100.0
0	33	3.9	39	2.8
1	79	9.3	130	9.3
2	167	19.6	268	19.2
3	193	22.7	345	24.7
4	163	19.2	277	19.8
5	86	10.1	154	11.0
6	45	5.3	70	5.0
7	13	1.5	32	2.3
8	16	1.9	20	1.4
9	7	0.8	9	0.6
10	1	0.1	4	0.3
11	1	0.1	2	0.1
12	1	0.1	1	0.1
Not given	46	5.4	48	3.4
Average score	3.30		3.36	

simple test of attitudes toward the church and the devising of a rough scale for recording these responses statistically.[1] The scale runs from 0 to 14. The most favorable attitude would score at 0 and the least favorable at 14, although none of the rural youth tested scored above 12. The score is based upon the number of endorsements or rejections of the 14 statements which compose the scale. The average for the youth in all eight counties is 3.34. (See Table 7.)

The variations by sex and between the different southern

[1] See Appendix B for method of scoring religious attitudes.

rural areas studied are slight, but interesting. As already noted, youth as a whole is less favorable to the church in the plantation counties (Coahoma and Bolivar counties, Mississippi, Greene County, Georgia, and Macon County, Alabama), than in the

TABLE 7

ADJUSTMENT OF RURAL AND URBAN NEGRO YOUTH TO THE CHURCH, BY COUNTY AND CITY, AND BY SEX[a]

As Indicated by Average Church Attitude Scores

County or City	Both Sexes		Boys		Girls	
	Number	Average score	Number	Average score	Number	Average score
RURAL SOUTH	2,156	3.34	805	3.30	1,351	3.36
Johnston County, N.C.	507	3.09	182	3.05	325	3.10
Davidson County, Tenn.	196	2.79	88	2.94	108	2.67
Shelby County, Tenn.	369	3.24	111	3.23	258	3.24
Coahoma County, Miss.	250	4.02	100	4.03	150	4.01
Bolivar County, Miss.	297	3.58	110	3.71	187	3.50
Madison County, Ala.	181	3.28	86	3.05	95	3.49
Macon County, Ala.	235	3.45	93	3.05	142	3.71
Greene County, Ga.	121	3.47	35	3.69	86	3.38
RURAL 4-H GROUP, NORTH CAROLINA	284	2.91	122	3.12	162	2.75
URBAN SOUTH	1,159	2.58	376	2.55	783	2.60
Atlanta, Ga.	265	2.08	91	2.19	174	2.02
Fort Worth, Tex.	266	2.47	64	2.00	202	2.62
Greensboro, N.C.	156	3.29	52	3.46	104	3.24
Nashville, Tenn.	221	2.75	74	2.91	147	2.67
New Orleans, La.	251	2.65	95	2.53	156	2.72
URBAN NORTH	540	2.36	202	2.60	338	2.22
Chicago, Ill.	225	2.41	87	2.69	138	2.24
New York, N.Y.	99	2.02	17	2.65	82	1.89
Philadelphia, Pa.	153	2.76	66	2.79	87	2.75
Springfield, Mass.	63	1.71	32	1.94	31	1.48

[a] Based on responses of 4,139 boys and girls

nonplantation counties and those rural areas within the influence of a large city (Davidson County, Tennessee, and Johnston County, North Carolina). (See Table 7.) The tests on which these attitude indices are based were given to 4,139 young people for purposes of intrasectional and intersectional comparisons.

There is an almost unbroken correlation between respect for

the church and degree of urbanization in an area. The difference between town and country is, on the whole, more pronounced than the difference among either the several urban or the several rural sections. The most favorable attitudes occur in highly urban areas of both the North and the South. The least favorable attitude toward the church is found in Coahoma County, Mississippi, the most definitely rural plantation county in the group, and the most favorable attitude toward the church was in the sample for Springfield, Massachusetts, where the selection reflects the influence of a nationally known Negro institutional church with one of the best children's camps in the country.

Intelligence and Respect for the Church

Keeping in mind the limitations of intelligence tests, the problem of what they measure, and the gross differences in intelligence quotients between rural and urban youth, our results indicate a direct correlation between intelligence quotients, as measured by the Kuhlmann-Anderson tests, and favorable attitudes toward the church. (See Table 8.) Further refinement of the statistics suggests that (a) respect for the church is associated with advanced social and economic status and parental education; (b) the church as an institution has values for this class in reinforcing claims to a status of respectability; (c) youth nearer urban centers respond to the superior quality of the ministry and to improved opportunities for self-assertion and self-expression; and (d) the most hostile attitudes toward the church appear among youth whom the church fails most conspicuously to reach, and who are, as a result of their lower status, at the same time more bitter and freer to express their criticism.

Church Maladjustment and Social Maladjustment

From the total group of religious and church attitudes as indicated by the tests, a selection was made of the highest and the lowest scores for a more careful examination of the personal history involved. One of the most unfavorable attitudes registered was that of Charlotta Regan, Johnston County, North Carolina.

Charlotta's religious attitude seems rooted in deep social resentment and emotional instability. Her teacher says she is smart "but something is lacking." Her friends say she is "bright but crazy." She does not respect her parents because they are hopelessly poor, and she "sasses" them for unaccountable reasons. She would stay out of school rather than "go there ragged." Her father refused a deacon's post, held for thirty years by his father, for no reason that he could give, but obviously because he lacked the economic and social security which his father had. He is a failure. His estimate of the interests of his daughter is that she "lives only to study and comb her hair." Charlotta has daydreams about money and getting away from farming, from the country, and from her own family. She is "tense" most of the time, and suspiciously weighs every occurrence which affects her in terms of exact fairness and justice. Parental favors to her sisters are measured with discerning exactness. She is loud, talkative, and self-assertive. Her cousin, similarly bright, made a brilliant record at Shaw University "and went haywire," apparently because of money difficulties.

Her church attitude is not distinguished from her school attitude or general social attitude, which is one of frustration, rebellion, and cynicism. She "got religion" after the pattern of the community, and conformed because everyone had to go through a certain type of conversion, but she thought it was "funny." She ridicules her own dissimilation at the same time that she concedes some emotional benefits from the experience of conversion.

Her father thinks she likes the church, but she admits that she goes only because she can meet some of her friends there. She is deeply resentful in most situations reflecting upon her social status, although she seldom articulates this bitterness. Her situation definitely reflects social frustration and unsuccessful adjustment. The attitude toward the church belongs in the same category with her attitude toward the school, neighborhood, color, the white community, and her family. Toward all of these she is testy and hostile.

TABLE 8

ADJUSTMENT OF RURAL NEGRO YOUTH TO THE CHURCH, BY INTELLIGENCE QUOTIENTS
As Indicated by Distribution of Church Attitude Scores

Church Score	All I.Q.'s	Intelligence Quotients									
		40–49	50–59	60–69	70–79	80–89	90–99	100–109	110–119	120–129	Unknown
All scores	2,250	7	120	281	598	513	232	66	16	1	416
0	72	—	4	10	24	14	5	5	1	—	9
1	209	—	6	21	52	57	25	11	5	—	32
2	435	1	17	34	123	113	64	16	5	1	61
3	538	1	23	52	155	143	58	19	2	—	85
4	440	—	18	57	123	105	48	8	2	—	79
5	240	1	17	36	62	49	19	5	—	—	51
6	115	1	13	25	27	17	6	—	1	—	26
7	45	1	4	12	8	3	2	1	—	—	14
8	36	—	5	6	10	1	2	1	—	—	11
9	16	1	1	4	—	2	—	—	—	—	8
10 and over	10	1	2	1	—	1	—	—	—	—	5
Not given	94	—	10	23	14	8	3	1	1	—	35
Average score	*3.33*	*4.13*	*4.13*	*3.80*	*3.19*	*3.04*	*2.97*	*2.48*	*2.48*		*3.79*

Church Adjustment and Total Personal Adjustment

Two of the most favorable attitudes toward the church and religion were registered by strikingly different personalities. One was a boy of 15 living in Coahoma County near the town of Clarksdale; the other was a girl of 14 living in Davidson County, Tennessee.

Robert Weems is a radiant, well-built boy who would readily be regarded as handsome. His complexion is brown and his straight brown hair is of fine texture. He is an adopted son, and his foster parents, who are in comfortable circumstances and darker in complexion, idolize him. Good in sports, he does not smoke, and has a normal and wholesome relation with girls. He likes school, makes good grades (I.Q. 107), and is ambitious to do something useful as a career. In school he easily assumes leadership and in spite of the serious tensions of the school community has no enemies and carries no youthful grudges against his playmates, teachers, or parents. At work or play he is vivacious and irrepressibly cheerful.

His foster parents are religious and well-balanced emotionally; the foster mother could even say this on the subject of racial attitudes:

> I just naturally got to love everybody. Some of the whites don't act so nice and do our folks bad, but the Bible say love everybody. Bible's all we got, so I have to do it. You gets along with 'em all right jus' so you knuckles down to 'em.

Church, to Robert, is obviously a social as well as an emotional satisfaction. His physical advantages are not personally exploited, and his general status of respectability is secure. This general state of emotional and social well-being favorably conditions his experiences in the church as well as in his other institutional relationships.

In contrast, Anna May Greene is a short, dark-brown girl of 14, with a pimply face, coarse features, and kinky hair. She lives with a great-aunt and great-uncle. She calls her great-aunt "mama," and her great-uncle "stepfather." Her own parents deserted her. Her great-uncle is blind, and it is her duty to lead him around on Saturdays as he begs. Her great-aunt often gets intoxicated, and whenever she has a few cents to spare sends Anna down to the "bootleg place" to buy whisky. The girl hates her great-uncle because he is blind and troublesome, her natural father because "he is black and looks like a monkey," and made her black and ugly. She hates her natural mother because she deserted her, and her great-aunt because she is course and intemperate. She is behind in school because she hates to go where the children make fun of her, and she feels that the teachers are "down on her." The only two people whom she admires are the school nurse, who spoke to her in a friendly way when she went to have her tonsils inspected, and a young student minister from a theological school who came over to her church to conduct a revival.

Anna May's experience with the minister led to her conversion and escape from an unpleasant reality. She first went to the church out of curiosity.

> I hadn't planned to join, but I went and this preacher came up to the boy sitting next to me and said, "Son, have you been touched?" Then he turned to me and said very soft and kind, "Anna May, you ain't never been touched, get down on your knees and start praying. It's not hard to pray." So I got down on my knees and started to pray. I don't know what I said, but somebody stroke my hand, and I got up. I'm going to be baptized next Sunday. The boy ain't never prayed. No, he didn't join the church. I was sorta scared during the whole thing. I reckon I feel better now, and I'm sure I'll be a better girl.

Anna May quite obviously made her escape into the church from a revolting home life, and found a new affection in the church through its sympathetic leaders. The personality of the minister was identified with the religious values of the church. Personal difficulties were abridged in this atmosphere of spiritual concern, and she even achieved superiority over the boy who failed to respond. Her re-orientation of behavior is probably based as much on a desire for ministerial as for Divine approval. A frustrated life found integration in the warmth of the church, secured to her by the personal interest of the minister.

SUMMARY

Not very distantly related to the sort of frustration phenomena reported is the current tendency observed in rural areas for traditional congregations to disintegrate and reassemble as "cult" churches. These churches of recent development have the advantages of smallness and homogeneity of membership, of doctrines newly interpreted and vigorously proclaimed, and of new procedures for the resolution of personal tensions in work, family life, and community relationships. In many of these rural communities, and in the towns and cities, the number of "cult" churches continues to grow, and in vigor and practical social value they are an interesting contrast with the traditional institutions.

It is an inescapable observation that the rural Negro church is a conservative institution, preserving in large part many values which, in the general cultural ferment of the Negro group, might well be altered. Its greatest present value appears to be that of providing emotional relief for the fixed problems of a hard life. As one woman put it, "It just seem like I can stand my worries better when I go to church." The secular institutions of the Negro community are changing slowly, but at a more rapid rate than the rural church.

The young people are dividing their loyalties between the church and the school and the overtly questionable agencies of commercial recreation. They require the church less than their parents for emotional release because they are both more mobile and less docile. Increasing literacy and education, and the increased value attached to education, emphasize the distance between themselves and the present church leaders, particularly in the plantation areas. All evidence points to the conclusion that the church will increasingly influence youth as its programs take their needs into account on a new and improved cultural level. Where this has been done, the church has tended to retain its role as a vital social and spiritual force in molding the wholesome and socially acceptable patterns of behavior.

CHAPTER VI

YOUTH AT PLAY

RURAL LIFE has its period of intense work and its period of dull and uneventful calm. When the soil is being broken and prepared for crops, all hands strong enough for the plow are engaged from early sunrise to sundown. Again when the crop matures and particularly when the cotton is ready for picking, idleness and leisure are costly. Between seasons the most common answer to the question about how and where the children play is likely to be "We don't do nothing, mostly just sit and talk."

As yet the benefits of guided recreational activities have been extended to few rural communities, and among the Negroes these advantages are almost unknown. Since the Negro child usually enters school at an older age than white children, the spontaneous play activities of the preschool period are important factors in his education. In a few progressive elementary schools, there are planned and directed play activities for the children. For the most part, however, play is restricted to competitive athletics between teams of older boys representing different schools. The social lag in providing wholesome opportunities for group participation in recreational activities which exists in many school systems is particularly evident in the rural Negro schools.

Suppers, picnics, entertainments, spelling bees, socials, and frolics are held under the auspices of church or school. Taverns, dance halls, and "honky-tonks" provide many undesirable and commercialized recreational opportunities for young and old. Apparently, no one feels a need for assuming responsibility for the development of wholesome recreational outlets for Negro youth in rural districts. Play activities which give zest to life and break the tedium of farm work, if noncommercial, are haphazard and, if commercialized, often vicious.

SWIMMING

"Besides swimming, we don't do nothing else for recreation 'cepting we go and see a girl every once in a while," said Tommy Cassey, an 18-year-old farm boy. In Coahoma County, Mississippi, one "swimming hole" is a flooded quarry, well known to all the boys. Another group of country boys swim naked in a lake twice a day. Rollicking horseplay bears eloquent testimony to their enjoyment.

Tommy, the best swimmer in the group, yells, "C'mon, you double-likkers! Let's get wet." A "double-likker," we should understand, is a boy who swims awkwardly by hitting the water with both arms and legs simultaneously. Only two or three boys can swim the 150 feet across the lake which is 50 feet deep. Tommy is one of them. The rest of the boys watch admiringly and exclaim:

> Look at that long nigger. He goes right fast. If I could overhand right good, bet I could make it.

> Look at Claude yonder—that little nigger ain't overhandin'. Reckon he'll make it.

> G'on Tommy, if you can't get over, we'll come get you.

As soon as Tommy gets across, the boys begin taunting him about coming back.

> Lindbergh got 'cross the ocean all right, but he come on back on a boat.

> Reckon we ought to get old man Hunt's boat and go after him?

> Naw, let's play 'gator, he'll come over then.

" 'Gator" is a game like water tag. The " 'gator" is "it" and he tries to catch the other fellows before they can swim to "home." Both players and " 'gator" swim under water, dive away, or use any means of moving that they can. Tommy swims back and joins in, but the game is broken up as Tommy tries a new stunt. "I'm going to read the Bible to y'all now. Looka here." Floating on his back he pushes off from the bank and, raising his hands above water as if holding a Bible, he swims out and around for a few minutes mimicking the rural preacher, "Git yourselfs straight, cause yo' time ain't long." Some of the boys attempt to do the stunt, but give up after several unsuccessful attempts.

Two of the boys on the bank begin throwing stones across the lake. "Nigger you can't chunk across there." "Jes' watch me—ain't *nothing* I can't do." Most of the fellows climb out and begin "chunkin." Only Paul, a great husky lad, can throw across. As soon as he does, two fellows grab him and throw him in the lake. The rest of the boys jump in and begin splashing and ducking each other.

While the boys are tussling in the water, a large soft shell turtle appears on the bank and one of the boys sees him and runs after him. These turtles travel at a very fast pace, but Henry rapidly overtakes it. "Yonder he goes, Henry," the boys yell, "Head 'em 'fore he gits in the lake." With a final spurt and headlong plunge, Henry catches him and brings him back. A discussion arises among the boys as to what it is.

He ain't nothing but a dry-land terrapin—I knows 'cause I done caught many of 'em. You can't eat him 'cause his meat is pisen.

G'wan nigger, you is jus' jealous 'cause you didn't catch him. Maybe you figger you won't git none of him when he's cooked.

Don't pay him no mind, he's one of them hill niggers what don't know nothing.

Now lissen at that! Many turtles, terrapins, and loggerheads as I done caught, I reckon I know. I tell you it's a terrapin and if any of you ignorant niggers eat him, you'll die.

Well, I'm going to tote him on, and we'll cook and eat him. I'll bet you is de first nigger is going to want to taste. Anybody know how to fix 'em?

Sho do! Old Mollie there can fix most anything, can't you Mollie?

Get me a knife and I'll fix 'em. C'mon, less go!

The boys put on their clothes and start up the hill. Crow leaps up to a limb on a cypress tree and pulls himself up on one arm. "Anybody can't do this ain't no man. I can do anything and I reckon I'm de best here." The boys stop and attempt this new display of strength. Several can do it, but most of them fail. "I'm the best nigger here!" Crow announces.

Another boy leaps a barbed-wire about four feet high and calls back, "All right, blue chile, less see you do that!"

"I can do anything, but I got to look out for these britches. How about next time." With that he runs off up the hill.

"How come you call him 'blue child,'" asks a big fellow called Bull Frog.

Another replies, "Man, can't you see he's so black that when he's wet with water he looks blue?"

With much loud laughter and many harmless but comic "jibes," the gang files through a cornfield back to their chopping.

BOXING

Unlike swimming, whose major equipment, "water and a hole," is provided by nature, boxing illustrates the type of recreational activity created through the initiative and ingenuity of the participants themselves. The success of Joe Louis in boxing has done much to stimulate interest among the rural youth in this type of activity. The following description of one of the regular Tuesday night boxing matches held in one county illustrates the ingenuity which is often employed in providing recreational facilities in rural areas, as well as the enjoyment which spectators and participants alike secure from such activities.

The bouts, scheduled for eight o'clock, usually start at nine and are over about ten o'clock. Admission is 20 cents. The ring in which the boxing takes place is a rather crude but serviceable affair built outdoors in a fenced lot. It is owned and operated by one of the colored citizens in the community. Wooden bleachers, made of rough plank, are built on three sides of the enclosure. The spectators number about 200, some 15 of whom are white men, who are seated in a special section at the right of the entrance.

The boxers are all young boys from 12 to about 20 except in the main event, for which any age is acceptable. The boys get about 50 cents for fighting and the opportunity to see the other bouts free. They fight stripped to the waist and barefooted unless they happen to have tennis shoes. Nothing is furnished except the gloves—no towels, sponges, or medical equipment, and there is no doctor. Boys fight at their own risk. Friends of the fighters volunteer as seconds to "work on them," and offer suggestions between rounds. The fighters sit on Coca-Cola cases and drink water from pop bottles. The referee and the timekeeper are either volunteers from the crowd or boxers who are not busy. The "bell" is an old tire rim that is sounded by striking with a hammer. The preliminary bouts between the young boys are scheduled for four rounds but are usually terminated by a knockout or a decision by the end of the second.

In the first bout, Leon, a popular local boy of 14, is matched with a new lad whom he severely trounces in less than one round. The crowd clamors for another opponent for Leon and a second boy goes in. Leon is so tired that he cannot hit the second fellow, and at the end of the second round the fight is called a draw.

The next match is the main event between Little Caesar, a 19-year-old local boy, and a 26-year-old man from a nearby town who is announced as being a champion from New Orleans. Little Caesar beats his opponent severely and knocks him out in the second round. The stricken contestant lies on the canvas unattended, bleeding freely from the mouth until a woman from the crowd climbs into the ring with a bottle of water and bathes his face and head. In a few minutes he gets up, unassisted, and climbs out of the ring. The ring is cleared and another bout is announced, but fifteen minutes elapse before two 16-year-old boys are found who are willing to fight. One boy, Man O' War, is a popular favorite who has fought before. His opponent quits after a round and a second partner is found for him. But Man O' War is tired and nearly gets whipped; the fight is declared a draw.

The spectators walk about the bleachers. They eat peanuts, peaches, and drink Coca-Cola. Most of the spectators are young and quite a few are women. They shout continuously to the fighters and the referee.

G'on, hit that nigger, Emmett!

Lay it on the coon, Little Caesar, you got him.

Hit him on top his head, son, he'll stop that dodging.

Nigger, stand up and fight.

The white men laugh but seldom call out to the fighters. They are the ones who call for the second opponents for the fighters and the referee turns to them without question, and says "Yes, suh, gentlemen," and proceeds to get the new fighter.

The referee often turns to talk to someone while the fight is going on. Frequently a spectator shouts, "Hey, 'ref,' pull those boys apart and make 'em fight!" The young fellows punch each other in clinches and use illegal blows without being stopped by the referee unless the spectators howl loud enough to attract his attention. Little Caesar referees one bout in which one of his "pals" is fighting. When he has occasion to separate the two, he either shoves his friend's opponent with his closed fist or butts him with his head. He aids his friend as much as he can.

Although the spectators continuously "razz" the fighters and officials, it is all taken as fun. Repartee passes back and forth between spectators and officials or fighters. The pugilists fight willingly and smile continuously. They do considerable clowning, at which the crowd laughs. They enjoy this as much as the actual fighting.

ORGANIZED RECREATION

Clubs and societies also contribute something to the social life of the rural community. Although these organizations may have a name which does not suggest any association with the church or its activities, virtually all of them have some relation with the church. Junior societies for young people also exist and, in a more limited field, serve the same function as adult clubs. These junior societies operate as control devices to reinforce the ideals and standards of the older generation.

Eighteen-year-old Elizabeth Lesley in discussing her social activities says:

We have a right nice time around here. We have clubs and things just like they have any place else. Oh, there are many of them—the Junior League Club, the Ever-ready Girls, the Christian Endeavor Society, and lots of others but I can't think of them now. We meet at various members' houses and play games—checkers most of the time. No, we don't play any card games because you see they wouldn't like that in the church. But we have a good time—that's better than doing nothing.

One of the other girls made this comment:

If it wasn't for the church giving suppers and picnics sometimes I don't know what we'd do for fun when school isn't going on. The boys can get around and manage to have a better time than the girls but there just ain't nothing to do around here in the summer excepting the church gives something.

Sometimes various members in the church give cream parties and socials for us. Yes, they invite the boys too. That's the way a lot of us gets to talk to our boy friends. Oh yes, sometimes our parents go too, but they don't go all the time.

Fifteen-year-old Sammie Parker of Greene County, Georgia, reports this interesting club project which was initiated by an adult member of the community in an effort to control the recreational activities and social life of the local boys.

Once a week we have club meeting. The boys round here were so rough Mrs. Taylor got up a club of us boys. All the boys who joined had to pledge not to cuss out loud, not to be out after ten o'clock, and not to be seen in bad places. The name of the club is the Tuxedo Club. I'm the president of it and Alonzo Brady is the secretary. I don't know why they elected me president. It's the first time I ever been president of anything. I like it pretty well, but I haven't learnt to do it so well yet. I know how to say "House to order," but I haven't learnt what you say when somebody do a motion and somebody say, "I second the motion." Mrs. Jackson promise to give me a book what tell you what to say but she ain't gave it to me yet. If she give it to me I could learn it easy.

We meets once a week at Mrs. Taylor's like I told you. At the meetings we plan new business and plan for parties. We had four parties already. Two of them was at my house, one of them was at Mrs. Taylor's, and one of them was a lawn party we had at Mrs. Perry's. All of them, except the lawn party, was for club members and their girls only. Most of the time we gives a party each one of us has to pay a quarter.

We plays fiddle-sticks and whist and we dance at our parties. Fiddle-sticks is a game where you have a whole lot of different colored sticks. You hold the sticks in your hand and let them fall out and then you supposed to pick up as many as you can without touching any of the rest. Different colors gets different scores. Whoever get 500 first win the game. . . . Yes, sir, mama let us play cards in the house when we has a party, but she don't allow us to play 'less it is a party. We can dance at home any-time we want to, though.

We started out with a lot of members in the club, but we ain't got but eight left. Some of them left when school turned out and some wouldn't go by the laws, and we put them out. . . . We put a lot of them out for not going by the laws. Mrs. Taylor say that the members is going to go by the rules if it ain't but two in it.

At the meetings if you been doing something you ain't got no business, the critics report you. We got some members which we elected to be critics. They don't tell nothing they heard about you, but if they see you, they report you. When you get reported, then the club deal with you. We take them out and ask them, "Are you willing to stop doing what you been doing?" When they says, "Yes," we fines them. First time the fine is 2 cents, the next time it's 4 cents and the last time it's 5 cents. We turn you out after you get fined three times.

One boy got turned out for cussing and for staying out 'til twelve and one o'clock at night. And one got turned out for going to the "Nook." That's a place where people get drunk and fight and cut each other up. That's where real rough people go. The "Nook" ain't Mr. Tom's restaurant. It's all right to go to Mr. Tom's. The "Nook" is across the field from Mr. Tom's.

We don't deal with them for drinking 'less'n they get drunk. Mrs. Taylor say drinking is all right so long as people don't get drunk. All of them [the boys] drink except Morris Mapp and I. I used to drink it in sugar and water and like that, but when I got up some size and seen how crazy it make other people, I won't drink it.

We got to deal with some of them for gambling, at the next

meeting. Yesterday some of them was round there by Mr. Tom's shooting craps for matches. That ain't exactly gambling but it's learning how to gamble.

They can come back in the club when they get turned out if they pledge all over again. Ain't none of those who got turned out asked to be took back.

The attitude of some of the youth who did not seem to be enthusiastic over the cream parties and socials of the organized clubs is illustrated by the comment of Freeman Edwards:

There ain't nothing to do around here in this old town. Sometimes we get together at these little old "sissy" parties—they let us play checkers and then serve us a little cream or something. I gets my fun mostly by jumping in the swimming hole. Every once in a while I gets to town and takes in a show. I goes to those "socials" sometimes just to get with the girls, but there ain't no fun in them. That's the only thing about down here. Me and the other guys was just talking about it the other night. After you finish working or in the night time there's no place to go. They used to have two movin' pictures here but now they ain't gonna have none, they ain't even got one.

The best accounts of the varied recreational activities are those given by the youth themselves. Minnie Lue, an 18-year-old farm girl, says:

Guess I like dancing better than anything else but that's another thing I don't like about this community. I had a party and we danced. One old man told papa that it wasn't fitting in the community for a deacon of the church to allow his daughter to have dances at her home. All they want us to do around here is attend those old dead church socials.

Emma Lee, a 17-year-old girl also commenting upon the community's attitude toward recreation, says:

I suppose we all like to dance more than we like doing anything else, but it ain't right to do it around here. Folks around here say if you dance you dance to the devil, so we just don't do nothing much but go to the church socials, and when school is going on play some of the games.

While the church makes possible the cream parties, socials,

picnics, and spelling bees, the school makes it possible for those who can attend to engage in more active recreation.

One boy, Phillips King, comments:

Now when school is going on we can play basketball, baseball, and football. Sometimes we even play tennis. We didn't play this year 'cause we didn't get the courts fixed; mostly everybody was working. I sure do enjoy myself when I'm playing these games.

Another youth whose recreational activities begin and end with the school season says:

I don't ever have any fun in the summer time. There just isn't anything to do around here. The most fun I ever have is when school is open, then I can play basketball, volleyball, dodge ball, and games like that. Of course there's a café that we go to sometimes at night. We can dance and play around but I don't enjoy that so much, but, that's about all there is to do in the summer time.

The few activities which the church and school offer fail, for the most part, to satisfy the recreational needs of these rural youth. Many of them are sensitive to this lack of recreational facilities or supervised activities. One 15-year-old girl from a middle-class family in giving a detailed description of existing conditions portrays youth's awareness of the great need for recreational facilities confronting young people in these rural areas.

That is the only thing I don't like about this place. There isn't anything at all for any of us to do. We have no social life at all. The grown folks here think it is terrible to do any of the things that you don't even twist a head over other places. They don't play cards or dance, or have any meeting place besides the church and naturally you don't expect people to do those things in church. The children should have roller skates, bicycles, and a place to go swimming. Children need those things to keep their bodies strong. The only thing these children have is a *hoe* and *spade*. I go to the movies once in a while but it's really too far to go to town just to go to a show. I'd like to have skates if there was any place to skate, but what would we look like plowing down these dirt roads on a pair of roller skates? There should be a club house of some sort where the children could gather and have games and clubs and learn how to sew. They have all these things up North but not here. Most of these children get into trouble at night just walking the roads, when all they need is a hang-out with someone in charge.

UNORGANIZED RECREATION

Since guided recreational activities are extremely rare in rural communities, most of the recreation is unorganized and haphazard. The lack of a plan for wholesome recreation leads to many diverse and undirected efforts on the part of youth to amuse themselves.

READING

Our study of the families of these rural youth shows that 25 per cent of the homes had some reading matter. The amount and type of reading engaged in depend upon available materials, which for the most part include whatever magazines and books are available at home, at the neighbors, or at school, and those which parents bring home from white families for whom they work. "Anything I can get to read, I read," more than one of these young people claimed. There are, of course, no libraries available for these youth and their reading is usually as casual as it is miscellaneous. Reading interests center around popular magazines and rural life journals in circulation in the area. A 16-year-old farm girl who said that she likes to read more than anything else gave this account of her reading:

I love story books. Don't matter what kind of stories—mysteries, detective, or love stories. I read the *Country Home Magazine* which we get also. I don't never read the newspaper. We don't carry none and I just don't see no papers. I didn't know that colored folks had papers of their own until you told me.

School teachers with an interest in reading have occasionally stimulated a kindred interest in the students. An 18-year-old youth confided wistfully:

I do like reading so very much and read everything I can get my hands on but mostly everything I get to read is detective stories, because that's what my father reads and I get the books from him when he's finished. I did hear a lot of talk up at the school one day when some older people were talking about a recent book *Gone with the Wind* but I haven't had a chance to even see what the book looks like. I don't suppose I'll ever read it, but I surely would like to. I certainly would read more than detective stories if I had more than that to read.

The county agent helped the reading interest of one youth, who said:

If I didn't have these books of Mr. Jones to read I don't know what I'd do. Things are so dry around here, but with these books to read it seems as if I go into another world entirely. I don't understand all of what I read but I find it interesting anyway. Some day I am going to get away from this place and go where they have some real libraries. Then I'll be able to select whatever I like to read.

Reading materials available around the home have helped one rural youth to decide upon his vocation. The doctor books of his deceased father are frequently read by 18-year-old Chester Brown:

Of course I don't understand everything I read in them—in fact, I could really say that I don't understand most of the things I read, but there is just something about those books that make me feel that I want to be a doctor. That literature appeals to me and somehow I have a feeling that I'd be a good doctor. I go to sleep with one of those books every night. I read all I can about what a doctor is supposed to be like. I think I could do more to help my people by being a doctor than anything else.

While the majority of the rural youth who read have to read whatever they can find, there are a few whose reading materials are more selective. Amanda Willis, a 16-year-old girl of a middle-class family, presents a strikingly different picture from those mentioned above.

I spend a great part of my leisure time reading. Oh, I've read most of the children's books and have read many of the classics —you want me to name some of them? It would be difficult to remember all of them, but some of the books I have read that I liked very much are: *Alice in Wonderland, Little Women, Uncle Tom's Cabin, The Chinaberry Tree,* and I have begun the *Idylls of the King*. I've read much more, but it's difficult for me to recall all of them right off.

RADIO AND MOTION PICTURES

The rural community is no longer a closed unit. Its boundaries have been broken in many places by the advent of modern transportation and communication facilities. The automobile, the motion picture, and the radio have become important forces in breaking down the isolation of the rural community. Many of the youth, and especially the rural nonfarm youth, report that they spend some of their leisure time listening to the radio and attending the movies. Reactions toward both moving picture and radio programs vary: some have favorite movie stars and radio programs, while others like all pictures and all programs, since they do not go to the movies or have a chance to hear the radio often enough to have favorites. The girls, for the most part, enjoy the love pictures, and most of all seeing the "pretty clothes of the movie stars," while the boys like the western pictures.

While some of the young people are able to get into town occasionally to see a motion picture, or are able to take advantage of the occasional pictures shown at the school, there are some who have never seen a motion picture or heard a radio program. A 15-year-old daughter of a sharecropper explained:

> We lives so far from town that I ain't never been to a movie in all my life. Even if I could get into town I don't reckon I'd have money enough to pay my way in the show so I guess it'll be a long time before I go. Yes, I know some other girls who ain't never been, too. We'd all like to go but we don't have none around here and we can't get into town.

Martha Reynolds is 16 years old, and has never seen a motion picture. Once the school had a picture program, but Martha had to work in the field that day and missed it.

> I sure did hate it because I was absent from school that day. You know when there's work to be done in the field there ain't no need of thinking about going to school. But I had been going pretty regular and the very day I had to stay out and work in the field is the very day they had the moving picture at the school. Gee, I was so sorry I was just sick, because I ain't

never seen one and I wanted to see one so bad. I hope I know
in advance the next time they have one at school so that I can
ask my folks if they'll let me go. No, I don't think there's much
chance of me seeing one any place else because we don't have
any lessen the school gives them. It's too far into town and it
takes too much money, too. I bet I sho' would like this moving picture thing.

While the radio has frequently invaded the most isolated
homes, many of the younger children indicated that they had
never heard a radio. Clarence Hodges, a 12-year-old farm boy,
says:

I've heard about the radio but I ain't never hears one play yet.
Mr. Mims got one and some of the kids go over there and listen
to his'n but I just ain't got over there yet. Mr. Mims he's white
but he's nice to the kids 'round here.

A farm girl in an isolated area said:

I'd just give anything if we had a radio to listen to. I ain't
never heard one but I just believe they'd be so much fun. I've
heard a lot about them though. I hear they play pretty music
and you can hear voices from way up in New York. It sure
would help a lot 'round here 'cause things are so dry. Papa said
he was going to get one, but I don't believe he's ever going to
get enough money to buy one. I sure do think one would be a
lot of company.

SINGING AND "JUST SITTING AND TALKING"

In the absence of a more formal type of recreation, many
rural youth, after the daily chores have been completed, spend
their leisure time in sitting either on their own porches or those
of their friends, singing, talking, and sometimes listening to the
conversations of older people. A 14-year-old girl in Madison
County, who had known only this type of activity from her very
earliest years, said:

When we gets through working well we do mostly the same
thing all the time. After supper we just sit down on the porch
and sometimes we sing and sometimes we talk. We ain't real
serious about our singing we just sing little jump songs. We
don't sing no hymns. We sings songs like—"Oh Mary Don't
You Weep, Don't You Moan," "Back, Back Train," "Good

Evening Everybody." Sometimes we go over to the neighbors'
and sing and sometimes they come over to our house. Sometimes it's a lot of fun visiting and sitting down talking to people. What do we talk about? Oh, everything—boy friends, other
girls who think they are so much, and those who ain't nobody,
too. Sometimes I go with my mother when she goes to visit,
then I mainly listens. Oh, they talk about everything, the folks
in the neighborhood and these fast girls around here. There
really ain't nothing else to do but jest sing and talk. Sometimes
on Sundays first one and then the other of us have cream din-
ners—ice cream and cake. We haves a real nice time talking then
because some of them that we haven't seen in a long time knows
a lots whats been going on and then we just have a good time
talking about everything.

TALL TALES AND RABBIT STORIES

Fifteen-year-old Sammie Hawkins of Macon County, Alabama, described his recreational activities as well as those of his
friends as follows:

Sometimes we sit down and tell tales. Oh, we tell all kinds of
tales, but most of the time they be about the fox and Brer
Rabbit. No, we don't make them up exactly. We heard all of
them some place before, but we add on to them if we can so
they be more funny. I know plenty of them. Here's one.

"The fox wanted to eat the rabbit, so he got some straw and
covered some dogs up with it. Then he went to Brer Rabbit
and told him that he knew where a potato patch was that was
covered up with straw and come on let's him and Brer Rabbit
go and dig it up. So they went on to where these dogs was
covered with straw. When they got there the fox said, 'Go
ahead and dig, Brer Rabbit.' But the rabbit said he would
wait for the fox to dig first. The fox went in and started scratch-
ing around and the dogs got after him and when he was running he hollered, 'Bear round, Brer Rabbit, bear round!' And
Brer Rabbit said, 'Bear round, nothing. I'm a straight through
man!' "

THE "DOZENS"

The "Dozens" is one form of "talking" recreation often engaged in by rural boys. It is usually played by two boys before
an appreciative, interested audience. The object of the game

is to speak of the opponent's mother in the most derisive terms possible. Many boys know long series of obscene ditties and verses concerning the immoral behavior of the mother of the one whom they are "putting in the dozens," and they sometimes recite for hours without interruption. The game usually ends pleasantly, but occasionally it is the spark which brings two unfriendly boys to blows—"talking about my mama." While the exact source of the name "Dozens" is uncertain, one theory is that it originated from the game of dice. In dice, twelve is one of the worst points one can throw. Therefore to be "put in the dozens" is one of the worst things that can happen to an individual.

COMMERCIAL AMUSEMENTS

While part of the social program of the more isolated sections is likewise current in the nonfarming areas, the program is supplemented in the latter case with urban amusements. The beer taverns, dance halls, and bootlegging "joints" carry over into the rural village the mores of the urban slum and underworld. The comment of one 15-year-old boy throws light on a type of recreation into which some of the youth have drifted:

> Some of the boys usta meet on the highway and chip in and buy liquor most every three or four nights. I got in with them and started buying it with them. We did it more for sport than anything else.

Sophronia Lew, an 18-year-old girl in Davidson County, Tennessee, gave this description of the activities of her "gang":

> Most of the girls in my gang range from 16 to 24. We put our money together and go to town to the Silver Lane or to the Crimson Red Home. Out at the Crimson Red Home we can drink beer and dance, but I don't guess you could call it a beer garden. We stay out until twelve or one o'clock. There is also a "fast house" out here called the Blue Lane Inn. It's just a beer garden; nothing else goes on there, but it isn't legal. We go there quite often but I don't like it there very much because they lock the door behind you when you go in. Some of the girls meet their fellows out there. Yes, we all drink but most of the girls drink only beer while the boys drink whisky. Well,

I don't suppose it's the best place in the world, but you gotta do something.

Wilbert Brince of Shelby County, Tennessee, described the recreational activities of his "gang" and himself as follows:

Nearly every Wednesday night we play whist or bridge. We play cards I guess about two hours. After playing cards we might dance a little or have a little something to eat. We go over to the café and play the nickelodeon. It isn't exactly a café, but it looks like a private home. That's the place where all the young people go. You know where the store is and you always see old men hanging out front, well, that's where all the old men go to raise hell and get drinks. Yes, most of me and my gang hang out there. There are a lot of women there, too, but I don't bother with them much. I'd rather fool around with the younger girls. Oh, yes, there are plenty of those around too.

PROBLEMS OF UNDIRECTED LEISURE

Seasons of relaxation from the stress of planting, cultivating, and harvesting of the crop are danger points for active youth without guidance. Certain of the summer months in particular permit considerable freedom from the responsibility and drudgery of work and, except in a few areas, the schools do not attempt to adjust themselves to this phase of the farm family's relationship to the crop.

The undisciplined impulses of rural youth find expression in a variety of activities, the most disturbing of which are those that, in an urban setting, would be classified under juvenile delinquency. Legally, there is little juvenile delinquency in the rural areas and among the youth studied. Actually, there are many offenses committed by rural Negro youth which contravene existing statutes, but rural areas are not policed as adequately as urban areas. There is a significant difference in rural and urban areas in what constitutes delinquency which is punishable by law. This is especially important in consideration of Negro juvenile delinquency, for much of the behavior that would, in the city, be considered a violation of a law, ordinance, or public policy, is assumed to be merely a part of "Negro culture." For example, the most frequent "offenses" charged against

Negro delinquents in the cities are immorality, truancy, incorrigibility, fighting, and stealing. These seldom come to the attention of rural authorities. In the first place, it would be impossible to distinguish truancy from necessary absence from school because of lack of transportation or the urgency of work. The sex mores in the rural area modify the offense of immorality. Moreover, this, like fighting and stealing, is most frequently interpreted as a phase of interpersonal relations that can be dealt with adequately by the parties concerned. Only when fighting and stealing reach extreme proportions do they come to the attention of the rural courts and then the treatment of the youthful offender is little different from that of the adult offender. In addition to these factors, there are in the rural areas fewer complaints made to courts, and there is no place for the special detention of Negro youth except the common jails. Most commonly the offenses are adjusted through personal arrangements between the complainants and the families of the youth, either with or without supervision of a court of justice, or if the offended party is a white person, he may settle the matter himself by punishing the youth.

The case of Jimmie Hicks illustrates how an act of petty stealing, which in an urban area might have led to a juvenile court, is handled in a rural area. Jimmie's own account of the situation follows:

When I was about 10 years old, me'n my cousin went out to a man's watermelon patch and took two big old melons. On the way out my cousin dropped his'n and broke it open. We divided it up and started to eat. He finished his up 'fore I did and wanted some of mine. I didn't want to give him none and he throwed sand on the piece I was eating. Course I went to fighting right there. The man that owned the patch heered the fuss and come up on us. He made both of us pick a croaker sack full of melons and tote them home. He went right along with us and wouldn't let us set the sack down to rest. When we got to the yard, we had to stand and hold the sacks while he talked to mamma. When he left, mamma whipped us good. We didn't had no business taking the man's melons 'cause he woulda gave us all we wanted. I just hated to ask people for anything. We had asked him the day before and I was shamed

to ask again. From then on though I allus asked for whatever
I wanted.

The fact that the rural cultural setting tolerates sexual laxity in the girls which might result in an urban setting in institutional confinement is discussed in Chapter VIII. Faced with a
need for companionship which is not satisfied through existing
school or play activities, or with a desire to achieve or maintain
group status, the rural girl has in numbers of instances turned to
sex. In these rural areas, therefore, sex instruction for both boys
and girls, if given, is more likely to take the form of admonitions of "being careful" than of abstinence. The delinquency,
thus, is seen very largely as a function of the cultural pattern of
the community, and may be viewed as a form of leisure-time
activity the chief control of which lies in the provision of a
more wholesome social and recreational life.

Play is a normal and necessary function of youth. Well-di-
rected and wholesome play, especially when purposefully planned and controlled, is both a form of social participation and a
means of social discipline. The testimony of the youth studied
leads to the conclusion that an important part of the discontent
with rural life and much of the antisocial behavior spring from
the same source—the poor and haphazard facilities for wholesome play. The narrow discipline and inadequacy of the rural
school, the traditional and cramping conservatism of the rural
church, the restricting and ever present shadow of the white
world with its limited tolerance, and the relentless economic
demands on youth of lowly status, combine to restrict this outlet,
and in the end have their inevitable effect on the life of youth.

CHAPTER VII

OCCUPATIONAL OUTLOOK
AND INCENTIVES

THE ROUTINE of farm life in which the occupations of rural youth are set is rigidly fixed and dictated by the seasons. Young people are inducted into this routine at an early age and continue it throughout their lives. By the time they reach the age of 14 or 15 they can do practically everything they will be required to do the rest of their lives. They can plow, and they can chop, weed, and pick cotton. They know how to milk a cow and kill a hog. They can do odd jobs around the farm; they can raise vegetables and chickens to feed themselves; and they can raise feed for the stock, if they have any. It is a hard life, and some of them like it. They have known and expect nothing else. Where agriculture is flourishing, it is possible to get a fair living from the soil; where it is in decline, the people are depressed without always knowing why. As in other vocations there are features that give zest to toil. This is the most wholesome aspect of work itself.

It is usually assumed that younger children will spend a large part of their day in school during the term. On the farm many children are unpaid family workers who accept it as a part of their home responsibility to help with definite farming jobs. Among Negro families the burden of making a living is so severe that the children's school attendance is frequently interrupted. As a result they are chronically backward in school, or they may be withdrawn from school entirely at an early age.

This chapter deals with the work of older rural Negro youth, but more especially with their occupational aspirations and prospects. It is conceivable that the goals to which youth aspire are as important in shaping their personalities as the more tangible environment to which they are exposed.

Work opportunities in rural areas are limited almost exclusively to the traditional farm operations associated with the work status of the most numerous class, the farm tenants. For the great bulk of them this consists of plowing, hoeing, and picking cotton. There are a few skilled and semiskilled jobs held by the boys, and domestic jobs, such as nursing, house cleaning, and cooking, held by the girls. Occasionally a few privileged young people may be found in white-collar jobs serving, for the most part, other Negroes. In general, pay for farm work is poor and all earnings are sorely needed in the home.

One of the most serious aspects of the present work of these youth is its unattractiveness. The Negro tenant families cannot emerge from their status into ownership rapidly enough to offer much prospect of independent rural living to their youth. As a result, the occupational outlook of most of them is keyed to the hope of escape from the drudgery, monotony, and poverty of their farming families and neighbors, escape into the prestige-bearing jobs of the community, or escape into the imagined world of improved economic opportunity in the large towns and cities.

COTTON PICKING

The work most commonly done by rural Negro youth is picking cotton. Since practically all of them learned early in life to pick cotton, one measure of occupational age is the amount of cotton that can be picked. Young children can pick from 50 to 75 pounds a day, older boys and girls from 100 to 200. Beyond this weight and age limit it becomes a matter of skill and endurance. Some youth take pride in this skill and earn reputations that make them the envy of their fellows and the boasted favorites of their landlords.

THE FASTEST COTTON PICKER IN COAHOMA COUNTY

Jimmie Hicks is a small, dark, wiry youth about 18 years of age, energetic and loquacious. He was born and reared on a farm in Coahoma County, Mississippi, near Jonesboro and began picking cotton when he was 7 years old. His own story has the tang of the John Henry legend, and his adventures, authenticated by observation, carry the atmosphere and the small but vital details of a farm youth's life in the kingdom of cotton.

I'll just tell you now—last year when me'n Bill was makin' a crop together, they was a nigger that a white man was carrying around and offering $5.00 to anybody that'd out-pick him. We was pickin' our own cotton out, but I heard about him and 'cided to give him a try if he stayed 'round long enough. I got a line on him 'fore I went over to where he was pickin'—right out from Jonestown. I knew I could pick over 400, and I figgered I could push him right smart even if I couldn't beat him.

I went on over one morning 'bout sun-up. He was a boy I reckon 'bout 19 or 20, and anyone 'tween 15 and 20 could pick with him for the $5.00. I was just 18 so I was all right.

I sat 'round and talked with him till long about nine o'clock—sizing him up, you know. He was waitin' for the dew to get off'n the cotton and that just hit me right. If I starts while the dew is on I can't do nothing 'cause it makes my fingers slick and I can't do no business. Meantime I eyed him up and down trying to figger out what his slight was.

Directly we got started. That nigger—he was a big old boy for his age—just straddled the row and got to goin'. For a spell I jus' watched him while I picked along right slow—just enough to keep where I could watch him. Directly I seed what they was to him and lit in on him and, pardner, I was a-swinging.

Well, such another going' you ain't never seen. We went down row for row all morning and I picked right along with him. At the end of the row—they was *long* old rows, too—when we weighted up he would have maybe a pound on me or maybe we'd be even up. I allus stayed behind him on my row and I never weighed up more'n him.

That a way he was 5 pounds on me by dinner time. When the bell rung, you know that wild nigger wouldn't stop to eat! I ain't never missed out on dinner, and he made me mad so I 'cided to rush him. We'd picked 'bout 200 apiece that morning, but then I lit in for fair. I was jus' as hot at him as corn bread on the stove.

I'd come up right close behind him and soon as he heard me he'd miss a heap o' cotton and jump way up the row. When I got to pushing him right fast, he got just as scary as a rabbit. Got so I'd just rattle the stalk close up behind him jus' to see him jump. I'd shake the stalk right hard and sudden and that nigger'd jump way ahead of hisself.

Tell the truth, they was some cottonin' done that evening. People stopped pickin' and begin to watchin' us. Directly they seed I was pushing that old boy and they 'gin to holler, "C'mon, Jimmie, beat that nigger." My hands was going so fast they scared me. It's the honest truth, I was each time weighing up 4 and 5 pounds more'n him at the end of the row. I was pickin' some cotton!

Well, suh, long 'bout sun-down when we finished up, I'd done picked 490 and him 475. He come over to me and said, "Nigger, I don't never want no more of you." He ain't been 'round since. But I ain't never picked cotton like I did that day.

OCCUPATIONAL PATTERN

In a relatively static society such as the more remote rural areas represent, the occupations of the youth follow rather closely the occupations of their parents. A first important indication, therefore, of the occupations and occupational outlook of the boys is the occupation of their fathers. In the group studied a preponderance of the fathers were farmers. But there were, of course, other occupations in which fathers were engaged, notably in such counties as Davidson, a mixed farming area near Nashville, where there is a wider variety of occupations, and Greene County in Georgia, where the breakup of the plantation system has resulted in greater occupational diversification.

Our information regarding the occupations of fathers was secured from 2,250 youth in the eight counties studied. In a large number of instances, work on the farm was not dignified by the title "farmer," and in still other cases the fathers were unemployed. Even excluding the large number of marginal occupations within the field of agriculture, the percentages listed as farmers ranged from 11.5 per cent in Davidson County, where many fathers worked in the nearby city of Nashville, to 50.8 per cent in Shelby County, Tennessee. If we exclude from the total number of fathers those cases in which no occupation is listed (largely dead or separated from the family), the proportions would range from 16.9 per cent in Davidson County to 66.3 per cent in Shelby County.

The occupations engaged in by the next largest number of fathers were unskilled labor, followed by skilled and semi-skilled work. The number of fathers who are professionals is small, averaging less than 3 per cent for the eight counties studied (2.6 per cent, if fathers with no occupation listed are excluded from the total). The lowest proportion was in Davidson County, Tennessee (1.5 per cent), and the highest in Johnston County, North Carolina, and Shelby County, Tennessee (4.2 per cent). In two counties, Greene in Georgia and Macon in Alabama, none of the youth studied had professional fathers. (There is a prominent Negro physician in Greene County, but he has no children, and there is no Negro physician in Macon County engaged in rural practice.) Teaching, however, accounts for most of the professionals where they are found.

For the girls the occupational pattern of the mothers is scarcely more stimulating than that of the fathers. In the active plantation areas, represented by Bolivar and Coahoma counties, Mississippi, farming was the occupation of the majority of those mothers whose occupations were given. In the declining plantation areas, represented by Greene and Macon counties, the greatest proportion of the working mothers were employed as servants. The servant group also accounted for the majority of the mothers in Davidson, Johnston, and Madison (Alabama) counties, but in Shelby a slightly higher proportion of mothers was engaged in farming. The number of mothers of girls engaged in professional occupations (practically all as teachers) is comparatively high in the active plantation areas of Coahoma and Bolivar counties, where 6.2 per cent and 6.5 per cent of the mothers, respectively, were in the professional class. The other three white-collar groups—proprietors, managers, and officials; wholesale and retail dealers; and clerks and kindred workers—were even more negligible for mothers than fathers.

A factor which operates to limit the occupational horizon of rural Negro youth is the almost total absence of Negroes in the nonagricultural occupations aside from the traditional unskilled labor field, the personal and domestic service occupations, and the overcrowded and poorly paid white-collar and skilled tasks of teaching, preaching, undertaking, and carpentry. Thus, these young people have in their communities few examples of Negroes to serve as inspiration, or as an index of wider occupational fields that are or might be open to Negroes.

OCCUPATIONAL TESTS AND INTERVIEWS

Inquiry was made into the vocational preferences and attitudes of 851 rural boys and 1,399 rural girls through the use of a detailed Occupation Ratings Test.

ESCAPE FROM AGRICULTURE

Only 62 of the boys wanted to engage in farming as a vocation in spite of the fact that the fathers of 302 of these boys were farmers. This does not mean, of course, that only 62 will eventually enter farming. The heavy hand of custom will inevitably prevail with many more who find nothing better to do, or who cannot get away. It is worth noting, however, that farming as a career attracts only a small number.

Examining further the occupational wishes of these 851 boys, it appears that of 302 sons of farmers, 38.1 per cent wished to enter the professions, 17.2 per cent wanted to enter skilled trades, 9.3 per cent wanted what might be called "clerical" work,[1] and 10.9 per cent preferred unskilled nonfarm labor and domestic service to farming while only 8.9 per cent preferred farm work. There is some indication in their comments that they rank farming, as they know it, as below even domestic service and unskilled labor, as they know these occupations.

Of the 16 sons of professional fathers none wanted to enter unskilled work or domestic service. Nine (56.2 per cent) of them wanted to enter professional work, one wanted to enter skilled

---

[1] "Clerical work" is *our* classification and not their description. The boys gave such responses as "insurance agent," "bookkeeper," and so forth, although some did say "clerk."

Table 9

PREFERRED OCCUPATIONS OF RURAL NEGRO BOYS, BY FATHER'S OCCUPATION
(In percentages)

Preferred Occupation	Father's Occupation										
	All Occupations	Professional	Proprietors, managers, and officials	Clerks and kindred workers	Skilled workers and foremen	Semi-skilled workers	Unskilled workers	Servants	Farmers	Unemployed	Not given
Professional	38.8	56.2	58.3	30.8	56.4	31.6	33.3	40.0	38.1	32.8	38.7
Skilled work	17.7	6.3	12.5	23.1	17.8	26.3	13.5	23.3	17.2	19.0	18.7
Proprietors, managers, and officials	0.9	—	4.2	—	2.6	—	—	—	1.0	—	1.7
Wholesale and retail dealers	2.0	—	—	—	5.1	—	3.1	—	2.3	3.4	1.7
Clerical work	10.1	25.0	8.3	7.7	—	5.3	11.5	20.0	9.3	8.6	10.6
Unskilled work	3.3	—	—	—	—	5.3	4.2	—	5.6	1.7	1.7
Personal and domestic service	3.8	—	4.2	7.7	2.6	2.5	6.3	—	5.3	3.4	1.7
Farm work	7.3	6.2	8.3	7.7	2.6	5.3	5.2	3.3	8.9	13.8	6.0
Miscellaneous	5.5	6.3	4.2	7.7	10.3	5.3	7.3	6.7	6.0	3.4	3.8
Not given	10.6	—	—	15.4	2.6	18.4	15.6	6.7	6.3	13.8	15.3
Number of cases	851	16	24	13	39	38	96	30	302	58	235

work, one farm work, and the other four desired clerical work. In this selection there is evidence of the influence of class status, and this also affects the sons of men engaged in skilled trades. Of 39 boys whose fathers were employed in skilled occupations, 22 wanted to enter the professions and only 7 wanted to enter skilled trades. The proportion of sons of fathers in domestic service who wanted to enter the professions was only slightly less than that for sons of skilled workers. Of 30 such boys, 12 desired a professional occupation.

This is only a measure of desire. These youth, as will be indicated later, were not wholly unrealistic about their desires and their actual chances.

The girls were more limited in their range of choice, and in all counties their desires were more heavily concentrated in the professions than those of the boys. This reflects, of course, the generally narrow range of observed patterns for girls in most counties. The general restrictions on sex add to the racial limitations. Of the 1,399 girls included in this study, 65.3 per cent desired to enter the professions as a vocation as compared with 38.8 per cent of the boys.

The counties show some differences in the preferences indicated which are, perhaps, important. For example, in Shelby, a cotton county near Memphis, Tennessee, 29.8 per cent of the boys wanted to enter the professions, but in Coahoma, a plantation county in Mississippi with no city, 46.2 per cent preferred a profession as a career. The wider variety of occupations in the nearby city exerts an influence which is not present in Coahoma County. Shelby County also had the highest proportion of boys who wanted to engage in farming as a vocation (12.1 per cent) while Bolivar County, another plantation-controlled county adjoining Coahoma, had the lowest proportion (4.4 per cent).

The girls were not only more pronounced in their desire for professional careers, but more positive in their rejection of farming as a vocation. Although women engage in farming as wives of farmers, farming is considered a man's vocation. The highest proportion of girls expressing a desire to engage in

TABLE 10

PREFERRED OCCUPATIONS OF RURAL NEGRO YOUTH, BY COUNTY AND SEX[a]

(In percentages)

Preferred Occupation	All Counties		Johnston, N.C.		Davidson, Tenn.		Shelby, Tenn.		Coahoma, Miss.		Bolivar, Miss.		Madison, Ala.		Macon, Ala.		Greene, Ga.	
	Boys	Girls	Boys	Girls	Boys	Girls	Boys	Girls	Boys	Girls	Boys	Girls	Boys	Girls	Boys	Girls	Boys	Girls
Professional	38.8	65.3	40.1	59.6	43.8	69.7	29.8	70.9	46.2	70.1	36.8	56.1	44.9	64.6	32.7	69.2	35.9	70.3
Skilled work	17.7	9.1	10.7	10.0	13.5	7.3	20.2	9.3	12.5	7.1	26.3	13.3	19.1	5.2	29.6	8.2	10.3	7.7
Proprietors, managers, and officials	0.9	—	—	—	2.1	—	0.8	—	—	—	1.8	—	2.2	—	1.0	—	—	—
Wholesale and retail dealers	2.0	1.2	2.7	1.5	2.1	11.0	0.8	0.7	—	0.6	1.8	1.0	2.2	5.2	1.0	0.7	10.3	1.1
Clerical work	10.1	10.3	8.0	9.1	5.2	—	18.5	7.8	12.5	14.3	8.8	13.3	12.4	7.3	6.1	8.9	7.7	13.2
Unskilled work	3.3	0.2	2.1	0.3	2.1	—	0.8	—	2.9	—	1.8	1.0	5.6	—	5.1	—	15.4	—
Personal and domestic service	3.8	6.5	3.7	6.8	2.1	10.1	5.6	6.7	1.9	1.3	4.4	9.2	1.1	7.3	6.1	6.8	5.1	2.2
Farm work	7.3	1.2	8.0	2.1	7.3	—	12.1	0.7	6.7	—	4.4	1.0	5.6	2.1	6.1	2.1	5.1	1.1
Miscellaneous	5.5	1.3	9.6	1.2	7.3	—	3.2	1.9	5.8	2.6	5.3	1.0	1.1	—	3.1	1.4	5.1	1.1
Not given	10.6	4.9	15.0	9.4	14.6	1.8	8.1	1.9	11.5	3.9	8.8	4.1	5.6	8.3	9.2	2.7	5.1	3.3
Number of cases	851	1,399	187	339	96	109	124	268	104	154	114	196	89	96	98	146	39	91

[a] For more specific preferences within major occupational groups, see Table 12, p. 202.

farming in any county was 2.1 per cent, and in two counties, Davidson in Tennessee and Coahoma in Mississippi, not a single girl expressed such a desire. Since most of them will be housewives, it might be assumed that they were responding only to a man's occupation. In Chapter VIII it is brought out that these girls were similarly opposed to being farmers' wives.

AREA DIFFERENCES IN PREFERRED OCCUPATIONS

If we group the counties studied into plantation and non-plantation areas, the gross differences in preference for professional occupations are not great (55.1 per cent in the plantation areas, 55.4 per cent in the nonplantation areas). However, the proportion of boys wishing to engage in farming was greater in the nonplantation areas (8.5 per cent in nonplantation areas, 5.6 per cent in the plantation area).

Among the girls 7.3 per cent in the nonplantation areas desired domestic service as compared with only 5.5 per cent in the plantation areas. This difference also is a measure of observed opportunity.

The plantation counties, when divided into active and declining areas, reveal some differences in the vocational desires of youth. For example, in the declining areas a smaller proportion of the boys look to the professions (33.6 per cent in the declining areas, 41.3 per cent in the active areas). More youth in the active plantation areas (12.5 per cent) desired clerical occupations than in the declining areas (9.1 per cent). There were decidedly more boys wanting unskilled work in the declining areas (8 per cent) than in the active areas (2.3 per cent). It has been suggested elsewhere that the declining plantation areas were forcing attention to other than the traditional plantation jobs. Girls in the declining areas were even more pronounced in their preference for professional and skilled occupations than they were in the active areas.

VOCATIONAL CHOICE AND INTELLIGENCE

There appeared to be some relation between the intelligence quotients for rural youth and the occupations which they de-

TABLE 11

PREFERRED OCCUPATIONS OF RURAL NEGRO YOUTH, BY INTELLIGENCE QUOTIENTS AND SEX

(In percentages)

Preferred Occupation	All I.Q.'s		40–59[a]		60–69		70–79		80–89		90–99		100–129[b]		Unknown	
	Boys	Girls	Boys	Girls	Boys	Girls	Boys	Girls	Boys	Girls	Boys	Girls	Boys	Girls	Boys	Girls
Professional	38.8	65.3	40.7	63.2	27.0	62.6	38.0	68.3	42.1	68.9	45.0	64.5	57.1	58.2	38.7	59.1
Skilled work	17.7	9.1	15.3	4.4	19.8	9.7	17.8	9.9	17.0	9.3	20.0	8.6	14.3	12.7	17.2	8.3
Proprietors, managers, and officials	0.9	—	—	—	0.8	—	0.9	—	0.6	—	2.5	—	7.1	—	—	—
Wholesale and retail trade	2.0	1.2	1.7	1.5	4.0	0.6	1.9	1.3	1.3	0.8	—	1.3	—	—	2.7	2.2
Clerical work	10.1	10.3	8.5	8.8	10.3	2.6	10.3	9.9	11.3	12.1	6.3	17.1	10.7	16.4	10.8	7.8
Unskilled work	3.3	0.2	3.4	—	6.3	—	4.2	0.5	1.9	—	—	—	3.6	1.8	2.7	—
Personal and domestic service	3.8	6.5	1.7	8.8	7.1	15.5	6.1	5.4	2.5	3.7	2.5	3.3	3.6	—	1.1	9.6
Farm work	7.3	1.2	8.5	1.5	6.3	3.9	8.0	0.3	5.7	—	10.0	0.7	3.6	3.6	7.5	3.5
Miscellaneous	5.5	1.3	3.4	—	7.1	1.3	2.8	1.0	10.1	1.7	7.5	2.0	—	3.6	4.3	0.4
Not given	10.6	4.9	16.9	11.8	11.1	3.9	9.9	3.4	7.5	3.4	6.3	2.6	—	7.3	15.1	9.1
Number of cases	851	1,399	59	68	126	155	213	385	159	354	80	152	28	55	186	230

[a] Includes 2 boys and 5 girls with I.Q. of 40–49

[b] Includes 5 boys and 11 girls with I.Q. of 110–119 and 1 boy with an I.Q. of 120–129

sire to follow. In general, the higher the intelligence quotient the higher the percentage of youth choosing professions as a vocation. Of the 59 rural boys, for example, with I.Q.'s between 40-59, 24 (40.7 per cent) desired the professions as compared with 36 (45 per cent) of the 80 whose I.Q.'s were between 90-99. However, it is significant to note that of the 28 boys with I.Q.'s over 100, 16 (57.1 per cent) expressed the desire to enter the professions. This proportion was much larger than the proportion of any other I.Q. group among the boys. Omitting the 40-59 group, the proportion of boys wishing to enter the professions increased as the I.Q.'s increased. Of the 28 boys with I.Q.'s over 100, only 1 (3.6 per cent) desired farming as compared with 47 (7.4 per cent) of the 637 whose I.Q.'s were below 100.

Skilled work was desired next to the professions by boys of each I.Q. group, but there was no significant pattern of variation in these desires.

Each I.Q. group among the girls showed an overwhelming desire for the professions, the lowest proportion being 58.2 per cent of the group with I.Q.'s over 100. In this group was found the highest proportion who desired skilled trades as well as a relatively high proportion who expressed a desire to do clerical work. The 60-69 and 40-59 groups were interesting in that these two relatively low I.Q. groups had the highest proportion of girls who desired personal and domestic service and farm work and ranked lowest in their desire for clerical work. In general, desire for clerical work among the girls increased with the I.Q. Of the 9 girls whose I.Q.'s were known and who desired farming only 1 had an I.Q. above 80, and 7 of the 9 had I.Q.'s below 70. None of the 55 girls with I.Q.'s above 100 desired farming.

OCCUPATIONAL PREFERENCE AND EXPECTATION

The occupations desired by these rural youth differ markedly from those they expect to follow. Although these rural youth were overwhelming in their desire for professional occupations, many expressed the opinion that, for one reason or another, these were not the occupations they actually expected to follow. For example, 38.8 per cent of the boys and 65.3 per cent of the girls desire to enter the professions, but only 26.4 per cent of the boys and 48.4 per cent of the girls actually expect to follow these occupations, and even this proportion is obviously overgenerous.

In the skilled trades the relationship between desire and expectation is closer. Of the boys, 17.7 per cent and of the girls, 9.1 per cent desire these occupations, and 17.2 per cent of the boys and 8.8 per cent of the girls expect to follow them. In the case of farming, the lack of relationship appears again in the reversal of the proportions of those desiring and expecting to enter the field.

Of the boys, 7.3 per cent desired farm work and 11.5 per cent expected to do it, while 1.2 per cent of the girls desired it and 3.4 per cent expected to pursue it. Here again an optimism is revealed which hard fact all too soon dispels.

The difference between the proportion of girls who desired personal and domestic service (6.5 per cent) and the proportion who expect to follow this type of work (17.2 per cent) is similar to the boys' responses on farming.

One other class of youth should be mentioned. Among the boys, 10.6 per cent expressed no preference for any occupation, 18.4 per cent had no opinion as to the occupation they would actually follow.

Differences between Counties

Coahoma County had both the highest proportion of boys who desired and who expected to go into the professions, 46.2 per cent and 39.4 per cent, respectively; Shelby County, with the lowest proportion of boys who desired the professions (29.8 per cent), had about the same proportion who actually expected to go into the professions (23.4 per cent) as Johnston (23 per cent) and Greene (23.1 per cent) and only a slightly smaller proportion than Madison (25.8 per cent), Macon (26.5 per cent), and Davidson (28.1 per cent) counties. Shelby County ranked first in the proportion of boys who preferred farm work

TABLE 12

PREFERRED AND EXPECTED OCCUPATIONS
OF RURAL NEGRO YOUTH, BY SEX

Occupation	BOYS				GIRLS			
	Preferred Occupation		Expected Occupation		Preferred Occupation		Expected Occupation	
	Number	Per cent	Number	Per cent	Number	Per cent	Number	Per cent
ALL OCCUPATIONS	851	100.0	851	100.0	1,399	100.0	1,399	100.0
PROFESSIONAL	330	38.8	225	26.4	913	65.3	677	48.4
Teacher—public school or unspecified	114	13.4	85	10.0	405	28.9	374	26.7
Teacher—college	5	0.6	2	0.2	4	0.3	—	—
Doctor	89	10.5	51	6.0	11	0.8	9	0.6
Nurse	2	0.2	1	0.1	354	25.3	221	15.8
Undertaker	12	1.4	8	0.9	10	0.7	7	0.5
Dentist	3	0.4	3	0.4	—	—	—	—
Artist	16	1.9	13	1.5	3	0.2	1	0.1
Supervisor of schools	4	0.5	2	0.2	1	0.1	—	—
Lawyer	11	1.3	9	1.1	4	0.3	1	0.1
Engineer	8	0.9	6	0.7	1	0.1	1	0.1
Musician	24	2.8	15	1.8	68	4.9	35	2.5
Librarian	—	—	—	—	4	0.3	5	0.4
Minister	5	0.6	2	0.2	4	0.3	1	0.1
Actress—actor	3	0.4	4	0.5	9	0.6	1	0.1
Dietician	—	—	—	—	3	0.2	—	—
Professional not specified	34	4.0	24	2.8	32	2.3	21	1.5
SKILLED WORK	151	17.7	146	17.2	128	9.1	123	8.8
Mechanic	38	4.5	37	4.3	—	—	—	—
Aviator	10	1.2	4	0.5	1	0.1	—	—
Electrician	6	0.7	5	0.6	—	—	—	—
Carpenter	15	1.8	12	1.4	—	—	—	—
Seamstress—tailor	12	1.4	10	1.2	47	3.4	45	3.2
Beautician	—	—	—	—	73	5.2	75	5.4
Policeman	3	0.4	3	0.4	—	—	—	—
Printer	4	0.5	6	0.7	3	0.2	1	0.1
Plumber	1	0.1	1	0.1	—	—	—	—
Skilled work not specified	62	7.3	68	8.0	4	0.3	2	0.1
PROPRIETORS, MANAGERS, AND OFFICIALS	8	0.9	9	1.1	—	—	2	0.1
Contractors	2	0.2	2	0.2	—	—	—	—
Proprietors, managers, and officials not specified	6	0.7	7	0.8	—	—	2	0.1

TABLE 12 (*Continued*)

Occupation	BOYS				GIRLS			
	Preferred Occupation		Expected Occupation		Preferred Occupation		Expected Occupation	
	Number	Per cent	Number	Per cent	Number	Per cent	Number	Per cent
WHOLESALE AND RETAIL TRADE	17	2.0	17	2.0	17	1.2	20	1.4
Grocer	1	0.1	2	0.2	—	—	1	0.1
Clerk in store	9	1.1	8	0.9	10	0.7	11	0.8
Storekeeper	4	0.5	4	0.5	6	0.4	5	0.4
Wholesale and retail trade not specified	3	0.4	3	0.4	1	0.1	3	0.2
CLERICAL WORK	86	10.1	61	7.2	144	10.3	121	8.6
Stenographer	3	0.4	4	0.5	70	5.0	54	3.9
Bookkeeper	10	1.2	6	0.7	20	1.4	15	1.1
Telephone operator	—	—	—	—	3	0.2	—	—
Mail clerk	52	6.1	33	3.9	1	0.1	1	0.1
Clerical work not specified	21	2.5	18	2.1	50	3.6	51	3.6
UNSKILLED WORK	28	3.3	42	4.9	3	0.2	2	0.1
Driver	24	2.8	28	3.3	1	0.1	—	—
Unskilled work not specified	4	0.5	14	1.6	2	0.1	2	0.1
PERSONAL AND DOMESTIC SERVICE	32	3.8	51	6.0	91	6.5	240	17.2
Cook	9	1.1	13	1.5	53	3.8	149	10.7
Maid	—	—	—	—	2	0.1	12	0.9
Porter	14	1.6	18	2.1	1	0.1	1	0.1
Laundry worker	1	0.1	1	0.1	8	0.6	18	1.3
Janitor	—	—	—	—	—	—	—	—
Personal and domestic service not specified	8	0.9	19	2.2	27	1.9	60	4.3
FARM WORK	62	7.3	98	11.5	17	1.2	48	3.4
Farm owner	4	0.5	8	0.9	—	—	1	0.1
Farm laborer	4	0.5	12	1.4	6	0.4	10	0.7
Farm tenant	—	—	—	—	—	—	—	—
Farm work not specified	54	6.3	78	9.2	11	0.8	37	2.6
MISCELLANEOUS	47	5.5	45	5.3	18	1.3	30	2.1
Housewife	—	—	—	—	4	0.3	10	0.7
Soldier	1	0.1	1	0.1	—	—	—	—
WPA worker	—	—	1	0.1	—	—	1	0.1
Prize fighter	9	1.1	6	0.7	—	—	—	—
Not specified	37	4.3	37	4.3	14	1.0	19	1.4
NOT GIVEN	90	10.6	157	18.4	68	4.9	136	9.7

(12.1 per cent), and at the same time ranked first with a much higher proportion (22.6 per cent) who expect to follow farming. In several of the counties, more boys expected to follow skilled work than actually desired such work. In every county, except Davidson and Macon counties, a larger proportion of boys expected to do farm work than actually desired it.

TABLE 13

PROPORTION OF RURAL NEGRO GIRLS DESIRING AND EXPECTING TO ENTER PERSONAL AND DOMESTIC SERVICE, BY COUNTY[a]

County	Personal and Domestic Service	
	Preferred	Expected
All counties	6.5	17.2
Johnston, N.C.	6.8	19.5
Davidson, Tenn.	10.1	27.5
Shelby, Tenn.	6.7	20.5
Coahoma, Miss.	1.3	7.1
Bolivar, Miss.	9.2	11.2
Madison, Ala.	7.3	15.6
Macon, Ala.	6.8	18.5
Greene, Ga.	2.2	15.4

[a] Based on interviews with 1,399 girls

The largest proportion of girls who desired the professions was found in Shelby County (70.9 per cent), and the largest proportion who expected to follow the professions was found in Greene County (60.4 per cent) which ranked next to Shelby in the percentage wishing to enter the professions.

The difference between the girls who desired and expected to go into clerical work was not great except in Greene County where 13.2 per cent desired clerical work and 7.7 per cent expected to follow it. This was not true, however, of personal and domestic service where there was a considerable difference in all except Bolivar County between the proportion who desired and expected to go into this type of work. In Bolivar County this type of work was desired by 9.2 per cent and expected by 11.2 per cent of girls.

Significantly, few girls in any county desired or expected to do farm work.

Boys in the plantation areas expected to go into the professions, the skilled trades, and clerical work in greater proportion than boys in the nonplantation areas; the latter expected to go into personal and domestic service and farm work in greater proportion.

Girls in both areas expected to go into the professions, the skilled trades, and farming in approximately the same proportion, but girls in the nonplantation areas expected to go into personal and domestic work in greater proportion than the plantation girls; the latter expected to go into clerical work in greater proportion.

Boys in the active plantation areas expected to go into the professions in a notably higher proportion than boys in the declining areas, while boys from the latter areas expected to go into unskilled labor and personal and domestic service in greater proportion than boys from the active areas. Girls in both areas expected to go into the professions in approximately the same proportion, but girls in the active areas expected to go into the skilled trades and clerical work in greater proportion than girls in the declining areas; the latter expected to go into personal and domestic service in greater proportion.

It appears that rural youth in the plantation areas desire and expect to go into the prestige bearing and comparatively better paid white-collar and skilled occupations in greater proportions than do young people in the nonplantation areas, and especially does this appear to be true of the active plantation areas. This points both to the greater rigidity of Negro society in the plantation areas, and to the greater desire of plantation area youth to escape from the system.

HOW VOCATIONAL CHOICES ARE INFLUENCED

Professional Work

Selection of vocations suggests the immediate influence of certain patterns and the general desire to escape to a new status. "Just want to be professional" is perhaps as far as many rural Negro youth have come toward selecting their future occupation. There was abundant evidence that many of them had not really thought seriously about a particular profession.

Foremost in their minds was simply the desire to escape from the drudgery of farm work which has kept and still keeps them and their families in a perpetual state of poverty. The vocational horizon is limited and their choices in the professional field were made, for the most part, on the basis of precedence in the community. Thus, among the professions, the majority—and particularly the girls—selected teaching because the teacher was usually the best educated Negro in the neighborhood, and the one with the highest status and most regular salary. Youngsters have more direct contact with teachers than any other professionals except, perhaps, preachers whose level of education is generally not to be envied. The social prestige offered by teaching, its relatively great remuneration, and the escape it offers from farm work together with its possible attainability made it attractive for boys and girls of all ages and from all socio-economic levels.

Among those who have selected the teaching profession as their future occupation is Mabel Perry, from Madison County, Alabama. She is 15 years of age and lives with her parents and stepsister on the property of one of the largest nurseries in the world. The Negro families connected with the nursery are said to be more secure economically than most families in that region. Her father is a laborer on the plantation, her mother a laundress. The surroundings of their home are pleasant and cheerful, with well-kept attractive shrubbery to beautify the property. The two girls help in the field and in the home. Mabel picks cotton though she says that she "can't pick much." It appears that Mabel has found her greatest satisfaction in her experience in a comparatively good school; when she compared the school setting with that in which she must live at home, she decided to escape the drabness of home by continuing to remain in school with the hope of becoming a teacher. She says:

> I've been wanting to be a school teacher ever since I started to school. I don't want my husband to farm. I want him to do something else like a school teacher. You can just live better if you have a good job like a teacher. Miss Weems is a teacher and she really lives good.

Even in instances where school work itself is difficult, teaching is selected as a means of escape from the insecurity of farming. Isabelle Holden, who lives in Madison County, Alabama, with sharecropper parents, furnishes such an example. There are ten in her family and the house is overcrowded and inadequately furnished for comfortable living. She is 17 years old, a gangling, awkward girl, extremely self-conscious and ill at ease around companions, especially of the opposite sex. She is obliged to work in the field and is whipped whenever she refuses to do so. Her work at school is difficult for her and often she has been punished because of inability to get her lessons. Nevertheless she says:

> I always did want to be a teacher, even before I started to go to school. I used to play school with other children. I would rather be a teacher than anything I know of. I certainly don't want to work in the field all my life. You either hurt your back picking or you burn up in the sun chopping. I don't know which is the worst.

The girl dislikes farm life and wants to escape from it. She indicates this when she expresses her desire to travel and describes the type of man she hopes to marry.

> I have never been away anywhere real far and I would just like to look over the world. I hope I do some traveling before I marry, because if you marry you just don't seem to get nowhere. I want to marry an educated man so that he would know how to make a living and I would not have to work in the field all my life.

It was interesting to note how many of these young people, in discussing vocations, mentioned their desire to travel and to improve their socio-economic position. It becomes difficult to isolate these two factors because they occur so often together. Amanda Nilson illustrates the desire to escape a depressing social and economic setting through migration. She is 13 years of age and left school five years ago when her mother died. There are nine in the family, and being the oldest, she has unwillingly assumed the role of the deceased parent. Amanda's father is a sharecropper and has been able to provide nothing better than a run-down shack for his children—the floor is littered, the boards insecure. The family appears to live in extreme poverty. Her desire to escape is clearly revealed when she states:

> The only thing I think about, and I think about it a lot, especially at night when everybody is asleep, if I could just save some money and leave from here. I just hate this place and I get so tired of workin' in the field and doing that heavy washing outdoors over the fire. I want to go North. I would like to go to Cincinnati. I have a half-brother up there. I am just so tired of this place. I get so tired of working and these children that sometimes I get real mad and curse everybody, including my father. I just can't help from swearing and cursing when I get mad, real mad. I really worry about it because I do want to go. If it wasn't for papa, I could go. He is the one that really keeps me from going because when I get mad and say I'm going he always tries to show me how much he needs me.

Amanda expresses an occupational preference which reflects the influence of her favorite teacher whom she still remembers from her earlier school days, as well as a desire to escape farming and a precarious economic state.

> I want to be a teacher, too, like Miss Benton. She is so kind and good. She takes time with the children and don't rush like some. She ain't never mean to nobody. I just think it's because she has such a good job and makes such good money that she's so nice. When you have to work in the hot sun farming all day and then never have anything, you just can't feel good. Then, too, I just want to 'mount to something some day.

Next to teaching, the profession most frequently selected by girls was that of nursing. Here, as in the case of those desiring to be teachers, the chief factors behind the choices are found to be mainly a desire for more material wealth, security, and escape. Although professional nurses are rare in the rural areas, a number of the girls selecting this career did so on the basis, apparently, of some personal contact. For instance, 13-year-old Ruby Ruggs, whose father is an electrician in a hospital, has observed the routine and selected her vocation because of what she saw. As she discusses her vocational choice, she appears quite intelligent and serious. The mother desires that her children get an education, but she seems more anxious that they leave

school and get "regular work that will bring them some pay."
Her daughter says, however:

> I don't want to be like mother meant [that is, leave school and
> work]. I don't want to work all the time. I want to be a nurse
> because I like to be around the hospital. Nurses make a lot of
> money too. I want to go to Tuskegee and learn. I want to marry
> a doctor, then we can work together in the hospital. I don't
> want to marry a farmer because that is too hard work. I really
> think I'll be a good nurse if I just get a chance. Mama says it's
> hard work, but it sure is good money in it.

Nursing is also chosen by a 16-year-old Greene County, Georgia,
girl, the seventh of nine children, whose parents own their own
farm and appear to be fairly secure. The family is a closely
organized unit and the parents express great interest in education for the children. This girl selected an auxiliary as well
as a desired vocation, the former to be used if she was not able
to find employment in her desired vocation. Stating this she
says:

> I want to be a nurse. I will study home economics too. I might
> not be able to do what I want to do, so if I have both courses I'm
> sure to get along. Domestic work pays too little for the amount
> of work you have to do.

A case illustrating the influence of community example in the
selection of nursing as a vocation is that of an 18-year-old farm
girl of Greene County. Her family is composed of a mother
and a half-brother. The father's whereabouts is unknown, and
the mother is obliged to work out of the home, forcing the girl
to spend most of her time with an aunt. Her mother has a friend
who is a nurse, and Elizabeth says that she wants to be one, too,
because of this woman she knows. However, she maintains
that she is also interested in nursing because she has patience
with people and enjoys waiting on them.

The majority of the young people who have no community
example to emulate secure inspiration from other less concrete,
but sometimes more romantic, sources. Such is the case of 18-
year-old Marjorie Hyman whose father is a farm manager on
a large plantation. She says:

I want to be a great nurse some day. I have read many stories about nurses and heard a talk on the radio about the profession.

Interest alone appears to be the influential factor in the choice of a 14-year-old Johnston County girl who selected nursing. Reflecting the poor economic status of her family, she says:

I want to finish college and be a nurse, but I may not be able to. It takes money to go to school and we don't have much, but I'm going to try. I just like being around sick people; I like to look after them.

Opportunistic thinking appeared to operate in the decision of 15-year-old Gloria Sweat, who states that she decided upon nursign when she recently learned that a certain lodge had decided to erect a hospital in the county and jobs had been promised to those who would study nursing. Rationalizing her change from teaching to nursing, she says:

My ambition is to become a nurse. I wanted to be a school teacher, but since so many people are school teachers and they don't get much money, I thought that I oughta be something that not so many colored people were in. It seems to me that a nurse can be of service to the race 'cause you certainly don't see so many of them down in these parts.

As the companion occupation to that of nursing selected by the girls, the boys select the profession of medicine, although many are unaware of the training or money required to follow this profession. Such is the situation of George Moore, a 15-year-old Johnston County, North Carolina, lad whose people are farmers who supplement their income by domestic work and carpentry. His family owns their home, however, and they have lived on their land for over forty years, a thing of which they proudly boast. The property is in great need of repair and is isolated from the rest of the community. When asked what he wants to be, George says, "I want to be a doctor so I can help people get well." But he adds:

I would also like to be like God. He can do powerful things. I would make poor people be better off than they are. I would fix it also so colored people would not have to work for white people.

When it was suggested that money and a long period of training would be required to become a doctor, he said, "I guess I won't be a doctor then. I would rather work in a grocery store and be a delivery boy."

Some boys, like Richard Edwards of Greene County, Georgia, who seem superior to many, have thought seriously of medicine as their future vocation. Richard works hard for his father, getting up at four o'clock in the morning to attend to his farm duties. He has seriously planned his future, and says, "I have wanted to be a doctor for two years. The reason, I guess, I think a doctor can do so much." His plans include Fisk University and Meharry Medical College, and he has heard much about both places. He worries a great deal over the fact that he has no money and possibly might not realize his ambitions. He says he dreams constantly of himself as the son of a wealthy man and his most constant worries are over his financial status. He thinks that perhaps he might become an insurance writer, and in this manner obtain the money to attend college.

Ray Hamilton of Madison County, a farm youth of share-cropper parents, wants to become a doctor chiefly for the prestige involved. He states:

> I don't know just exactly what I wants to be when I grow up. I wants to stand for a great point. I wants to be eddicated and stand in a high place and teach others. I wants to be a doctor, because it is a large place. Doctors are just big people. They can get folks around here to do anything; that's why I want to be one. They call you in to ask your advice about everything—I'd like being a doctor more than anything else.

The absence of Negro undertakers in his community made this vocation appear particularly attractive to 19-year-old Herman Bing, who has thought quite seriously of this vocation, even to the point of having obtained information concerning the type and cost of training. The request of a cousin in Cleveland to come and live with him has been refused because of this boy's desire to follow this vocation in his local community.

> I always did say if I could get a trade it would be embalming. There ain't no colored undertakers here. The closest one is

Madison. I reckon I could make money here if I was an under-taker. I wrote to Georgia State College and they said I could take the course for $66. I'll take it if I can find work and pay for it as I go along.

Samuel Green looks upon embalming as something that is easy and offers prestige and money, as is obvious from his com-ment:

I guess I'd like to be most of all a undertaker. Seems like you can make so much money. Mr. Jones, the undertaker in this town, don't do no work at all now. He got people working for him and he just ride around. He got two or three cars, I reckon. The folks around here do anything he say. I think I'd like to be a undertaker more than a doctor, because it don't take you so long to learn it, and you have money and just ride around all the time. You know colored folks believe in spending their money on big funerals. So if you just know how to take care of the dead, you don't never have to worry about money.

Edward Carson's induction into the ministerial field illus-trates the influence of subtle uncontrolled factors. Sometimes in the evening the family would read the Bible and have prayers together. He said:

Daddy mostly read the Bible to us and most every Wednesday we had prayers.

Sometimes daddy led or mamma, or me, or anybody who felt like it. I reckon that's how I got started at preaching.

Edward was 13 years of age when he actually began to preach.

I just got an appointment in a church at Big Creek and stayed there till 'long in '35. I was called to preach when I was 11. Every time I was asleep and got right quiet, I'd just go on off to preachin'. I had visions. Sometimes they was when I was sleep or maybe just when I was quiet I'd see myself leading people or preachin' to them. Sometimes I'd tell my mother about them, but she'd just "shoo" me off and tell me I was playing wid her. When I got my church and began preaching, she was glad.

Most of the preachers are fine and help me along, but some is jealous because I'm young. Sometimes they gets up behind me and tries to tear down what I said. They don't worry me none. I like preachin' and aim to keep right on. I want to get educated so I can be a good one. I'll preach anywhere. It ain't the money I'm worried about. God will give me money if he sees fit and I am worthy.

A combination of experience and incidental methods furnished Edward his training for the ministry.

The only practice I ever got was in church making 'sponses and just talking. I allus was doing something in the church. I was a junior deacon and the junior pastor. My boy friends thought it was fine I was preachin'. They is mostly junior deacons themselves. I been preachin' right along, but I ain't had no church since '35 when I ran away from home to Chicago.

The direct as well as subtle factors which enter into the occupational preferences and choices of these rural youth, their awareness of the type and amount of training required for these fields and the possibility of obtaining such training can perhaps be best revealed by a description of actual occupational choices and the factors influencing their selection. By grouping similar choices it will be possible to see how different influences may operate in the selection of one specific vocation.

Clerical Work

Selection of a clerical occupation offers an escape from agriculture without the necessity for professional training. Those youth who desire clerical jobs made their choices, for the most part, with little enthusiasm or logic. These jobs appeared attractive because of the office setting, imagined remuneration, and possible escape from the area and from farming. Sara Hinton, an 18-year-old girl of Madison County, Alabama, illustrates the uncertain frame of mind of those who select clerical occupations.

I like to type. I guess that's my hobby but I don't know the touch system yet. They teach it at school, and I'm going to take it as soon as I can because I want to be a stenographer. I used to want to be a home economics teacher but I changed my mind when I saw what teachers have to go through. Oh, they have to do so many different kinds of sewing and cooking, and it just took so much time. I plan to take two years college before I stop. I have no idea where I'll get a job, but if I can't be a stenographer I'll just get some kind of office work. I don't like teaching and I don't like farming either. It's too hard working in the hot sun and you have to work too long all day. Office work is easy and I'm going to try to get something to do in one. You don't have to go to school a long time to learn that.

Dora Lewis, a 17-year-old farm girl of Johnston County, stated that she wanted to be a secretary to "some big person like the big insurance men in Durham." Her vocational interests seemed spasmodic but she was interested at the moment in learning how to use the typewriter.

The boys usually select among this group of occupations that of government mail clerk because of the pay and prestige involved. This is one type of public job in which they know Negroes have been employed. Samuel Warren, 18, of Madison County, said, "I want to be a mail clerk because that's a government job and because I will get a good salary." Later, while discussing his wishes, he said, "I wish I was the president of a big high school, had a big farm, and had a bank account."

Of the boys who indicate a desire to work in the field of insurance, the comment of Lonnie Rayford is typical:

I think I'll be an insurance man. I don't think it will be hard to sell 'cause I guess just about everybody wants insurance nowadays. It's real easy work too. All you have to do is just walk around. I think some day I might get to work in a office selling insurance and that will be even easier. You get a lotta money outta it, too, and it really ain't no real work to it at all.

Comments about vocations generally indicated more desire for prestige and security in terms of money and position than direct interest in or knowledge about the vocation. Among those who selected occupations outside the professional fields, there were a number who chose private business as the field of their future vocational activities. The factors behind these choices were similar to those operating in the selection of the professions —wealth, security, and escape from the farm—with the additional factor, perhaps, of the imagined satisfaction to be gained from "being one's own boss" or the importance of having an office and working behind a desk. The business occupations selected tended to be related to community experience more closely than occupations in the professional group. The girls almost unanimously selected beauty culture, while the boys generally selected mail clerk, insurance, and other occupations for which there existed some community precedent for Negroes.

Skilled Work

Roberta Davie, 15 years of age, and Pauline Monroe, 17 years of age, live in Shelby County, Tennessee, and want to become beauticians. Roberta lives in a dilapidated house with her mother. Her father has deserted the family. The mother works irregularly in domestic service and wants her daughter to attend college in order to "get a better type of job." Roberta says, however:

> I'd like to have a beauty shop. I already fix girls' hair. I don't charge them, but if I had a real shop I would. I just think I'd be able to sell at that type of work. Then, too, it isn't hard, and there's good money in it.

Pauline became tired of school and dropped out. Her desire to become a beautician probably reflects as much her attraction for city life, with which she has had some contact, as it does her interest in the work itself. She rationalizes her out-of-school status as follows:

> I wanted to be a beauty culturist and I wasn't learning that in school. I ain't never going back. Miss Elder in Memphis got a shop she's building. She's going to let me come there and work for her and learn me all about beauty culture for nothing. I am to go as soon as the shop is finished. I believe it will make me an independent living, and I won't have to be bothered with trying to go to college so I can be a teacher.

Susie Crawford of Davidson County, Tennessee, is another girl whose desire for city life probably equals her interest in the work as a factor influencing her choice of beauty culture. Her family appears to be an industrious, closely knit group with high ideals about the future education of their 17-year-old daughter. One son is studying in a seminary while two other daughters are attending college. Susie's plans include college, but she inquires, "How long does it take to finish a beauty culture course? Do you think I could make a living out of it?" Susie has a father who drinks and this she resents deeply. It is perhaps a major factor in her desire to leave and go to a large city where she can become independent.

Emmalena Coe, 15, and Lucinda Akins, 16, who also want to be beauticians, are children of Johnston County, North Carolina, farm families. Emmalena's house, though isolated and simple, is clean and well kept. Her people own their home. The mother lived in New York for a short time and constantly expresses her desire to return there because she dislikes farming. The mother, however, wants Emmalena to remain behind when she leaves, in order to attend college. But Emmalena says, "I want to be a beauty culturist, and you really don't need to go to college for that; so I don't know." The mother wishes that she could dissuade her daughter from such an idea. Emmalena, however, likes pretty things and "likes to look at pretty people." If she did this type of work, she continues, she "could help to make people beautiful."

Lucinda's home is not as well kept as Emmalena's and she has to work more and is often accused by her grandmother of being useless about the field work, which she detests. Her home life is uncomfortable because the family is constantly moving, and this is another thing which she does not like. She is very conscious of her shabby appearance, as she reveals when she describes her school life:

> Everybody looks down on you when you don't know much. I used to feel bad about not having the things some of the other children had. I stopped having anything to do with the children who had better clothes than I had and just went around with children that dressed like me. They make you feel the difference because they just go around with children that dress well like they do—and the smart children go around together. It's better to go with people on your own equal.

The desire to improve her own appearance figures greatly in Lucinda's choice.

> I want to graduate from Clayton High. Then I want to take up beauty work. I used to want to be a teacher, but even if you

go to college you may not get a job, so I changed. I want to take a beauty course. Then I could fix up myself and other people too. My aunt in New York has a girl with her who is taking a beauty course. That's just what I want to do. Aunt Lissa says that if I finish high school here, they will try to get me with her sister in New York to take beauty work.

Special mechanical aptitudes and short training periods prompt some youth to select trades as a future vocational career. Many boys indicate a desire to practice trades. Some feel that they have definite aptitudes, like one lad of Coahoma County who says, "I wants to be a carpenter. I kinda got a knack at that kind of work." Phillip Morris wants to be a mechanic because:

It just seems like anything I put my hands on I can do something with it. Sometimes I just take things apart so I can put them together again. No, I ain't never had no lessons, but I don't believe there's a thing I don't know about cars. I sure do want to be a mechanic bad.

Often experience in a given trade is an important factor in occupational choice. The incidental manner in which vocational training is secured and some vocational choices are made is illustrated by the case of 15-year-old Hamilton Ware, who relates his ambitions and experiences as follows:

I might go to A. and T. College and take up the shoe trade. I wonder if they teach you how to make a whole shoe, mend it and all that. I could go in business for myself, but I don't know enough about machines and how to fix them if anything happens to them. I learned the shoe business by working in a shoe store up town. I've been there about four years. I started to shine shoes there and later on the boss taught me how to use the machines and fix shoes. I would like to be a shoemaker.

The girls who want to enter the trades frequently are those who are generally interested in sewing and have usually had some experience in such work in the community. Typical of these is Sadie Menkins of Bolivar County, Mississippi, who says:

I like to do any kind of work, but I like to do sewing best. If I had a machine I could make lots of money. I can make anything. People around here worry me to death asking me to sew for them. I learned at the training school.

Milton Lee, like many others who select the trades, has this to say about it:

> I think I'd like to be a printer more than anything else 'cause you don't have to stay in school so long to learn it. It's good money in it and easy, too. I know a man who has a printing place and he just sets down all day and lets them machines do all the work.

Domestic and Personal Service

Some feel they can find greater security and new experience in certain forms of domestic and personal service. Some wanted the prestige as well as the travel attached to such a job as pullman porter, a traditional occupation for Negroes. One Bolivar County farm youth saw prestige in still another type of job. His uncle is a janitor in one of the large buildings in Chicago, and this boy commented:

> I don't know that I want to stay on the farm. I wouldn't mind being a porter or a janitor in one of those big apartment houses in a big city.

A few of the youth felt that the remuneration for some domestic and personal service occupations is such as to make them attractive. This was the case of one Madison County, Alabama, boy who wanted to be chef in a restaurant, and a Davidson County, Tennessee, girl who wanted to be a charwoman in the post office. The latter comments, "I knew a woman who was a charwoman and she made $60 a month. That's a lotta money." Other reasons given for selecting this type of vocation are expressed by a Madison County girl who says "I want to be a house cleaner because it's the easiest work I know," and a Greene County, Georgia, girl who says she wants to be a cook because "I like to cook and I cook mostly."

Farming

As indicated, few of the youth expected to be farmers and fewer still desired farming, but not all looked with dread upon this occupation. One Coahoma County, Mississippi, boy who wanted to be a doctor said:

I expect I'll end up farming, though. That's all right, though. I'd do it right. First I'd rent a few acres and work it scientifically. Soon as I got a little money I'd start to buy and pretty soon I'd have a pretty fine place. I kinda like farming. I'd enjoy being a big farmer if I had the money. I'd buy a couple hundred acres right here around our house and I'll bet I'd make good. I'd grow nothing but cotton too. I believe I could do all right with it.

Most rural youth, however, though born and reared on farms, have little desire to remain there. This, in many cases, is because of the inherent social and racial discomforts as well as the economic hardship. Jimmie Hill does not like sharecropping:

You jes' can't make anything at it. A man has a better chance if he rents. Then he can manage his own business and it's up to him to get out when he can. They don't even let you see the 'counts, and you know they're cheating you but you can't do a thing about it.

I was with my uncle one time when he was settling, and the white man had cheated him out of pract'ly everything. We told him to go back and tell the man that he thought he had made a mistake in figgering up the settlement. That ole peckerwood scratched his head and said, "Wal, now les' see. They was the time you got this, and then you got this on such and such a day." Well, time he got through figgering again my uncle had to give him back $6.oo of the settlement. I was mad as a hen 'cause the crop wasn't nothing and he sure needed all he could get; but I had to laugh. My uncle jes' said "Yassuh, thank you, suh"; and went on home. They don't let you keep books on 'em, and if you dispute 'em, that's how they do you. But there ain't gonna be no farm for me.

Elmer, who started plowing when he was 12 years old, observed:

I wanted to start bad, but I was sorry I ever had to learn. I started learning and using a turning plow. I plowed in the evening until sundown. No, I don't like to farm; you got to work too hard for nothing. I don't like sharecropping for you don't make any money. The owners take it all, just plain take it. You have to go on your way, too, 'cause they's very few that will correct a mistake when you show it to 'em. Then the agents bother so much. I know a lady got into a argument with an agent, a colored lady on a place, and he made her move off just for arguing with him.

Thirteen-year-old Kelly Dobbs, from a farm family, although he had made no positive occupational choice, very definitely had a negative attitude toward farming. He said:

> I don't know what I want, but I don't want to stay on no farm. I wouldn't mind being a porter or a janitor in one of those big apartment houses in a big city. I got an uncle who does that kind of work in Chicago. But I just don't want to be a farmer.

Lucile Miller made this comment:

> No, I don't want to be a farmer. I don't like all this hard work. It don't matter to me if I never work. I want to be a secretary, where I can sit down and work. Farming is too hard.

This desire to escape the status and drudgery of farming was the unmistakable shadow across the vocational interests and selections and the total occupational attitude of a decided majority of these rural youth. Nevertheless there were some who liked farming and planned to follow this occupation as a career. For one thing, some of the youth felt that their vocational limitations restricted them solely to farming. This attitude was expressed by 17-year-old Alfred Williams, of a farm family.

> I guess I'll be a farmer. That's all I'm 'pared to do. I know everythin' about raisin' a crop, so I guess I'll be around this neck of the woods all the time. I'd like to own me a little piece of land that I could make my crop on every year.

Others felt, likewise, that in a narrow occupational range from which they could choose, farming was preferable. Emma Wesley said, "I would rather be a farmer than a teacher. The children worry you to death if you're a teacher." Another said:

> If we didn't have this farm we couldn't get along. The thing I like about farming is that even if you don't clear nothin' you can always eat. You can get a livin' out of it anyway. I think I'll do farming all my days.

Fourteen-year-old Maude Ware had no plans or ambitions for the future, found complete satisfaction in farming, and thus had never given the question of occupational choice any serious thought:

> I likes farming. I likes to pick cotton. Reckon I picks faster than any of 'em on Mr. Tony's place. I pick close to 200 pounds a day.

There were also those who expressed a desire to do "vocal" farming and give instructions to practicing farmers. The following comment from 18-year-old Harold Marsh expresses the sentiment of a group:

> I would like to be a vocational guidance teacher. I would like to demonstrate to farmers new ideas pertaining to the farm. I would be able to ride around and give advice to other people. I wouldn't want to be a teacher. You got to take too much stuff from the kids. Farming as such is too hard, and then, too, it would be a real help to the farmers. I like to be able to advise them about their farms, but I don't care about doing the farm work.

The Limiting Influence of Racial Stereotypes

In an attempt to gauge the extent to which rural Negro youth felt that racial factors operated to limit their freedom of occupational choice and practice, a checklist of relatively common occupations was submitted to them, with careful instructions to indicate those which they felt Negroes could do as well as whites, those which Negroes could do better, and those which Negroes could not do as well as whites. Generally, the unskilled and low status occupations and the traditional "Negro occupations," such as field hand, porter, singer, farmer, chauffeur, road laborer, or cook were indicated as the occupations which Negroes could do as well or better than whites. These were the occupations which these youth had seen Negroes practice, and for which they felt Negroes had a peculiar aptitude. Moreover, these occupations were or had been sanctioned by the community as open to Negroes. One 12-year-old girl from Davidson County, Tennessee, whose father was a carpenter and whose mother, although not working now, had previously worked as cook, said:

A Negro just makes a better porter than a white person. Some
white people wouldn't wait on a colored person as well as a
colored person would wait on another colored one. When it
comes to farming, white people think they are too good to work
on a farm. Colored chauffeurs are just better than white ones;
and you'll see all rich people with colored chauffeurs. Negroes
are better cooks too. I guess I think that because my mother's
a cook. Ain't no need of colored people thinking about banking.
A colored person can't get a job in a bank because people
wouldn't trust him with money.

From this same area, another girl expressed similar prejudices
concerning the ability of Negroes to perform certain occupations. She believed that many types of jobs filled by whites are
closed to Negroes because they are too lazy and depend too much
upon other people.

I guess that Negroes can do all jobs as well as white people if
given a chance. But now take a banker—I'd rather trust a white
man with my money than a Negro. It just seems to me like
Negroes ain't never had anything, and if they were given a lot
of money they'd probably run away with it. Negroes make better
farmers and cooks than white folk. It just looks like they can
stand more hard work. It just seems to be for a Negro to farm.
I guess maybe it started from slavery times when they were
taught to do this. I guess they know it better. Negroes can
certainly sing better than white people. You've never heard
white folk sing jubilee songs like Negroes can.

Negroes make better laundresses than white folk. White people
always give Negroes all their washing to do. It just seems that
Negroes know how to do it better. When Negroes are washing
and ironing, white people are doing better things. All white
people would rather trust a Negro to drive them. But as to a
lawyer, I'd rather have a white lawyer than a Negro. It seems
that when a case comes up in court a white lawyer's word would
go further than a colored one. A Negro just wouldn't have a
chance against a white lawyer. I prefer white policemen, too.
Negroes would be a "mess." Since they know that they could do
anything they wanted and get away with it, they would kill up
more people. White policemen are mean enough, but Negroes
would be worse. I think I'd rather have a white letter carrier.
It's true that there are colored letter carriers in town, and if you
get one you can trust it's all right, but I think that they might

bother with the mail. It seems to me that Negroes are weaker because they have never had a chance, and if you just give them any job that has too much attached to it, they might go wrong.

SUMMARY

Differences in the various areas as to desired and expected occupations have been treated statistically elsewhere in this chapter. In summary, however, it should be noted that the choices made and the various reasons given reflect the cultural setting of the areas. In the plantation areas of Bolivar, Coahoma, Greene, and Macon counties, the dominating attitude appears to be one of escape from farming with apparently less knowledge of the requirements or possibilities in the chosen fields than was present in the nonplantation areas of Davidson, Johnston, Madison, and Shelby counties. In all areas the occupations chosen tended to be those for which there was some known precedent establishing them as Negro occupations. The proportion desiring to enter already overcrowded professional occupations and trades reflected the desire for security, escape from farming, and for greater material wealth. The girls wanted to be teachers, nurses, beauticians, seamstresses, and occasionally stenographers, and the boys wanted to be doctors, teachers, and undertakers, or to follow one of the traditional trades.

These youth felt the racially restricted situation within which they were compelled to make their choices and responded to it. A basic problem appears to be one of securing further education to increase their training as well as their knowledge of the requirements of the vocations which they desire or expect to follow.

The gap between occupational expectation and reality is at present so great as to suggest that the expectation itself borders on fantasy. Certainly there is a pronounced psychology of escape in the occupations selected, escape from status and from the region itself in many instances. Youth require the stimulation and incentive of intimate and achievable career patterns, but even more important, they require confidence in their social environment.

CHAPTER VIII

ATTITUDES TOWARD SEX
AND MARRIAGE

Sɛx taboos in a culture based upon puritan theology complicate the adjustment of post-pubescent youth. Adolescents of all races in this culture are forced to repress their sex impulses and to accept a complicated system of taboos. The result is that expressions of sex behavior assume an importance wholly unknown in such primitive social orders as those, for example, investigated by Margaret Mead. During the period of adolescence innumerable mental conflicts result when normal biological impulses run counter to our powerful mores. The personality of Negro youth is influenced not only by difficulties which face all American adolescents, but also by peculiar circumstances which arise from the status of the Negro in America.

YOUTH AND SEX

The setting of rural Negro youth in the South has certain special features which have importance for their sex behavior and attitudes. In the first place, the sex mores for a large part of the Negro population are not always consistent with the ideals of the larger society. The rural Negro family as a carrier of the social tradition has been under the handicap of imperfect organization and has had no real opportunity for the full development of rigid sex regulations in terms of the dominant American culture. This deficiency is more a matter of culture than of race, for the African cultures from which the ancestors of these young Negroes came have well-defined and rigidly enforced sex controls, but the African cultures were shattered by the impact of New World conditions of life. At no time in the early history of Negroes in the South was sex in Negroes regarded by the dominant society as much more than a commodity. The slave tradition of breeding carried a certain psychological preparation for reproduction. Sex practice was the means of reproduction and under encouragement by the dominant white society the prowess of the male was developed. Reproduction had no value to the slave but free sex practice was followed as an end in itself; to the white society, reproduction among Negroes, however, had value and free sex practice was therefore tolerated. This traditional attitude survives to some extent in both the white and the Negro societies. In the former it appears in the attitude of tolerance of sexual behavior in Negroes which is at variance with the assumed patterns of the white society, so long as this behavior does not affect or threaten to affect the white world. In the latter it appears in a large margin of tolerance of sex freedom in the mores of the group. One of the most vital indices of Negro family organization and cultural advancement is the change in the sex mores which has occurred since slavery. The development of stricter standards has accompanied the formation of higher social classes within the Negro group.

THE "FOLK NEGRO"

Sex attitudes and behavior take on special significance in the cultural contrast between the "folk Negro" and other social groups within the rural Negro population. Historically, there has been more sex freedom in the "folk Negro" group generally, not only with respect to sex experimentation in youth, but also with respect to the more stable adult relationships. It would thus be expected that the conflict between sex drives and social taboos would be less acute.

In this group sex is not, apparently, an acute problem. In the first place, the greater freedom from the traditional sex controls is rooted in an economy which gives greater weight to the economic than to the romantic factor in family organization. There is less formal marriage and greater freedom of separation. So important is this factor of flexibility in maintaining a balanced economic unit that it has, for this group, become a part of the survival technique itself. In this sense, freedom from the traditional controls of the larger society is an asset. Within this special organization of family life certain forms of sex control do, however, exist. For example, there is less incest than appears in some culturally isolated white groups, there is less homosexuality and other forms of perversion, and there are certain group sanctions which distinguish between types of sex behavior. But the fact remains that taboos relating to extramarital sex relations and sex play in children are less rigid in this group than in other groups of the Negro population.

The living conditions of this group re-enforce its defective cultural inheritance. Most of the families are large, irregular in organization, and poor. Their homes are small, poorly constructed cabins. For the most part, parents and children sleep in the same rooms, and privacy in the exercise of adult sex functions is impossible. Sex play becomes matter-of-fact behavior for the youth, who have little or no access to sound sex instruction. They tend to regard it with the same glamourless interest that attends their observation of animal behavior on the farm. One youth of this group observed casually about his uninhibited sex life, "I ain't never thought of there being anything wrong about it." The mother of one youth, when asked the name of her latest child, said without apparent concern, "Oh, him? His name Willie Jackson. He my baby, my husband ain't had nothing to do with him."

It was observed that many of the youth talked about sex without very much embarrassment; in numbers of instances young boys apparently felt no reticence and discussed sex freely with the women interviewers. A number of the girls discussed details of their sex experience with no more apparent concern than they felt in discussing other personal habits. Sex play in some instances began young—as early as 7 and 8. Sometimes the children were imitating an older couple. In some instances they were of different ages and the older child would be the initiator. The ages most frequently mentioned for beginning this sex play were 12 to 14.

In a social situation that does not rigidly censure common-law marriage among adults, a moderate emphasis on restraints for the children would perhaps be expected. The frequency with which the youth mentioned having sex experiences around home, in the field, at school, and in familiar local rendezvous suggests that parents more or less accepted it as likely and probable. In some instances apprehension on the part of the parents was noted regarding girls, but this concerned their having babies that would not be supported by the fathers during the non-productive period of infancy and early childhood. In some other cases the parents were suspected by the children of objecting to sexual freedom although they had not warned them specifically against it.

In still other instances there was awareness that sexual freedom resulting in pregnancy was a violation of the new standards to which the group was being introduced, but no actual social inconvenience was experienced as a result of the censure of the group. For example, Savola Carter, an 18-year-old daughter in a tenant farm family, in explaining why she was not attending school mentioned, incidentally, that she had no one to take care of her baby. She said:

> I was going with a boy and he got me in trouble last year. He ain't no bad boy, he's pretty nice. We was in love and just couldn't wait to get married. I wanted to finish school here before I got married and maybe teach over at Boyle or somewhere. I thought a heap of that boy. He's living out here in the county now, working with his papa. His name is Connie Sims. Well, we just got caught, that's all. At least I was the one that got caught. I had to quit school. My baby is 6 months old now. I'll tell you the truth, I still loves Connie. He comes over to see me and treats me and the baby nice. We wants to get married soon's he can make a little more money.

Savola's recreation has changed with the coming of the baby. Once she went out occasionally to places where the young people could dance and amuse themselves. Now she is limited in her recreation to the church and Sunday school. She teaches the small children in the Sunday school when the regular teacher is absent, and sometimes sings in the choir. Her mother's chief complaint about Savola's having the child was economic; her husband had been away for over two years and sent little money for the support of the six children in the family. She said,

"Savola, she had to go get herself in family way and that meant one more mouth to feed."

Sex attitudes are linked in the mores of the group with the belief that continence is responsible for certain illnesses and "poor health" in girls and women; that in some way "soon's they get a man they be all right." These youth are blocked off from most of the avenues of approved self-expression. They live in a limited cultural world, with few patterns for emulation or stimulation. In their play groups they frequently use sex experience and prowess as a means of attaining status. This is a type of activity unchallenged by the white world. One of these boys, dull in school, ungainly in appearance, and living on a hopelessly low economic plane, when interviewed, was hesitant, slow, and indifferent in most matters. When sex was mentioned he brightened up, and his entire attitude changed as he strove to report his sexual prowess. Many of the phrases and allusions of gang conversation appear to attach high value to accomplishments in this line. The conversational game referred to in Chapter VI under the name of "The Dozens" is a further index to the wide limits of sex tolerance. This game taxes the imagination of the youth in imputing fantastic excesses of sexual indulgence to the mother of the boy who is "put in the dozens." A boy may give warning that he does not "play the dozens." Middle-class Negro boys do not indulge in this sport, and the upper-class boys are revolted by it.

The attitudes of these youth regarding sex can best be represented in their own words. One young cotton picker of unusual skill exhibits an apparently equivocal position in his personal sex code. He does not believe in common-law marriage, for example, although he "knows heaps of people around here who do it." The people in the community, he says, don't bother about it. But he justifies premarital sex relations on the grounds that "we all do it." He would marry a girl who had had sex experiences, but not one "who had a name for it." He does not approve of "chasing after a heap of women," but he thinks it is all right to have a "regular girl." He would marry her if any compromising consequences developed, because he would only "mess with" a girl he was willing to marry.

MIDDLE-CLASS YOUTH

It is not possible either to draw a sharp line between the social groups of the rural Negro population, or to determine by the social group what the sex behavior will be. There are, however, attitudes with regard to sex in the group with more advanced economic and cultural standards, which are not so conspicuous in the "folk Negro." Among middle-class youth there is considerable sex play, but there is also some recognition of the social censure of this behavior and increased fear of social consequences. For example, there is a disposition to make a sharper distinction between "nice girls" and "girls who run around," and more rigid moral standards are applied to girls whom middle-class boys expect to marry. One youth explained:

> We go 'round with girls after Sunday school on Sunday. We boys ride out on our bicycles to their houses if their mothers don't care. I like a girl that is about my equal, that is in age, school, and things like that. I wouldn't go off with a girl that didn't go to church. But I wouldn't have a bad girl. A bad girl is anybody's girl.

Another 17-year-old youth, in discussing his sex activities, gave a similar indication of discrimination between girls. He said:

> Most all the girls like me and like to dance with me. There are some that I run around with and can do anything to. And there are some who won't let you mess with them. I don't mess with girls I go with because they are nice girls, and I don't believe it's nice to bother nice girls.

A boy of 15 who had referred to experiences with girls made this observation:

> The girl I go with is a real nice girl and still goes to school. She's the kind of girl I'd like to marry, but I don't know if I'd marry her or not. She may go off to school and might not come back.

The girls of this group who engage in sex play have two important concerns. One is that they might become pregnant, and another is that they might be talked about. It was noted that in most of the areas cheap devices for preventing conception were in use. In Madison County, Alabama, for example, it was discovered that there were men peddling these devices to the school boys.

The intensity of concern about biological and social consequences is another mark of distinction between this group and the "folk Negro." One rather intelligent 16-year-old boy in Macon County, Alabama, who had begun his sex life at the age of 14, expressed this concern.

> Sometimes I get scared that something might happen, and I won't be able to finish school. I guess I would run away if I got into any trouble with any girl.

A seventh-grade girl in the same county showed a similar fear. She said, "I don't want no one to fool or ruin me. Having a baby would kill me."

Information on venereal diseases, taught in the school, is also a deterrent. An eighth-grade Johnston County, North Carolina, girl reflects this type of fear in her comment:

> I'm not going to get myself in trouble that way. That's how people get the bad disease like syphilis. One teacher in our club in school told us about that. It eats up your body and makes your skin peel off. So I don't fool with boys. It's all right after you get married.

The success of parental instruction in sex matters appears in numerous reported experiences of these youth, particularly among the girls. A tenth-grade Madison County girl, in discussing her relations with her boy friends, said:

> David is my boy friend. I really don't know so much about him. I just started going with him two or three weeks before school closed. He's mostly just a friend too. I have had lots of boy friends, but Walter is the only one I really went with. My sister didn't like Walter's ways and he had some kind of breaking out on his face, so I just let him go. I get a goodnight kiss from David once in a while, but sometimes not that. I have never been in contact [sexually] with boys. Mother always told us not to let boys make a fool out of us and to wait until we were

married before we have anything like that to do with a boy. I believe if I lost my head and did anything like that I would kill myself. If I didn't I guess my brothers would kill me and Clinton, too. Clinton is just like one of the family; he tells us what to do and what boys say about girls and not to let them fool with us.

UPPER-CLASS YOUTH

Among upper-class girls active sex experience usually does not occur before marriage. With the exception of this group, sex experience among rural Negro youth seems, in general, to begin at about the age of 14. Boys in the upper class appear to be the only boys who feel that extramarital sex relations are wrong. A major characteristic of upper-class families is a rigid moral code. In many cases this is accompanied by strong parental admonitions and attempts to keep the boy from contacts which might lead to a breach of the sex code of this class. With few exceptions, girls at all levels give verbal allegiance to the idea of premarital chastity. Boys believe in it—for girls. However, only in upper-class families do the boys apply the moral code to themselves. In some cases upper-class boys abstain completely from sex relations, and in general they are restrained from sex activity by "moral scruples" or by fear of consequences. Some of them feel that girls will interfere with their education, work, or career.

Girls from upper- and middle-class families usually express puritanical views about sex. In addition to having the advantages of superior instruction and high social standards to maintain, they are subjected to much more careful family supervision. While young lower-class girls are frequently not allowed to go out at night, in upper-class families such restrictions are often applied to older girls as well. Marie Harper, a 16-year-old girl whose parents are community leaders in Johnston County, reported:

Yes, I have a boy friend. He calls on me and takes me to socials. Sometimes mama lets me go to movies with him in the afternoon, but if he goes with me at night papa and mama go too.

With reference to sex relations, Marie said:

> Yes, I know lots of girls do, but I just haven't wanted to. It's
> not that I'm afraid. I just think it's something you enjoy more
> if you wait until you are married. Mama and I talk about that
> a lot, and she says that it is the thing to do—wait until you're
> married. I can't say what the other girls I go with do. All I can
> say is what they tell me, and they claim they don't.

Marie felt that girls who have illegitimate children should be
ostracized, although she felt that no stigma should attach to the
child.

> Girls that have babies and aren't married shouldn't be allowed
> to associate with girls who live right. There are two or three
> girls at school who had babies and the principal let them back
> into school. Some don't have enough nerve to come back, but
> the ones that do play basketball and do what the rest do. I
> don't think they should be allowed to.

CHANGING SEX MORES

In general, sex attitudes of rural Negro youth and those of
white youth appear to be rapidly approaching each other. In
the Negro group there has been a large increase in the rigidity
of sex standards with some increase in the restraints on actual
sex experience, while at the same time in the white group there
has been a relaxing to some extent of the restraints in sex experience. As a result, girls of both groups have attitudes which evidence disapproval of extramarital sex relations, a strong fear
of consequences, and more actual sex experience than the codes
condone. Boys of both groups have the same nominal standards
for sex conduct as girls, but in practice these standards apply
with greater force to women than to men.

WHEN SEX ACTIVITY BEGINS

Active sex experience among rural Negro youth seems to begin about the age of 14. Girls' statements are somewhat vague,
but girls younger than 14 show little interest in or familiarity
with sex. Among boys the division is sharper. Boys of 12 and
13 express little interest in girls and usually say that they have

not had sex relations. Boys of 14 may express indifference, but most of the boys of this age admitted having had such experience.

The older boys refer to sex experiences beginning at the age of 12 or younger. Sex play between children of 6 to 8 years is not uncommon, and active relations may occur at 12 or 13. These early experiences are somewhat casual. It is likely that the 12- and 13-year-old boys interviewed had had such experiences, but were rather confused and did not mention it. With older boys, embarrassment about girls more often gave way to a pride in sexual prowess and a feeling that having intercourse is a necessary, proper, and usual thing. Variations in sex experience differentiate youth at different social levels. In the lowest socio-economic class sex experience may start earlier, intercourse occurs more frequently, and discussion of sex is franker.

SEX BEHAVIOR AND SOURCES OF INFORMATION

Boys acquire sex information principally from the talk of contemporaries and older boys. Most of them are unable to recall exactly how sex information was acquired. In a few cases information was supplemented by books or instruction in school:

> I first learned about girls when I was 11 years old in school. I learned some things from these boys and my older brother. One professor over at school called all the boys together. He said that a boy ought to use a girl in the right way. He ought not to mess up a girl. He [the teacher] saw some of the fellows with a magazine called *Pop Eye* [a cheap magazine describing various techniques of sexual intercourse].

Girls in families that are more stable and advanced culturally are usually warned by parents against having sex relations. Mothers usually give the girls instructions on the care of themselves during menstruation.

> When my monthly periods began, mama told me not to be around boys, because boys draw lightning. She told me not to get wet or get cold and hot and be careful of myself.

Mothers frequently couch their instructions in terms calculated to frighten the girl from any thought of sex relations:

> Mama just said I was old enough to know how to act and to be careful with myself. She pointed out some girls she didn't want me to be like. They were young girls who were not married and had children.

Some of the girls, and particularly the younger ones, seemed ignorant about sex. A 13-year-old farm girl in Greene County, Georgia, stated that she had never heard where babies came from but "she figured the doctor brought them." This girl has observed sex play between her 15-year-old cousin and a boy friend. She peeped and laughed, but had no desire to experiment with it. She had been given no instruction regarding sex or menstruation.

Girls also acquire information about sex from friends, although this source is not so important for girls as for boys. One 12-year-old girl, for instance, was told by some of her friends how babies come and she realized that they were telling her the truth. Her mother had never talked to her about relations with boys.

Another girl said:

> My grandmother said an old lady brings them to the mother. But I do know where babies come from, for a girl told me that the mother has to have something to do with the father and then it starts the baby. I hear girls and boys say the baby comes by the mother. Then, my mother told me not to have nothing like that to do with boys because I might get a baby.

Social Diseases

Although contraceptive devices are frequently used by rural Negro youth, the rates for syphilis and other venereal diseases are high. Several of the youth interviewed had had venereal infections. Owing to absence of facilities for treatment, the death rate from venereal disease among Negroes is comparatively high. If syphilis mortality only is considered (omitting general peresis and gonococcus infections), the rate for Negroes was 289 per 10,000 deaths in 1935,[1] over five times the rate for whites

[1] *Mortality Statistics, 1935* (Washington: U. S. Bureau of the Census, 1937).

(52.2 per 10,000 deaths). Mortality from syphilis in the age range from 15 to 29 shows a similar ratio (Negroes, 240.7; whites, 52.9). The rates are also about the same if only rural areas are considered.

Information about prophylaxis in venereal disease has not yet reached Negroes in rural areas. Once a venereal disease is contracted, the probability of mortality is undoubtedly higher among rural Negroes than among any other group. The urban syphilis death rate among Negroes is higher than the rural rate, but this is due to the greater frequency of infections in urban areas. The fact that 2 out of every 100 deaths among rural Negroes are due to syphilis (a preventable and curable disease) indicates the urgent need for development of health services in these areas.

YOUTH AND MARRIAGE

Despite considerable laxity in their own sex standards, boys demand a high moral level in their prospective wives. A few of them said they "might" marry the girl with whom they were having relations at the time. Some said they did not expect their wives to be virgins, but on the whole they did not seem to want for a wife a girl who "ran around." The prospective wife's behavior is as important as her appearance. Of the boys reached in the tests and interviews, 21.3 per cent mentioned beauty, youth, good looks, or some similar quality in the preferred mate. About the same proportion (19.3 per cent) said they wished to marry a "nice," or "decent" girl. Next to appearance and respectability, the most frequently preferred quality in a future wife was education or intelligence ("good sense"). These qualities were mentioned by 18.7 per cent of the boys. A typical picture of the preferred mate is that of a 16-year-old boy in Johnston County, North Carolina. He is the son of a sharecropper.

> I would like to marry a girl who had plenty of sense. I wouldn't mind if she danced, but I don't want her to cuss, drink, or chew snuff. I wouldn't want to get one who is too ugly. I wish she had an education; then she could do things I couldn't do. I could help her to do things she couldn't do.

Economic Security

The rural Negro girl is beginning to revolt against her traditional position as principal bearer of the family burdens. The demand for a husband "who will support me" is constantly repeated. There is a particular aversion to the drudgery of farm life. Farmers are frequently mentioned as undesirable husbands. So frequent are such statements that it might appear that the Negro farmer today must make a strenuous search to find a wife willing to assume the burdens of a sharecropper's "helpmate." Many of these girls will inevitably marry farmers but few seemed pleased by such a prospect:

> I don't want to be no farmer's wife. You have to work too much in the hot sun. I don't like to work in the sun. I want my husband to work in town or something like that. I don't want as many children as my mother's got. Two or three will be plenty for me.

> I'd marry, or like to marry, a nice boy that likes to work and won't fuss. I just want him to be nice and to be tall and dark. Darker than me. I'd just like for him to be that way. I don't want him to farm. I want him to do something else like a school teacher.

Among the qualities preferred in their mates, rural girls generally place wealth-getting ability above appearance. Another qualification frequently commended was education, which was mentioned by 21.2 per cent of the girls. Next in frequency (15.9 per cent) was preference for a man in some profession, usually teaching or medicine. Together these accounted for over one-third of the choices. In the rural Negro community, economic security is associated with education and professional occupations. The interviews indicate that these qualities are emphasized by girls for their economic values:

> I'm going to marry some day—a doctor, I guess. They make money and I'd have a house that's fine.

> I'd want a husband who worked steady and looked after home affairs. He'd have to be educated. I wouldn't marry a man who had less education than I have and I'd want him to have more,

but he would not have to be a college fellow. They think they are better than anyone else and they ought to think so too. I wouldn't have a drunkard for a husband nor a loafer. Looks don't matter so much; looks don't get it nowadays; it's what you know and how much money you can make that counts.

The emphasis of the girls in choosing a mate is practical. Only 7.9 per cent of the girls mentioned good looks, youth, or beauty as preferred qualities in the husband. These were the qualities most frequently mentioned by boys. On the other hand, 17.6 per cent mentioned wealth as the primary characteristic of the preferred mate. One of the three primarily economic qualifications (education, a profession, or wealth) was thus mentioned by more than half of the girls.

The emphasis on economic success is strongest among girls of the middle and upper classes. Of 125 girls whose fathers were in white-collar and skilled occupations, 55.4 per cent preferred husbands with education, a profession, or wealth. For these girls, wealth was most frequently mentioned (by 24 per cent of the girls). Of the girls whose fathers were farmers 63.2 per cent checked one of the three primarily economic categories. On the other hand, good looks, youth, and so forth, were mentioned by only 3.2 per cent of the girls whose fathers were in white-collar or skilled occupations, while the proportions for daughters of farmers was 7.2 per cent. Girls with fathers in semiskilled or unskilled occupations showed marital preferences similar to those of the daughters of farmers.

The marital requirements of girls in lower-class families are less exacting than those of girls from upper-class families. The principal demand of these girls is that their prospective husbands should have a job and that marriage should not be undertaken with the irresponsibility characteristic of destitute men. The interviews reveal a desire to avoid the disadvantages of marriage with which the subjects are personally familiar:

I wouldn't marry a man that was too rich or he'd be lazy and wouldn't work and I wouldn't marry one too poor 'cause then you couldn't eat. I want him to have a job and work and give me his money for food and clothes for the children. I just would not have a man who drinks. They get mean. Both my father and stepfather drink, but not enough to hurt people, but it just ain't right to drink. I wouldn't want a man who would be accusing me of doings I hadn't done. Some men accuse their wives of courting. By that, I mean going with other men. My husband must be tall and brown-skin. I don't want no black husband and he must be neat and clean and go to church and Sunday school weekly.

Appearance

Lower-class girls were more apt to emphasize appearance than were girls from upper-class families. A typical statement of an upper-class girl ("Oh, looks don't matter so much . . . it's what you know and how much money you can make . . .") has already been quoted. Lower-class girls may specify skin color, or height, or merely say that their future husband must be "nice looking." The preferred skin color is brown. A number of the statements already quoted mention this color. A few girls wish husbands darker than themselves, although none wished one who was "black." Girls also seem to avoid husbands with very light skin. A common feeling within the Negro group is that light-colored men are undependable and do not work as hard as men with darker skin. Color preferences in the interviews are borne out by the results of the Color Ratings Test. In responding to this test, the girls most often mentioned brown and light-brown as the skin color of the handsomest boy they knew, and black (and to some extent, dark-brown, yellow, and white) as the color of the ugliest boy they knew. The results of this test are treated more fully in Chapter X.

FAMILY EXPERIENCES AND MARRIAGE

Unfortunate marital experiences in the families of rural girls frequently result in unfavorable attitudes toward marriage. Some girls emphasized unfortunate marital experience in their own families in explanation of their extremely cautious, and sometimes negative, attitude toward marriage:

I would hate to get married and have a lot of children and later be left by my husband. That's what my father did to my mother, so I'm going to try and be careful. That's why I don't want to marry.

Mama doesn't want us to marry; not even my brother who married and now lives in Arkansas. I reckon I'm afraid of marriage anyhow 'cause most of them around here turn out so badly and so terrible.

The sight of mothers worn out by overwork and too much child-bearing acts as a powerful deterrent to hasty marriage:

> I never want to have as many children as my mother did. I wouldn't mind having about two maybe. One thing my mother worked too hard. She had too many children and she liked chickens and her garden and things and she just tried to do everything herself. Her dying affected my going to school some because I said if I could get the little ones to go to school I'd get along.

> I want to marry somebody who can make me a good living because I don't want to work for someone who can't support himself. I don't want a husband who argues all the time and gets drunk. When I do marry I don't want more than two or three children because if I had more I couldn't take care of them like they should be. If I had some money right now, there's so much I'd like to do for these children around the house.

COMMON-LAW MARRIAGE

A part of the general revolt against conditions of married life in lower-class families is the antipathy expressed toward common-law marriage. In the past such relations have been perfectly acceptable in rural areas (and, to some degree, in urban areas also). In contrast with community indifference to nonobservance of the legal formalities of marriage, the girls are outspoken in condemning it:

> I don't think it a bit right to live with a man and not be married to him. That is a sin. Plenty people right here in Selma do that. They make believe they are married, but they aren't.

> It is wrong to live with a man until you are married. I know some people around here what do and pretend they be married. Well, that is wrong and God puts a curse on people what do things like that.

> It don't look well for a man and woman to live together if they ain't married and people talk about them too. All the folks around here what lives with men is married.

Very few boys had opinions about common-law marriage, but those who did expressed opposition to the practice.

I just don't think it is right. If a man is going to live with a woman it's no more than right that he marry her. I know a heap of people around that do it but I wouldn't. They are sometimes people I know, but I can't hold any respect for them. People in the community don't bother about it. They think it is okay except when they are in church. The same people would talk out against folks not married living together in the church, but wouldn't say anything against it outside. I don't think it's right to do that. I got a girl and I would marry her. The girl I marry must be well thought of, nice around home, not so much in dress, but neat and careful of herself. I don't think I'd marry a girl who smokes or drinks.

MARRIAGE AND CAREERS

Girls at higher economic levels are less concerned about the morals of prospective husbands and their ability to support a wife. They take these things for granted and demand, in addition, education and an income sufficient to provide comforts and luxuries beyond mere subsistence. In some cases, these girls are concerned about careers for themselves and disinclined toward the dubious advantages of matrimony:

I feel like this—I want to accomplish something in life. Life is given to us to do something with aside from getting married. If you spend time talking to boys, they will get in your way and the time you spend talking to boys you can be doing something to help yourself. It's all right if a person has getting married in mind, but I think it's a waste of time to spend money, your good money, to go to college and to prepare yourself to do something and then come out and get married. I want to go to college and get my education and do something with it.

SUMMARY

The whole trend of rural Negro youth is towards stricter sex standards and a more stable family life. Sex standards, while verbally at a higher level than formerly, are frequently disregarded in practice. Sexual promiscuity is fairly common in the lower classes, although it is not regarded by youth with the complacency typical of older generations of rural Negroes.

In expressing marital preferences, boys are as much concerned about the behavior as about the personal appearance of their future wives. Undesirable characteristics in a wife are drinking, smoking, cussing, and "running around."

Girls in lower-class families are principally concerned with securing husbands able to maintain a more stable family life than that to which they are accustomed. They are in revolt against community toleration of common-law marriage and of desertion, and of easy, irresponsible separations. They wish to avoid the large families and hard work which their mothers have been forced to bear. Rural Negro girls are no longer willing to suffer the disadvantages of rearing large families, of being the family's major wage earner, of working in the fields as a farm hand, of putting up with drunken and shiftless husbands.

Girls of upper-class families do not ask for the things specified by lower-class girls since these things are taken for granted in the higher income groups. Upper-class girls demand more than mere ability to support a wife. They expect to marry well-educated professional men, with substantial incomes.

CHAPTER IX

INTRARACE ATTITUDES

THE ATTITUDES expressed by Negro youth toward other Negroes and toward themselves as members of a racial minority group may be regarded as a further index to social and emotional security. All individuals seek identification with some group for the benefits which such identification can contribute to their status and prestige. In the South the prestige of the Negro group suffers from persistently unfavorable judgments on the part of the white community; of equal significance is the fact that Negro youth do not as a rule take pride in the qualities for which Negroes are most appreciated by the whites. Only a few of them, for example, recognize loyalty, uncomplaining industry, and patience as having racial prestige value comparable to the importance given these traits by the white group when they wish to speak favorably of Negroes. It is a convenience in the biracial situation to be regarded as loyal, tractable, happy, and hard working; few of the interviews with these youth revealed, however, that they were proud of these racial virtues. Indeed, few of the comments assumed these virtues to be racial, or the qualities to be virtues.

Some of the youth recognized a racial contribution in a special type of music and, in theory, the importance of Negro labor to the support of the dominant agriculture of the South. Those who saw these values objectively, however, were usually the ones farthest removed from the source of such contributions. There was little indication in the communities that there was anything in their racial past from which they could draw prestige or anything of unique prestige value to which they could aspire in the future as a racial group.

INFLUENCE OF DOMINANT CONCEPTS

To a very large degree, the development of race pride has been limited by the biracial system. As in the case of color values, noted in Chapter X, self-estimates by the Negro are profoundly influenced by the attitudes of the white community. To use an extreme example, Denmark Vesey, a Negro who resisted slavery and led an insurrection in the effort to throw off the oppression, is a type which contradicts the assumption that Negroes are innately docile as a race and were content with slavery. In a sense, Vesey represents the spirit of independence for which the founding fathers of America are praised—an insurrection is merely an unsuccessful revolution. But Denmark Vesey is a symbol of a spirit too violent to be acceptable to the white community. There are no Negro schools named for him, and it would be extremely poor taste and bad judgment for the Negroes to take any pride in his courage and philosophy. There is, indeed, little chance for Negro youth to know about him at all.

The personality of the southern rural Negro is to a large extent organized around values outside his own racial group. The "center of gravity" is outside the race, a circumstance for which the long adventitious role of the Negro has been responsible. The behavior and reputation of the Negro mass, particularly the lower-middle and lower classes, can definitely militate against the attainment of status or success by an individual Negro. The white community throws all classes of the Negro population together; this assumption of the physical and cultural uniformity of Negroes all too easily retards the progress of aspiring Negro youth. So heavy is the weight of this cultural backwardness on the individual seeking recognition that he frequently tries to elevate his own status by criticizing the censurable qualities of the mass rather than by showing pride in his minority group. In fact, among the rural Negroes there appears to be more group loyalty than group pride. Group loyalty, fellow-feeling, and a disposition to defend the group against external criticism appear to spring more from consciousness of a common lot when faced with outside coercion than from the pride of the individual in the merits of this group.

RACIAL IDEOLOGIES

The one outstanding example of articulated racial ideology affecting southern Negroes was the Garvey Back-to-Africa Movement.[1] This, however, was essentially an escape device. An incidental but significant feature of this movement was the attempt to impute new and attractive meanings to blackness to rid Negro psychology in general of the unfortunate emotional connotations of blackness. This movement sought further to provide for these Negroes such needed symbols of status as are gained through titles, uniforms, high-sounding offices, and conspicuous group ownership of the tools of trade and commerce. The movement failed, but while it lasted it served an important psychological need. The motivation of the movement, however, was never formulated in terms of a philosophy and when the excitement abated the individuals lost themselves in the problems of personal adjustment to their environment.

There have been large scale migrations of Negroes from South to North, in the course of which racial sentiments favorable to these mass movements were generated. The migration of 1916 to 1920 in particular reached a high point of racial self-concern, in which the escape motive was dominant. Large groups of southern Negroes acting together under the stimulation of crowd hysteria abandoned their homes suddenly and moved North not so much as workers seeking improved economic opportunity, but as a self-conscious race escaping oppression.

PATTERNS FOR EMULATION

Rural Negro youth have been limited in their contacts and access to the outside world; in most instances they do not know of any major contributions by Negroes or of any prominent Negroes of whom they can be proud in any sense comparable to the knowledge available to white youth for building race pride. In the course of the testing of these youth regarding their knowledge of types of work that could be performed by Negroes, many did not believe that Negroes could be lawyers, bankers, pharmacists, skilled mechanics, engineers, or artists, because they had neither seen nor heard of a Negro in these roles. Again, in

---

[1] In 1917 Marcus Garvey, originally from the West Indies, organized the Universal Negro Improvement Association to restore Africa to the Africans. Over 1,000,000 American Negroes contributed funds, but the movement was impracticable and Garvey was finally arrested for using the mails to defraud.

response to the question, "Whom would you like to be like?" only 17 per cent of the boys and 6.4 per cent of the girls mentioned a famous Negro. On the other hand, 12.1 per cent of the boys mentioned some white historical character, and 5.1 per cent mentioned wealthy or prominent white persons (such as Henry Ford, John D. Rockefeller). The largest number of boys (20.7 per cent), in evidence of limited patterns, mentioned casual relatives of about their own status as persons whom they would most like to emulate.

One youth, in appraising the relative racial aptitudes, said:

> Colored people can do farming better than white people because they will stick to the work no matter how hot the weather becomes. They don't have other things on their minds as white people do. The colored people can stand the weather better than the white people. White folks make better storekeepers than colored. Most colored stores I know anything about ain't kept as clean as stores run by white men, and so the colored people don't get as much trade. White men are able to be better lawyers than colored because in the first place they have a better opportunity for education as soon as they start school, and they have the money to get the schooling to be lawyers. I never seen a colored lawyer.

Another youth in Madison County was less discriminating in his judgment. He said:

> Colored folks have as good a chance as white folks, but some of the colored folks don't have sense enough to have nothing or keep nothing. Whenever they get a little money or anything they go and drink it up. Some white folks does that too, but it's more colored.

This youth is expressing a type of generalized resentment against a certain class of Negroes which is not uncommon in the rural areas. His estimate is obviously exaggerated, but the overstatement itself is an interesting symptom of the state of mind provoking it. Actually, these youth appear more often to be class conscious than race conscious. When the question of race pride was raised in the interviews, they had the greatest difficulty in formulating an answer, as if this subject were one farthest from their minds.

Recently, however, there have been indications of pride in one type of racial hero who symbolizes certain qualities and a degree of success which compel public admiration. This new hero is the Negro athlete. Prize fights and, in a few instances, track events have been so widely discussed that the news has penetrated the rural areas. Eleven per cent of the boys in the group studied, in telling whom they would like to be like, mentioned Joe Louis, Henry Armstrong, Jesse Owens, or some such well-known Negro athlete. This racial superiority in the field of athletics has contributed more to race pride than any other single factor in recent years. Admiration of the prowess of Negro athletes in the prize ring, indeed, provides other incidental and vicarious satisfactions. These youth, who cannot resent insults, or pit their strength fairly with that of white youth, or resist malicious aggression without incurring the danger of wholesale reprisals from the white community, are more than normally thrilled and vindicated when the special racial handicap is removed and a Negro reveals his superior physical quality. In a few areas of the South, the disposition of Negro youth to celebrate too jubilantly the fistic triumphs of Joe Louis has been brusquely and sometimes violently discouraged, indicating that the symbolism was as significant for the white as for Negro youth.

RACE PRIDE AND EDUCATION

Race pride is most pronounced among youth who are advanced in education and sophistication. Frequently these young people are seeking to justify their claims to recognition in terms of past or potential contributions of Negroes to American and world civilization. For rural Negro youth in general, the sources of information and inspiration are all too meager—even for those who can and do read. School texts, which have been prepared primarily for white youth, give little attention to Negro characters or to anything else on which race pride might be based. The assumption is, presumably, that Negro youth will form their principles from acquaintance with exemplary characters of American life and history as other American children do, even while they are acutely conscious that their actual roles are limited and the white patterns of success are for them essentially meaningless. It is only when the horizon of life has been extended to include a wider range of experience that new estimates of racial worth are possible.

ATTITUDES REVEALED BY TESTS

The following tabulation shows the responses of these southern rural Negro youth to selected statements. These responses indicate, for the most part, unfavorable attitudes toward Negroes as a group.

TABLE 14

JUDGMENTS OF RURAL NEGRO YOUTH ABOUT THEIR OWN RACE, BY SEX[a]

As Indicated by Proportions Responding "True" to Statements on Race Attitudes Scale

Statement	Percentage Responding "True"	
	Boys	Girls
Negro doctors are just about as good as other doctors.	92.0	94.0
Only a few Negroes become famous, but a large number would if given a chance.	85.0	84.6
Negroes are always fighting and cutting each other up.	83.2	79.3
Negroes will take strangers in.	80.0	84.6
Negroes drink too much.	71.1	70.7
It's harder to work for a Negro than for anyone else.	62.9	60.5
Negroes are more interested than other people in getting an education.	48.6	53.6
If you don't know who committed a crime, you always bet it was a Negro.	41.4	42.6
Negroes are cowards.	28.7	32.0
Negroes are the meanest people in the world.	12.5	11.8

[a] Based on responses of 833 boys and 1,402 girls

There is an interesting inconsistency in these responses. On the one hand, there is criticism of the disorderly behavior of the lower-class Negro, particularly with respect to fighting and drinking. There is, also, strong indication of preference for white over Negro employers. On the other hand, there is recognition of the barriers to distinction, and there is confidence in the ability of Negro doctors. In this respect Negro youth are more liberal in their judgment than older rural Negroes, who have not yet developed full confidence in Negro doctors.

The sensitiveness among the youth regarding the disorderly behavior of the larger Negro group is reflected in their response to the statement "Negroes are always fighting and cutting each other up." This was endorsed as true by 83.2 per cent of the boys and 79.3 per cent of the girls. A similarly high proportion of boys and girls checked the statement "Negroes drink too much." The young people who amplified these unfavorable responses with further comment show the effects of their isolation within the Negro world. Their comparisons of Negroes with whites reveal the fact that they are unacquainted with the intimate life of the whites and probably exaggerate the difference on the basis of this inadequate knowledge. One of them said:

> Colored people get a little money and don't keep it, but most whites don't throw their money around like colored does. Everywhere you go it's going to be someone don't act right. You hardly ever hear anything about white ones acting up at their picnics and things. Colored can do as much as white folks if they had sense and knowed how to act.

A casual observer might suppose that at least one basis of racial pride would be the business establishments started by enterprizing Negroes, but curiously this factor often operates in just the reverse manner. The intense struggle of the small Negro entrepreneur with his limited funds, in competition with larger and stronger businesses, often results in failure or at best in limited success in comparison with the flourishing white establishments, and in the end has an unfortunate effect upon Negro youth, who cannot see the larger factors operating in this competition. They tend to attribute the difficulty to weaknesses in Negro qualities. One 15-year-old boy in Coahoma County, Mississippi, thought that Negroes did not have successful businesses because they could not stick together. He said:

> Just ever so often you see our folks sticking together. Most of the time they are pulling apart. That's the difference 'tween our folks and white folks. If a Negro got a store and another one got a store they'll fight each other tooth and nail all the time, and won't pull together, not ever; but white people can be fighting like mad and if you go in either their stores they going to stay

off fighting one another for a minute and get together to beat you. Then after you leave they might go back to fighting at themselves. But they always come together long enough to lick the other fellow, no matter how mad they is at each other. A nigger won't do that for I notice such things in this community.

There were, however, interesting evidences of the beginning of racial respect in several minor incidents observed. One youth made a point of calling a Negro insurance agent "Mr." in the presence of white men, knowing that it would prove irritating, and that nothing directly could be done about it. Another said, "I calls anybody 'Sir' if they be a man. I got as much right to call a colored man 'Sir' as I is a white man."

DIFFERENCES BETWEEN COUNTIES

The racial attitude scores[2] make possible a comparison between counties and sections. These scores indicate that the most favorable attitudes of Negro youth toward their own race (that is, the lower scores) are in Davidson County, Tennessee, and the least favorable (that is, the higher scores) are in Shelby County, Tennessee, and Coahoma County, Mississippi.

TABLE 15

ADJUSTMENT OF RURAL NEGRO YOUTH TO THEIR
OWN RACE, BY COUNTY AND SEX

As Indicated by Average Race Attitude Scores

County	Boys		Girls	
	Number of cases	Average score	Number of cases	Average score
All counties	766	7.33	1,330	7.20
Johnston, N.C.	167	7.37	327	7.45
Davidson, Tenn.	78	5.72	93	4.63
Shelby, Tenn.	110	8.40	257	7.67
Coahoma, Miss.	102	8.19	145	8.21
Bolivar, Miss.	106	7.02	190	6.94
Madison, Ala.	79	6.38	90	6.50
Macon, Ala.	92	7.51	145	7.54
Greene, Ga.	32	7.50	83	6.58

[2] See Appendix B for procedure in scoring of tests.

Coahoma is a plantation county and contrasts interestingly with Bolivar, another plantation county in Mississippi, in these scores. They are similar in practically all respects save for the presence in Bolivar of one of the few all-Negro towns in the South. Mound Bayou was settled in 1888 by Isaiah T. Montgomery, and has continued through its various economic vicissitudes to maintain active group consciousness, and to strive actively to develop conscious race pride. A few of the present leaders have distinguished themselves both locally and nationally and have brought favorable publicity to the town. The effect in terms of race consciousness generated in Mound Bayou is pronounced. It not only stimulates a different attitude toward the Negro race but also promotes a general sense of well-being even under unfavorable economic circumstances. A 14-year-old boy in Mound Bayou said, for example:

> I like it here. I like it because it's an all-colored town. You don't have to be around white people. You can laugh if you want to here. Down in Marigold or some place like that the white folks would be saying, "Nigger, do this and do that," but here you can play ball right out here in the street and nobody will run you away.

Following Davidson County in favorable attitudes toward race for both boys and girls is Madison County, Alabama. Following Shelby and Coahoma counties in unfavorable attitudes are Macon County, Alabama, Greene County, Georgia, and Johnston County, North Carolina. In one of these counties is an active Negro institution of considerable prestige. However, the high degree of maladjustment in other respects, as a result of a seriously disorganized rural economy, may account for the result observed in intrarace attitudes. In general, racial self-estimates are lower in the poorer areas.

ATTITUDES AND INTELLIGENCE

While there is no clear relationship between age and favorable race attitude scores, favorable attitudes do seem to have considerable correlation with intelligence. The youth of lowest I.Q. were most unfavorable in their judgment regarding their own race, and those of highest I.Q. most favorable.

TABLE 16

ADJUSTMENT OF RURAL NEGRO YOUTH TO THEIR OWN
RACE, BY INTELLIGENCE QUOTIENTS

As Indicated by Average Race Attitude Scores

I.Q.	Number of Cases	Average Score
40–59[a]	121	7.65
60–69	269	8.09
70–79	586	7.37
80–89	492	6.89
90–99	224	6.58
100–109	64	5.91
110–129[b]	16	4.38

[a] Includes 7 youth with I.Q.'s 40–49 and 114 with I.Q.'s 50–59
[b] Includes 1 youth with I.Q. 120–129 and 15 with I.Q.'s 110–119

Other tests and interview materials further indicated that the higher I.Q.'s tend to appear in the nonplantation and more urban counties, and that the more intelligent youth tend to be those who have better educated parents, who have had broader experience and larger reading interests, and who have attended schools with more race conscious Negro teachers.

Some of the youth in families of higher economic and educational rank have the advantage of more careful instruction in racial matters than others. They thus develop more racial poise. One mother reporting her experience in adjusting her daughter to her own physical characteristics and social status in the effort to preserve her self-respect, said:

I don't see how any Negro parent in the South can very well do otherwise than explain to the children the meaning of the differences which they observe. Race prejudice takes such queer forms that a child is very apt to run into it unexpectedly, and I think he or she should be prepared. I explain that the difference is really just in the minds of the whites. I tell my children that Negroes are every bit as good as whites. They [the whites] make the difference they think is there apparent so that they can control Negroes. It just happens that the laws are made by whites and that Negroes perforce must in certain instances submit to humiliation because they can't do otherwise and live. This situation, however, should not fundamentally affect the Negro's pride in himself. Negroes must realize that exterior features do not affect the inner being. I don't believe that we

should let this prejudice discourage us and our faith in our-
selves. I think my children understand and believe this. It is
possible for Negroes living here never to have contacts with
whites for months.

Another mother emphasized an interesting variant of this
policy of compensatory explanation. Her daughter asked her
one day, "What is a nigger?" She explained that a "nigger" was
any person who acted in a very ugly manner. The little girl immediately applied the term without racial significance, leaving
a large unsolved problem. Later she asked her mother why she
could not go to a certain section of the theater, and why all people
like her were sitting in the balcony. The mother commenting
upon her reply, said:

> It was suggested that ofttimes some members of the group do
> not act right or, if they are poor, do not clean themselves up
> before going to the theaters—and while this was true sometimes
> of the whites too, still it was used as an excuse to bar Negroes
> or else to give them separate sections in which to sit. My
> daughter has not yet been told that the Caucasian feels a
> superiority because it was desired that she first establish a high
> degree of personal respect and respect for the group, and a
> realization that Negroes are as capable of rating very high as
> another group. Then, if later the theses of racial superiority
> and inferiority are suggested to her, it is believed that she will
> not accept them even "with a grain of salt."

URBAN AND RURAL ATTITUDES IN THE SOUTH

In the South, urban Negro youth are, on the whole, more
race conscious and have more race pride than rural youth. Race
attitude tests were made in the following five southern cities:
Atlanta, Georgia; Fort Worth, Texas; Greensboro, North Carolina; Nashville, Tennessee; and New Orleans, Louisiana. A comparison of the average scores in these cities with the average
scores for the rural areas indicates that urban Negroes have a
more favorable attitude toward other Negroes than do rural
Negroes. This is no doubt partly due to the greater degree of
personal dependence on whites in the rural than in the urban
settings. But it is also partly due to the larger range of reassuring
examples of success in the cities, to better schools, and to the practice in many of the schools of supplementing the text discussions

with data useful as a basis for a re-estimate of the race. (The lower the score, the more favorable the attitude.)

Table 17

ADJUSTMENT OF SOUTHERN AND NORTHERN URBAN NEGRO
YOUTH TO THEIR OWN RACE, BY CITY AND SEX

As Indicated by Average Race Attitude Scores

City	Boys		Girls	
	Number of cases	Average score	Number of cases	Average score
SOUTHERN CITIES	381	5.65	752	5.43
Atlanta, Ga.	96	4.73	171	4.25
Fort Worth, Tex.	71	4.99	176	6.30
Greensboro, N.C.	49	6.12	104	5.83
Nashville, Tenn.	72	6.14	139	6.32
New Orleans, La.	93	6.47	162	4.71
BORDER CITY (Baltimore, Md.)	37	4.30	121	5.01
NORTHERN CITIES	209	4.70	379	3.80
Chicago, Ill.	79	3.54	129	3.29
New York, N.Y.	18	4.47	124	3.42
Philadelphia, Pa.	82	5.41	95	5.03
Springfield, Mass.	30	5.97	31	3.68

The manner in which standard public school course outlines are frequently supplemented with Negro data by race conscious Negro teachers in urban centers is related by one public school official who gave as the first purpose of Negro history "to instill race pride." He said:

> The study of the ancient Negro culture is nowhere to be found in the course of study [of the city public schools] as given in the printed outline. . . . Nowhere do we find the slightest mention or even reference to any member of the ethnic group with which we are identified. Now one of the functions of a supervising principal in our system is to interpret the course of study. I perform this to the best of my ability. With regard to the teaching of history every requirement is met, yet by the interpolation of facts as given by the best authorities, the interweaving of historical data in the proper chronological sequence, without bitterness or prejudice we have made our children cognizant of "the missing pages of American history."[3]

[3] John C. Bruce, "How and Why We Teach the Negro," *Journal of Negro History*, XXII (January 1937), 38-43.

Another very important medium for re-estimate of the race, and one whose influence has been felt largely in cities, is the Negro press. There are few southern cities of any size which do not have either a local weekly newspaper or some circulation of a national newspaper devoted almost exclusively to the presentation of events affecting Negroes as well as current and historical Negro achievements. It is not altogether without significance that Atlanta, whose Negro youth had the most favorable attitude toward their race of the southern cities tested, boasts "America's only Negro daily newspaper." These local papers usually circulate only in the areas where they originate, but there are imported into practically all southern cities other Negro newspapers and magazines whose news, circulation, and influence are national in scope. Indeed, it is not infrequent that these national newspapers have a wider circulation in some localities than newspapers indigenous to those areas. It would be regarded as a phenomenal instance of cultural isolation for any youth in these southern cities to report, as some did in the more isolated rural areas, that they "didn't know Negroes had their own newspapers."

NORTHERN AND SOUTHERN ATTITUDES COMPARED

The tests were extended, for purposes of comparison, to several northern areas. The cities included were: Chicago, New York, Philadelphia, and Springfield (Massachusetts). Northern urban youth, on the average, are more race conscious and have more race pride than southern youth, rural and urban.

A possible explanation of the lower average score in the northern cities is that Negro youth in these areas, being more detached from the unfavorable weight of race, are more impersonally accepted on the whole. They feel some limitations as members of a racial minority, but are, on the other hand, exposed to a larger range of favorable information, and can make a more satisfactory rationalization of Negro status. It can be observed that northern youth have been more diligent in providing for themselves a historical background from both fact and fancy, and they have a more clearly articulated racial ideology, which not only defends the race but offers constructive compensation for some of the popularly recognized inadequacies. Northern Negro youth are both less prejudiced toward whites, according to our statistical indices, and more favorable in their attitudes toward other Negroes. This is not necessarily a self-contradiction, for increased race pride contributes to the security of identification with some acceptable group, and in the end this security tends to decrease the racial maladjustment which expresses itself in bitter antiwhite racial feeling.

SUMMARY

The general results of this phase of the study lead to the tentative conclusion that southern rural Negro youth get little emotional security or constructive stimulation from identification with the Negro group and that this is due not only to the institutionalized race attitudes of the region regarding the group, which disparage it, but to the fact that few examples of value on which genuine pride can be based have been available to them through experience or literature. The Negro youth of broader education, and those in areas more effectually detached from widespread economic hardship and cultural backwardness as well as from the racial concepts associated with this status, have greater apparent respect for their own race. Moreover, for Negro youth living in the North (which is the haven of escape for southern Negroes) no further geographical escape is possible, and they have sought the needed security of group membership by attempting to reconstruct the Negro's past, by glorifying the naïve folk contributions of the Negro, by separating themselves as a racial category apart from southern Negroes, and by attempting to develop new defensive racial ideologies.

CHAPTER X

COLOR AND STATUS

THE NEGRO population, as a result of a long history of interbreeding of races in America, reveals in its physical traits a wide range and variety of features and complexions. Estimates of the extent of Negro-white race mixture vary considerably. Melville Herskovits, professor at Northwestern University, suggests, on the basis of sample studies in the North and South, that white or Indian and white-Indian crossings with Negroes are evident in nearly two-thirds of the Negro population.[1] His findings were based very largely upon studies of Negroes in colleges and this may exaggerate the true proportion. Nevertheless, there has been considerable race crossing in the past, although the number of direct crossings are fewer today than they were a generation ago.

The southern rural Negro does not appear to have been affected by this race crossing to the same extent as the urban Negro. Miscegenation is on the whole an urban phenomenon. Mixed-bloods tend to migrate to the cities. Negro-white admixtures are usually thought of as being mulattoes. "True" mulattoes are direct crossings of white and Negro stock. Actually, admixtures of from one-eighth white to one-eighth Negro, when they are discernible, are classified as Negro. Crossings within the sociological category "Negro" are constantly widening the population range of admixture without encountering the racial problems involved in direct crossings. One biological factor of sociological significance in this connection is the frequent occurrence within the same family of children of different shades of complexion and texture of hair.

What is more important, however, from the point of view of this study is the social and aesthetic evaluation placed upon color, and the meaning of this for Negro youth. The mixed-

[1] Melville Herskovits, *The American Negro* (New York: A. A. Knopf, 1928).

blood has received in the past, by inference at least, a higher rating in view of his conformity to the Caucasian norm. Intelligence, culture, and achievement have been assumed to vary directly with the amount of white blood. This has been a lay judgment, but for many years it had the support of some scientific students of race.

Conditions under which mixed-bloods originated have contributed to give the mulatto a more favorable position than the black Negro in the American social hierarchy. Mulattoes have often been the offspring of wealthy slave owners and persons of consequence in society. Living in and nearby the "big house," they have been closer to the carriers of the dominant culture than the field hands. They were the first to get the benefit of the schools, and they shared, to some small extent at least, the prestige of their masters and progenitors. Occasionally they inherited bits of property, were granted freedom, or were permitted to purchase it. On the whole, their lot was easier than that of their darker plantation kin.

Along with the advantageous social position of the mulatto there has been a pronounced disadvantage for blacks in the ideological heritage of society generally. The concept of blackness has held, in the popular mind, an unfavorable connotation. "Black as evil," "black as sin," "black as the devil," are phrases which suggest the emotional and aesthetic implications of this association. The evil and the ugliness of blackness have long been contrasted in popular thinking with the goodness and purity of whiteness. Whether with respect to men or things this color association has been deeply meaningful; it is an inescapable element of the cultural heritage.

It is a fact frequently overlooked that American Negroes in sharing to a greater or lesser degree the American culture, take over the ideas of those very institutions which disparage their physical and mental traits. The conflict of career drives in Negro youth and these color concepts which stamp the race as innately inferior are, in a vast number of cases, the source of deep emotional disturbance. This situation calls for constructive adjustment if Negro youth is to live a normal, well-balanced life. But successful adjustment is seldom achieved. One frequent attempt at emotional adjustment is to deny or deprecate in one way or another the fact of a color problem. This may be done by trying to act as if one is not conscious of the problem, or by incorrect self-appraisal. Frequently there is an attempt, usually unconvincing and unsuccessful, to rationalize the situation.

JUDGMENTS REVEALED BY TESTS

The importance of the color factor in the personality development of Negro youth was recognized early in this study, and two methods of appraising the extent of its influence were developed. A simple test was devised to draw out responses from the youth to a selection of pleasant and unpleasant stimuli in terms of color associations. A familiar color classification was employed as follows: black, dark-brown, brown, light-brown, yellow, and white. The individual was asked merely to check the color of (*a*) the most stupid boy (or girl) you know, (*b*) the most handsome boy (or girl) you know, (*c*) the smartest boy (or girl) you know, (*d*) the boy (or girl) you dislike most, (*e*) the boy (or girl) you like best, and a list of 30 similar value judgments. The results appear to be extremely significant. Approximately 500 of the 2,214 rural youth so tested were later interviewed for further information and insights into the status problems associated with color.

BLACKNESS

Considering the southern rural Negro youth as a whole, our results show a decided tendency to classify as black a disproportionately large number of negative judgments. For example, 39.5 per cent of 837 boys checked black as the color of "The ugliest girl you know," 10.8 per cent checked yellow, and only 6.5 per cent checked light-brown. On the other hand, only 4.7 per cent of the boys checked black as the color of "The most beautiful girl you know," but 43.8 per cent checked light-brown, and 14.5 per cent checked yellow.

The girls revealed similar color value judgments. Of 1,377 girls who checked the color of "The ugliest boy you know,"

42 per cent checked black and only 5.6 per cent checked light-brown and 9.9 per cent yellow. On the other hand, of those 1,377 checking the color of "The most handsome boy you know," only 5.5 per cent checked black, while 41.7 per cent checked light-brown, and 6.4 per cent, yellow. Table 18 shows the response of 837 rural boys and 1,377 girls to a selection of 30 value judgments involving color.

Just as aesthetic judgments appear, in these results, to be given value in terms of color, so do moral judgments. For example, the question regarding the color of "The best man you know" shows 16.7 per cent of the boys checking the color black, and 20.2 per cent checking light-brown. A similar question to the girls regarding "The best woman you know" shows 5.5 per cent checking black and 33.6 per cent light-brown. A population factor might be suspected in this disproportion if the figures did not so completely reverse themselves when the opposite value is involved. Of the boys responding to the question regarding "The meanest boy you know," 42.3 per cent checked black, 14.6 per cent dark-brown, and 8.7 per cent light-brown; and of the girls, 22.5 per cent checked black for "The meanest girl you know," while 22.1 per cent checked dark-brown, and 11.7 per cent checked light-brown.

The interviews revealed results similar to those of the tests. Some of the reactions to blackness were as follows: "Black is too black," "Black is ugly," "Black people are mean," "Black isn't like flesh," "Black is bad because people make fun, and I don't think it looks good either," "Black people can't use make-up," "Black people are evil," "White looks better than black," "No black people hold good jobs," "Black people can't look nice in their clothes," "You can't get along with black people," "Black looks dirty," "Black people have to go to the kitchen and scrub," "Even in college they don't want to take in black students." Black youth are called by such derisive names as "Snow," "Gold Dust Boys," "Blue Gums," "Midnight," "Shadow," "Haint," "Dusty," "Polish," and "Shine."

Several factors should be taken into account in order to understand this situation. In the first place, most of the southern rural

TABLE 18

COLOR VALUE JUDGMENTS OF RURAL NEGRO YOUTH, BY SEX[a]

(In percentages)

Descriptive Judgments	Black Boys	Black Girls	Dark-brown Boys	Dark-brown Girls	Brown Boys	Brown Girls	Light-brown Boys	Light-brown Girls	Yellow Boys	Yellow Girls	White Boys	White Girls	Not given Boys	Not given Girls
GENERAL DESCRIPTION														
The poorest person you know	41.7	33.2	12.5	15.2	6.7	7.9	3.6	5.1	3.1	2.2	18.3	21.6	14.1	14.9
Your teacher	6.2	2.0	17.6	14.2	16.2	14.9	34.5	41.0	13.0	14.3	2.9	3.3	9.6	10.5
Principal of your school	5.7	2.3	29.7	29.0	15.2	15.6	30.7	34.6	10.3	12.5	1.6	1.2	6.8	4.8
The person your father works for	4.3	2.4	4.5	3.6	3.5	3.8	6.3	4.3	2.4	2.0	51.0	54.9	28.0	29.0
The richest person you know	3.8	2.9	5.9	3.8	2.9	3.5	6.5	7.3	1.8	4.6	68.0	69.3	11.2	8.6
The person your mother works for	3.0	2.5	4.8	3.6	4.5	3.6	6.0	5.8	1.9	1.8	36.2	38.8	43.6	43.9
FAVORABLE DESCRIPTION—MALE														
The smartest boy you know	13.9	8.1	20.6	21.7	21.2	18.3	25.5	34.5	4.9	5.5	4.1	1.9	9.8	10.1
The best man you know	18.5	13.9	20.9	21.8	23.9	19.1	21.4	28.4	4.3	4.1	1.2	1.2	9.8	11.4
The nicest boy you know	16.7	9.7	22.3	23.8	20.4	18.7	20.2	28.2	4.7	7.0	6.3	2.2	9.3	10.3
The boy you like most	13.9	8.1	18.8	22.3	22.9	20.6	28.3	33.9	5.7	5.8	1.1	0.5	9.3	8.9
The man you look up to most	13.6	4.1	21.4	21.1	20.4	17.2	27.5	43.0	5.0	4.5	1.2	0.7	10.9	9.4
The most handsome boy you know	11.6	7.4	20.5	22.3	19.7	17.3	20.7	31.6	4.8	5.4	13.3	5.6	9.4	10.4
The most handsome boy you know	9.0	5.5	19.8	18.7	20.0	16.7	34.9	41.7	5.0	6.4	1.4	0.9	9.9	10.0
FAVORABLE DESCRIPTION—FEMALE														
The smartest girl you know	8.2	4.9	17.5	18.8	18.3	20.8	34.5	35.2	9.6	7.9	2.6	2.0	9.3	10.3
The smartest girl you know	12.7	6.2	21.0	20.0	20.0	22.1	26.4	31.2	9.6	7.6	1.3	1.8	9.1	11.1

[a] Based on responses of 887 boys and 1,377 girls

TABLE 18 (*Continued*)

Descriptive Judgments	Black		Dark-brown		Brown		Light-brown		Yellow		White		Not given	
	Boys	Girls	Boys	Girls	Boys	Girls	Boys	Girls	Boys	Girls	Boys	Girls	Boys	Girls
FAVORABLE DESCRIPTION— FEMALE (*Continued*)														
The best woman you know	10.3	5.5	19.7	18.2	20.0	21.6	30.5	33.6	5.9	7.3	3.3	2.3	10.4	11.5
The nicest girl you know	8.2	4.6	18.2	21.8	20.1	22.5	33.2	32.5	10.5	6.8	1.8	0.8	8.0	11.0
The woman you look up to most	7.6	5.0	21.1	18.7	18.3	20.2	31.5	34.8	6.9	8.6	5.3	3.8	9.2	9.0
The girl you like most	6.0	3.8	13.7	21.4	17.2	22.4	40.5	35.1	10.4	6.5	1.0	0.9	10.3	9.8
The most beautiful girl you know	4.7	4.4	11.2	13.1	14.1	16.1	43.8	44.4	14.5	10.5	3.0	2.4	8.6	9.2
UNFAVORABLE DESCRIPTION— MALE														
The ugliest boy you know	32.0	28.3	16.2	19.3	10.6	12.1	8.9	9.9	8.0	8.6	14.1	10.3	10.2	11.6
The meanest boy you know	46.7	42.0	9.6	14.7	6.1	6.5	5.6	5.6	9.2	9.9	11.7	9.1	11.1	12.2
The worst man you know	42.3	37.0	14.6	17.4	10.0	11.2	8.7	9.4	4.5	5.6	9.8	7.2	10.0	12.2
The boy you dislike most	30.2	27.6	15.9	16.0	6.8	10.5	7.2	7.9	5.9	7.4	23.9	17.9	10.0	12.6
The most stupid boy you know	28.3	27.9	14.9	18.2	8.5	12.4	7.8	9.3	9.2	10.5	18.6	11.0	12.7	10.7
The most shiftless man you	24.6	19.5	25.3	28.0	14.3	17.4	10.9	11.5	10.0	9.2	6.9	4.1	7.9	10.2
know	20.1	16.0	17.0	21.2	17.6	14.5	13.3	15.9	9.1	8.8	13.5	12.3	9.6	11.4
UNFAVORABLE DESCRIPTION— FEMALE														
The ugliest girl you know	24.7	17.7	17.2	20.4	12.5	16.4	12.0	13.0	9.2	11.3	12.9	9.2	11.4	12.1
The meanest girl you know	39.5	28.0	16.1	18.5	6.6	12.1	6.5	9.7	10.8	11.5	10.5	8.7	10.0	11.6
The girl you dislike most	29.5	22.5	18.2	22.1	12.4	15.0	11.5	11.7	9.7	9.2	6.5	7.2	12.3	12.3
The most stupid girl you know	22.3	14.0	14.2	13.0	12.4	16.4	10.4	13.6	8.5	14.4	19.4	9.8	12.8	13.8
The worst woman you know	21.5	14.4	22.3	26.4	17.7	19.8	13.0	14.2	7.4	9.7	6.8	4.0	11.2	11.6
The most shiftless woman you	19.2	16.8	15.5	19.0	12.1	14.6	11.7	11.2	8.4	10.9	19.8	13.9	13.5	13.7
know	16.0	10.7	16.7	18.2	14.1	20.3	19.1	17.8	10.6	12.0	14.5	11.6	9.0	9.4

Negroes are of dark complexion, and unmixed in appearance. Moreover, they are perhaps more dependent, psychologically and economically, upon the white group than other Negroes. They are in a measure immune to factors that intensify self-consciousness with respect to race. Their ideas and their values reflect the ideas and values of the white world, even when those values are derogatory to Negroes. Color values are no exception to this rule.

In the second place, the belief that "black people are mean" can easily make such people "mean" if the behavior toward them is habitually based on such an assumption. In the end the reaction of such dark persons reinforces the stereotype. One young girl declared that she hated both her parents and herself because she was black and because the children "laughed at her." Few of these youth are able to make satisfactory adjustments to such a social "handicap."

YELLOWNESS

The tendency to favor lighter shades of complexion meets certain conflicting factors in other value judgments. In the white society "yellow nigger" has a somewhat unfavorable meaning. Although mulattoes on the whole appear to be proud of their lighter complexions, they are at a disadvantage when the question of paternity is raised by their darker associates. Such derisive terms as "Yellow Pumpkin," "Yellow Bastard," are used in this connection. The youth commenting on this shade of complexion made such statements as these: "Yellow people are not honest" (meaning that they are probably illegitimate), "Yellow is the worst color because it shows mixture with whites," "Yellow is too conspicuous" (like black), "Yellow people don't look right," "Real yellow people ain't got no father," "Yellow don't have no race, they can't be white and they ain't black either," "Anything that is too light looks dirty," "Yellow is mixed bad blood," "Light people get old too quickly," "Yellow don't hold looks so long," "White colored people is all bastards." Under the circumstances youth of light complexion encounter difficulties of adjustment to their social surroundings, similar to those of youth at the other extreme, particularly since in the rural areas they are in a minority.

Girls seem to be more color conscious than boys, or at least they are less successful in building up for themselves defenses against assaults upon their self-consciousness. The formidable weight of this factor appears not only in constant minor taunts and slights, but in tragedies of a serious nature. Eva Mae Williams, in Greene County, Georgia, explaining why one of her uncles killed a man, said:

> This man was brighter [in color] than my uncle and he was making fun of my uncle's color. Uncle told him to leave him alone or they'd be trouble. One word led to another and this man was making to kill my uncle and he killed him first.

"THE WORST COLOR TO BE"

The statistical results from the tests provide an interesting distribution of judgments regarding "the worst color to be." Table 19 gives percentages for boys and girls according to color preferences expressed, and indicates that black and yellow are the least desirable colors from the point of view of these youth.

TABLE 19

JUDGMENTS OF RURAL NEGRO YOUTH ON "WORST COLOR TO BE," BY SEX[a]

(In percentages)

Worst Color	Both Sexes	Boys	Girls
Black	34.9	34.5	35.1
Dark-brown	1.9	2.5	1.6
Brown	1.4	1.9	1.1
Light-brown	1.4	0.9	1.6
Yellow	28.2	28.8	27.9
White	32.1	31.3	32.6

[a] Based on responses of 635 boys and 1,161 girls

The judgments regarding "white" are in part racial and in part color evaluations. Some Negro complexions are described as "white," but in most instances the term is interpreted in a racial sense. Where the former interpretation is indicated, the association with "yellow" is apparent; when the latter is used, the subject is expressing a judgment regarding the white race as symbolized by the trait of color. For example, one youth said "I wouldn't want to be white because they are mean to colored," and another "White people can get the best jobs so I rather be white." Generally considered, then, it appears from the tabulations that the extremes of color are regarded more unfavorably than other complexions.

Basis for Judgment

The tests sought further to discover the youths' reasons for classifying a certain color as the "worst to be." The largest volume of negative reactions to a specified color is based upon the judgment that it is "ugly." Table 20 gives the distribution of the basis of color judgments.

TABLE 20

REASONS GIVEN BY RURAL NEGRO YOUTH FOR JUDGMENTS ON "WORST COLOR TO BE," BY SEX[a]

(In percentages)

Reason	Both Sexes	Boys	Girls
Because it is ugly	56.0	52.6	57.8
People don't like it	19.5	20.2	19.1
Because it is "mean"	10.7	13.3	9.3
Because it shows dirt plainly	5.8	6.4	5.4
Because of lack of opportunity	5.2	5.0	5.3
Because I am not that color	2.5	2.4	2.6
Other	0.3	0.1	0.4

[a] Based on responses of 420 boys and 771 girls

"THE BEST COLOR TO BE"

In the list of "favorable" descriptions by both boys and girls, light-brown shows by far the highest ranking. Among the boys 38.3 per cent and among the girls 46.5 per cent regarded light-brown as the most desirable color. The next preference was for "brown," with 23.5 per cent of the boys and 20.1 per cent of the girls indicating this color as desirable.

The interviews again support the statistical results with such statements as these: "I'd rather be light-brown, but I wouldn't want to be yellow," "It is better to be brown or light-brown, because one is too conspicuous when he is all black or yellow," "If I could be any color I'd be light-brown, it looks the best," "I like light-brown first, because it's pretty and you are able to wear any color when you are that color," "Black people can't use make-up, but light-brown people can; that's my color."

The invariable convergence of color preference around "light-brown" not only has the sociological and psychological significance which the comments indicate, but may, indeed, be linked with the observed "biological" trends toward a new "brown" race. This has been noted by Melville Herskovits[2] and Edwin Embree.[3]

SELF-APPRAISALS OF COMPLEXION

It was observed in the testing program and in the direct interviews with the youth that they consistently rated their own complexions a shade or more lighter than they appeared to be. This prompted the study to attempt a more careful measurement of a tendency which seemed to have some significance. It suggested a type of unconscious response to the color evaluations which they gave in other situations. They could escape, in their own minds at least, some of the unfavorable association, by appraising themselves as lighter than they were.

The basis of the "true" estimate used by the study was the consensus of the group of interviewers and testers, and comparisons made with the aid of the color top. It was observed that the complexion of the appraiser influences to some extent the color estimate. Appraisers who were of dark complexions tended to rank complexions lighter than did the appraisers who were of light complexion. An absolutely objective index was impossible, but the results of the estimate seem fairly significant.

In 721 cases estimates were made by the testers of the youth's complexions. The testers' estimate and the self-estimate were closest together for the category dark-brown and farthest apart for the categories black and light-brown. Of the boys, 7.5 per cent placed themselves in the category black as compared with

[2] *Ibid.*
[3] Edwin R. Embree, *Brown America* (New York: Viking Press, 1931).

28.1 per cent estimated by the testers. Among the girls 2.4 per cent appraised themselves as black as compared with 23.3 per cent as estimated by the testers. On the other hand, 35.8 per cent of the boys and 40.2 per cent of the girls estimated their complexions as light-brown as compared with 6.5 per cent and 9.9 per cent, respectively, in the testers' estimates for boys and girls.

In addition to appraising their own complexions "favorably," the youth tended to reflect their emotional attitude toward school principals, teachers, and relatives in their color classifications. When the principal or teacher was popular he was rated lighter than his real complexion, and darker when disliked. Consistent with the preference shown by the youth for their mothers over their fathers, the results show not only higher proportions of mothers checked as being light-brown (43.2 per cent of the boys and 46.7 per cent of the girls), but both boys and girls consistently rated mothers lighter than fathers.

SECTIONAL DIFFERENCES IN COLOR VALUES

Interesting intersectional differences appear in the comparison of northern and southern Negro youth, reflecting slightly different social orientations. The northern urban data here used are based on tests made in course of the study in New York, Chicago, Philadelphia, and Springfield (Massachusetts). In the test certain items were included that could be checked by the investigators, as for example, "The color of your principal." The first difference appears in the factual item. In the southern area only 1.4 per cent of the principals were checked as white as compared with 66.8 per cent in the northern cities. There were, so far as observed, no principals in the southern rural schools in which tests were made who were classed as belonging to the white race, but a few of the principals were of light enough complexion to be described as "white" in complexion. In two of the northern schools in which tests were made the principals were Negroes. Again, in the southern rural areas, "The poorest person you know" was checked black by 36.4 per cent of the youth as compared with 13.5 per cent of the youth in the northern cities, where other groups share conspicuously the Negro's poverty.

A significant general difference appears in the fact that southern rural youth check more favorable descriptions (10.3 and 6.2 per cent) as black than northern youth (4.6 and 3.4 per cent) and also more unfavorable descriptions as black. In the southern group 29.7 per cent, and in the northern group 16.3 per cent, checked as black their unfavorable descriptions of males, and corresponding percentages for unfavorable descriptions of females were 20.4 and 11.3. The two groups are similar in their preference for light-brown (31.1 and 35 per cent for southern youth, 30.8 and 36.7 per cent for northern). Slightly more southern than northern youth checked as yellow the color of "The most beautiful girl you know." Table 21 gives these ratings for southern and northern youth.

CONFLICTS BASED UPON COLOR

The social values associated with color have extremely serious consequences for Negro youth. Conflict situations may develop between families and arise within families. It often happens that darker children in families feel that their parents give preference to the children of lighter complexion. Even such inadvertent and casual comparisons as "better hair," "nicer complexion," "prettier skin," "nicer shade" affect the more sensitive young people and contribute to their feelings of inferiority. Children may apply color values unfavorably to one or the other of the parents, or find themselves apologizing for the dark complexion of a parent. They may even harbor resentment against the parent who was biologically responsible for their own undesirable appearance. By far the most frequent instances of color sensitivity, however, occur outside the home as the child attempts to make adjustment to new groups.

Elsie Carter's family is poor. Her father is a day laborer in a sawmill, and her mother works the farm. There are six other children in the household, including brothers, cousins, and half-sisters. Elsie is 15, and very dark, with hair about an inch long and straightened. She is above the average in intelligence among children in the area (I.Q. 99). Wherever she goes, however, she is made conscious of her color. She says, "Black is just ugly and

TABLE 21

COLOR VALUE JUDGMENTS OF SOUTHERN RURAL NEGRO YOUTH AND NORTHERN URBAN NEGRO YOUTH[a]

(In percentages)

Descriptive Judgments	Black Southern	Black Northern	Dark-brown Southern	Dark-brown Northern	Brown Southern	Brown Northern	Light-brown Southern	Light-brown Northern	Yellow Southern	Yellow Northern	White Southern	White Northern	Not given Southern	Not given Northern
GENERAL DESCRIPTION														
The poorest person you know	36.4	13.5	14.2	20.6	7.5	22.0	4.5	9.1	2.5	4.6	20.3	14.0	14.6	16.2
Principal of your school	3.6	0.8	29.3	0.8	15.4	4.2	33.2	23.5	11.7	2.4	1.4	66.8	5.6	1.5
Your teacher	3.6	0.3	15.4	3.9	15.4	11.2	38.5	28.1	13.8	3.9	3.1	46.9	10.1	5.6
The richest person you know	3.3	3.5	4.6	6.2	3.3	14.1	7.0	10.6	3.5	3.0	68.8	51.0	9.6	11.5
The person your father works for	3.1	1.1	4.0	1.8	3.7	4.4	5.1	4.2	2.1	1.4	53.4	57.2	28.6	29.9
The person your mother works for	2.7	0.6	4.0	1.1	4.0	4.6	5.9	3.9	1.9	1.8	37.8	37.9	43.8	50.1
FAVORABLE DESCRIPTION—MALE	10.3	4.6	21.3	13.1	19.4	33.0	31.1	30.8	5.3	4.4	2.7	3.3	10.0	10.8
The smartest boy you know	15.7	7.6	21.5	13.5	20.9	29.6	25.7	29.1	4.2	5.8	1.2	5.8	10.8	8.3
The best man you know	12.4	5.3	23.3	16.4	19.4	30.7	25.2	24.7	6.1	5.3	3.7	4.7	9.9	15.8
The nicest boy you know	10.3	3.3	21.6	16.4	21.5	36.7	31.8	28.5	5.8	3.2	0.7	0.5	9.0	11.4
The man you look up to most	9.0	5.2	21.6	14.4	18.2	33.4	27.5	27.9	5.2	2.4	8.5	3.8	10.0	12.9
The boy you like most	7.7	3.0	21.2	10.3	18.4	39.3	37.1	35.1	4.7	4.1	0.9	1.2	9.9	7.0
The most handsome boy you know	6.8	3.0	19.2	10.6	17.9	28.2	39.1	39.0	5.9	5.8	1.1	3.6	10.0	9.7
FAVORABLE DESCRIPTION—FEMALE	6.2	3.4	18.3	10.3	19.9	30.8	35.0	36.7	8.6	5.5	2.2	2.5	9.9	10.6
The smartest girl you know	8.6	5.3	20.4	10.0	21.3	32.2	29.4	34.3	8.4	5.5	1.6	4.1	10.3	8.6
The best woman you know	7.3	4.1	18.7	11.7	21.0	28.4	32.4	30.2	6.8	6.2	2.7	3.0	11.1	16.4
The woman you look up to most	6.0	3.0	19.6	12.1	19.5	31.6	33.6	36.4	7.9	4.6	4.3	2.1	9.1	10.2
The nicest girl you know	6.0	3.5	20.4	10.9	21.6	35.7	32.7	30.2	8.2	4.9	1.2	1.7	9.9	13.2

[a] Based on responses of 2,214 southern rural youth and 659 responses of northern urban youth

TABLE 21 (Continued)

Descriptive Judgments	Color Rating													
	Black		Dark-brown		Brown		Light-brown		Yellow		White		Not given	
	South-ern	North-ern	South-ern	North-ern	South-ern	North-ern	South-ern	North-ern	South-ern	North-ern	South-ern	North-ern	South-ern	North-ern
FAVORABLE DESCRIPTION—FEMALE (*Continued*)														
The girl you like most	4.7	2.1	18.5	8.8	20.5	31.6	37.5	45.5	8.0	4.4	0.9	0.9	10.0	6.7
The most beautiful girl you know	4.5	2.6	12.4	8.5	15.4	25.6	44.2	43.4	12.0	7.7	2.7	3.3	8.9	8.8
UNFAVORABLE DESCRIPTION—MALE														
The ugliest boy you know	29.7	16.3	18.1	23.9	11.5	17.0	9.5	11.2	8.4	7.1	11.7	7.0	11.1	17.5
The meanest boy you know	43.8	26.4	12.7	23.5	6.3	12.4	5.6	7.6	9.7	8.8	10.1	7.4	11.8	13.8
The worst man you know	39.0	21.5	16.4	23.1	10.7	17.5	9.1	12.6	5.2	5.3	8.2	5.0	11.4	15.0
The boy you dislike most	28.6	16.1	16.0	23.4	9.1	13.8	7.6	8.8	6.8	6.2	20.1	10.5	11.7	21.2
The most stupid boy you know	28.0	13.7	16.9	26.1	10.9	14.6	8.7	11.7	10.0	8.2	13.9	5.2	11.4	20.6
The most shiftless man you	21.4	9.9	27.0	24.3	16.2	23.7	11.3	14.4	9.5	8.5	5.2	7.1	9.3	12.1
know	17.5	10.3	19.6	23.1	15.6	20.3	14.9	12.3	8.9	5.5	12.7	6.7	10.7	21.9
UNFAVORABLE DESCRIPTION—FEMALE														
The ugliest girl you know	20.4	11.3	19.2	19.5	14.9	21.8	12.6	13.0	10.5	8.5	10.6	6.6	11.8	19.2
The meanest girl you know	32.3	20.5	17.6	21.7	10.0	17.9	8.4	9.6	11.2	8.2	9.4	5.5	11.0	16.7
The worst woman you know	25.2	11.8	20.6	20.2	14.0	22.3	11.6	14.3	9.3	10.2	6.9	6.4	12.3	14.9
The girl you dislike most	17.7	10.0	17.7	16.4	13.6	21.7	11.4	11.2	9.9	7.9	16.2	8.5	13.5	24.3
The most stupid girl you know	17.2	10.2	16.6	20.9	14.9	19.7	12.4	12.7	12.1	9.9	13.4	6.1	13.4	20.5
The most shiftless woman you	17.1	9.1	24.8	20.9	19.0	25.8	13.8	15.2	8.8	7.9	5.1	5.6	11.5	15.5
know	12.7	6.4	17.7	17.0	17.9	23.1	18.3	15.2	11.5	7.0	12.7	7.7	9.2	23.7

black people have to be ashamed of their color. People make fun of you all the time." She would be happier if she were "only brown." "This," she asserts, "is a prettier color and you can look nice in different colors of clothes." The white children seem to single her out more often for their epithets, because she is more conspicuous; when the Negro girls select their friends they leave her out, and even when she permitted a boy to have sex relations with her, in the effort "to get a fellow," he did not respect her enough to keep it secret. He told it as a joke, and all her schoolmates teased her about it. Other girls she knows are generous in their favors, but the boys treat them with more consideration.

Sadie Thompson is dark-brown, but she classifies herself as light-brown, and has made partial adjustment to her color by this reassurance to herself and by pointing out that yellow is really as bad as black. She says:

> If you're a Negro and yellow then you are half-white. That means your blood is mixed and that ruins the race. I'd rather be black than my own color. I guess I'm light-brown; that's what I think, but since I'm a Negro I'd rather be a real black one. I've seen lots of black people and I think some are pretty. Most of the children laugh at black girls, and say they are mean. They ain't mean. You'd be mean, too, if someone was always calling you "black nigger." If you don't take it, they want to fight. The colored girls at school are mean to the black children, and worst to the yellow ones.

Nettie Stamps is the 15-year-old daughter in a family that is above the average in economic status and in general living standards. They have a comfortable home and such conveniences as electricity, a radio, and a small automobile. She is dark-brown in complexion, but refers to herself as brown. Her own color worries are projected to other girls of her identical complexion, whom she describes as black. It is evident that in so doing she can express at the same time her dislike of blackness in people, and her bitterness toward lighter Negroes who make black children uncomfortable. Both of her parents are of very dark complexion. Nettie says:

> Black is the very worst color you can be. It's ugly, and people treat black people so mean. I really think colored people are

worse to black people than white people are. They are first to call names like "black" and "nigger." It's bad when white people call that, but worse for colored to call their own race names. They are all colored together.

Seems to me like black people don't have the advantages that brown and yellow people have. I can't exactly think of what advantages I mean, but around school the real dark children don't get much attention. Some of the teachers don't like them and call them "black" and "dumb."

Black people just look ugly. I'm between black and yellow; I think brown, but I'd rather be light skin. You look better, but best of all I'd rather be real light-brown. Any color is better than black!

Melvina Ingram is a mulatto girl of 17, in a comfortably well-off family. Her complexion is light, and she has curly hair. Her sister Constance is of the same complexion. Although apparently adjusted at home, they both have had such difficulty with the children at school that the family plans to move to another community. The children call the two girls "yellow pumpkins," and make insinuations about their ancestry, although their parents are married and are similarly of light complexion. Melvina says:

I don't get along at all with the children at school. They are always sneaking around and talking about you. They are just a selfish bunch. Some of the girls wrote letters to me and didn't sign their names. I showed these letters to Professor Giles. They don't like me because I change my clothes every day and they wear a dress a whole week. I always raise my hand to recite, and they say that I think I'm smart. I cry about the whole thing, and then they started talking about the principal and me.

In spite of the economic advantages which the girls have in their family, they have persistent difficulties in school which seem to be rooted in color. Melvina's contacts in the community are limited to only two families, and they are persons of light complexion. She says:

I get along with the Carters because they are light. It just seems that black people are evil. I have one friend who is dark. She lives in a part of my aunt's house. She is so sweet and friendly you just can't help but like her. I guess I select my friends on the basis of color, as all my friends are light. I just can't get along with dark people.

My parents don't permit me to discuss color. If they talk about it at all we never hear it. They say it's ugly to say things about a person's color. My father has to be nice to people of all colors because in his business that is necessary. They have friends of all colors, too—but now that I think about it, I think most of their friends are light.

In Ruth Parker's family there are six children, four light and two dark. The father is light and has black curly hair. Ruth says:

Me and Arthur have the worst hair in our family. Arthur bought some kind of hair oil and put it on his hair, and it looks real good, and curly too. But you can't use it on women's hair. They say it will take women's hair out. I wish I could use it. I straighten my hair. It used to be good like Elsie's till mama cut it about four years ago.

All the children took hair after my daddy except Arthur and me. Honey got hair just like him—long and pretty and curly.

Ruth is considered the "slow" child in the family. She has a smouldering resentment against her mother, who seems inordinately proud of her lighter children. On one occasion when her mother was showing some pictures of the children, she omitted the picture of Ruth. A visitor asked to see it, and Ernestine, one of the lighter children, said impulsively but devastatingly, "I don't see what you want that ugly thing for." The mother and all the children except Ruth laughed nervously. Ruth explained to the visitor, "All my sisters are better looking than I am." The mother ignored this, but later remarked again about another daughter's beautiful long hair, and talked at length about how well she had done in school. Ruth had missed one grade in school because when her father was ill she was the one selected to stay at home with him.

CLASS AND COLOR

Our results indicate that there is little correlation between class and color in the southern rural area. Differences in complexion and hair create problems of adjustment, but do not mark class lines within the rural Negro group. Such advantages as light complexions have, in the sense of conformity to the white norms, are qualified by (*a*) the present unfavorable social conditions under which direct crossings occur; (*b*) the fact that increasing numbers of Negro professionals, who constitute the upper classes, are of dark complexion; (*c*) the movement of light males away from the area and sometimes into the white group; (*d*) the apparently stronger and occasionally successful drive of darker men for recognition and status; and (*e*) the prejudice against very light Negroes on the part of darker individuals who are numerically dominant in the southern rural areas.

CHAPTER XI

RELATIONS WITH WHITES

IN THE foregoing chapters major attention has been given to the normal routine of life of rural Negro youth with its problems and tensions; the familiar institutions of the Negro community; and the characteristic responses of these youth to their problems and to their social status. It has been impossible to escape the shadow of the white world over their lives, whether in their contacts with the economic institutions of the area or in the intimacy of their own humble homes. The whole complex of life for these youth and their families, their work, their play, their relations with their fellows generally, their outlook and aspirations, their opportunities for development and self-expression, their attitudes and sentiments, are conditioned in one way or another by the traditionally sanctioned patterns of race relations in the area. It is the purpose of this chapter to discuss these relationships and the effects of the impact of the race system, with its taboos and compulsions and, not infrequently, its violence, upon the personality of these youth. It is this racial situation that defines their minority status.

RACE SYSTEM OF THE SOUTH

The Negro in the South is still involved in the processes by which one people is incorporated into the life and culture of another. Progress in this respect has at times been halted, at times accelerated, by crises and conflicts of various sorts. The social order that has evolved in the South has not been one that merely conformed to the rigid conditions imposed by the soil and the climate, but one which offered a reasonably satisfying *modus vivendi* between the races thrown together by fate and necessity. Although constituting, formally, at least, a separate society, Negro society has never yet been free to pursue, as some have thought it should, an independent career as a race, nor to develop social values peculiarly its own. Until comparatively recently the population has remained in the slow moving rural areas, rooted in a system of agriculture which is no longer prosperous. In this situation the Negro's native adaptability has somehow enabled him to maintain an original zest for life which has contributed a vicarious vitality to the habits and customs (in short, the institutions) to which he finds himself so vitally related. One of the questions which disinterested students of southern conditions of life have asked is this: "What is it that has preserved down to the present day the continued existence in the South of an obviously obsolete agriculture?" The answer is, in part at least, the accommodating disposition of the Negro tenant farmer. Another explanation is the persistence of a tradition of frontier individualism in the mores of his competitor, the white farmer.

All this becomes extremely important in any consideration of the personality development of Negro youth. For it must be understood at once that the Negro child is born not only into the intimate social world of his family, but into a larger social world rigidly defined for him by the peculiar status of his group and its adventitious role in the total social economy. The Negro child must learn not only to live in his own world and like it, but he must find some zest in the very necessity of conforming to the conditions imposed upon him by a more inclusive social order, an order that insists on treating him, in some senses and to some degree, as an alien.

The personal and racial aspirations of the Negro have been developed within the framework of occidental culture and, because of his limited participation in the intellectual life about him, they have developed on a level lower than would otherwise have been the case. Isolation ensures stability but limits progress. Furthermore, the chronic economic inadequacy of the southern region has contributed in numerous ways to the retardation of the Negro who has been at the bottom of the economic structure. The slow but steady decline of the economic fortunes of the area has forced many of the insecure white population to accept a status originally identified with the Negro. But despite all this, over the years there have been marked changes, and particularly with respect to the Negro community.

The race problem for Negro youth is not in the fixed role of the Negro but in the changing racial patterns and values as these youth seek to achieve a personal and racial career. The racial role of the Negro has been implicit in many of the matter-of-fact economic and social relations described as parts of the normal routine of life. The fundamental difference between the present status of the southern rural Negro and the white of the same economic class is that a change in economic status does not permit the Negro the same measure of social or political participation that such a change would make possible for the white. Race in this case reinforces the economic disabilities, and by so doing retards the general cultural development of the group.

What constitutes the race problem is not the fixed character of the relations, but their dynamic character. There would be no race problem if the Negro group uniformly accepted the status assumed for it. The present patterns of these relations are, in the large, different from what they were fifty years ago, or even twenty years ago. They vary with localities and backgrounds and with social classes within the Negro and white groups. The simplest method of presenting the present racial pattern of relations is by indicating what *can* and *cannot* be done by Negroes within the racial mores of typical rural areas of the South.

RACIAL ETIQUETTE OF THE RURAL SOUTH

The social life of the white and Negro rural populations in its more intimate aspects is traditionally separate. In the eight counties studied a careful check has been made for each of a large list of possible contacts and relations. The exceptions to the general rule are most often those in which the new Negro professional and business classes are involved in relations with similar classes of the white population, and among the occasional intelligentsia, artists, nonprovincials, criminals, and other "free" classes not rigidly bound by the mores. These exceptions are usually in private relations and thus escape the more serious censure of public opinion.

The two universally tabooed practices are intermarriage and interdancing. Interdining is generally prohibited in all counties, but occurs in minor instances in some. The exceptions are more significant in some than in other areas. In one county eating together is tolerated for a few at school exercises, in another county when whites are invited to a barbecue. Whites and Negroes play games together in semiprofessional baseball practice in Greene County, Georgia, and at dice in Bolivar County, Mississippi. Young children play together in any area, older ones occasionally in Macon County, Alabama, and Davidson County, Tennessee. Whites use "Mr." and "Mrs." only when as salesmen they are selling goods. Salesmen and department store clerks in Madison County, Alabama, selectively employ the titles when making sales or seeking patronage. The terms employed when titles are not used are "boy," "John," "Aunt," or "Uncle." Teachers and well-to-do Negro farmers and businessmen in Bolivar are sometimes addressed by their last names.

The exceptions in the case of entering white homes by the front door are business and professional calls, and when a Negro knows a white person personally. The practice depends upon the individual white man. Negroes and whites occasionally shake hands under a variety of conditions: when a salesman is trying to sell goods, when a former employer meets a respected Negro who has worked for him, when whites are attending public programs or meetings of Negroes, and occasionally on the streets. The white man makes the first approach.

The following are, in general, the rules of racial etiquette in the eight counties studied as typical of the rural South.

Where taboos are rigid

1. Negroes may never marry whites in any of the counties studied.
2. Negroes may never dance with whites in any of the counties studied.

3. Negroes may never eat with whites in any of the counties except Bolivar and Coahoma (Mississippi), and Davidson (Tennessee).

4. Negroes may never play games with whites in any counties except Bolivar, Davidson, and Madison (Alabama).

5. Negroes must always use "Mr." and "Mrs." when addressing whites in all counties.

6. Whites never use "Mr." and "Mrs." when addressing Negroes in Bolivar, Coahoma, Johnston (North Carolina), Macon (Alabama), and Shelby (Tennessee).

7. Negroes never drink with whites in Madison and Shelby counties except occasionally among the lower classes.

8. Negroes never enter white people's houses by the front door in Coahoma and Johnston.

9. Negroes must give whites the right-of-way on the sidewalks in Bolivar and Madison.

10. Negro men must take off their hats in banks, stores, and so forth, where whites need not, in Madison.

11. Negroes cannot touch a white man without his resenting it in Bolivar and Madison.

12. Negroes must always say "Yes, sir," and "Yes, ma'am," when addressing whites in all counties except Davidson and Johnston.

Where the etiquette is relaxed

1. Negroes drink with whites sometimes in Bolivar, Coahoma, Davidson, Greene, Johnston, and Macon.

2. Negroes and whites shake hands sometimes in all counties.

3. Negroes enter white people's houses by the front door sometimes in Bolivar, Davidson, Greene, Madison, and Shelby.

4. Whites use "Mr." and "Mrs." sometimes in Davidson, Greene, and Madison when addressing Negroes.

5. Whites and Negroes play games together sometimes in Bolivar, Davidson, and Madison.

6. Negroes must use "Yes, sir," and "Yes, ma'am," sometimes in Davidson and Johnston.

7. Negroes may touch a white man without causing resentment in Davidson, Johnston, Macon, and Shelby.

Where the etiquette is confused

1. Negroes attend theaters patronized by whites in all counties but Madison.

2. Negroes can try on hats in all stores in all counties but Shelby.

3. Negroes can try on gloves in all stores in Bolivar, Davidson, Johnston, and Macon, and in no stores in Greene.

4. Negroes must occupy a separate section while being waited on in all stores in Coahoma, Macon, and Madison; in some stores in Davidson, Greene, Johnston, and Shelby; and in no stores in Bolivar.

5. Negroes may sit in all public parks in Bolivar, Coahoma, Greene, and Macon; in some parks in Davidson and Shelby; and in none in Johnston and Madison.

6. Negroes use hotels with whites in none of the counties.

7. Negroes use some restaurants with whites in Coahoma, Davidson, Madison, and Shelby only, and these are separated by partition.

8. Negroes serve on juries sometimes in Coahoma, Greene, and Shelby, never in Bolivar, Johnston, and Madison.

9. Negro lawyers may try cases in all counties except Madison.

10. Negroes are segregated in all courts except in Coahoma.

11. Whites work *for* Negroes sometimes in Bolivar, Davidson, Greene, Johnston, and Madison; never in Coahoma, Macon, and Shelby.

12. Whites work *with* Negroes usually in Coahoma and Greene; sometimes in Davidson, Johnston, and Madison; seldom if ever in Shelby.

13. Whites are served by Negro doctors in Davidson, Greene, Johnston, Madison, and Shelby; not in Bolivar, Coahoma, and Macon.

14. Negroes usually vote in Coahoma, Davidson, Johnston, Macon, and Shelby; sometimes in Greene and Madison.

15. Negroes and whites worship together sometimes in Coahoma, Davidson, Greene, Macon, and Madison; never in Bolivar, Johnston, and Shelby.

16. Negroes drink with whites in drug and liquor stores in

Coahoma; at beer "joints" in Bolivar; when each party is about half drunk from whisky in Greene; and among the lower classes occasionally in all counties.

The taboos, prohibitions, and coercive symbols indicated here in summary form and embedded in the traditions of the area constitute a vital element in the social environment of southern rural Negro youth. This influence is pervasive and constant and, like the awkward and at times defective patterns of family organization, can warp personality profoundly from infancy.

STEREOTYPE OF THE SOUTHERN RURAL NEGRO

In the historical literature and much of the familiar lore, the "folk Negro" is presented as a simple, trusting servant, addicted to petty crimes and sexual looseness, but feeling a deep and grateful devotion to his masters. He might have deceived them in small things, but he knew that he was understood and would be protected. His masters could be confident of his loyalty in times of stress, and equally confident of his unreliability and irresponsibility in the daily routine of life. He knew his place and had no desire for independence or for social, economic, or any other kind of "equality." He lived a carefree, happy life, confiding his simple problems to his master, who always solved them with a few kindly, jovial words and perhaps a dollar bill. This stereotype was most nearly and most often approximated by the Negroes during slavery and immediately following emancipation.

The present generation of Negro youth presents somewhat different social and psychological characteristics than those of the stereotype of the southern rural Negro. This is not a sudden development. The popular conception of the Negro as described in the preceding paragraph has little basis in fact; it has always been confused by pervading doubts and exceptions. Some of the contradictions within the old stereotype have resulted in the postulating of special types, some of which have been based on fact and others on myths as highly fictionalized as those which formed the basis for the original stereotype. Clashes have occurred from time to time between Negroes and whites; violence within the Negro group has conflicted with the picture of the simple, easygoing, tractable, submissive character of the stereotype; the old dogma that the Negro must be kept in his place has not been in complete accord with the assumption that the Negro is content and accepts that place; it has not always been possible to reconcile the loyalty and affection of the Negro for his white "master" with the belief that Negroes will assault white men and endanger white women if given the opportunity to do so.

Two of the most common of the various special types postulated because of contradictions in the stereotype are the "bad nigger" and the "uppity nigger." These are here described because they represent quite opposite extremes. The "bad nigger" is conceived to be an abnormal individual whose innate perversity makes him indifferent to law and common sense. He drinks, swears, gambles, and indulges in various other vices. He carries a lethal weapon and is ready to use it. He is a coward and can be easily handled by white men who know how to treat "niggers," but he will attack from the rear if given a chance. The "uppity nigger," on the other hand, does not "know his place" and dangerously disturbs race relations by trying to be what he is not and never can be. In most cases his obnoxious conduct is attributable to too much education. He fails to realize that his real racial role is fixed regardless of education, occupation, or other personal characteristics. He demands rights instead of requesting favors. He stirs up other Negroes by "inventing" wrongs. He is, if anything, more dangerous than the "bad nigger," because he is more subtle in linking his annoying pretenses with values otherwise approved by the culture.

In all sections of the South it is possible to find Negroes who have developed traits of easygoing docility and respectful humility, or at least those who can affect that manner convincingly in the presence of whites. It is likewise possible to find the violent, drinking, gambling "bad nigger"; and the Negro who, despite the formula for "getting along," prefers what he regards as independence to favors, and tries to act upon this principle.

There were among the youth reached by this study several who might easily be included in the classification "bad nigger." Although detested by whites they were sometimes silently endorsed by other Negroes who shared their racial attitudes but could not afford their irresponsible independence.

A number of youth in our study would be termed "uppity" in the sense in which the word is understood. There were, also, several who expressed feelings toward whites reminiscent of the faithful house slave. None of the youth, however, were without some measure of criticism of the bearing upon their lives and aspirations of the restricting institutions of the white world.

WHITE SOCIAL CLASSES AND THE RACE PATTERN

In order to understand the racial pattern in the South it is necessary to take into account the social and cultural stratification of the white population, and the unique relations existing between these classes. Historically the white planter and Negro tenant have been in many respects, in closer relationship than the white planter and the poor white. The latter has had no place in the plantation system and has had only a bare foothold in other rural areas. The result has been bitter antagonism on the part of the poor white toward the Negro who, under the protection first of slavery and later of the plantation system, kept the poor white impoverished, and there has been similarly, a contempt and dislike on the part of the Negro for the poor white. Over recent decades the increasing social mobility of the whole rural population has brought some changes in relations. The most notable of these changes have been the result of the increased political importance and expansion of the middle-class whites. This group plays a role in the racial situation distinct from that of the traditional poor white or rich white. They possess neither the bitter antagonism toward Negroes of the poor white nor the close personal relations which frequently obtain between Negroes and the white aristocracy. However, the traditional distinction between rich and poor whites remains in considerable measure in the complex patterns of relations and in the attitudes of Negroes. The distinction and the conflict of interests have, in fact, found continued usefulness in the newer economic relations of the area.

Although the Negro sharecropper and domestic are employed and often exploited by well-to-do whites, personal relations tend to obscure this fact in the thinking of the Negro group. White employers are frequently generous and kindly in dispensing small personal favors. This generosity does not often extend to the point of adequate wages because it is believed this would upset both the wage scale and the Negro scale of living. The Negro worker senses vaguely that he is being victimized but he does not direct his resentment against the "good white folks," who have listened so often and so patiently to his personal troubles. His resentment is directed to his economic competitors, the poor whites.

Typical of a traditional attitude of the rural Negro are the comments of a 20-year-old farm laborer in Coahoma County, Mississippi:

> Now the poor white folks is them that ain't got nothing, but thinks they is somebody. They like to pick on Negroes. They cheat them, 'buse them and meddle with them. An aristocratic white person is more decent about it. 'Course they cheat Negroes too, but they's nice about the way they do it. Some rich people are just poor white folks too. Money don't change them none, it's all in the way they act.

The difference in status between the wealthy and the poor whites is reflected in the objects of attention in the racial situation. The poor white pursues the noneconomic suppression of the Negro with greater vigor than the wealthy white person. The white plantation owner or successful businessman is secure in his position. He has ample opportunity for casual display of superiority without resort to direct personal reminders of his superiority. His position as employer automatically keeps his Negro employees "in their places." The poor white cannot always secure this automatic deference. His behavior suggests that he is uncertain of his position as "a white man." Economically he is frequently as impoverished as the Negro, and he is jealous of the fact that the Negro's relation to the employing group enables him to secure favors denied the poor white. Although the poor white's antagonism toward the wealthy white is denied expression by considerations of economic and legal expediency, Negro dependents of hated landowners or other employers offer vulnerable targets for suppressed antagonisms. The poor white utilizes every opportunity for asserting "white supremacy," partly because in his case it is a very meager and uncertain superiority, partly as an outlet for the hatreds generated by the social system of the South. Thus, the Negro is the target of the poor white not only because he is a competitor but also because of the Negro's identification with the upper-class white group of the South.

The reluctance of white employers to offer overt protection to Negroes from the antagonisms of the poor whites is an aspect of the situation which does not appear to be consciously comprehended by any of the three participating groups. It is to the advantage of the white landowner to keep his tenants docile. Various studies have emphasized this concern of the landowner. Thus Marsh Taylor, in *These Are Our Lives,* comments that "the Negroes who started farming in those high price times (1923) are much harder to handle than the older farmers."[1] Landlords prefer Negro tenants because they are "easy to handle," and the racial system of the South helps to keep the Negroes docile. The same landlords who refuse to engage poor whites as tenants have at times been observed to cooperate, at least passively, in the periodic aggressions of these poor whites against Negroes. These aggressions are in many respects the bulwarks of the race system, and the race system continues even now to be the bulwark of the plantation system.

ATTITUDES TOWARD THE RACIAL SITUATION

The response of Negro youth to the southern race system varies significantly between individuals and between areas. It is important to know not only the varieties of responses, but something of the quantitative distribution of the various types

[1] Federal Writers Project, *These Are Our Lives* (Chapel Hill: University of North Carolina Press, 1939), p. 120.

of response. Accordingly, we have employed both the interview and test methods in the results presented. Included in the group of tests was a Race Attitudes Test, designed to provide an index to the feelings of Negro youth toward members of the white community. Results of this test are presented in this chapter.

In addition to providing some indication of the numerical distribution of types of attitudes toward particular items of behavior, these tests served as a basis for the selection of youth for intensive interviewing.

CHARACTERISTIC ATTITUDES

Among the youth of all areas, social classes, and individual temperaments, two characteristics were observed which were fairly common: (a) they were race conscious to the extent of recognizing themselves as different and apart from the rest of the community; and (b) they entertained a conviction that Negroes, as a race, were treated unfairly and were suppressed economically. This latter attitude was held even by those who felt that they personally had escaped the more serious aspects of this status.

The extent of this feeling is suggested in the numbers endorsing test statements which reflected censure of white behavior. For example, of the statements concerned with behavior of white people towards Negroes, the two most frequently endorsed were "I think white people could do more for colored people but they won't" and "White people call Negroes bad names." Over 70 per cent of the southern rural Negro youth who took the Race Attitudes Test endorsed the statements in Table 22.

In our interviews the most frequent complaints were that white people try to keep Negroes down economically, and that whites insult and ridicule Negroes. The feeling that whites bar Negroes from economic advancement is probably the reason for the large number endorsing the statements "I think white people could do more for colored people, but they won't" and "White people think all Negroes should be servants."

Among the statements unfavorable to whites on the Race Attitudes Test is number 29, "White people are mean and stingy." The attitude reflects various types of situations in the rural areas involving direct, personal contact of these youth or their parents with individual whites. For example, Martha Grimes, a 16-year-old Shelby County, Tennessee, girl based her attitude on experiences in the country store. She said:

> I don't like white people at all. They are mean and hateful and selfish. They try to keep the colored people from having a thing. I know Mr. Spencer—he's that big, fat man in the store—every time, he will try and give me the wrong change, just because he wants to keep colored people poor. They are all like that—them what I know.

Table 22

STATEMENTS ON THE RACE ATTITUDES TEST ENDORSED BY
OVER 70 PER CENT OF RURAL NEGRO YOUTH[a]

Statement	Percentage Endorsing
There are all kinds of white people—some are good and some are bad.	95.6
I think white people could do more for colored people, but they won't.	91.3
White people call Negroes bad names.	90.5
Sometimes I think white people treat Negroes all right, and sometimes I don't.	86.4
Most of the big businesses are owned by white people.	83.8
White men have done wonderful things to make the United States a great country.	83.6
Most white people make fun of Negroes and laugh at them.	80.8
White people think all Negroes should be servants.	78.7
Sometimes white people make me mad, but they are no worse than other people.	75.1
The white race has produced some of the best and some of the worst men in history.	74.9
White people will always take care of a Negro who works hard and minds his own business.	71.7

[a] Based on responses of 2,235 boys and girls

Amos Dobbs, a 15-year-old Madison County, Alabama, boy, was motivated by a family experience with white neighbors of, presumably, a similarly low economic level when he said:

> A colored man said to my grandfather the other day that it's a wonder the white folks haven't poisoned his hogs because they're so big. White people don't like to see you have anything, and they try to make you get rid of your things. White

people want to borrow my grandfather's horses and don't even want to pay him for them.

Over half of the youth (58.4 per cent) endorsed the statement "White people are mean and stingy."

Economic Suppression

Low wages paid to Negroes are a common grievance. Lower-class Negro youth in particular are conscious of economic exploitation by whites. Many of them work as errand boys, maids, nurses, or at odd jobs. Two and three dollars a week are the usual wages received. On the Race Attitudes Test, 46.7 per cent of all youth felt that most white people did not pay Negroes fair wages.

Personal Humiliation

Sensitiveness about being called "bad names" which is so common among these youth suggests a considerable concern about preserving their own self-respect against behavior interpreted as attempts to humiliate. The following examples from the comments of these youth help to explain this attitude.

I was just 8 or 9 years old when white children first meddled me. I don't think I'd thought anything about them before. I don't think I'd felt any difference in white and colored till that day. I got in a fight with some little white children and they called me "nigger." That's not what we was fighting 'bout. We started fighting 'cause they tried to sic the dogs on me and I jumped on 'em.

Most white people I don't like. Some is nice. I used to play with white children when I was small and I liked them then, but since I grew up I don't bother with white people. If I did somebody might call me a name, and I'd sure fight 'em. It makes me mad if white children call me "nigger." I did fight a white girl once. I was about 15. She called me "black nigger" and I called her a "peckerwood." Then she got mad and slapped me. I pulled her hair and slapped her face. Ain't nobody done nothing about it. Nobody said nothing. She didn't have no right to start meddling with me.

As long as they [white people] don't fight and bother me, I like them. Some call you "black nigger" or worse names, but some white children have good manners and wouldn't say things like that.

Segregation

Segregation is not resented by Negro youth as vigorously as are economic suppression and insults from whites. While these youth are aware of the restrictions imposed by the racial mores, most of them have adjusted themselves to these restrictions. Unlike the injustices of white employers and the insults of white children, segregation does not seem to generate active resentment. Most youth feel that segregation imposes only minor deprivations. In most cases the youth expressed themselves as preferring not to associate with whites, and viewed their segregation with indifference. It is true, of course, that cause and effect may be somewhat confused here, since avoidance of whites is as much a consequence of segregation as it is a cause of the passive acceptance of segregation. The awareness of restrictions imposed by segregation and the rationalizations employed in th process of making adjustment are apparent in the comment of 15-year-old Raymond Towers, who said:

> I can't do everything a white person can. I can't go in a white café. I don't think it's fair 'cause they let you go there and buy everything else, but it never did bother me, I never wanted to sit down in there anyway, and I get plenty of milk at home.

The form of segregation most frequently resented is the restriction of recreational facilities to whites. Where recreational and other facilities are available within the Negro community, segregation does not seem to affect Negro youth very much. As indicated earlier, however, few desirable recreational and amusement facilities are open to Negroes. Carter Jones expressed the sentiments of many of them when he lamented:

> We don't have nothin'. The white people don't even think about colored children. You can't go to the movies because there ain't none. We don't have no parks or nothin' at all. The white boys and girls have a club house where they can play games and have a good time. In the back of the house they even have a playground with swings and everything. That's only for the

rich. The colored children ain't even allowed to watch them play.

The general attitude toward segregation is an excellent example of the manner in which adjustment is made to the interracial situation. These adjustments are both physical and psychological.

VARIATIONS IN ATTITUDES

There is a wide range in the types of response of Negro youth to racial situations. This can be indicated, first, statistically, in the distribution of race attitude scores, which are the number of statements unfavorable to whites endorsed by the youth. The favorable attitudes register at the lower extreme of the scale. There are slightly more girls than boys at the favorable extreme. This distribution is given in Table 23. Specific attitudes are

TABLE 23

ADJUSTMENT OF RURAL NEGRO YOUTH TO WHITE RACE, BY SEX
As Indicated by Distribution of Race Attitude Scores

Race Attitude Score	Boys		Girls	
	Number	Per cent	Number	Per cent
All scores	766	100.0	1,330	100.0
0	21	2.7	60	4.5
1	48	6.3	85	6.4
2	84	11.0	147	11.1
3	87	11.4	155	11.7
4	100	13.1	194	14.6
5	100	13.1	176	13.2
6	106	13.8	164	12.3
7	91	11.9	161	12.1
8	67	8.7	85	6.4
9	40	5.2	59	4.4
10	12	1.6	31	2.3
11	9	1.2	11	0.8
12	1	0.1	2	0.2
Average Score	*4.93*		*4.72*	

indicated in Table 24 which employs the individual statements endorsed by these youth. Some of the statements involve feeling in interracial situations while others are value judgments. The

Table 24

JUDGMENTS OF RURAL NEGRO YOUTH ABOUT THE
WHITE RACE, BY SEX[a]

As Indicated by Proportions Responding "True" to Statements on
Race Attitudes Scale

Statement	Percentage Responding "True"	
	Boys	Girls
There are all kinds of white people—some are good and some are bad.	94.2	96.4
White people call Negroes bad names.	91.5	89.9
I think white people could do more for colored people, but they won't.	89.6	92.3
White men have done wonderful things to make the United States a great country.	84.8	82.9
Most of the big businesses are owned by white people.	84.0	83.7
Sometimes I think white people treat Negroes all right and sometimes I don't.	83.4	88.2
Most white people make fun of Negroes and laugh at them.	81.0	80.6
The white race has produced some of the best and some of the worst men in history.	75.6	74.5
White people think all Negroes should be servants.	75.4	80.7
Sometimes white people make me mad, but they are no worse than other people.	74.1	75.7
White people will always take care of a Negro who works hard and minds his own business.	72.5	71.3
White people are human and have the faults of other human beings.	66.4	64.1
White people work hard and save their money.	65.1	61.9
No matter how nicely he treats a colored person, a white man doesn't really mean it.	63.5	65.3
Negroes would still be heathen savages if it were not for the work of white people in educating them and bringing them Christianity.	62.2	50.4
White people are mean and stingy.	60.5	57.2
White people don't treat Negroes any worse than other Negroes do.	58.1	61.7
I neither like nor dislike white people.	57.7	63.4
White people have better homes than other people.	57.4	54.1
Most white people give Negroes fair pay for the work they do.	56.8	51.2
White people are poor Christians.	51.7	48.9
The South was a beautiful place before white people came in and ruined it.	51.6	44.6
White people have built up the best civilization in the world.	50.4	38.7
All Negroes want from white people is to be let alone.	48.4	44.2
I never think about white people.	42.5	44.9
White people have done more for the world than any other race.	41.9	34.4
White people never did me any harm or any good.	40.6	37.7
White people are the cruelest people in the world.	37.6	37.7
White people don't take care of each other.	26.3	22.5
White people don't know how to have a good time.	20.5	18.3
Negroes should hate all white people.	16.7	11.8
I'd rather be dead than ask a white man for anything.	10.7	10.7

[a] Based on responses of 833 boys and 1,402 girls

highest percentage of endorsements, it is interesting to note, is on a statement which makes some distinction between white persons. A comparatively small proportion (10.7 per cent) endorses such an extreme statement as "I'd rather be dead than ask a white man for anything."

With this statistical distribution as a structure it is possible to evaluate more closely the significance of the free comment of the youth on racial status and relations with the white community.

Friendly Acceptance of Whites

The most favorable response to the white community is that of preferring whites to Negroes. This was noted in a few instances, in all of which the subordinate racial role of the Negro youth was taken for granted. In such instances, also, there was evidence either of contacts limited to certain classes of the white population or of some disagreeable experience with other Negroes. Elmira Fields, an 18-year-old Shelby County, Tennessee, girl, was fond of white people. Her attitude, however, revealed a careful distinction between classes of whites. She confided:

> I sure do like white folks. I like 'em better than colored most times. When I was small I played with white children around here. They don't fight and seem more 'greeable. They don't growl like colored children. The white people what got money treat colored folks fine. It's the poor ones that be jealous and treat colored bad. I never been in a fight with white children but had plenty of 'em with colored.

Janie Henderson, a 17-year-old Davidson County, Tennessee, girl, expressed a more favorable opinion of whites than most of the youth interviewed, even though her statements contained some reservations. She said:

> I sho' do like white people. I don't know why. They just nice. I don't visit none, but I know the man in the store and Mr. Schwartz, and all of them that knows me treat me well. I don't like white people as good as colored people because I'm colored —but I like 'em.

Very close to the traditional attitudes are the opinions expressed by Mary Graham, a 15-year-old girl in Macon County,

Alabama. Her father has deserted the family and Mary and her mother are share renters. Mary said:

> We got right smart white people up in town. I think a lot of them. 'Deed I do like white folks. All them I know in town is real nice. They talk nice to me and treat me all right. If we be nice to them, they be nice to us. I know Mr. Tatum. He's the white man what runs the store. He's smart, too. He treats me fine. Sometimes he gives me cookies or candies when I go to buy something. I sure do think white folks be smarter than colored. They got money and can go to school and they learn what the colored don't know. I don't wish I was white, but I just like white people. They can give me more than colored folks 'cause all the colored folks be poor like me.

Where Negroes and whites live in the same community, the children very often play together. This is particularly true in rural communities where the choice of playmates is limited. In other cases a Negro mother who works out in service may bring her younger children with her, and her children play with the children of her employer. Walter Petit was an only child and for several years was carried along by his mother when she went out to work. Walter explained:

> I got some young white boy friends. I knew them when we used to shoot marbles. I used to shoot halves with them. They liked to shoot halves with me 'cause I could shoot so good. I talk to them now, and today I showed some of them how to throw a curve [with a baseball].

Younger children in unstrained situations play normally. As they grow older they either take on more of the racial etiquette or break off relations entirely. Elsie Matthews referring to her own family explains the attitude engendered by these early relations and further suggests the differences in response that occur with increased age.

> White people next door is all right. They little child come over and play at our yard sometimes. I speaks to them every day. I calls them Mr. Newton or Miss Louise—that's the white lady. Call the boy Gerald or Dip—that's the name they give him. Willie, he like to play with that little white girl. He 'bout her age. They around 4 or 5. He do more for them white folks than he do for his own people.

Charlie Weems has worked with his father and learned from him how to act in the presence of whites. He does not feel restrained by the racial situation.

I meet a lot of white children when I go out with my father. Most of them are right nice, and we usually talk quite a good deal. I call them by their first name or I don't call them anything. I learned to treat the grown folks by watching how my daddy [a fish vendor] treats them. Many times these white people give me clothes. I can do most anything I want to do, it don't seem to me that white people prevent me from doing anything what I want. It might be that I've lived here all my life and I know I can do this and not that; but I feel perfectly happy here.

Ella Manders defines the white persons for whom she often worked as "good white people," and she observes no difference in their behavior toward her since she grew up.

I used to work with white people on the farm, but they were good white people. We stayed close to them and played with the children, and they was always over to our house. Their mother died and my mama helped them with the young baby. I see them sometimes now, and they treat me just like they always did.

In Davidson County there are small, scattered Negro communities. However, some Negro children met whites when their parents went out to work for nearby white families. Carrie Jenkins' experience with white children has left her with a favorable attitude. She said:

This is a colored community and I don't know of but one white family around here. My aunt washed for them and I used to go with her sometimes. They seemed nice. I have always played with white children where my aunt and mother worked, and I never had any trouble with them. I guess I was about 9 years old when I first started playing with them. My mother was working there and she told me to go play with the children. I didn't know them and they looked so white I didn't want to go. She said "Go on and play with them just like they was colored. They are children just like you." So I went on with them, but we fussed I guess like other children. One of them went away and she still writes me. Whenever I meet any of them in town we stop and talk about the good times we used to have and how we are getting along. They act just as friendly as they did when we were little.

Young people who occasionally play with white children may really prefer to play with Negroes. The Negro child usually learns very early that relations with whites are delicate matters requiring considerable diplomacy. In the cases quoted immediately above relations seemed natural and unstrained. In other cases the Negro child is never quite at ease with white playmates. Eddie Mays said:

> I ain't never had no fights with white boys. I played with them though. Once I went over there with my daddy, and while he was talking I played with them. I still play with them sometimes. We ain't never had no fuss or nothing when we playing, but I don't like to play with white boys. I don't like white folks nohow.

Back of the restraint is fear, not so much of the children themselves as of the race system. This is well illustrated in the comment of the young girl who said:

> I don't fool with them [white children]. I see 'em on the streets, but I never have nothing to do with 'em. When we lived in the country a little old po' white girl used to come up to see us. I guess we were both about 12 years old. She lived near our house and was always running over to play. I didn't take up much time with her and she finally stopped coming. Well, you see, she liked to play and I just wouldn't play with her much, because if you play with white children and hurt 'em you might get into trouble. Yes, my mother did tell me that if you fool around and hurt 'em it would be all on you. I liked to play and I'd play with her some, but I was just careful. Mama had tole me not to do nothing to 'em if they hit me. I guess I was about 11 then.

Avoidance of Whites

The most common response to white people is avoidance. About two-thirds of the rural Negro youth interviewed avoided contact with whites as much as possible. In some cases this avoidance is based on dislike of whites and discomfort in their presence. In other cases avoidance is simply a precaution. There is no active antipathy, but the youth prefer to avoid whites because of possible conflict. The latter group is willing to have contact with whites but considers it inexpedient. The former group feels that even friendly contacts with white people are undesirable.

On the Race Attitudes Test, while 67.5 per cent of the youth stated that they stayed away from white youth as much as they could, 41.4 per cent said they would not play with white children if they could, and between 25 and 30 per cent asserted that they definitely disliked white people.

The interviews confirm these test results in distinguishing three types of avoidance. There are youth who have little contact with white people but would have no objection to such contacts if there were favorable conditions. There are youth who prefer Negroes and are unwilling to associate with white people but do not actively dislike them. And there are youth who dislike white people. All of these young people consciously or unconsciously avoid whites. Each of the first two groups contains about 20 per cent of the rural Negro youth studied while the group which dislikes white people represents about one-fourth. There are also, of course, youth who do not avoid whites. These constitute about one-third of the group. The following comments illustrate the avoidance patterns of Negro youth.

Yes, them white folks is mighty nice, but I stays as far away from 'em as I can. I treats 'em nice when I comes in contact with 'em, but I don't have much to say. I don't never forget they's white. If colored folks do good or if they do bad, I'm always with 'em, 'cause they's my race.

I don't like 'em [white] and I don't hate 'em. I just stays out of their way. You know we don't see many white folks up this way. Mama told me a long time ago white folks didn't like to see colored folks get along, and if they dressed too well the white folks would whip 'em.

I get along with white people all right, but I don't bother with them. I see them in town and in the stores, but go on about my business and they let you alone. They are nice to you when you go into a store because they want your trade. If they weren't nice, colored shouldn't go there. I keep out of their way and there is no trouble.

I don't like white people. I wouldn't play with them. If they were kind I would, but they are mean and I don't have nothing to do with them. No'm, I don't know any white children at all. I ain't never played with them.

I gets along with white folks fine 'cause I don't have nothin' to do with them. I don't associate with them at all, but I just stay with the colored folks. That's the best way to get along with white folks—stay away from them. But they don't bother you much out here, though. I ain't heard of them beating up no colored folks for a long time. They do's pretty well out here, I guess. But white folks ain't to be made friends with too much.

White people are mean. I don't like them. I'm glad I live where there ain't none. I don't know no white people, but I know I don't like them. They don't like colored people and try to fight them and down them. That's why I don't like them.

I don't like white people. I don't know why except they don't like colored people. Everybody out at this school is colored, and I'm glad. I don't like to be near white people. I want to be true to my race, and I can't be true to my race and like white people, too, can I?

I sure don't like white folks. Me and Juliette [sister] hates 'em. They always laughin' and pokin' fun at colored people. They don't want colored to have nothin' either. Seems like they try to hurt your feelin's. They never call me no names. I ain't never been in a fight with none. If I did, I'd be in trouble. Ain't no tellin' what they'd do to me if I hit a white girl. I stay out of their way.

Dissimulation

Among some of the youth outward conformity concealed inner discontent. Since resentment is more easily attached to persons than to things, the antagonisms of these Negro youth were directed against white people, and particularly against poor whites. It was not uncommon to find attitudes of Negro youth toward whites in conflict with behavior toward whites. The traditional race system makes the expression of antagonism inadvisable and even dangerous. Outward submissiveness and respect may thus be, as often as not, a mask behind which these youth conceal their true attitudes. George Cater is an example of this behavior. He has learned to flatter and to conceal his own feeling as a means of preserving his own estimate of himself.

Papa told me not to start no fight with them [whites], but if they start to fighting me for me to fight back. I first used to make nickels and dimes off them, going different places, and then I started cutting off yards. When I'm around them I act like they are more than I am. I don't think they are, but they do. I hear people say that's the best way to act.

Parents teach their children to restrain themselves in situations involving contact and possible conflict with white children.

I've had white children meddle me. They call me "little black nigger" and "chocolate drop" and things like that. Mama told me not to pay them any attention and not even to look at them, so I don't. But I'd be thinking I'd like to beat them up. I'm not scared of them, but I'm scared of their parents 'cause I know they'd get a crowd and come and beat me good.

Resistance

Negro youth in the rural South as a rule try to avoid overt conflicts with white youth. Fights between Negro and white children occur, but most Negro youth will fight only when the provocation is extreme. At an early age they learn that fighting with whites is dangerous. When assaulted and unable to escape, the Negro boy will defend himself, but Negro youth do not often initiate fights with whites, and defense against aggression is usually a last resort.

I like to had a fight with some white boys not so long ago. A white boy jumped on one of my buddies when we was coming home. My buddy left—he must of got scared or something. I didn't do nothing and they throwed a rock at me. I didn't throw back till they kept on throwing. I throwed and hit one, and he say he going to get me, but he ain't done nothin' yet, and I seen him sometimes since. I told mama about it, and she say not to bother them, but don't let them do nothing to me.

Youth in the upper class are more apt to resist aggression. Upper-class parents attempt to keep their children from contact with whites in so far as it is possible. The youth do not work for white people and only play with white children when family acquaintance makes this safe. Lower-class parents cannot keep their children from contact with whites. In lower-class families the youth frequently must work, and this usually means that they must work for white people. Lower-class youth soon learn to avoid conflicts with whites. Parental instructions emphasize staying out of fights with white children. Upper-class youth do not acquire such habits of submission and, since their parents attempt to keep the children from contact with whites, warnings against conflict are less explicit. When attacked by a white youth, an upper-class Negro boy may resist vigorously. Elton Summers' experience suggests this sensitiveness and the mode of response.

> I have had lots of fights with white boys down here. I guess the biggest fight I had was at a carnival they had here a few years ago. They had a greasy pig out there, and a white fellow was trying to catch it. When he got all greasy a group of colored boys I was with laughed at him. He came over where we were and said, "What you niggers laughing at?" Nobody said anything to him, and he wiped his greasy hands across my face. I hit him three times before he hit me once. People stopped the fight quickly—white and colored people stopped it. If they hadn't there would have been a race riot. I didn't tell mama and dad about it because I was afraid they might not let me go to the next one.

If white and Negro boys meet where there is no possibility of adult intervention, the Negro boy may obtain revenge for humiliations. One Madison County, Alabama, youth said:

> I never had no trouble with white people much, except some little old boys over in factory town. When me and my cousin used to go over there, two or three little boys tried to be bad. They got behind a house and chucked us. But when they came down on the railroad to pick blackberries we got them. We'd catch them, but we wouldn't do nothing but make pretend we was going to hurt them. We didn't hurt them though, 'cause we 'fraid we'd get in some trouble.

Not all such youth, however, are as timid in their aggressions as the boy just quoted. There is, for instance, the so-called "bad nigger," who is less restrained by the powerful race mores, who will fight if attacked, and who refuses to be humiliated. These individuals become social problems of the adult white population who regard such an attitude as dangerous to race relations and an irresponsible defiance of the prestige of the white race.

While comparatively safe from individual attack by white boys, these aggressive Negro boys are likely to be punished on the smallest provocation or suspicion by the police or self-deputized white adults.

Resignation

In spite of the brave talk and wishful thinking of many of the youth, there was in their comments a pervasive strain of resignation and futility. It appeared in their manner and inflections of speech where it was not present in their words. Occasionally this background of resignation was articulated. It was more a passive than an active fear, but it exercised a cramping restraint. Guy Miller of Shelby County, Tennessee, provides the words and the mood when he says:

> I like white folks all right, but I just don't want to have no trouble with them. Oh, if I did get in trouble with 'em I wouldn't do nothing. I couldn't do nothing. They'd kill me. White folks don't play with no colored folks. You have to do what they want or else your life ain't worth nothin'.

Desire to Escape by Migration

Reference was made in Chapter II to the number of southern rural youth who expressed a desire to get away from their environment. Where a definite preference for the North is expressed, the presumption is strong that racial as well as economic handicaps are the motivating factor. Sixty-one per cent of the girls and 65 per cent of the boys expressed a desire to move away from the South and go to the North or West. In some cases racial attitudes are explicit and vigorously expressed. Robert Calloway of Coahoma County, Mississippi, looked to the North, because there "You don't have to be cowed like you do here." He said:

> I know I'd like Detroit, and I'd like to go now. I've never been there, but I like it from the way they [relatives in Detroit] describe it. There is so much to see, and you can learn more in a shorter time. You wouldn't have to work like you do here, and you have more freedom there. You don't have to be cowed like you do here. The white people here want to be first, and my people who live in Detroit don't like it here at all. I been here and I'm used to it, but I'd like to get away. They [whites] think

they should be first in everything. Even in the stores they want to be waited on first. If I'm in a hurry and they wait on them first, I walk out, but if it's something I want I'll stay and wait. Then some of them look at you so underhand; seem like they're angry with you, and sometimes they meddle. Most of the time they call you "old nigger."

Southern rural youth who have been in the North express a decided preference for northern race patterns even though they might be emotionally attached to the South in other respects. This is true despite the lack of consistent differences between northern and southern urban youth. However, the few rural youth interviewed who had been North had been to Chicago or Detroit. No tests were conducted in Detroit, but Chicago youth were the most favorable to whites of any group tested. While the preferences expressed for the North may be specific reactions to Chicago and Detroit, it is reasonably certain that the youth have in mind the general advantages of the North for living. An important factor in these attitudes is the contrast between North and South as it impresses the southern migrant. To the northern born Negro, discriminations against Negroes in northern cities (particularly economic barriers) are painfully apparent. To the youth newly arrived *from* the South or recently arrived *in* the South, the vastly greater freedom of the northern Negro overshadows the racial and economic difficulties which northern cities still impose upon Negroes. Youth who had been to Chicago spoke most favorably of race relations there. What impressed Ernest Greene of Bolivar County was that "You don't have to 'Yassuh' and 'Nossuh' every old white man." He said, further:

I liked Chicago fine, 'specially how white and colored got on together. Colored people go right in the front door and ride right on the streetcars with white folks; and practically do anything. They has colored policemen there. Northern white people are just nicer than southern ones. They don't bother you and try to keep you where they think you belong.

Some differences in attitude exist between adults and youth on the matter of remaining in the South and in the capacity for judging happiness in the southern society. Many of the adults look forward to no change in their status and find such satisfactions as are possible from their set circumstances. Whether they lived there originally or not, many of the youth, on the other hand, entertain some hope of change either in their environment or their geographical relationship to it, and this hope continues whether they see any prospect of change or not. Moreover, this attitude is not confined to those of superior advantages or experiences. The boy whose statements are quoted immediately above is a typical plantation hand. He has worked in the fields from the age of 10, and boasted of his prowess in picking cotton.

Desire to Be White

Another attitude expressed itself in the desire to be white. The number who accept such an escape from the race situation is, however, small. Of 2,241 youth responding on this item, only 89 or 4 per cent endorsed the statement "I wish I were white" on the Personal Attitudes Test. This response seems to be associated with a high degree of maladjustment. These 89 youth score 20 points above the general average in the total maladjustment score, the average being 56.6 for the 89 youth who wish to be white, and 36.7 for the whole group of rural Negro youth.

The Negro community is built around the idea of adjustment to being a Negro, and it rejects escape into the white world. Community opinion builds up a picture of whites as a different kind of being, with whom one associates but does not become intimate. Without much conscious instruction the child is taught that his first loyalties are to the Negro group. He may criticize Negroes and even dislike them, but he is a Negro and must not even wish to be otherwise. This doctrine is reinforced by stories of the meanness and cruelty of white people. To wish to be white is a sacrifice of pride. It is equivalent to a statement that Negroes are inferior and, consequently, that the youth himself is inferior.

Henry Stubblefield wished to be white. He also said he preferred to play with white rather than colored boys. His other responses indicate serious maladjustment. His is a marginal personality in an acute sense, a mulatto youth who reflects to an exceptional degree the struggle of loyalties between his biological relationship to the white world and his admiration for it, and his only opportunity for comfortable living in the Negro world. On the Personal Attitudes Test he also checks as "true" such statements as: "Sometimes I feel so blue I'd like to kill myself," "I wish I could go away and live somewhere else," "I'm usually the last to be picked for a team," "I like to be around grownups more than around fellows of my own age," and "I find it hard to get along with other people in school."

These are statements endorsed by 25 per cent of the boys, or less. Only 29 per cent of the rural boys said that Negroes are cowards, and only 13 per cent said "Negroes are the meanest people in the world." Henry Stubblefield agreed with both of these statements. Although he endorsed only one statement on the scale of statements unfavorable to whites, he endorsed nine unfavorable statements on the Negro scale. The most beautiful girl he knows and the man and woman he looks up to most are all white.

Henry is generally disliked among the boys and girls because they accuse him of feeling "better than the others because his father was a white man." A schoolmate said:

> He's low-down and always trying to get away with something. I believe he's had a fight with most every boy at school, and he always gets whipped.

The principal at the school said:

> Henry is a fellow of not too much ability who looks down on the other fellows. He doesn't compare very highly with most of the boys, socially, physically, or scholastically; so he has set up a "color bar" to satisfy his desire for prestige. He is not a good student, and just does avoid being a discipline problem.

Henry's interview does not completely reveal the extent of his maladjustment. The interviewer notes: "He is very furtive and reluctant about talking; he appeared ill at ease in the presence of a stranger." Indirect evidences of Henry's maladjustment are present in the interview. One source of this boy's difficulties is the fact that his father was white. He, himself, is a slender, weak-looking adolescent of 16, with light-brown wavy hair, blue eyes, Nordic features, and a "poor white complexion." His face is full of blemishes and has a sickly pallor. Henry has had several conflicts with other Negro youths, all of them centering around his maladjustment within the Negro group and his wish to be white. He boasted in the interview that one of his bosses called another boy " 'nigger' and never called me out of my name." The following, in his own language, is the type of situation in which Henry gets involved:

> I got in a fight with one of the boys [on his first job, waiting table at a night club] about playing the slot machine, and we got fired. This old boy said that I promised to go halves with him, and after he had put in about 50 cents he grabbed me and said "Come on, pay your share." I just hit him in the mouth, and the fellow that ran the place fired us. This was a real dark boy, and he didn't like me much because the boss called him "nigger" or "black boy" and he never called me out of my name.

> I don't know why, but white people always treat me better than other boys. They never call me names and never whipped me, but they often do other ones, 'specially dark boys. They even give me easier work to do. They don't give me any more privileges, though. I'm still considered colored.

Most rural Negro youth state that they prefer to be colored. The reasons given are varied: "race loyalty," "white people's meanness," or no reason at all. As one of the boys said:

> White people just think they own the world. They won't give Negroes no chance at all. 'Course, we don't run into white folks much, living down here, but I'm talking about other places. They just make me tired. I wouldn't be white for a million dollars.

Another youth, discussing the subject of being white, said:

> White people can work in offices and in the mill and clerk in stores and banks, and colored can't do that. White children have finer schools and better clothes to wear, and better houses. I'd like to clerk in a store, but I can't do that because I'm colored. I wouldn't like to be white so I could do all that. I'd rather stay colored. Some people say they wish they was white, but I don't 'cause some white folks don't have no more than colored. No'm, even if they was rich, I'd rather stay colored, because there's

some colored just as rich. I don't think I'd like to go to school with white children even if they do have better schools. I'd rather go to the colored school. I'd just feel better with my own color.

FACTORS DETERMINING ATTITUDES TOWARD THE RACIAL SITUATION

Several major influences appear to be important in molding the attitudes of Negro youth toward whites. These are (1) the community, (2) class position, (3) family training, (4) individual experiences, (5) age, and (6) intelligence. In some cases all six influences may operate. In other cases only one of the factors seems to have much influence.

THE COMMUNITY

The influence of the community in molding race attitudes is suggested in the differences in race attitudes observed between

TABLE 25

ADJUSTMENT OF RURAL NEGRO YOUTH TO WHITE RACE,
BY COUNTY AND SEX

As Indicated by Average Race Attitude Scores[a]

County	Boys		Girls	
	Number of cases	Average score	Number of cases	Average score
All counties	766	4.93	1,330	4.72
Johnston, N.C.	167	5.06	83	4.65
Davidson, Tenn.	78	4.05	93	3.34
Shelby, Tenn.	110	4.59	145	4.45
Coahoma, Miss.	102	5.13	327	5.01
Bolivar, Miss.	106	5.50	190	5.38
Madison, Ala.	79	4.72	90	4.57
Macon, Ala.	92	5.42	145	5.30
Greene, Ga.	32	4.16	257	4.27

[a] Attitude is measured by average scores on a racial attitude scale. A score of 0 indicates the least amount of maladjustment toward whites, and a score of 13 indicates the greatest degree of maladjustment

the different areas studied. Table 25 gives the average scores on the test of Negro attitudes toward white people. (A high score indicates an unfavorable attitude.)

Of the rural youth tested, Davidson County, Tennessee, youth were the most favorable in their race attitudes. Average scores of boys and girls differ somewhat, but both listings agree that Davidson County youth were most favorable to white people, while Bolivar County, Mississippi, and Macon County, Alabama, youth were least favorable. The results of the Personal Attitudes Test also show less antagonism to whites among Davidson County youth. Although 27.6 per cent of the rural youth in all counties combined stated that they hated white people, in Davidson County only 14.8 per cent hated whites. On the other hand 30.1 per cent of the Bolivar County youth hated whites.

Plantation Influence

Differences in test results seem to be based on community characteristics. Bolivar County, for example, is in the heart of the plantation belt. It has the most exacting racial restrictions of any of the counties studied. Segregation is rigid and the racial etiquette is strictly enforced. The white persons, other than the large and sometimes benevolent landlords, are economic competitors of the Negro, directly or indirectly, and share a tradition of hostility to him. On the plantation the ownership units are larger and personal relations between landlord and tenant are less frequent than in other counties where small farms are operated. Illiteracy is high and exploitation of tenants is common. The limitations of life in the plantation area generate bitter, hopeless attitudes. The heart of this area is the Mississippi Delta. A common belief in Negro communities outside Mississippi is that it is the worst place in the entire country for Negroes. To some extent this opinion is shared by Negroes in Mississippi. The mother of one Bolivar County youth expressed this feeling rather succinctly when she said "Mississippi is awful." She continued:

> All the important things Negroes can't do. This is the last state in the world. Ought not to belong to the Union. They ought to drop it out like they did Jim's birthday.

All-Negro Community

Mound Bayou, an all-Negro community in Bolivar County, has fostered a tradition of race consciousness. Youth in this town have little contact with whites, and they were nearly unanimous in expressing sentiments of racial solidarity. Their attitudes on race were more often based on community sentiment than upon individual experience. They have more race pride than most of the other southern Negroes, and more pronounced hostility to whites. Most of this hostility is based upon fear which is untempered by the adjustment possibilities discovered in daily contact situations. The following are expressions of the youth of Mound Bayou:

> I don't like white folks. They kill you. No, they don't kill everybody. Ain't nary one done nothin' to me, but I'm scared they might kill me.

> I don't believe in white and colored mixing together. That's why I likes Mound Bayou, you don't have to mix with the white folks. Everything is run by colored people. If white folks lived here, you know we wouldn't have that big, three-story school house and all them teachers. Colored folks feel better when they don't have white folks around.

> We don't see much of them [white people] around here, but when we lived in Clarksdale there were some around. Some of them are mean and hateful to colored people and go out of their way to bother them, even though they never did anything to me.

As the interviewer and a youth rode through a small town near Mound Bayou, the boy said:

> This is a bad town for colored people. The police get you for little or nothing, and beat you up. They don't like for Negroes to come here, and Negroes don't stop unless they have to.

> People around here don't like Mr. Roberts [one of the most successful citizens of Mound Bayou] much because he gives in to white people too much. He has tried to get elected mayor, but the people don't want him because he'll let white people tell him how to run the town. We can run our town, though, and get along without them.

Occasionally the attitude becomes contemptuous as in the case of the youth who said in describing whites, "they look like ha'nts." This was intended as fearless indifference to the lower-class whites of the area.

> I don't pay them peckerwoods no mind. They don't bother you less you monkey with 'em, and I don't have nothin' to say to 'em. They tickle me, they look like ha'nts.

Nonplantation Area

Although many Davidson County, Tennessee, youth had almost as little contact with whites as youth in Mound Bayou, attitudes were much more favorable. They do not live in a community of organized racial sentiment; they are in less exacting competition with whites and have a different traditional background. One young girl said:

> Oh, we get along pretty good with white folks out here. Don't have much trouble. If you don't bother them they ain't gonna bother you none. Just keep to yourself and you'll be all right. I ain't exactly crazy about white folks, but I don't hate them either. They is all right in they place.

The following are comments of other nonplantation youth:

> I like white people all right. Them I know around here is all right. In Indianapolis I played with white boys. They were all right. We'd play baseball together. I like them all right.

> I don't have much contact with white people. The people across the street who run the walnut factory are white and I know them all well enough to call them by their first names. They call us by our first names, too; but they call my mother "Mrs." Stokes. They are always borrowing something from us like garden tools, scissors, and wash tubs, but we don't borrow from them. One thing about them is they always return the things that they borrow. We get walnut hulls from them to burn in our stove.

> I like to talk with the white people in my neighborhood as they are very friendly. I have eaten at their homes and they have meals at my home. Many parents come to visit my entire family. The lady who owns the grocery store comes every Saturday and sits a while. They [the white people in this community] only associate with my family, my aunt, and another family.

The relatively friendly race relations reflect the absence of the plantation system, which was never successful in Davidson

County. The rural parts of the county are primarily nonfarm areas. In the other counties studied, 50 to 70 per cent of all families are farm families. In Davidson County only 23 per cent are farm families. This implies different types of Negro-white relationships than the traditional white planter and Negro tenant or poor white and Negro relationships.

Racial taboos in Davidson County are present, but are relaxed. Negroes and whites occasionally eat together, shake hands, and play games together. Rules for addressing white people are not rigid and whites usually, but not always, are willing to address Negroes as "Mr." and "Mrs." Negroes frequently enter homes by the front door. In most stores Negroes and whites receive identical service. Negroes are not segregated in courtrooms, and Negro lawyers try cases, although Negroes do not serve on juries. Negroes vote without interference, and Negro professional men occasionally have white patients. Whites work with Negroes and occasionally for Negroes.

Some of these practices occur in the other counties studied, but they are not as common as in Davidson County. In common with other counties, Davidson has a segregated school system; segregation on streetcars, buses, in railroad waiting rooms, in theaters, parks, hospitals, and libraries. Except for the provision of separate toilets, Davidson County does not discriminate against Negroes in public buildings, that is, Negroes use the same doors and other services as whites. In securing licenses, paying taxes, and so forth, Negroes in Davidson County wait in the same line as whites, and are served in their regular turn.

Community Differences as Measured by the Tests

Race attitude scores of urban youth support the conclusion that rural plantation life is associated with unfavorable attitudes toward whites. Average scores of race attitudes indicated less hostility to whites on the part of Negro youth in Atlanta, Baltimore, Chicago, New Orleans, New York, Fort Worth, and Greensboro[2] (North Carolina), than in any of the rural counties

---

[2] Springfield, Massachusetts, conforms to these results.

except Davidson. Davidson County youth are closer in their rating to the urban youth than they are to the rural youth. This may be partially due to the fact that this is a predominately urban county. A rural group of 4-H club members tested in Greensboro, North Carolina, resembled the other rural youth in having a relatively unfavorable race attitude.

The two factors that appear to account for differences in attitudes between the plantation and nonplantation areas are the economic operation of the plantation system itself and the social distance between Negroes and whites in the plantation areas. In the first place, the system leaves the Negro tenant with the feeling that he has not been treated justly. Our family interviews make frequent reference to the fact that whites expect Negroes to work for little or no wages, that white landlords turn over to the tenants little cash in return for their year's work. In the second place, the farm youth, as indicated earlier, have little direct personal contact with whites. They may have played with white children when younger, but this is more common in the villages and in the areas near towns than in the farm areas. The relation of Negro tenant to white landlord is an increasingly impersonal one. Contacts with whites are brief. The tenants see the landlord when they make their agreement, sometimes when they get their supplies, when the landlord inspects the farm, and at settling time. In many cases all of these transactions are conducted by managers, overseers, or even clerks. Contacts are made by the family head and the youth rarely participate. They hear frequent comment about white people, in complaint or appreciation, and have no personal experiences which might tend to contradict the stereotypes of the communty. Attitudes are developed toward whites in general and not toward individuals.

Village youth more often have personal contact with white people as playmates and as employers. Some of these contacts are pleasant and some are unpleasant. They serve, however, to disturb stereotyped concepts. To them some white people seem to be "all right." The fact that Davidson County is more suburban than the rest may account for the more favorable attitudes of Negro youth toward whites as compared with youth in Bolivar County, Mississippi, and other plantation counties.

Urban youth appear to have fewer personal contacts with whites than village or suburban youth. In the city community opinions are less organized and less effective, however, and stereotypes are not as well developed as in the small, intimate rural communities. For this reason urban youth, like village youth, show attitudes more favorable to whites. There is a difference, however, in that the urban youth's feeling toward whites is likely to be one of indifference, while the village youth's feelings are complicated by the conflict of personal observations and community stereotypes.

Urban as well as rural attitudes vary with community differences. Average scores on the test of attitudes toward whites appear in Table 26.

TABLE 26

ADJUSTMENT OF SOUTHERN AND NORTHERN URBAN NEGRO
YOUTH TO WHITE RACE, BY CITY AND SEX
As Indicated by Average Race Attitude Scores[a]

City	Boys		Girls	
	Number of cases	Average score	Number of cases	Average score
SOUTHERN CITIES	381	3.40	752	3.52
Atlanta, Ga.	96	2.86	171	2.65
Fort Worth, Tex.	71	3.13	176	3.54
Greensboro, N.C.	49	3.12	104	3.77
Nashville, Tenn.	72	4.68	139	5.06
New Orleans, La.	93	3.30	162	2.92
BORDER CITY (Baltimore, Md.)	37	2.35	121	2.34
NORTHERN CITIES	209	3.80	379	3.12
Chicago, Ill.	79	1.94	129	2.11
New York, N.Y.	18	3.06[b]	124	3.02
Philadelphia, Pa.	82	5.43	95	4.78
Springfield, Mass.	30	4.67	31	2.65

[a] Attitude is measured by average score on a racial scale. A score of 0 indicates least amount of maladjustment toward whites, and a score of 13 indicates the greatest degree of maladjustment.

[b] Unreliable, due to small sample

Both northern and southern cities appear among the highest and lowest ranking cities. The order for boys and girls is about the same. Although Springfield, Massachusetts, shows a large shift in position when boys and girls are compared, the three groups with attitudes most favorable to whites (Chicago, Baltimore, Atlanta) and the two with the most unfavorable attitudes (Nashville and Philadelphia) are the same for boys and girls. This, together with other evidence, indicates that race attitudes are more dependent upon specific community settings and the racial mores and adjustment to them than upon regional location or upon sex.

The operation of community opinion may be subtle and indirect. An 18-year-old Madison County, Alabama, boy said that no one had told him how to act toward white people, but his comments indicate that he acquired definite adjustment patterns, and these patterns are those prevalent in his community.

> Ain't nobody tell me how to act around them [white people]. I just knowed how to tend to my business and let them tend to theirs. I knowed if I didn't, there'd be trouble. I was scared of white folks when I was small. I thought they had the rule. I don't know the reason why I thought that. I can't remember nobody telling me that. I don't never fight with no white people, and I don't play with them neither. Some of them call me "nigger." I don't do nothin'. I just keep going. I know that's what I is—a nigger—so I keep on. I don't get mad. I know that's what I'm supposed to be, and it don't make me mad.

CLASS POSITION

In families on the upper levels more youth wish to migrate to the North. There is no consistent relation between the father's occupation and the place the youth wishes to live. Fifty-five per cent of the youth with unemployed fathers, and 59.7 per cent of the youth whose fathers were farmers, wished to live in the North or West, while 62.6 per cent of all youth wished to live in the North. The highest per cent of youth wishing to migrate is found in the skilled workers' group (74.4 per cent).

Desire to migrate is more closely related to the father's education than to his occupation. Of youth whose fathers had completed only the second grade or less, 45.8 per cent wished to live in the North or West, compared with 70.5 per cent of those whose fathers had completed the tenth grade or more. A slight correlation between mothers' education and desire to migrate also appears. For the mothers the corresponding percentages were 60.9 and 68.9.

Upper-class families are more conscious of the difficulties of being a Negro in the rural South. The greater sensitivity of the upper-class Negro to racial discrimination is attributable to two factors: (1) his greater familiarity with political and social thought, and (2) the contradiction between his personal achievements and his social position. The upper-class Negro is more aware of the regional variations in racial prejudice. He sees the race system of the South as a local phenomenon, while the less educated Negro is apt to regard white domination as part of the order of the universe. The upper-class Negro also feels himself entitled by training and ability to achieve a high social position in the community—a position denied by reason of race alone.

Upper-class parents find migration inconvenient for themselves but pass on their feelings to their children. These youth, unencumbered by the responsibilities of homes and businesses, frequently carry into practice the desire of their parents to migrate. This is particularly true of those who succeed in acquiring a college education. Despite the greater opportunities for college graduates as teachers in the Negro colleges and separate school systems in the South, about one-fourth of the southern born Negro college graduates are living in the North. Only 19 per cent of the Negro college graduates return to their home towns to live there permanently. Of Negroes listed in *Who's Who in Colored America*, 77 per cent were born in the South but only 39 per cent live there.[3] While Negroes as a whole are leaving the rural South, the rate of migration is clearly higher for persons at the upper economic and educational levels, and particularly for the younger Negroes. The established professional men, of course, do not find it expedient to leave.

[3] Charles S. Johnson, *The Negro College Graduate* (Chapel Hill: University of North Carolina Press, 1938), pp. 41-54.

Reactions of an upper-class youth to race relations in a northern city indicate the motives prompting this group to migrate. This boy was sent to Chicago by his father, a very successful businessman in Madison County, to take advantage of superior school facilities there.

I was 11 when I went. When he [his father] first told me I was going to Chicago, I was glad, but when I sat down and thought, I got scared. I had read about gangsters in Chicago, in the paper, and I got to thinking about them. After a while, though, I decided that a lot of other people were living there and hadn't got hurt, so I wouldn't get hurt either.

We went in a car. I liked Chicago right away. I liked it because there are a lot of big buildings; people are always on the go; the beautiful lakes, streetcars and the "El's."

I went to St. Elizabeth. That's a Catholic school. It's different from the school down here. The discipline is better. I mean there is a regular routine of work. The teachers seem interested in you and your work.

There weren't but a few white students in St. Elizabeth. You see it's right in the middle of a colored section. I was in a class with a white boy. I felt scared because I didn't know any of the children or anybody. I didn't know how to act. I didn't like that white boy who was in my class at first either. I had some prejudice against white children when I went up there, I guess. When I left I had in my mind that there were two kinds of white people, poor whites who were mean, and nice white people who were all right.

Well, this boy in my class looked to me like one of the poor white kind. I guess that's why I didn't like him at first. He was part Italian. He said something to me first. We used to shoot marbles together and play ball. I forgot he was white sometimes. While I was up there I lost a lot of my prejudice against white people.

After I finished St. Elizabeth I went to DuSaible High. All the students there are colored, but they have white and colored teachers. One thing I noticed at first, and used to think a lot about, was that the students didn't like a teacher just because she was colored. The teacher that was liked best was a white teacher.

It's hard to come back down here and live after you've been in Chicago for five years. That prejudice I lost against white people is coming back because of these poor white crackers in Mill Town. If you go down there they call you "nigger" and run you. Only the low-class white people do that. Sometimes I just sit down and wonder what can be done about the race problem. I think about such things after I read about a lynching.

Sometimes I forget I'm colored when we are around playing, but something will always happen to make me remember that I am colored. Well, sometimes I see a pretty white girl on the street and I would like to say something to her, but I know I'm colored and I can't. I start thinking about that after I see these pretty moving picture stars in the theater and then come out and see some white girls that look like them. No, I never had anything to say to any of them down here, and I never will.

FAMILY TRAINING

While many parents make no attempt to influence their children's attitudes toward white people, other than to protect them from danger, parallel opinions of parents and children often appear in the interviews. A 17-year-old-Macon County, Alabama, girl echoed her father's opinion that white people "try to keep Negroes down." This girl had little personal contact with whites and her statements were evidently not based on personal experience. Statements of father and daughter show interesting similarities. The father said:

> White folks are all right long as a man stays in his place. Down here in the South a Negro ain't much better off than he was in slavery times. We work all the time but we don't get nothin' for it 'cept a place to live and plenty to eat. I ain't got nothin' 'gainst white people, but they won't give Negroes a chance. We all equal and ought to have an equal chance, but we can't get it here. In this settlement there ain't no white folks. Folks live peaceably here and tend to their own business, so I consider it a good place to be.

The daughter of this man said:

> I don't like white people. I don't know why. There ain't no reason 'cept they think they are better than colored and try to keep the colored people down. Maybe all white people ain't alike, but I don't like none of them.

A Johnston County, North Carolina, girl from a culturally impoverished sharecropping family had attitudes based on her family's experience with white people. Her father said:

> White folks around here don't bother you none. It's the niggers doing all the fighting and talking. Mr. Parker [their landlord], he's just like my own brother—gives me whatever I want, like food. I know all the white folks roundabout, and they are good people. 'Cos, there ain't none close to us 'cept Mr. Parker—they live down the road a piece, 'bout a mile or so—but they come up here sometimes to see Mr. Parker.

The community in which this family lives is not particularly favorable to whites. The family is not popular in the Negro community and dislikes its Negro neighbors. The father commented, "People round here pretty bad themselves, yet they talk about my family." The daughter shared her father's opinion of white people, although she showed no antagonism to the Negroes in the community.

> The white people here are nice. They give you food if you need it, and if anyone is sick they will help you. I don't know many, but Mrs. Parker, she is fine to us. Yes, I like white people all right. They are nice, but I'd rather be colored. Don't know why. Just because I am, I guess.

In Bolivar County a sharecropper commented:

> You got to treat white folks like they a silk handkerchief on a barb wire fence. They'll bump you off if you don't. They'll sho bump you off.

This man's 13-year-old son expressed similar feelings regarding the temperament of white people.

> I guess white people are all right. They ain't never done me no kinda way, but they real mean to a lotta people.

That many racial attitudes of rural Negro youth are based on the opinions of parents or other adults in the community rather than on personal experience is indicated by the fact that youth who have had little or no contact with white people express attitudes as definite as those of youth who have had a great deal of personal contact with whites.

INDIVIDUAL EXPERIENCE

Individual experience has a marked influence on the feeling of Negro youth toward whites in some cases. These experiences generally tend to reinforce or modify the stereotyped attitudes of the community.

Frances Hall's mother died under circumstances which embittered her against white people. Although Frances was a small girl when she lost her mother her bitterness has only increased with the years, possibly because the need and desire for a mother became stronger as the girl matured.

> I don't like white people. I hate some of them. Maybe some are all right, but I don't like any of them. There ain't no colored doctors around here. If you get real sick you have to call a white doctor or just die. The white doctors are so mean they won't come to see colored no matter if you're almost dead, unless you have the money. I was only about 5 years old when mama died. I don't remember her much. Gertrude [her sister] remembers her. I remember she was kind and sweet and good, and I was real happy then. I loved my mama. Well, she got real sick and didn't nobody know what was the matter. Papa called the white doctor, 'cause there ain't no colored ones, but he wouldn't come 'til we got enough money and then the doctor came to mama. He gave her a little medicine and told papa not to call him any more, 'cause he couldn't do nothing for mama. The doctor said to send her to Wilson to the hospital there. Well, that was the year that all the colored people who went to the hospital at Wilson died. Well, the doctor wouldn't come to mama, so they sent her to Wilson, and sure enough, she died too. I remember everyone crying, and they brought her back dead.

Lynchings

In some communities incidents have occurred which have left a vivid imprint on the minds of youth. When George Thompson, a farm boy in Coahoma County, was 12 years old a lynching occurred in his community. Although some lynchings are relatively quiet affairs and are accepted with resignation as "private" concerns or as justified punishment for the indiscretion of some irresponsible Negro, others are mob outbursts which leave deep scars of horror, fear, and dismay. The lynching described by George, a youth of 17, was one of this type. Several years after the event the memory was still vivid and detailed.

I was down in Drew when a white man shot a colored man and the colored man killed him. He ran to the woods and a mob got up and took after him. They finally crowded him into a sewer pipe in some bayou, poured gasoline in it and burned him out. He killed some of them 'fore they got him, though. All he had in there with him was a breech-loading shotgun. After he was dead they tied him to a truck and drug him all through town.

Must have been 500 or 600 in that mob. They had guns and pistols, and even machine guns. It was just like they was hunting a bear. Some was walking, some in cars, and some had hounds. They even had an airplane circling the bayou trying to spot him. You see they was three days gettin' him out. This mob had all the niggers in town scared but the one was carrying food to the fellow in the bayou. None of 'em would come out on the streets much. 'Course I jes went anywhere I wanted to go. That mob would push you around and beat you up if you acted funny. They went through all the niggers' houses and nobody tried to stop 'em. This all happened about 1930. For a long time the niggers was even scared to mention anything about it and went about town very quiet.

Lynchings usually follow a pattern. The mob, the man hunt, the brutality, the terrorization of the entire Negro community are standard features. The effect on children is profound and permanent. After a time the Negro community returns to "normal." Life goes on, but Negro youth "let white folks tend to their business." Contacts with whites are avoided as far as possible. The youth may work for white people but intimacy is avoided. The Negro servant or laborer continues friendly to his employers. The employers may even be liked and regarded as "good white folks," but ultimate trust is held in abeyance.

The effect of lynchings depends largely on the area in which they occur. Of the counties studied, the largest number of lynchings between 1900 and 1931 occurred in the following: Bolivar, Mississippi, 8; Coahoma, Mississippi, 7; and Shelby, Tennessee, 5. These are Mississippi Delta counties in which the plantation system still flourishes. Also, they have the largest Negro populations. In these counties lynching or the possibility of lynching is a part of the culture pattern. A type of adjustment to it exists. During and shortly after a lynching the Negro community lives in terror. Negroes remain at home and out of sight. When the white community quiets down, the Negroes go back to their usual occupations. The incident is not forgotten, but the routine of the plantation goes on. The lynching, in fact, is part of the routine.

In counties in which lynchings are infrequent more permanent effects may occur. Following an argument a white man was shot by a Negro in Greene County, Georgia, in 1920; the Negro ran away and "800 white men with nothing else to do went out scouring the country for him." After the lynching a mass migration of Negroes took place. Certain other factors contributed to the migration (decline of cotton and opportunity to work in another area) but the lynching was a powerful stimulant. The mass migration from other areas had started three years earlier. A man who had been through the 1920 Greene County lynching commented:

> You see them woods over yonder. They used to be just thick with people, but it's nothing but empty houses. Two things made them leave, the boll weevil and the row. The weevils was bad and niggers couldn't make nothing, and then when that row come along they was done so bad by white folks they just left.

Other Types of Individual Experience

Extensive contact with whites tends to modify the stereotyped attitudes toward them. Velma Cain, a 15-year-old girl in Madison County, Alabama, dislikes some white people. Furthermore, her reactions are less stereotyped than the responses of most youth in this county and are determined by her individual experience.

> Most of the neighbors is colored and we get along pretty well. We visit them and they visit us too. All the white ones treat me pretty well and I treat them pretty well. I see them every day. I work with them. Sometimes we talk together. White children have more because their folks can make a living for them. Some of them I hate. Some of them meddle with me.

Johnston County, North Carolina, youth, in general, were not particularly favorable to whites. Erma Cartwright, a 14-year-old girl, however, has had friendly contacts with whites and relatively few contacts with Negroes. As a result, her attitudes were much more favorable to white people than the average for the county. This is again a case of individual rather than stereotyped response.

> White people around here are real nice. After you pass my grandmother's house there aren't any more colored people. There's just our two families [colored] between Four Oaks and Benson [about seven miles], so we have all white people around here. They come to the house, sit down and eat with you and are just as nice as can be. One lady comes over here every day. She'll be here before you go, 'cause she never misses. She sits out here and talks to mama most of the day, and they sew. Sometimes her husband has to go away overnight, and if she sees a storm coming up she brings the little girl and comes over here and gets right in the bed with any of us and stays all night. She's real afraid of lightning. When her husband comes home, if she isn't home he comes right up here, 'cause he says he knows just where she'll be if she ain't home. No, he doesn't care if she comes here. He's the one told her to.

In some cases individual responses to particular white people coexist with contradictory feelings about white people in general.

> Papa told me how to get along with white people. He say "Don't raise your voice but talk quiet like. Don't talk too much. Let them talk. Let them have their way." If I wanted to do my way they might get angry and start trouble. I don't be around any of them any more than I can help. None except this family up here [the Jessups, white neighbors]. They acts just like colored folks, you can't tell the difference. Selma Jessup is just as nice as she can be. She comes over here and talks. We usually jokes a lot—like about the mule being so poor there wasn't enough for his ribs to meet, and things like that.

AGE AND INTELLIGENCE

Between the ages of 10 and 15, Negro children tend to withdraw from all contact with whites. Children younger than 15 have little contact with whites as employers. On the other hand, playing with white children begins to become taboo for Negro children at about the age of 10. In some cases childhood associations with whites are dissolved earlier than this and in other cases they persist until the beginning of puberty. Youth older than 15 only associate with whites in an employer-employee relationship. In a few cases childhood friendships are preserved, but usually on a basis of distant friendliness. Negro youth may greet white friends in the street, but they do not visit each other's homes.

In many cases childhood associations between Negroes and whites are abruptly ended in some overt conflict. One boy said:

> I used to wrestle and play ball with white boys. The last time I played ball with white boys was about five years ago. I was playing ball about three miles down the road. One of the white boys said that it wasn't my time to bat. I said it was. He wanted somebody else to be up. He tried to take the bat away from me. He hit me with the ball. He and I got into a fight. Nothing happened afterwards. You see a lot of white folks were standing around and they saw how it happened.

Avoidance of whites is more closely associated with the adolescent period than with any other period. Adult Negroes are of necessity in close contact with white people except in such all-Negro communities as Mound Bayou. Relations between adults are of the employer-employee type. Although many of the younger boys and girls included in this study worked for white people, their relations were in general irregular, that is, a boy or girl might work for a short period and then return to school or to work on the family farm. Younger rural Negro youth, it appears, do not often become permanently attached to a particular employer. A majority of those interviewed were not employed by white persons at all. They were in school, or helping on the family farm, or in the home, or unemployed. Relations of Negro youth to whites as employers are, therefore, no obstacle to avoidance behavior. This probably accounts for the higher racial maladjustment of adolescents as compared with youth who had found a basis of adjustment in the personal relations supported by the employer-employee relationship.

Where the older youth work regularly for a white employer,

avoidance of white people may be absent. In many cases, an intimate relationship develops between a white employer and a Negro youth. George Hollins, who is 18, is an example. He works in a small hotel in Greene County and is on good terms with his employers. When they go on trips George usually accompanies them. He has been to Atlanta with them several

TABLE 27

ADJUSTMENT OF RURAL NEGRO YOUTH TO WHITE RACE, BY AGE
As Indicated by Average Race Attitude Scores

Age	Number of Cases	Average Score
12	219	5.20
13	271	5.40
14	332	5.21
15	358	4.89
16	325	4.68
17	251	4.36
18	194	3.98
19	81	3.68

times. George's comment indicates that similar friendly relationships exist between some of his friends and their employers.

About fourteen months ago I got this job I'm working at now. Frank Weeks had it, but that white woman that he had been working for so long wanted him to come back. He says that she near 'bout raised him, and he couldn't deny her nothin', so he left the hotel and went back to work for her.

The older and the more intelligent youth show less antagonism to white people. Tables 27 and 28 give the average scores on race attitudes of rural Negro youth toward whites, by age and intelligence quotient. The averages decrease (that is, the attitude becomes more favorable toward white people) fairly regularly from the 12-year-old to the 19-year-old group, and from the lowest to the highest I.Q. group. The correlation coefficient of the attitude score with age is —.20 and with the I.Q. it is —.27. These correlations are low but statistically significant. Control of other factors affecting race attitudes (community opinions, family attitudes, and individual experiences) would probably yield even higher correlations.

Relationships of race attitudes with age and intelligence seem to be attributable to the rejection of emotional stereotypes by the older and the more intelligent youth. Examination of individual items on the race attitudes scale indicates that differences in attitudes between younger and older youth are principally due to differential acceptance of such stereotyped phrases and concepts as "white people are mean and stingy." Table 29 lists the statements about whites for which there was a significant differ-

TABLE 28

ADJUSTMENT OF RURAL NEGRO YOUTH TO WHITE RACE, BY INTELLIGENCE QUOTIENTS

As Indicated by Average Race Attitude Scores

I.Q.	Number of Cases	Average Score
40–59[a]	121	5.97
60–69	269	5.68
70–79	586	4.76
80–89	492	4.35
90–99	224	3.87
100–109	64	3.44
110–129[b]	16	2.31

[a] Includes 7 youth with I.Q.'s 40–49
[b] Includes 1 youth with I.Q. 120–129

ence between 12-year-old and 18- and 19-year-old youth. In Group A are the statements endorsed by more 12-year-olds than 18- and 19-year-olds. Statements in Group B were endorsed more frequently by older than by younger youth.

The nine statements in Group A are, with one exception, general assertions. The older youth tended to label these statements false because of their sweeping character. The younger and less intelligent youth agreed with the statements, since they are representative of community stereotypes. The largest difference between the two age groups is in the responses to the statement "White people are mean and stingy." It has already been pointed out that this statement is a community stereotype in many areas, and it is therefore significant that it is more frequently endorsed by younger than by older youth.

All of the statements which were more frequently endorsed

by older than by younger youth (see Table 29, Group B) are of a more balanced and mature character than those of Group A. One is actually a statement of fact ("Most of the big businesses are owned by white people") and difference in response of the

TABLE 29

JUDGMENTS OF RURAL NEGRO YOUTH ABOUT WHITE RACE,
BY SELECTED AGE GROUPS

As Indicated by Proportions Responding "True" to
Statements on Race Attitudes Scale[a]

Statement[b]	Percentage Responding "True"	
	12-year-olds	18- and 19-year-olds
GROUP A: (12-year-olds more favorable)		
White people are mean and stingy.	67.7	45.5
Most white people give Negroes fair pay for what they do.	62.2	41.1
White people are poor Christians.	51.8	37.5
The South was a beautiful place before white people came in and ruined it.	50.6	33.6
White people are the cruelest people in the world.	43.4	23.8
White people don't take care of each other.	31.1	17.3
White people don't know how to have a good time.	18.7	9.4
Negroes should hate all white people.	17.5	5.4
I'd rather be dead than ask a white man for anything.	17.1	4.0
GROUP B: (18- and 19-year-olds more favorable)		
There are all kinds of white people—some are good and some are bad.	91.6	97.8
Most of the big businesses are owned by white people.	80.9	91.0
The white race has produced some of the best and some of the worst men in history.	67.7	81.2
White people are human and have the faults of other human beings.	57.4	71.1
I neither like nor dislike white people.	55.4	69.0

[a] Based on responses of 251, 12-year-olds and 277, 18- and 19-year-olds
[b] The statements selected are those showing a statistically significant difference, that is, a difference over 3 times its standard error.

age groups indicates the more intimate acquaintance of the older youth with the national economic system. Fifty-five per cent of the 12-year-old youth neither liked nor disliked white people, compared with 69 per cent of the 18- and 19-year-old youth. Table 30 shows by age groups the responses to statements about whites on the Personal Attitudes Test. Here, again, the younger groups more often endorse statements of a general stereotyped nature. The statements which show no differences between age groups are those relating to individual behavior or feelings (for example, "I keep away from white boys [girls] as

TABLE 30

HOSTILITY OF RURAL NEGRO YOUTH TO WHITE RACE, BY AGE

As Indicated by Proportions Responding "True" to
Statements on Personal Attitudes Scale

Statement	Age						
	12	13	14	15	16	17	18 and 19
I keep away from white boys (girls) as much as I can.	68.8	71.6	68.0	63.9	72.6	57.5	62.3
I wouldn't play with a white boy (girl) if I could.	45.2	46.7	37.7	42.8	40.5	40.1	38.8
It makes me mad because white boys (girls) can do things I can't.	26.5	31.6	25.3	30.7	30.7	26.3	32.0
Listening to white people talk makes me mad.	30.6	39.3	29.2	27.3	25.0	21.2	20.6
White people are to blame for my father's being out of a job.	39.9	38.4	33.4	25.9	28.0	22.0	18.5
I am going to get even with white people when I grow up.	34.5	32.6	22.6	24.6	21.4	22.3	15.7
I hate white people.	39.9	39.6	26.2	24.9	28.0	22.3	15.3
Number of cases	253	285	359	374	336	274	281

much as I can") and not dependent upon stereotyped community attitudes.

The decreased acceptance of stereotypes by older youth is largely due to their greater contact with white people. Older youth are in many cases employed by white people. This contact makes their attitudes in general *appear* more favorable to white people. However, the actual situation is more complex than a mere quantitative shift. More 18- and 19-year-old youth than 12-year-old youth felt that white people did not pay Negroes fairly. This difference and the other age group differences noted point to a less stereotyped response in older youth rather than a mere increase in friendliness with whites.

DYNAMICS OF THE RACE SYSTEM OF THE SOUTH

The southern race system has been described as a caste system. Unquestionably, resemblances to caste do exist. Most prominent of these is the ban on intermarriage. There is also a certain linkage between racial classification and occupation. There is segregation in residences and social activities which bears at least superficial resemblance to that obtaining under a caste system. There is the tacit support by the church and custom of lines of separation between the races. As in a caste system, racial position is fixed at birth and cannot be altered by personal achievements or experience. Nevertheless, examination of the psychological implications of the southern race system discloses fundamental differences between it and a caste system as ordinarily conceived. The four basic qualities of a caste system seem to be prohibition of intermarriage between castes, the absolute impossibility of altering caste status, the religious sanctions, and the mutual acceptance of and adjustment to the fixed status. These restrictions are established by custom and are accepted without apparent resistance by the participants in a caste system.

The southern race system does not, however, appear to meet fully the description of a caste system. It fights overtly and specifically against change of status. A caste system does not need to fight against change. If, for example, interracial marriage were conceived of as impossible this would undoubtedly be termed caste. In the South, however, intermarriage is not accepted as impossible. It does not occur, but the fact that legal restrictions are imposed indicates the lack of faith of the white group in the efficacy of traditional taboos against intermarriage. In a caste system legal prohibitions are unnecessary, since intermarriage is inconceivable. Moreover, the South does not exist *in vacuo*. Intermarriage occurs to some extent in the North.

With regard to change of status, the southern race system also differs from a caste organization of sects. Negroes do not become *white*, regardless of personal characteristics or achievements, but the terrific energy expended in "keeping the Negro in his place" is evidence of the failure of traditional regulation. Unlike a caste system, the southern race system is highly unstable. There is not only tension between races but actual uncertainty in the minds of both groups as to the significance of race lines. A caste system is not only a separated system, it is a stable system in which changes are socially impossible; the fact that change cannot occur is accepted by all, or practically all, participants. Legal sanctions are unnecessary since revolt against custom is absent.

No expenditure of psychological or physical energy is necessary to maintain a caste system. Although frictions occur within a caste system, they are mainly minor individual outbreaks. The southern system, with all its restrictions, does not conform to this picture. Probably the salient feature of the southern race system is the friction between races demanding an enormous amount of energy and elaborate legal restrictions to maintain the status quo. Segregation laws in the South are necessary because the race system is not a caste system, because traditional sanctions are "inadequately" observed. Furthermore, in spite of the stereotyped traditions and customs, there is also a wide variety of practice in the racial etiquette of the South which does not lend support to a caste theory.

With regard to occupational stratification, despite discrimination against Negroes in many occupations, there is no strict caste association of occupation and race. Although certain occupations have been traditionally Negro and others white, the dividing line is far from rigid. Negroes can and do enter skilled and white-collar occupations supposedly reserved for whites and, as the recent depression has painfully demonstrated, whites enter "Negro" occupations, frequently displacing Negroes entirely from fields in which they formerly had a monopoly.

The differences between the southern race system and caste are less in the objective situation, although such objective differences exist, than in the attitudes of the participants. While the southern white traditionalist likes to believe that the race system is accepted as natural and proper, in actuality he and all other participants know that it is not. The race system in the South is preserved by legal sanctions and the threat of physical violence, quite as much as by the mutual acceptance of traditional modes of behavior. Furthermore, the attitudes of the white group are constantly changing, and at many points in the relationship between the two races there is a blurring of caste distinctions. In general the Negro continues to occupy a subordinate position, but the fact that he is struggling against this status rather than accepting it, and that the white group is constantly redefining its own status in relation to the Negro, indicates that in the future, if one cannot safely predict progress in race relations, he can at least predict change.

MEMORANDUM ON A PSYCHI-
ATRIC RECONNAISSANCE

Harry Stack Sullivan

An intensive psychiatric study of a few American Negroes of northern urban habitat having inspired in the writer an intense interest in the possibilities of obtaining significant data on interpersonal relations, he was persuaded to undertake a visit of exploration in the deep South. Nothing of optimistic expectation as to results was developed, despite the encouragement offered by Hortense Powdermaker and Charles S. Johnson. Such preliminary formulations as came of the experiment are largely to be credited to the group of graduate students at Fisk University, who were most cooperative in supplying personal data, to the assistance of the white and the Negro leaders in the area chosen, and to that of two clergymen who superintended a school there.

Throughout my work with marginal individuals, I have heard a variety of all-inclusive generalizations about the Negro group. In work with persons representative of more privileged American society, I have observed the coexistence of these generalized beliefs with contradictory individualized thinking and behavior towards members of this group. The "logic-tight compartment" principle is conspicuous here. It appears that the generalized (often derogatory) belief is an essential part of one's emotional make-up, whereas the more valid individual formulations are much less emotionally significant.

In a few words, it was easy to discover not one general type but very wide differences of personality among Negro youth in the southern area. It is impossible to find much of anything that is

NOTE: The research which is reported in this volume represents a sociological approach to the personality problems of the southern rural Negro. It was felt that an added contribution could be made if an independent investigator, experienced in the psychiatric approach, were to observe for a period some of the same subjects in their setting. Dr. Harry Stack Sullivan, director of the William Alanson White Psychiatric Foundation, chiefly out of interest in the problem itself, spent several weeks in one of the rural communities of the deep South interviewing a number of these youth. Because of the limited period of observation, the results are presented very largely as the personal impressions of a psychiatrist rather than conclusions from extended inquiry. These impressions, however, reveal interesting insights and contain a considerable measure of confirmation of this study's findings regarding the effects of minority status upon the personality of Negro youth.—C.S.J.

unique or general in American Negro personality, excepting only an almost, if not quite, ubiquitous fear of white people. These inter-racial attitudes always came to the front; one of my three best in-formants in this area shocked himself by realizing belatedly that he was telling me how deeply he hated all whites. Here, too, we seem to have a generalization essential to the self; again, one that is no bar-rier to quite contradictory specific beliefs and behavior. This particu-lar young man was quick and accurate in perceiving the nuances of our relationship, and, aside from this one instance of painful embar-rassment, expressed himself with rather astonishing freedom from re-straints.

The personnel studied included highly talented people, rather mediocre individuals, and at least one amiable imbecile. They made themselves available for a variety of reasons, rather generally with some vague hope that an improvement of their individual lot might perhaps come from the interviews. The spread of this general hope varied from a wide consciousness of the need of the whole colored population to a narrow, sometimes very shrewd, self-seeking. The formulation of the hope varied extremely—sometimes approximating the surmised eternal diffuse optimism of the Negro, sometimes reach-ing no further than an anticipation of a little money. In a few, it was formulated in terms of the distant future, with realism and excellent logic. In one, whom unforeseen accident had but recently thrown out of a vassalage[1] relationship with a white plantation supervisor, it rapidly focused on the re-creation of such a situation with me. Begin-ning as a fleeting fantasy that he expressed among several "thoughts" about the immediate future, I was able to observe its progression to a resolve to break with everything familiar to him and trust his fate to me—all this with no expression of emotion. At one stage, however, he showed a transient disturbance of personality, a period of troubled sleep followed by the dream-like detachment which the psychiatrist associates with the schizophrenic forms of mental disorder.

An abortive experiment in more intensive psychiatric study was undertaken with this individual. He was removed to New York City and supposedly headed towards a more independent career. He showed good capacity for controlling the anxieties that the actual translation included, but he was felled by his almost complete il-literacy and came to suffer such nostalgia that he returned home—at once to become a vessel of regrets and of urgency to return to the North.[2]

[1] See "A Note on Formulating the Relationship of the Individual and the Group," *American Journal of Sociology*, 44: 936.

[2] It is to be noted that this young man is not included among the three most

Everyone was encouraged to talk of the Negro community. Everyone commented more or less directly on its lack of organization, and of the inability of Negroes to cooperate in long-term projects. Almost everyone spoke of the unreliability of Negro leaders. I saw one of the prominent Negro clergymen and came to feel that distrust of his integrity was not in any sense abnormal. The outstanding Negro leader of the community, on the other hand, impressed me favorably. He suffered so vividly, however, from rage at the whites that one of the elements of distrust expressed to me about him seemed all too well founded. One of the young men remarked that this leader was going to "get himself in trouble"; another said that it would not be long before he "get killed resisting arrest"—the local improvement on lynching. I think that this leader—though he came to express himself with great freedom about some topics—progressed in our acquaintanceship only from a distrust of my motives, through a distrust of my judgment, to a vague wondering if I might actually be a detached observer without blinding preconceptions and group loyalties hostile to him and his people. He seemed to me one of the loneliest of men; a well-trained professional man of rather keen sensitivity, isolated in the nexus of several fields of hostility, so driven by some complex of motives (which proved mostly inaccessible to me) that it seemed wholly unpredictable how long his remarkable judgment of people would suffice to insure him from retaliation for the anxieties and fears that he tends to focus.

The Negro's hostile attitudes toward whites are partly a reaction to discriminatory custom, an important example of which is the "Mr.–Mrs." taboo. No Negro is to be addressed as Mr. or Mrs. In general, they are to be called by their given name and not by their surname. I three times made the mistake of using the formal address; once from ignorance, with the result that the laborer concerned became highly suspicious of my *bona fides,* twice from preoccupation in seeking out a particular one in a group. In all cases, I created a dis-

---

useful informants above mentioned. One of them was in fourth-year high school, one—nearly incredibly—was a student of aviation, and the third, while of but lower grammar school education, had kept closely in touch with events and was quite unusually well informed. The boy of the experiment had an effective formal education amounting to a good second grade, an intelligence that would have carried him through at least junior high school. His career had encouraged him to but little curiosity about events external to his narrow personal horizon. He had, however, rather firm ideals as to working for a living which, too, suffered in the debacle of the northern translation, in no small part, doubtless, because of my inability to assume a useful role in the transitional phase. I was away most of the time on the study in a border area.

turbance such that the individual concerned was of no further use as an informant.

Besides these measures to "keep the nigger in his place," there are incidents of violence, some of them official in character in that they are initiated by the police. I learned that lynching, which had long since ceased in this particular area, was practiced recently in a neighboring town. The poor whites have a good deal to do with lynching parties. This may be determined in part by economic factors as the Negro is often preferred as tenant or as laborer; it is partly determined, I surmise, by the need of a thrill, for these whites suffer almost as great a dearth of recreational activities as do the Negroes. There are, however, some middle-class lynching enthusiasts, some of whom are reputed to be unusually kind to "their niggers" when things are going well.

The occasions of great violence towards the Negro arise chiefly in connection with the master taboo of the society, the prohibition of any intimacy between a Negro male and a white woman. The force and importance of this taboo can scarcely be exaggerated. I have been told that the integrity of the whole social system rests on its inviolability. I know that mere unsubstantiated rumor of its violation has necessitated the prompt evacuation of the accused youth to a northern city, in the interest of civic quiet. Several of the young men interviewed remarked on the unwisdom of looking at a white girl if there were any "peckawoods" (poor whites) around. One of them had been beaten for staring at a girl whom he insists he had not even seen. It must be understood also that this taboo is absolute; nothing declasses a white woman and nothing exempts a Negro man. A white prostitute's pursuit of a Negro taxi driver culminated in her calling him from the yard which serves as cab stand, showing him $50, and remarking that he would take the money and come home with her or she would tell the police he had made advances to her. He refused, repeating his oft stated "I don't want to mess around with no white woman." The protector of the civil peace had shortly thereafter to provide him with means for leaving town for good. Mongolians may or may not be "white" for taboo purposes—it varies in different states—but certain Eurasian immigrants who are darker than light Negroes, *are* white for taboo purposes and woe betide the Negro male who proves attractive to one of these women.

Knowing the channels of rebellious attitudes, one might expect covert violations of this taboo to occur. They are probably much less frequent than many people surmise. I make this statement on the strength of observations of a probable instance, with persistent severe anxiety, and on reports of dreams. There are indications that in many Negro personalities in this area this taboo carries with it a large component of awe. The sophisticate of the border and the northern areas should not be taken to be a characteristic denizen of the Negro population in America.

The sanctions which restrict Negro personality and which fix Negro men as inferior to the most degraded white woman are probably the prime factors in determining the ubiquitous hatred of the white. The unwavering performance of the rituals which emphasize these sanctions is an index of the meaning of the Negro patterns incorporated in the white personalities concerned. I must pause here to mention the occasional phenomenon of the "nigger-lover"—a white who fraternizes with the Negro in preference to the white. Such a person is ostracized, if possible; he is regarded with a more complex attitude than mere contempt. The suggestion that one may be a nigger-lover usually suffices to cure any tendency to diverge from the white pattern. Northerners who settle in this region find it expedient to become "meaner" than the native southern families.

I have gone to some length to indicate the factors in the interracial situation that must have extraordinary effects on personality development. There are equally interesting factors in the Negro family patterns which still reflect economically conditioned practices of the slavery period. There are factors inhering in the single-crop agriculture of the plantation. There are factors in the disenfranchisement of the Negro and the more recent fall of the plantation owners from political power and the ascendancy of the poor whites.

The Negro of the deep South seldom escapes serious warping influences and a large proportion of them doubtless come to be measurably close to the reality underlying the prevailing white views of the Negro. I did not succeed in establishing contact with any of those who were described by my informants as "just average niggers." I learned in the first few days that I could not bridge the cultural gap with most of the plantation workers. The Negro seems to have a notably great capacity for sensing by intuition interpersonal reality. This faculty led to a good many pseudo-conversations, early in my stay. It may be worth mentioning that one informant carried on in some eight hours of conversation an account of the consequences of a highly improbable experience—later found by collateral channels to be almost certainly mythical—without showing any of the phenomena by which I am customarily warned that an account is becoming wishful rather than valid. The one other detail of my provisional hypothesis which may merit mention bears on the *amiability* of the Negro as compared with whites and Chinese with whom I have worked. A timeless, formless optimism about life in general seemed to be remarkably widespread—even in obsessional personalities that

I encountered. Something of this attitude also persisted in two thoroughly disillusioned and rather definitely embittered intellectuals who assisted me in various ways. I could not help but conclude that the Negro had escaped in some way those cultural-personal necessities which had compelled the Western Europeans to look to another world. Religious practices have importance in life in the deep South, but the effective religious beliefs, attitudes, and behavior do not seem to be functional counterparts of the circumambient white culture.

In conclusion, it may be said that psychiatry as the study of interpersonal relations has a difficult but a most rewarding field in the American Negro, that the Negro of the deep South seems in many respects the most promising for a beginning, and that he and his social situation, with its chronologically well-separated variations from the influx of new elements, constitute one of the most significant social science research fields.

METHODOLOGY

The data used in the study of rural Negro youth were collected by three different methods, two of them essentially quantitative and extensive, and the third qualitative and intensive. Under quantitative methods are included the tests which were given to youth in the county schools and schedules obtained from rural families. Intensive qualitative data were obtained by interviews with a smaller number of rural youth. In determining the composition of the sample to be interviewed, material in the tests was utilized.

The families sampled by the schedule method all had one or more children in the age range from 12 to 20. Some, but not all, of these children were also included in the testing program. The families sampled are fairly representative of the families of the children tested, although the two samples were not identical. Schedules were obtained from the families of all youth interviewed.

The interpretation of the schedules and of the interviews is fairly straightforward and simple. A word of explanation is necessary, however, to aid in interpreting the test data. For this study five new tests were developed by Eli S. Marks in collaboration with Lily Brunschwig.

The most conventional and familiar of the tests used was the Intelligence Test (Kuhlmann-Anderson Test). From this test the measure used was the "intelligence quotient" (I.Q.). While the I.Q. is a familiar measure, it would be quite erroneous to suppose that it was used in this study for the purposes with which we are familiar. A vast body of research has clearly indicated that intelligence tests are completely useless for comparisons of inherited intelligence between groups of dissimilar background and nonequivalent educational opportunity. However, intelligence tests can be used as a measure of the effects of cultural and educational differences, provided it may be assumed that the groups tested are basically similar in inherited ability. Since all the children tested come of substantially the same hereditary stock this assumption is not an unreasonable one. Objection may be made that northern children and urban children represent a selected sampling of the Negro population. The work of Klineberg and others, however, seems to disprove very definitely any such hypothesis.

In the comparison of groups, therefore, the I.Q. is used in this study as an indicator of the effects of cultural and educational differences between children assumed to be essentially the same (as groups) in inherent capacity. Within a group from the same community, differences in I.Q. may validly be taken as representing *true* differences in capacity. Therefore, within a particular county the I.Q. has been used as a guide in determining the essential capacity of individual youths, although even this is not done without other material which verifies the I.Q. since particular individuals within a relatively homogeneous community may nevertheless suffer educational disturbances additional to those encountered by youth as a whole.

The Personal Values Test requires very little explanation. A series of questions were asked, and the young people filled in the answers themselves. The responses in each category were prepared.

In the Personal Attitudes Test the youth were presented with 125 statements to be marked *true* or *false*. These statements related to the individual's feelings about six spheres of activity: home, school, church, race, social adjustment, and general emotional life. Marking a statement *true* indicates a particular symptom of maladjustment in a given sphere. Thus, to mark statement number 16, "I hate my father," *true* may be considered symptomatic of maladjustment in the home and family life. The score assigned on a particular scale is the number of maladjustment symptoms marked true;[1] the higher the score the greater the degree of maladjustment indicated. While it is valid to compare the scores on a particular scale of two different persons or groups of persons, direct comparisons between scores on different scales are not valid. For example, 31 statements are included in the home scale, so that the maximum score possible on this scale is 31. In the school scale there are only 16 statements, giving a maximum score of 16. In addition to the differences in maximum score there are differences in the degrees of extremeness of statements on different scales. For example, there is probably no statement on the church scale comparable in its symptomatic value with the statement "I hate my father" on the home scale. However, patterns of responses on the different personal attitude scales may be

[1] On this test (but not on the Race Attitudes Test) a response of "uncertain" (X) was scored as $\frac{1}{2}$. On this test an "uncertain" usually meant that the person did have the particular maladjustment symptom but hesitated to reveal it completely. While these half-scores were added into the total, odd halves were dropped in the tabulation. Thus 2 halves and 3 halves both counted as 1.0, 4 halves and 5 halves as 2.0, and so on. This procedure may have misrepresented the attitudes of particular individuals (any testing procedure does this in any case) but it probably gave fairly valid group averages. The results of other experimenters with attitude tests indicate that simple scoring methods give, in general, substantially the same results as more elaborate weighting techniques (see for example R. Likert, "A Technique for the Measurement of Attitudes," *Archives of Psychology*, 1930, No. 140). Examination of various methods of scoring the Race Attitudes Test confirmed this conclusion; the highest reliability was recorded for the simple scoring technique which was finally adopted.

validly distinguished. For example, two young people showing about the same total amount of maladjustment may differ in the maladjustment patterns—one showing maladjustment concentrated around home matters and the other maladjustment centered around school work.

In the scoring of the Race Attitudes Test, the methods were similar to those used for the Personal Attitudes Test. It was found, however, that omission of certain statements gave more reliable results. The Race Attitudes Test is separable into two scales: one of attitude toward whites, consisting of 14 statements to be marked *true* or *false,* and the other of attitude toward Negroes, consisting of 16 statements. High scores on the white attitude scale indicate an unfavorable opinion of whites; high scores on the Negro attitude scale an unfavorable opinion of Negroes.

Since the Occupation Ratings Test failed to yield results of sufficient reliability for general comparisons, it will not be discussed here. In specific cases interesting items of information were obtained from the Occupation Ratings Test. These are discussed in connection with the topics to which they relate.

The sixth test used was the Color Ratings Test. Here the youth were asked to circle the word describing the skin color of "the boy you like most," "your teacher," "the most beautiful girl you know," and so on. These responses were divided in terms of the way in which the person rated was described, that is, "the girl you like best" is a favorable description of a female; "the meanest boy you know" is an unfavorable description of a male. Frequency tabulations of responses to each item were prepared, and also an aggregate of responses to items in a given category. In addition, a median was obtained of all responses in the favorable categories and of all responses in the unfavorable categories, counting "black" as 1 and "white" as 6. Since "brown" would be 3 and "light-brown" 4 on this scale, a median of 3.5 would represent a general response between "brown" and "light-brown." While this particular scoring method has many disadvantages, it seemed to be the only method available for getting a simple index of the general trend of an individual's color ratings responses. The median for favorable categories may validly be taken as the color preferred by the youth. It is therefore referred to as the "median preferred color." Similarly, the median for unfavorable categories is referred to as the "median disliked color."

All these indices must be used with a certain amount of caution. In individual cases a particular index may be quite unrepresentative of the individual's true responses (partly due to the mechanics of scaling and, in some cases, partly to failure of the youth to express the response unequivocally). In group averages, however, the errors made with individuals will tend to cancel out, and the average may be validly taken as a fairly accurate index of the group's position on a given matter. In individual cases the indices have proved valid when checked against interview material. It is not felt that this is universally true, but very few of the tests seem to warrant dismissal as meaningless. In one case in particular, for example, the tester felt that the youth tested was confused about the meaning of questions, yet examination of the pattern of this youth's own statements in an extended interview seemed to validate the test results, for to a remarkable degree they agreed with certain almost unconscious emotional tendencies revealed by the interview.

(The five special tests devised for use in this study are given in the following pages.)

Staff

FIELD INTERVIEWERS

Virginia Argrett
Eunice Adamson
Joseph Douglass
Edmonia Grant
Willie C. Holt
Isham Jones
Anne D. Johnson

William Layton
E. Nelson Palmer
Joy McDowell
Gertrude Porcher
Paul Phillips
Lincoln Sawyer
Ophelia Settle

TECHNICAL STAFF

Eli S. Marks
Melissa Forrester

Estella H. Scott
Bonita Valien

SPECIAL CONSULTANTS

Harry Stack Sullivan, M.D.
Lily Brunschwig

Hortense Powdermaker

PERSONAL ATTITUDES TEST

DIRECTIONS: Place *T* on the line in front of each statement which is true.
Place *F* on the line in front of each statement which is false.
If you can't decide whether the statement is true or false,
place *X* on the line in front of it.

—— 1. It seems as if I never can answer my teacher's questions right.
—— 2. When I get mad I'd like to beat up everybody who comes near me.
—— 3. They never teach us anything useful in school.
—— 4. I feel bad because I am bigger than the other boys in my class.
—— 5. It is better to be white than colored.
—— 6. I often say things and then feel sorry I said them.
—— 7. The boys in my gang often make fun of me.
—— 8. I don't have any good clothes.
—— 9. I wouldn't play with a white boy if I could.
—— 10. I wish I were lighter in color than I am.
—— 11. I lose my temper easily.
—— 12. Sometimes I feel so blue I'd like to kill myself.
—— 13. The preacher tells you to do a lot of things that he doesn't do himself.
—— 14. Talking to white people scares me.
—— 15. My father spends too much money for liquor.
—— 16. I hate my father.
—— 17. The other boys in my class are smarter than I am.
—— 18. I usually worry a long time over things that happen to me.
—— 19. I wish I could go away and live some place else.
—— 20. My teacher is down on me.
—— 21. I feel scared when I get into a fight.
—— 22. My father doesn't amount to much.
—— 23. My brothers and sisters always act as if they are a lot better than I am.
—— 24. I don't like to play any games unless I can be leader.
—— 25. Sometimes I have felt that I was doing wrong but went ahead and did it anyway.
—— 26. I only go to church because my girl goes.
—— 27. I never understand what they are talking about in church.
—— 28. I sometimes lie awake a long time before I fall asleep.
—— 29. I always get blamed for everything that goes wrong in class.
—— 30. Girls make fun of me.
—— 31. I hate white people.
—— 32. I don't have as many friends as other fellows.
—— 33. I hate going to church.
—— 34. I wish I were white.
—— 35. My folks would like to get rid of me.

—— 36. I wish I had a different mother.

—— 37. I often sit down and make believe I am someone else.

—— 38. My folks are always making me do things I don't want to do.

—— 39. I'd like to beat up my teacher.

—— 40. I can't sit still long.

—— 41. I keep away from white boys as much as I can.

—— 42. People say a lot of things that aren't true about my family.

—— 43. White boys get a lot more from their folks than I do.

—— 44. My father is too lazy to go out and make money.

—— 45. I wouldn't go to church if my folks didn't make me.

—— 46. My teachers make me do too much work.

—— 47. I don't like girls.

—— 48. My folks are always fighting.

—— 49. I guess I won't amount to much when I grow up.

—— 50. I'd like to beat up a policeman just once.

—— 51. I sometimes have bad pains in some part of my body.

—— 52. No one at home ever does anything for me.

—— 53. I rarely have a good time at a party.

—— 54. I don't stay around home unless they make me do so.

—— 55. Going to church doesn't make people any better.

—— 56. Most other boys have better homes than I have.

—— 57. Sometimes I like to start a fight just for the fun of it.

—— 58. Sometimes I wish I had never been born.

—— 59. My folks won't let me do the things other boys do.

—— 60. I'm not so good playing games, but I can beat the fellows doing other things.

—— 61. Praying never did me any good.

—— 62. If I could, I would rather play with white boys than with colored boys.

—— 63. Most of the time, the others at home get more to eat than I do.

—— 64. Girls don't like me as well as they do other boys.

—— 65. Most of my friends get more from their folks than I do.

—— 66. There are some people I'd like to kill if I could.

—— 67. My mother wouldn't care if I never came home at all.

—— 68. White people are to blame for my father's being out of a job.

—— 69. Lots of times I get blamed for things that weren't my fault.

—— 70. If you have to go to church to be good I'd rather be bad.

—— 71. What the preacher says in church scares me.

—— 72. I can't make good marks in school no matter how I try.

—— 73. I wish we had a better place to play.

—— 74. I wish I were bigger.

—— 75. It makes me mad because white boys can do things I can't.

—— 76. I like to be by myself more than I like to be with others.

—— 77. It makes me mad when people try to boss me around.

—— 78. I don't want to be like my father when I grow up.

—— 79. I get tired very easily.

—— 80. My mother thinks more of other things than she does of me.

—— 81. Sometimes I worry over the things I dream about.

—— 82. I bite my fingernails.

—— 83. I wish I didn't have to go to school.

—— 84. I'd like to run away from home.

—— 85. Sometimes I love my folks and other times I hate them.

—— 86. My father beats my mother.

—— 87. I'm not much interested in school work.

—— 88. People never want to answer my questions.

—— 89. My mother isn't fair to me.

—— 90. My mother is always picking on me.

—— 91. The sight of blood makes me feel sick.

—— 92. It makes me mad when my side loses a game.

—— 93. I get all mixed up when the teacher calls on me in school.

—— 94. I'm usually the last to be picked for a team.

—— 95. I like to be around grown-ups more than around fellows my own age.

—— 96. People always fight in church over a lot of things that don't make any difference.

—— 97. I often wish I were grown up.

—— 98. My mother can't ever understand the things I want to do.

—— 99. I wish I were dead.

—— 100. Listening to white people talk makes me mad.

—— 101. I don't care what anybody thinks about me.

—— 102. Most of the things in the Bible aren't true.

—— 103. I don't care for my brothers and sisters much.

—— 104. I am scared of my father.

—— 105. The boys in my class make fun of me.

—— 106. I get tired of having to be polite to people.

—— 107. Sometimes people make me feel so bad that I'd like to cry.

—— 108. I wish I had more friends.

—— 109. I worry a lot about dying.

—— 110. I often get so mad I can't talk.

—— 111. Most of the guys in my gang can lick me.

—— 112. My mother could do more for me if she wanted to.

—— 113. People are always praising my brothers and sisters and not me.

—— 114. Some churches are all right, but others are all bunk.

—— 115. Sometimes I feel that nobody cares about me.

—— 116. I am going to get even with white folks when I grow up.

—— 117. All ministers want to do is to get as much money out of people as they can.

—— 118. I find it hard to get along with other people in school.

—— 119. I'm not smart enough to get into college.

—— 120. There is no use going to school since it won't help me any later on.

—— 121. I never get enough to eat at home.

—— 122. Religion is a lot of bunk.

—— 123. My folks treat me like a baby.

—— 124. My folks are mean to me.

—— 125. College fellows usually think they are better than anybody else.

NAME ——————— GRADE ——————— SCHOOL ——————— DATE ———————

PERSONAL ATTITUDES TEST

DIRECTIONS: Place *T* on the line in front of each statement which is true. Place *F* on the line in front of each statement which is false. If you can't decide whether the statement is true or false, place *X* on the line in front of it.

——— 1. It seems as if I never can answer my teacher's questions right.
——— 2. When I get mad I'd like to beat up everybody who comes near me.
——— 3. They never teach us anything useful in school.
——— 4. I feel bad because I am bigger than the other girls in my class.
——— 5. It is better to be white than colored.
——— 6. I often say things and then feel sorry I said them.
——— 7. The girls I go with often make fun of me.
——— 8. I don't have any good clothes.
——— 9. I wouldn't play with a white girl if I could.
——— 10. I wish I were lighter in color than I am.
——— 11. I lose my temper easily.
——— 12. Sometimes I feel so blue I'd like to kill myself.
——— 13. The preacher tells you to do a lot of things that he doesn't do himself.
——— 14. Talking to white people scares me.
——— 15. My father spends too much money for liquor.
——— 16. I hate my father.
——— 17. The other girls in my class are smarter than I am.
——— 18. I usually worry a long time over things that happen to me.
——— 19. I wish I could go away and live some place else.
——— 20. My teacher is down on me.
——— 21. I feel scared when I talk to boys.
——— 22. My father doesn't amount to much.
——— 23. My brothers and sisters always act as if they are a lot better than I am.
——— 24. I don't like to play any games unless I can be leader.
——— 25. Sometimes I have felt that I was doing wrong but went ahead and did it anyway.
——— 26. I only go to church because my boy friend goes.
——— 27. I never understand what they are talking about in church.
——— 28. I sometimes lie awake a long time before I fall asleep.
——— 29. I always get blamed for everything that goes wrong in class.
——— 30. Boys make fun of me.
——— 31. I hate white people.
——— 32. I don't have as many friends as other girls.
——— 33. I hate going to church.
——— 34. I wish I were white.

341

—— 35. My folks would like to get rid of me.
—— 36. I wish I had a different mother.
—— 37. I often sit down and make believe I am someone else.
—— 38. My folks are always making me do things I don't want to do.
—— 39. I'd like to beat up my teacher.
—— 40. I can't sit still long.
—— 41. I keep away from white girls as much as I can.
—— 42. People say a lot of things that aren't true about my family.
—— 43. White girls get a lot more from their folks than I do.
—— 44. My father is too lazy to go out and make money.
—— 45. I wouldn't go to church if my folks didn't make me.
—— 46. My teachers make me do too much work.
—— 47. I don't like boys.
—— 48. My folks are always fighting.
—— 49. I guess I won't amount to much when I grow up.
—— 50. I'd like to beat up a policeman just once.
—— 51. I sometimes have bad pains in some part of my body.
—— 52. No one at home ever does anything for me.
—— 53. I rarely have a good time at a party.
—— 54. I don't stay around home unless they make me do so.
—— 55. Going to church doesn't make people any better.
—— 56. Most other girls have better homes than I have.
—— 57. Sometimes I like to start a fight just for the fun of it.
—— 58. Sometimes I wish I had never been born.
—— 59. My folks won't let me do the things other girls do.
—— 60. I'm not so good playing games, but I can beat the girls doing other things.
—— 61. Praying never did me any good.
—— 62. If I could, I would rather play with white girls than with colored girls.
—— 63. Most of the time, the others at home get more to eat than I do.
—— 64. Boys don't like me as well as they do other girls.
—— 65. Most of my friends get more from their folks than I do.
—— 66. There are some people I'd like to kill if I could.
—— 67. My mother wouldn't care if I never came home at all.
—— 68. White people are to blame for my father's being out of a job.
—— 69. Lots of times I get blamed for things that weren't my fault.
—— 70. If you have to go to church to be good I'd rather be bad.
—— 71. What the preacher says in church scares me.
—— 72. I can't make good marks in school no matter how I try.
—— 73. I wish we had a better place to play.
—— 74. I wish I were bigger.
—— 75. It makes me mad because white girls can do things I can't.
—— 76. I like to be by myself more than I like to be with others.
—— 77. It makes me mad when people try to boss me around.
—— 78. I don't want to be like my mother when I grow up.
—— 79. I get tired easily.
—— 80. My mother thinks more of other things than she does of me.

—— 81. Sometimes I worry over the things I dream about.
—— 82. I bite my fingernails.
—— 83. I wish I didn't have to go to school.
—— 84. I'd like to get away from home.
—— 85. Sometimes I love my folks and other times I hate them.
—— 86. My father beats my mother.
—— 87. I'm not much interested in school work.
—— 88. People never want to answer my questions.
—— 89. My teacher isn't fair to me.
—— 90. My mother is always picking on me.
—— 91. The sight of blood makes me feel sick.
—— 92. It makes me mad when my side loses a game.
—— 93. I get all mixed up when the teacher calls on me in school.
—— 94. I'm usually the last to be asked to a party.
—— 95. I like to be around grown-ups more than around girls my own age.
—— 96. People always fight in church over a lot of things that don't make any difference.
—— 97. I often wish I were grown up.
—— 98. My mother can't ever understand the things I want to do.
—— 99. I wish I were dead.
—— 100. Listening to white people talk makes me mad.
—— 101. I don't care what anybody thinks about me.
—— 102. Most of the things in the Bible aren't true.
—— 103. I don't care for my brothers and sisters much.
—— 104. I am scared of my father.
—— 105. The girls in my class make fun of me.
—— 106. I get tired of having to be polite to people.
—— 107. Sometimes people make me feel so bad that I'd like to cry.
—— 108. I wish I had more friends.
—— 109. I worry a lot about dying.
—— 110. I often get so mad I can't talk.
—— 111. Most of the girls I go around with are prettier than I am.
—— 112. My mother could do more for me if she wanted to.
—— 113. People are always praising my brothers and sisters and not me.
—— 114. Some churches are all right, but others are all bunk.
—— 115. Sometimes I feel that nobody cares about me.
—— 116. I am going to get even with white folks when I grow up.
—— 117. All ministers want to do is to get as much money out of people as they can.
—— 118. I find it hard to get along with other people in school.
—— 119. I'm not smart enough to get into college.
—— 120. There is no use going to school since it won't help me any later.
—— 121. I never get enough to eat at home.
—— 122. Religion is a lot of bunk.
—— 123. My folks treat me like a baby.
—— 124. My folks are mean to me.
—— 125. College fellows usually think they are better than anybody else.

COLOR RATINGS TEST

I. Here is a list of some people whom you know. Read the name of each person in the list. What color is he? Draw a ring around the word after his name which tells what color he is.

1. Principal of your   Black Dark-Brown Brown Light-Brown Yellow White
   school
2. Your teacher   Black Dark-Brown Brown Light-Brown Yellow White
3. The richest person   Black Dark-Brown Brown Light-Brown Yellow White
   you know
4. The poorest person   Black Dark-Brown Brown Light-Brown Yellow White
   you know
5. The person your   Black Dark-Brown Brown Light-Brown Yellow White
   father works for
6. The person your   Black Dark-Brown Brown Light-Brown Yellow White
   mother works for
7. The boy you like   Black Dark-Brown Brown Light-Brown Yellow White
   most
8. The girl you like   Black Dark-Brown Brown Light-Brown Yellow White
   most
9. The meanest boy   Black Dark-Brown Brown Light-Brown Yellow White
   you know
10. The meanest girl   Black Dark-Brown Brown Light-Brown Yellow White
    you know
11. The ugliest boy   Black Dark-Brown Brown Light-Brown Yellow White
    you know
12. The ugliest girl   Black Dark-Brown Brown Light-Brown Yellow White
    you know
13. The smartest boy   Black Dark-Brown Brown Light-Brown Yellow White
    you know
14. The smartest girl   Black Dark-Brown Brown Light-Brown Yellow White
    you know
15. The most hand-   Black Dark-Brown Brown Light-Brown Yellow White
    some boy you know
16. The most beautiful Black Dark-Brown Brown Light-Brown Yellow White
    girl you know
17. The most stupid   Black Dark-Brown Brown Light-Brown Yellow White
    boy you know
18. The most stupid   Black Dark-Brown Brown Light-Brown Yellow White
    girl you know
19. The man you look   Black Dark-Brown Brown Light-Brown Yellow White
    up to most
20. The woman you   Black Dark-Brown Brown Light-Brown Yellow White
    look up to most

21. The nicest boy you know   Black   Dark-Brown   Brown   Light-Brown   Yellow   White

22. The nicest girl you know   Black   Dark-Brown   Brown   Light-Brown   Yellow   White

23. The boy you dislike most   Black   Dark-Brown   Brown   Light-Brown   Yellow   White

24. The girl you dislike most   Black   Dark-Brown   Brown   Light-Brown   Yellow   White

25. The best man you know   Black   Dark-Brown   Brown   Light-Brown   Yellow   White

26. The best woman you know   Black   Dark-Brown   Brown   Light-Brown   Yellow   White

27. The worst man you know   Black   Dark-Brown   Brown   Light-Brown   Yellow   White

28. The worst woman you know   Black   Dark-Brown   Brown   Light-Brown   Yellow   White

29. The most shiftless man you know   Black   Dark-Brown   Brown   Light-Brown   Yellow   White

30. The most shiftless woman you know   Black   Dark-Brown   Brown   Light-Brown   Yellow   White

II. List the members of your family in order from oldest to youngest, including yourself. Then draw a ring around the word after each name which tells what color the person is.

     Name   *Color*

1. ———————— Black Dark-Brown Brown Light-Brown Yellow White
2. ———————— Black Dark-Brown Brown Light-Brown Yellow White
3. ———————— Black Dark-Brown Brown Light-Brown Yellow White
4. ———————— Black Dark-Brown Brown Light-Brown Yellow White
5. ———————— Black Dark-Brown Brown Light-Brown Yellow White
6. ———————— Black Dark-Brown Brown Light-Brown Yellow White
7. ———————— Black Dark-Brown Brown Light-Brown Yellow White
8. ———————— Black Dark-Brown Brown Light-Brown Yellow White
9. ———————— Black Dark-Brown Brown Light-Brown Yellow White
10. ———————— Black Dark-Brown Brown Light-Brown Yellow White
11. ———————— Black Dark-Brown Brown Light-Brown Yellow White
12. ———————— Black Dark-Brown Brown Light-Brown Yellow White
13. ———————— Black Dark-Brown Brown Light-Brown Yellow White
14. ———————— Black Dark-Brown Brown Light-Brown Yellow White
15. ———————— Black Dark-Brown Brown Light-Brown Yellow White

III. Write down the members of your family in the order you like them. Put the person you like best next to number *1*, the person you like next best next to number *2*, and so on:

1. ———————————————————————— (Person you like best)
2. ————————————————————————
3. ————————————————————————
4. ————————————————————————
5. ————————————————————————
6. ————————————————————————
7. ————————————————————————
8. ————————————————————————
9. ————————————————————————
10. ————————————————————————
11. ————————————————————————
12. ————————————————————————
13. ————————————————————————
14. ————————————————————————
15. ————————————————————————

IV. Which color do you think it is best to be? ————————————————

Why? ————————————————————————————————————

Which color do you think it is worst to be? ——————————————

Why? ————————————————————————————————————

Which color would you like to be? ——————————————————

Why? ————————————————————————————————————

PERSONAL VALUES TEST

A. Suppose that you could have three wishes come true. What would your wishes be?

1. ——

2. ——

3. ——

B. Suppose that you could be born as somebody else. Who would you like to be?

——

Why? ——

C. If you had to be somebody else, who would you *not* want to be?

——

Why? ——

D. If you could be free to move to any part of the United States that you wanted, where would you go to live?

——

Why? ——

E. If you could visit any place in the world that you wanted to, where would you want to go?

——

Why? ——

F. a) After you have finished school, what kind of work would you like to do best of all?

——

Why? ——

b) What kind of job do you expect to have?

——

Why? ——

G. a) What kind of person would you like to marry?

_____ _____

Why? _____

    b) What kind of person do you think you really will marry?

_____

Why? _____

H. Of what three things are you most afraid?

    1. _____

    2. _____

    3. _____

I. What are the three things that are worrying you most?

    1. _____

    2. _____

    3. _____

J. What is the best thing that ever happened to you?

_____

_____

Why? _____

K. What is the worst thing that ever happened to you?

_____

_____

Why? _____

OCCUPATION RATINGS TEST

DIRECTIONS: Below are listed in the first column a number of jobs. Opposite each job which Negroes cannot do as well as whites you are to put a check in Column 3 (under heading "Negroes cannot do this job as well as whites"). If Negroes can do the job just as well as whites, put a check in column 4. If Negroes can do this job better than whites, put a check in column 5. Leave column 2 blank until later.

COLUMN 1	COLUMN 2	COLUMN 3 Negroes cannot do this job as well as whites	COLUMN 4 Negroes can do this job as well as whites	COLUMN 5 Negroes can do this job better than whites
Field Hand				
Doctor				
Porter				
Auto Mechanic				
Singer or Musician				
Druggist				
Engineer or Architect				
Teacher				
Dressmaker				
Laundress (washes and irons)				
Politician				
Janitor or Caretaker				
Minister				
Farmer				
Road Laborer				
Carpenter				
Banker				

Column 1	Column 2	Column 3	Column 4	Column 5
		Negroes cannot do this job as well as whites	Negroes can do this job as well as whites	Negroes can do this job better than whites
Driver or Chauffeur				
Aviator				
Cook				
Storekeeper				
Nurse				
Lawyer				
Railroad Worker				
Barber				
Dentist				
Policeman				
Secretary or Stenographer				
Waiter				
Letter Carrier or Post-office Clerk				

1. Which of these would you most like to be? ——————————

   Next choice? ——————————————————

2. Which of these would you least like to be? ——————————

   Next choice? ——————————————————

3. Which of these jobs is most important? ——————————————

   Next most important? ————————————————

4. Which of these jobs is least important? ——————————————

   Next least important? ————————————————

5. Go back and put a check in Column 2 next to each job that a Negro has a good chance of getting if he wanted it.

RACE ATTITUDES TEST

DIRECTIONS: Place *T* on the line in front of each statement which is true. Place *F* on the line in front of each statement which is false. If you can't decide whether the statement is true or false, place *X* on the line in front of it.

——— 1. I think white people could do more for colored people, but they won't.

——— 2. Sometimes white people make me mad, but they are no worse than other people.

——— 3. White people call Negroes bad names.

——— 4. White people don't know how to have a good time.

——— 5. Most of the big businesses are owned by white people.

——— 6. White people will always take care of a Negro who works hard and minds his own business.

——— 7. All Negroes want from white people is to be let alone.

——— 8. I neither like nor dislike white people.

——— 9. Most white people give Negroes fair pay for the work they do.

——— 10. Most white people make fun of Negroes and laugh at them.

——— 11. No matter how nicely he treats a colored person, a white man doesn't really mean it.

——— 12. I never think about white people.

——— 13. White people think all Negroes should be servants.

——— 14. White people never did me any harm or any good.

——— 15. White people have better homes than other people.

——— 16. White people are poor Christians.

——— 17. White people are human and have the faults of other human beings.

——— 18. White people don't treat Negroes any worse than other Negroes do.

——— 19. The South was a beautiful place before white people came in and ruined it.

——— 20. The white race has produced some of the best and some of the worst men in history.

——— 21. There are all kinds of white people—some are good and some are bad.

——— 22. I'd rather be dead than ask a white man for anything.

——— 23. Negroes should hate all white people.

——— 24. White men have done wonderful things to make the United States a great country.

——— 25. Sometimes I think white people treat Negroes all right and sometimes I don't.

——— 26. White people don't take care of each other.

——— 27. White people have done more for the world than any other race.

——— 28. White people have built up the best civilization in the world.

—— 29. White people are mean and stingy.

—— 30. White people are the cruelest people in the world.

—— 31. Negroes would still be heathen savages if it were not for the work of white people in educating them and bringing them Christianity.

—— 32. White people work hard and save their money.

—— 33. Negroes are always fighting and cutting each other up.

—— 34. Most of the criminals found in prisons are Negroes.

—— 35. The greatest general of history was a Negro.

—— 36. Negroes are the best singers and dancers in the world.

—— 37. If you don't know who did a crime, you can usually bet it was a Negro.

—— 38. Negroes have done more for the world than any other people.

—— 39. Negroes always work hard and try to improve themselves.

—— 40. Negroes are the meanest people in the world.

—— 41. Negroes never speak well of each other.

—— 42. Negroes drink too much.

—— 43. Negroes and white people were made by the same God, and He meant them to be equal.

—— 44. It's harder to work for a Negro than for anyone else.

—— 45. Most Negroes are superstitious.

—— 46. Negroes are cowards.

—— 47. Negroes should not be praised for the things they do since other people do the same things just as well.

—— 48. Negroes are more interested than other people in getting an edu-
—— cation.

—— 49. Negroes would be nice looking if they didn't have such bad hair.

—— 50. The United States couldn't have won any wars without the help of Negroes.

—— 51. Negroes are always worrying about the things that don't matter.

—— 52. Negroes think more about singing and playing around than they do of making something of themselves.

—— 53. Negroes will take strangers in and treat them well.

—— 54. There are just as many bootleggers and law-breakers among Negroes as among other people.

—— 55. Some of the best athletes in the world are white and some are Negro.

—— 56. Negroes don't have the courage to fight for their rights.

—— 57. I see no reason for either liking or disliking anyone just because he is a Negro.

—— 58. Drunken Negroes are bad but so are drunken white men.

—— 59. Negroes always think that people are putting things over on them.

—— 60. Negroes are as smart as other people but no smarter.

—— 61. Negro doctors are just about as good as doctors of other races.

—— 62. Only a few Negroes ever become famous but a large number could if given a chance.

—— 63. Negroes take their troubles with a smile while other people are always kicking and complaining.

—— 64. Sometimes I get mad at the way Negroes act, but I don't think they are any different from other people.

LIST OF TABLES

INDEX